M000317458

The Representation of
(In)definiteness

Current Studies in Linguistics Series
Samuel Jay Keyser, general editor

The Representation of
(In)definiteness

edited by Eric J. Reuland
and Alice G. B. ter Meulen

The MIT Press
Cambridge, Massachusetts
London, England

First MIT Press paperback edition, 1989

© 1987 by The Massachusetts Institute of Technology

All rights reserved. No part of this book may be reproduced in any form by any electronic or mechanical means (including photocopying, recording, or information storage and retrieval) without permission in writing from the publisher.

This book was set in VIP Times by Village Typographers, Inc., and printed and bound by Halliday Lithograph in the United States of America.

Library of Congress Cataloging-in-Publication Data

The Representation of (in)definiteness.

(Current studies in linguistics series ; 14)
Bibliography: p.
Includes index.
1. Definiteness (Linguistics).   I. Reuland, Eric J.
II. Meulen, Alice G. B. ter.   III. Series.
P299.D43R47   1987   415   86-27307
ISBN 0-262-18126-6 (hardcover)
       0-262-68059-9 (paperback)

To Merijn, Timen, and Emma

Contents

Contributors

Sandra Chung   Board of Studies in Linguistics, University of California, Santa Cruz

Franciska de Jong   Philips Research Laboratories, Eindhoven, The Netherlands

David Gil   Department of Linguistics, Tel Aviv University

Irene Heim   Department of Linguistics, University of Texas at Austin

James Higginbotham   Department of Linguistics and Philosophy, Massachusetts Institute of Technology

C.-T. James Huang   Department of Modern Languages and Linguistics, Cornell University

Edward L. Keenan   Department of Linguistics, University of California at Los Angeles

David Pesetsky   Department of Linguistics, University of Massachusetts at Amherst

Tanya Reinhart   Department of Poetics and Comparative Literature, Tel Aviv University

Eric J. Reuland   Institute for General Linguistics, Groningen University

Kenneth J. Safir   Program in Linguistics, Rutgers University

Alice G. B. ter Meulen   Department of Linguistics, University of Washington

Janis S. Williamson   English Language Program, University of California, Santa Barbara Extension

Series Foreword

We are pleased to present this book as the fourteenth volume in the series Current Studies in Linguistics.

As we have defined it, the series will offer book-length studies in linguistics and neighboring fields that further the exploration of man's ability to manipulate symbols. It will pursue the same editorial goals as its companion journal, *Linguistic Inquiry,* and will complement it by providing a format for in-depth studies beyond the scope of the professional article.

By publishing such studies, we hope the series will answer a need for intensive and detailed research that sheds new light on current theoretical issues and provides a new dimension for their resolution. Toward this end it will present books dealing with the widest range of languages and addressing the widest range of theoretical topics. From time to time and with the same ends in view, the series will include collections of significant articles covering single and selected subject areas and works primarily for use as textbooks.

Like *Linguistic Inquiry,* Current Studies in Linguistics will seek to present work of theoretical interest and excellence.

Samuel Jay Keyser

Preface

This book constitutes a collection of original articles presenting new research in different grammatical frameworks on a common and central theoretical issue: the representation of (in)definiteness in linguistic theory. Definiteness is mostly studied as a property of NPs, where it plays a crucial role in the linguistic analysis of predication and quantification. The contributions in this volume offer various competing theoretical characterizations of the distinction between definite and indefinite expressions and consequently provide different theoretical insights and results, using arguments based on distinct background assumptions and proposing alternative explanations for the linguistic data that constitute their common ground.

The roots of this book lie in the Fifth Groningen Round Table, held in June 1984 and organized by the Institute for General Linguistics of Groningen University, where the ideas explored in each chapter were extensively discussed. Because of the large number of participants at the conference, it was not possible to publish the proceedings. Instead, we decided to bring out a book setting forth the most important ideas and results, which we believe to be representative of the work on this issue within current theoretical syntax and semantics in general. Contributors were challenged to pay particular attention to alternative analyses offered by other theories, promoting cross-fertilization of both syntactic and semantic ideas, concepts, and argumentation. As editors, we have attempted to combine a high degree of internal coherence with breadth of theoretical scope. The project is grounded in the belief that genuine progress can be made in theoretical linguistics when alternative, seemingly incompatible approaches are explicitly compared and that this not only encourages further developments but in fact is essential to improving understanding of the nature and structure of natural language. Although we would not deny that antithesis often does result in progress, here we have taken a synthetical, rather than an antithetical, position. We believe that many of the insights in semantically and syntactically based approaches to the study of natural language are complementary and in principle compatible. We trust that the synthesis we have endeavored to provide in chapter 1 supports that position. Finally, we hope that the nature of this collection and the perspective in which we have placed the various contributions will both sufficiently identify the important issues and provide a fruitful basis for further research.

The authors and editors have profited immensely from the presentations and comments by other participants of the Round Table, notably Rainer Bäuerle, Paz Buenaventura Naylor, Annabel Cormack, Deborah Dahl, Urs Egli, Jan van Eijck, Jacqueline Guéron, Mike Hannay, Erhard Hinrichs, Richard Kayne, Sebastian Löbner, Peter Ludlow, Michael Lumsden, Chris Lyons, Edith Moravcsik, Pieter Muysken, Ann Reed, Henk van Riemsdijk, Susan Rothstein, Remko Scha, Barry Schein, Anna Szabolcsi, Henk Verkuyl, and Yael Ziv. This finds its reflection in the bibliography. We appreciate the time and effort spent by the anonymous referees. Comments by Sjaak de Mey have been crucial in shaping our initial ideas, and we would also like to thank him for his help in organizing the Round Table. In organizing this meeting, we have greatly benefited from the success of the previous Round Tables organized by Frank Heny. The Round Table, and therefore this book, would have been impossible without the financial support of both the Faculty of Letters of Groningen University and the Royal Dutch Academy of Sciences, which we hereby gratefully acknowledge. Hennie Zondervan's assistance and energy have been invaluable throughout the whole enterprise. We are very much indebted to her. We would also like to acknowledge the help we received from Jet van Everdingen and from other members and students of the Institute for General Linguistics. Finally, we express our sincerest gratitude to all those around us who have so freely donated their time and set aside their needs in helping us to bring this project to completion.

Eric Reuland
Alice ter Meulen

The Representation of
(In)definiteness

Chapter 1

Introduction   Eric J. Reuland and
Alice G. B. ter Meulen

In this introduction we will provide general background information on (in)definiteness, summarize the content and major results of the individual contributions, and briefly assess the state of the art, open research problems, and potential theoretical developments growing out of the work reported here.

The distribution of definite and indefinite noun phrases (NPs) differs widely in various constructions across languages. Independently of any theoretical characterization of the notion of (in)definiteness, the linguistic environments in which either a definite or an indefinite expression is exclusively acceptable are said to exhibit a *definiteness effect* (DE). Environments where the indefinite is preferred are said to exhibit a *definiteness restriction* (DR), as a special case of a DE.

Since definiteness is at least partly a semantic property of expressions, and assuming that semantic structure is relatively little subject to cross-linguistic variation, one would expect a number of universal environments to exhibit a DE. This expectation is indeed borne out by the results reported in the following chapters. The conditions on anaphora with indefinite antecedents, found in so-called donkey-sentences, do not vary much across languages (see the discussions by Higginbotham in chapter 3 and Reinhart in chapter 6). The objects of inalienable possession or units of measurement in amount terms similarly exhibit strong universal characteristics (see the discussion by De Jong in chapter 11). Other examples of such universal environments present additional support for the hypothesis that definiteness is at least partly a semantic property and should be represented as such in the grammar.

However, some environments with a DE seem to be best characterized syntactically. In many languages, for instance, there is a strong correlation between the presence of an expletive subject and some indefinite argument elsewhere in the clause. Other languages bar indefinites as syntactic subjects or as topics. Even if these phenomena are not genuinely universal, they constitute recurrent patterns in otherwise widely divergent languages.

The central question is to what extent a universal linguistic characterization of (in)definiteness may be detected underlying this cross-linguistic variation. In striving for a linguistically universal characterization of (in)definiteness, various restrictions on and cross-linguistic variations in DEs must be explained by analyzing the interaction of their properties with other structural or semantic properties. This pattern of interactions may provide a clue to how (in)definiteness is to be represented in the grammar.

A much-studied DE construction consists of an expletive element such as *there* in the structural subject position and a true VP-internal argument that must be indefinite, as in (1).

(1) There ensued a/*the riot on Mass. Ave.

Milsark (1974) calls this the *quantification restriction;* Safir (1982) calls it the *definiteness effect.* Any explanation of this fact should indicate the interpretation of such sentences as well as explain the patterns of variation found across languages. Constructions of this type occur in languages as diverse as Chinese, Chamorro, Dutch, Finnish, French, German, Hebrew, Hungarian, Italian, Papiamentu, and Spanish. For an overview based on more than 30 languages distributed over a number of different language families, see Clark 1978. The Case of the restricted NP varies across languages. In many languages, as for instance in English, it bears the Case assigned by Inflection. In the German *es gibt-* and Spanish *hay*-constructions the Case of the restricted NP is accusative. Dutch has constructions with a nominative and a dative NP, both VP-internal, where the DR requires just one of the two to be indefinite. In Finnish the restricted NP may have partitive or accusative Case (see Safir 1982, Torrego 1983, Reuland 1985, and Renault 1984 for discussion of these facts, and Clark 1978 for discussion of a wider range, largely showing the same pattern). The expletive element is also subject to cross-linguistic variation. In some languages it must be overtly realized—for instance, in English by *there,* in French by *il.* In others it must or may be empty, as in Chamorro, Chinese, Hebrew, Italian, Papiamentu, Spanish, and certain dialects of Dutch. In some languages the construction is subject to few restrictions. In Dutch, for example, almost any verb appears to allow the thematic subject to occur as an indefinite VP-internal argument with an expletive structural subject. In other languages the construction is limited to a small number of verbs, or even to just one. Spanish, for example, freely allows constructions where the thematic subject is in a noncanonical position and the structural subject empty, that do not exhibit a DR; only when *haber* is construed with an (empty) expletive subject does the DR apply. Despite obscuring factors, in Italian a DE appears to be generally associated with the VP-internal subject of ergative verbs (a first systematic overview of these facts is given in Belletti 1985). It is an important task to identify what is constant within this varying pattern and to account for it systematically in a general theory of indefiniteness. The authors represented here discuss many other interesting DE environments, considerably extending the range of data and empirical evidence concerning DEs in various languages. It is to be expected that this will significantly constrain the number of theories of this domain that have to be considered.

1.1 Three Accounts of Definiteness

We turn now to three influential theoretical accounts of the DE with expletive subjects, each of which is in its own way a precursor of the current analyses and theoretical viewpoints.

Milsark (1974) explains the DR with expletive subjects in the structure *there be NP Pred* by claiming that *there be* represents an existential quantifier that must bind some variable. Quantificational NPs like *John, every man, most men* do not provide such a variable free for binding by *there* and hence are unacceptable in such a structure. Cardinal NPs like *a man, some man, two, three, n men* are not quantificational and do provide a variable to be bound by *there*. Some NPs like *some men* and *many men* are ambiguous between a quantificational and a cardinal reading. Although a sentence like (2) is grammatical, it lacks one of the readings associated with sentence (3).

(2) There are many men in the garden

(3) Many men are in the garden

Sentence (3) may mean either that a large proportion of the existing men is in the garden or simply that a lot of men are in the garden. Sentence (2) admits only the latter interpretation, implying nothing about relative proportions of men inside and outside the garden (on this point, see also Higginbotham's discussion in chapter 3). Milsark (1977) introduces the terms *strong determiner* for determiners in quantificational NPs and *weak determiner* for determiners in cardinal NPs. For Milsark, the distinction between definite and indefinite NPs appears to be completely subsumed under this distinction between strong and weak determiners.

Pursuing a suggestion by Richard Montague, Barwise and Cooper (1981) develop a theory of NP-interpretations as generalized quantifiers, that is, as sets of sets of individuals. They show that various relevant semantic differences between NPs and determiners are captured by set-theoretic conditions and properties of set-theoretic constructions. They also provide a set-theoretic formalization of Milsark's notions of strong and weak determiner, which classifies a determiner as (1) positive strong (*every*), (2) negative strong (*no, neither*), or (3) weak (*some*), if the interpretation of the sentence *Det N is a(n) N/are Ns* is respectively (1) tautologous, (2) contradictory, or (3) contingent. Barwise and Cooper account for the DR with expletive subjects by interpreting *there is/are NP* as requiring the universe of individuals of an interpretation to be a member of the NP-interpretation. For positive strong determiners this interpretation will always be a tautology, and for negative strong ones it will always be a contradiction. Only for weak determiners will it be a genuinely informative contingent statement. The traditional notion of a definite determiner is actually more restricted than either Milsark's or Barwise and Cooper's notion of a strong determiner. The presupposed existence of the referent of an NP with a definite determiner is imposed in Barwise and Cooper's analysis by requiring in addition that the N-interpretation is not empty. These two requirements capture the traditional notion of definiteness. Unlike Milsark, Barwise and Cooper do not distinguish the quantificational and the cardinal interpretations of *many* and *some* (plural). Despite acknowledging that there may be an issue here, they treat such ambiguous determiners as weak. A noteworthy result of this set-theoretic analysis of determiners is that for a weak determiner the verification of a sentence *Det N is/are Pred* is based only on the intersection of the N- and Pred-interpretations, that is, information provided by the sentence itself, whereas strong determiners require for their verification consideration of some other set, often already given in the interpretation or otherwise available as part of the conversational background or common ground. Although all NPs are quantifiers on this theory of generalized quantifiers, the verification of a sentence, conceived of more dynamically, depends on the nature of the determiners in its NPs. Neither Milsark's nor Barwise and Cooper's analysis incorporates such factors traditionally thought to belong to the realm of pragmatics, characterizing the contrasts between definite and indefinite NPs in a static manner.

On the contrary, Heim (1982) introduces an essentially dynamic approach to the interpretation of definite and indefinite NPs. Heim bases her analysis on the traditional view that a definite NP refers to an entity that is in some sense given in the conversational common ground, whereas an indefinite NP refers to an entity that is newly added to the conversational domain. Indexed NPs in a discourse are interpreted relative to a set-theoretic file structure, which consists metaphorically of a set of cards with entries of properties and relations; the structured file is interpreted in standard set-theoretic models by a modified satisfaction definition. Interpreting an indefinite NP requires adding the index of that NP to the file on a new card and entering the property interpreting the noun on that card, after checking to make sure that index does not already occur in the file (the Novelty/Familiarity Condition). Definite NPs with indices already on file are interpreted as coreferential with the "referent" of the initial card. This dynamic analysis of the process of interpretation in a set-theoretic model-theory integrates a number of purely semantic satisfaction conditions with more pragmatic factors such as given-new information and conversational background, while appealing essentially to a representational level of Logical Form (LF). On Heim's account, indefinite NPs contain a variable that may be unselectively bound by quantificational NPs. For instance, in the so-called donkey-sentences (such as *Every man who owns a donkey beats it*) the indefinite NP *a donkey* is bound by the universal quantifier *every man* and the subsequent pronoun picks up the referent from this bound indefinite (here, *it* is interpreted as 'the donkey he owns'). Heim (1982) does not provide an account of the DR with expletive subjects, but Reuland (1983, 1985) suggests along the lines of Heim's file change semantics that *there* should be analyzed as an indefinite that bears no referential index, since it is semantically empty. The logical form of such constructions is assumed to have a subject with semantic content as proper input for the interpretation; hence, another argument must be linked to *there*, preserving its indefiniteness. Heim's contribution in this volume (chapter 2) addresses the DE in contexts with variables dependent on various kinds of NPs and outlines the necessary conditions for a satisfactory account of the DE.

Comparing these approaches brings up an important question. Four oppositions have been described, which seem conceptually independent: (1) quantificational versus cardinal NPs (including Milsark's strong-weak contrast), (2) Barwise and Cooper's positive and negative strong versus weak determiners, a division that treats all NPs as generalized quantifiers, (3) definite versus indefinite NPs, and (4) the Novelty/Familiarity Condition of Heim's dynamic interpretation. The classifications these notions induce on the NPs or determiners overlap to a large extent, indicating that probably there is still a common insight to be captured.

1.2 Existential and Presentational Sentences

Two aspects of the DR environment in (1) and more generally the class of *existential sentences* (E-sentences), which we may take here to include the presentational sentences, have been the subject of much dispute and have received rather divergent analyses.

First, *there* has been claimed to have lexical meaning or locative force (Bolinger 1977; Kuno 1971), to be a definite topic (Rando and Napoli 1978), a scope marker (Williams 1984), an existential quantifier (Milsark 1974), or a dummy subject (Safir 1982), or to mean the universal property *thing* (Barwise and Cooper 1981) (see also Safir's overview in chapter 4). The question is whether these divergent claims are irreconcilable, or whether a coherent and illuminating account can be developed on the basis of the insights they express. Since there are languages with E-sentences lacking an overt expletive subject, the only plausible approach toward reconciling these divergent analyses is to derive the properties attributed to *there* from other properties of the construction.

The second major point of disagreement among existing analyses concerns the structure of the *coda* (the nominal element and the optional predicate) governed by the existential verb. Disagreeing with Jenkins (1972), Milsark (1974) argues that the coda cannot be an NP. Stowell (1981) and Safir (1982) argue that it has the structure of a small clause. Williams (1984) claims again that in English the coda is an NP. But is this an issue of Universal Grammar, or just an issue of the grammar of English? Even if the coda in English E-sentences is an NP, it surely is no ordinary NP. The question remains whether its unusual character can be explained by other properties of the coda. For instance, does the predicative part of the coda modify the nominal part, as one would expect in NPs, or does some kind of predication relation obtain, as in a small clause, or can the two parts be construed in yet another way? And at what level do the DE and DR apply? Do the conditions involve surface syntactic properties, or can they be stated at LF or at some representational level between syntax and semantic interpretation, or can they be formulated in purely semantic terms?

1.3 Summaries of Contributors' Views on (In)definiteness

Each chapter in this book contributes in some way to the central issues outlined in the previous sections.

In chapter 2 Heim answers the fundamental question, "At what level does the DR apply?" Her investigation of inversely linked readings in *with*-complements and the conditions under which the coda of *there*-sentences may contain a trace of *Wh*-Movement, involving the *who-what* contrast, comparatives, and various types of relatives, shows that the DR must apply at a level at which scope ambiguities have been disambiguated and at which *wh*-elements that have been moved are restored to the position at which they are interpreted—in other words, at LF. Analyzing individual variables as strong and hence definite (that is, referentially dependent upon a variable assignment already fixed in the interpretation), she argues that any account of the DR must explain why such variables are prohibited after expletive subjects. She shows that the lack of wide-scope readings for the admissible NPs in the coda of E-sentences follows from her analysis of the DR. Wide-scope readings would require movement and would give rise to a (definite) variable. The position of *there* may mark the scope of the NP in the coda, without being a lexical scope marker. Thus, its role becomes virtually identical to that of zero-marking in languages lacking overt expletives.

In chapter 3 Higginbotham discusses a variety of domains with DEs, focusing on the relation between restrictions on predicate nominals and restrictions in *there*-insertion contexts. He argues that the common factor in these DEs is that they arise from the various meanings of a quantificational specifier and especially conditions on predication. The DR on predicate nominals follows from the fact that predicates must be unsaturated. In argument NPs the role of the specifier is to saturate the predicate by binding the open position in N'. In predicate nominals specifiers with an adjectival character, interpreted as cardinal determiners, are admitted that do not bind the open position. The predicational use of the copula *be* selects predicates, whereas the identity *be* takes only singular terms. Hence, in predicative constructions with *be* open Nps are allowed as well as closed Nps that quantify over extensions of predicates; but only such closed Nps are found as predicates of small clause complements without copula. The semantic interpretation of the predicate nominals is therefore the relevant level, resulting in the restriction against specific use of indefinites. In E-sentences, however, the DE is explained strictly by the nature of the specifier. Higginbotham shows that on Williams's (1984) assumption that the coda in English E-sentences is an NP, this NP itself must be able to function as a sentence. As quantifiers undergo raising at LF, the N′ cannot move along with the specifier in E-sentences, since that would leave the sentence without a predicate. In these cases the binder must receive an unrestricted or absolute meaning, because the usual restrictive predicate in the N′ no longer serves that function. Since *there* is not lexically a scope marker, Higginbotham's results apply equally to languages lacking overt expletives. An important question is how these results can be extended to *there*-sentences with other verbs than *be*. Higginbotham argues that in a number of cases analyzing such sentences as quantifying over events is the correct solution.

In chapter 4 Safir presents an important overview of the methodological issues involved in the choice between current alternative approaches to the DR in E-sentences, demonstrating that no lexically based account will do. Safir argues that *there* is Case-marked and that the NP in the coda is not; the latter must be linked to *there* in order to receive Case. Since nonanaphoric, nonpronominal NPs must be free (Principle C of the binding theory in Chomsky 1981), such linking is generally ruled out. Safir suggests that linking is possible just in case the NP is understood predicatively, requiring an open NP, which explains the DR. In extending his analysis to further data, Safir argues, like Higginbotham but on different grounds, for quantification over events.

In chapter 5 Pesetsky provides direct support for Heim's (1982) claim that not all NPs are quantificational. Basing his suggestion on a crosslinguistic study including English, Polish, and Japanese, Pesetsky makes a fundamental distinction between quantificational *wh*-expressions that move at LF and are sensitive to Subjacency and conditions on empty categories, and nonquantificational, discourse-linked *wh*-expressions that are interpreted in situ. Scope assignment is shown to be possible on the basis of unselective binding, just as it is for the nonquantificational NPs in Heim (1982). Pesetsky argues forcefully for the necessity of a level of LF intermediate between S-structure and semantic interpretation.

In chapters 6 and 7 Reinhart and Williamson present further convincing evidence from other environments that the NPs admissible in the coda of E-sentences are nonquantificational. Reinhart discusses anaphora in donkey-sentences, based on Heim's (1982) analysis of singular indefinites, and extends it to plural open NPs with cardinal determiners. To explain the role of S-Structure conditions in such anaphora, Reinhart distinguishes two types of binding: specifier binding and referential binding. On the basis of conditions statable at S-Structure, specifiers may bind open variables in indefinite NPs with cardinal determiners as well as variables dependent upon them.

Williamson investigates relative clause formation in Lakhota, where the head remains internal to the relative clause: $[_{NP}[_{S'} \ldots NP_i \ldots] \text{Det}_i]$, where NP_i is the relativized NP. She finds that the determiners in the NP_i in such constructions are precisely the cardinal ones discussed by Milsark (1974), whereas the Det_i carries no restriction as determiner of the entire NP. She proposes that the S' should be interpreted as containing an open NP_i, free for binding by Det_i.

Chapters 8 and 9 by Chung and Huang constitute a very interesting pair. Chung shows convincingly that the coda of an E-sentence in Chamorro is an NP, whereas Huang equally convincingly shows that the coda of an E-sentence in Chinese cannot be an NP. Together these analyses imply that a universal explanation of the DR in E-sentences, if it involves such structural properties, must appeal to them only indirectly.

Chung demonstrates that Chamorro E-sentences, lacking overt expletives, have the structure $[_S \emptyset [_{VP} V_{exist} \text{Coda}]]$. The coda may be realized by a single NP, marked oblique, or it may be complex and contain an additional predicative constituent, which is shown to share crucial characteristics with relative clauses. Moreover, Chung notes, Chamorro lacks small clauses in general. This leads to the conclusion that the coda here must be an NP. Chung observes that the construction does not have all the characteristics of Chamorro relative clauses, since in the structure $[_{NP} NP_i [_{S'} \text{Comp} [_S \ldots t_i \ldots]]]$ the path between NP_i and the variable has the properties of the path found in questions. This fact is accounted for under the assumption that, unlike standard relatives, this construction is formed by a movement rule. Thus, the coda is an NP whose predicate is realized by a nonstandard form of relativization. This NP has the property we expect by now: it may only have a cardinal determiner. The facts suggest a relation between the DR on the NP and the special form of the relative clause. What this relation is poses a challenge to any account of the DR, a challenge to which we will return.

Huang analyzes the rich variety of existential constructions in Chinese. The linear form of these constructions can be given as $(NP_1) \, V \, NP_2 \, (XP)$, where NP_1 is the optional subject and the XP in the coda is a predicative expression. Huang notes that the structure of Chinese NPs is strictly head-final, which entails that their general pattern prohibits analyzing the string $NP_2 \, XP$ as an NP. Hence, the structure of the coda in Chinese must differ from the structure of the coda in Chamorro. NP_2 exhibits a DE, partly depending on other features of the context. When the coda contains a predicate phrase, the DR obtains without exception. If the XP position is empty and the verb is the equivalent of *be* (literally *have*), the DR is mitigated when the NP_1 position is filled. In sentences with a verb of (dis)appearance the absence of an XP leads to the absence of a DR in other than assertive uses. For other choices of the verb the DR does not hold at all. Finally, Huang observes that just in case the coda contains a predicate, NP_2 must be not only indefinite but also specific. Although some of these facts may follow from other analyses, none of them would explain the effects associated with the presence of an XP.

In chapter 10 Gil helps answer the question, "To what extent do the four contrasts quantificational-cardinal, strong-weak (in Barwise and Cooper's sense), definite-indefinite, and given-new differ?" From his considerations it must be concluded that the definite-indefinite contrast constitutes a distinction in its own right, since, according to him, configurational NPs are obligatorily marked for this contrast but other NPs are not. Crucially, however, the configurationality parameter affects only contrasts corresponding to that expressed in English by *the/a*, not, for instance, contrasts expressed by *most/many*. The fact that these oppositions are affected differently indicates their different status, which squares with Heim's view that the definiteness–indefiniteness contrast is restricted to nonquantificational NPs. Gil also provides evidence that the quantificational-cardinal contrast is distinct from Barwise and Cooper's strong-weak contrast. To account for the lack of stacked numerals in configurational languages, Gil assumes that in such languages numerals are interpreted as determiners, mapping properties into sets of properties. In nonconfigurational languages numerals are interpreted like adjectives, mapping properties into properties. Since the strong-weak contrast applies only to mappings of properties to sets of properties, numerals from nonconfigurational languages cannot be subsumed under it. On the other hand, the notion of a cardinal determiner is directly applicable in such cases, just as certain uses of weak determiners are cardinal. The range of the quantificational-cardinal distinction is therefore wider than the range of the strong-weak distinction.

In chapter 11 De Jong addresses two important issues. One involves the model-theoretic basis of Barwise and Cooper's strong-weak contrast and the question of how restrictions on partitives are to be represented. Barwise and Cooper (1981) suggest that the restrictions on the Det_2 in $[_{NP} Det_1$ of Det_2 N] are related to their notion of definiteness. De Jong reconstructs their strong-weak contrast in terms of determiners that presuppose that the N-denotation is not empty and determiners that do not carry such presuppositions. She reanalyzes their notion of definiteness as inclusion of the subject N-interpretation in the interpretation of the predicate. All other determiners are cardinal according to De Jong's classification, including *most*. De Jong treats *all* and *the* alike, although (as Gil points out) only one of them is affected by the configurationality parameter. This raises a new question: To what extent does this model-theoretic analysis interact with the configurationality of a language?

The second issue De Jong addresses concerns the DR in contexts such as *NP have Det brothers, NP be Det meters long, NP be Det years ago*. Other contexts with relational nouns such as *brother* and measure nouns such as *meter* and *year* do allow strong determiners. Because of its relational character, De Jong argues, *brother* is not interpreted in every model as the set $\{x \mid$ there is a y, x brother of $y\}$, but rather as a function giving for each such y the set of y's brothers. In other words, relational nouns are interpreted with respect to an "anchoring point" in the model, a notion that deserves further study and proper formalization. Expressions denoting dimensions in space or time must similarly be anchored with respect to the objects they are dimensions of. The contexts above are typically anchoring contexts, and after anchoring such relational expressions behave just like other referential expressions and have the standard properties of definite NPs.

Most of the contributors limit their consideration to simple determiners, but in chapter 12 Keenan presents a rigorous definition of the notion "existential NP" covering complex cases as well by defining what basic existential NPs are and showing how existentiality is or is not preserved under various operations. Determiners in existential NPs are not just the cardinal determiners but also some determiners that are not logically constant. Some complex determiners turn out to be acceptable in existential NPs, despite being strong in Barwise and Cooper's sense. Keenan shows that his notion of existential NP makes the right distinctions in these cases. He also offers an important explanation of the DR in E-sentences, showing that no appeal to triviality should or need be made. Keenan's analysis assumes that *there* is semantically empty and hence transfers easily to languages lacking an overt expletive. He does not assume that the coda in E-sentences must be an NP, since the XP is a separate constituent that determines properties of individuals. A sentence of the form [there [be NP XP]] can only be interpreted compositionally as expressing that the NP-denotation has the property denoted by the XP, semantically equivalent to the interpretation of [NP be XP]. This in turn is on an existence reading of the copula equivalent to [NP XP exist]. Keenan shows that these equivalences hold only if the NP is existential. His analysis does not rely on any syntactic conditions on the relation between the NP and the XP in the coda. A syntactic analysis in which Nom + XP would form an NP is also admissible, provided it would still allow the proper interpretation of the XP. The DR on relational nouns with possessive verbs (as in *John has many friends studying law*) can be derived, if the subject of the clause (here, *John*) is interpreted as argument of the object noun (here, *friends*). This leaves the clause without a subject argument and forces the same kind of treatment as in E-sentences. Keenan's statement that such relational nouns are maps from sets of properties to sets of properties is quite compatible with the idea that such nouns require their values to be anchored.

1.4 Conclusions and Open Problems

From the variety of DEs discussed in this book three general factors may be identified. First, a DR obtains if an NP must be bound by a specifier external to it, as in donkey-sentences and Lakhota relative clauses, which requires the NP to be nonquantificational. Second, a DR is also observed on predicative NPs, since they are unsaturated and must contain a free variable, requiring them to be nonquantificational. Third, a DR obtains if the meaning of a sentence requires some NP to be discourse-linked or (yet) unanchored. We have seen that in relational expressions the last factor alone is sufficient to force a DR.

Assessing these results, we must conclude that all properties of E-sentences have still not been adequately explained and moreover that at least two analyses are in apparent conflict. Consider first the fact that the NP "introduced" by an E-sentence is subject to a DR. On one level this follows from the discourse function or force of E-sentences in a manner to be discussed later. But from this it does not yet follow that a clause with the structure of an E-sentence but with a definite NP substituted for the indefinite one should be ill formed or even odd. It follows only that such a clause could not have the force of an E-sentence. Higginbotham derives the relative ill-formedness of E-sentences with definites from their structural properties (the expletive subject and the assumption that the coda is an NP). How, then, can this DR be explained for languages where the coda is not just a single NP? Keenan accounts for the lack of an existence reading when the NP in the coda is not existential by the interaction of syntactic structure and semantic interpretation. His analysis raises the questions of how the DR follows for languages where the coda is a simple NP, and why E-sentences quite generally appear in a form that favors NPs with an existential interpretation, unlike canonical sentence forms like *John exists*. Both analyses leave open the questions, "What is the role of the expletive subject and why do so many languages construct E-sentences with expletives?" and "What is the role of the XP in the coda, how does it force a DR in Chinese, and why does it have such a special form in Chamorro?"

By way of conclusion, it is worthwhile to develop some tentative answers to these questions. With regard to the first, we have seen that the analyses converge toward the claim that the scope-marking properties the expletive appears to have are independent of any of its own properties but should follow from the properties of the other elements in the structure. There is no need to construe the expletive as an existential quantifier, since the DR follows without that assumption. In general, the expletive cannot have locational meaning. There remain the claims that it is a definite topic, that it is interpreted as the universal property *thing*, or that it is simply an empty subject. These claims share the intuition that E-sentences contain a position occupied by the expletive of which the VP is predicated. Then why would a language contain a structure where the VP is predicated of a semantically empty subject?

Milsark (1977) discussed the difference between *Many unicorns exist*, where existence is predicated of a previously established set of unicorns by a *quantificational use* of the NP *many unicorns*, and *There exist many unicorns,* which newly introduces unicorns into the conversational domain with a *nonquantificational use* of the same NP *many unicorns.* We believe a generalization of his insight should provide the foundation of a proper account of (in)definiteness, based on the claims that (1) NPs can be used either quantificationally or nonquantificationally, (2) the context of an NP determines how it is used, and (3) this distinction can only be explained and formalized in terms of a dynamic theory of information conditions formalizing the informative content of any expression of natural language in its context of use. *Quantificational* uses of NPs require for their interpretation a set of assignment functions that assign values to referential markers (not to be identified with the individual variables of predicate logic) from a given set of objects, fixed prior to and independently of the interpretation of the sentence. The set of reference markers available for the interpretation of such quantificational uses of NPs constitutes what we have informally called the conversational domain. Other uses of NPs modify the conversational domain in various ways, introducing new referential markers, identifying or unifying given referential markers, requiring certain sets to be empty, restructuring sets of available referential markers by new dependency relations, or constraining the mapping of referential markers into model-theoretic structures by imposing specific requirements on the satisfaction or embedding functions or on anchoring functions. The interpretation of an NP used to modify the conversational domain cannot be defined in terms of the hitherto current domain but must appeal to elements outside this current domain. Specifically, its interpretation cannot be a generalized quantifier in Barwise and Cooper's sense. We call such uses of NPs *nonquantificational* and claim that they are directly discourse-linked. Representations of nonquantificational uses of NPs may contain a new referential marker and enter into dependency relations with already available referential markers or assignment functions. It remains an open question to what extent such ideas may be formalized in a genuinely compositional framework, and the state of the art does not warrant any conclusions concerning the ultimate necessity of a representational level between the natural language syntax and the purely semantic interpretation. It should be clear, though, that this question is to be viewed as a strictly empirical issue concerning the structure of the linguistic system.

Returning to the DE with expletives, on the basis of Milsark's discussion, but also supported by other linguistic studies, we may argue that the semantic characteristic of the (normal) syntactic subject is its quantificational nature, using this notion now in the manner just outlined. Hence, the nonquantificational, indefinite NP that introduces novel elements into the conversational domain cannot occur in subject position in E-sentences; instead, it must be part of the coda. If the subject in E-sentences were an argument, it would require a thematic role. Then the sentence would fail to be an E-sentence but instead would express the existence of a relation between an already identified object and a newly introduced one, as in *John saw a man*. If a sentence is to have merely the force of introducing some element(s) or requiring their absence in the conversational domain, then, its subject must be semantically empty.[1]

What about the claim that *there* is a definite topic or is interpreted as the universal property *thing?* The essence of these claims is in some sense implicit in what we have suggested. If the subject is always quantificational, this must be true of expletives as well. Since an expletive lacks semantic content, its denotation can only be fixed by some general principle and should not have any informative value. Plausible candidates are either the universal property *thing* (the entire set of objects or universe of discourse in the model), as Barwise and Cooper suggest, or the empty set. In a dynamic approach to the interpretation of E-sentences the first alternative seems ruled out, since the entire universe of objects contains the interpretation of the indefinite NP, which by hypothesis should not already be part of the conversational domain. This leaves the empty set as denotation of an expletive, to which the properties interpreting the VP are attributed. This may capture the basic insight shared by theories as diverse as those of Bolinger (1977), Kuno (1971), Rando and Napoli (1978), and Barwise and Cooper (1981): the expletive establishes the link between a hitherto current conversational domain and newly introduced objects.

It will be clear that both *be*-type and *have*-type verbs can be expected to occur in E-sentences. The *be*-type verbs establish a link by causing the content of the NP in the coda to be added to the conversational domain and attributed to the empty set. The *have*-type verbs, varying from the Spanish *hay* to the Chinese *you*, may be viewed as simply expressing a limiting case of the possessive anchoring relation between the empty set and the newly introduced objects. If this suggestion is at all on the right track, subtle differences may be expected between the two constructions. One possible difference may concern the structure of the coda. For instance, in Chinese, which has a *have*-type verb, the predicate of the coda is not part of the NP. Guéron's

(1984) analysis of existentials in French, which has *have*-type E-sentences, depends on the coda having small clause character. Based on this, one would expect the E-predicate in Chamorro to be of the *be*-type. Whether this is indeed the case and whether there is such a connection remain open questions. This leaves the matter of the structure of the coda and especially the relation between predicative constructions and the DR.

Let us first consider at a more general level the types of relations that might conceivably exist between the nominal and the predicative expression in the coda. Huang discusses four options: (1) a small clause-like analysis, (2) restrictive modification, (3) nonrestrictive modification, and (4) predication.

Consider small clause constructions such as (4).

(4) Cindy considers many lovers romantic fools

The object of *consider* is a "proposition" or a truth-value-denoting expression. As argued earlier, *many lovers* in subject position should be quantificational. In any event, this type of complement seems to have all the properties of a quantificationally closed or saturated expression (see Higginbotham's discussion in chapter 3). Huang notes that in all but one of the existential constructions in Chinese a small clause analysis is highly implausible, since the verbs involved are not of the kind one would expect to select a truth-value-denoting expression. In the one remaining case a small clause analysis is still not necessary. In English E-sentences a strict small clause analysis of the coda would require *be* to select a truth-value-denoting expression just like *consider*. Independently necessary are only the identifying and predicative uses of *be* (discussed by Higginbotham in chapter 3). All these considerations support the idea that the coda of an E-sentence is not a small clause in the standard sense (see discussion by Higginbotham in chapter 3 and Keenan in chapter 12). The other three options all have in common that the verb is construed with an NP-type denotation. What should be accounted for is that in the relevant Chinese cases the absence of XP allows a definite NP, whereas the presence of XP forces the NP to be indefinite and nonquantificational. Although we have nothing to say in particular about the character (list or nonlist) of the readings, we will attempt to provide some reasons for this correlation.

A similar situation, although obscured by some other factors, may be observed in the English pairs (5)–(6) and (7)–(8), where there appears to be a difference in the relation between the NP and the XP.

(5) There is the car in the garage

(6) There is a car in the garage

(7) There is everyone who has passed his orals
    (Context: Who is up for the Ph.D. exam?)

(8) There is a student who passed his orals

Sentence (5) is acceptable with a list reading with *in the garage* construed as a restrictive modifier of *the car*. In (6), on the other hand, *in the garage* is not understood as a restrictive modifier of the indefinite NP. Although not all speakers agree on the acceptability of universal NPs with expletives (see De Jong's discussion in chapter 11 on the two uses of universal NPs), list readings are more easily obtained in interrogative contexts and (7) shows such a reading with a restrictive relative clause. In (8) the relative clause cannot be restrictive to the indefinite NP, however, as is the case in (6). If we can somehow claim that in Chinese XP cannot be a restrictive modifier, the Chinese facts can be reduced to the English facts.

Tying in with Reinhart's result that the restrictive term of an operator is defined by the nodes it c-commands at S-Structure, the following empirical assumption seems a plausible general principle holding for English and Chinese alike and allows the required distinction to be derived.

(9) A restrictive reading of a Nom–Pred construction implies a
    structural NP.

Since English has postnominal modifiers, *the car in the garage* can be analyzed as an NP and has a restrictive reading. On the other hand, since Chinese lacks postnominal modifiers, this principle would rule out readings that indeed are lacking in Chinese. For a restrictive reading to obtain, the XP must be in the scope of the determiner of the NP. This is illustrated by the difference between restrictive and nonrestrictive readings of (10).

(10) Cindy noticed the man on the street

The nonrestrictive reading of (10) is defined only in models that contain one already identified man. The restrictive reading admits any number of men, provided that just one of them is on the street. This suggests that the restrictive reading of the NP is associated with a logical form or representation like [Det [man & on the street](x)], obtained from

[Det [[man (x)] & [on the street(x)]]]. In the nonrestrictive reading the modifier is obviously not part of the restriction on the quantifier. Hence, the modification relation must be expressed otherwise. We employ coindexing to represent referential markers that must be free for unselective binding but that also, if so bound, must receive identical interpretations. Without implying that coindexing is the correct or even the most illuminating way to do so, we represent this relation in nonrestrictive readings of (10) as [Det man(x_i)] & [on the street(x_i)]. We will assume the standard interpretation of predication—that is, the property denoted by XP is a member of the set of properties denoted by the NP, on a par with the property denoted by the noun. From a logical point of view it may be worthwhile to explore the formal properties of such dependencies of "free" referential markers, since in ordinary predicate logic variables are required to be interpreted by the same objects only if they are bound by the same quantifier and free variables cannot be required to be interpreted coreferentially.

Consider now what this entails for E-sentences that introduce new objects into the conversational domain. Whatever principle allows definite descriptions, proper names, or even universal NPs to occur in E-sentences with a list reading, it should make such uses of them nonquantificational in our sense. Philosophical discussions on definite descriptions in the context of metaphysical and epistemological studies of reference have never abated. But consensus has been obtained that a definite description may be used both to refer successfully to an object or individual even though the property is not true of it/him (Donnellan) and to assert existence of its referent (Russell). More recently arguments have been presented that universal NPs can be used in either a quantificational or a nonquantificational way. All we want to claim here is that, if such an NP is used in the coda of an E-sentence, it must be interpreted nonquantificationally. As a consequence, the set of properties interpreting such an NP is highly restricted, containing only the properties interpreting the predicates overtly expressed in the NP but no properties interpreting some XP predicate. Whatever the nature of the relation between an NP and an XP in the coda of an E-sentence, it cannot be the standard predication relation, if the sentence is used felicitously. An alternative construction of the NP-XP relation would be a conjunction of their properties. This process, we would like to claim, either involves free coindexing of free referential markers in the NP and XP predicates or requires them to be unselectively bound by the same sentential operator, which need not be overt (see Heim 1982).

Since NPs with a noncardinal specifier lack a free referential marker, even on their nonquantificational use, this option is available only for standard cardinal NPs. Hence, in structures like [Expl V_{exist} [$_{NP}$ Det $N'(x)$] [$_{XP}$ X$'(y)$]]] the XP cannot be truthfully predicated of the NP under some standard concept of predication. The coda as a whole can be interpreted by the conjunction of properties N' & X' only if both x and y can be coindexed or unselectively bound by the same operator. This requires that Det does not bind x, in other words, that Det is cardinal. So in the presence of an XP the requirement that the NP be nonquantificational in our general sense is not sufficient.

This gives us the correlation between the presence of an XP and the strengthening of the DR in Chinese. The facts in English are in principle similar but are obscured by other factors such as the presence of postnominal modifiers in NP. Given the different properties of inflection in Chinese, it may well be the case that unselective binding by a sentential operator is less readily available, leaving free coindexing of referential markers as the preferred option. This may provide a basis for the specificity found in the Chinese examples.

The special form of the relative clause in the XP of the coda in Chamorro E-sentences, discussed by Chung in chapter 8, may also be attributed to factors involving the relation between the NP and the XP. This relative clause requires a predicative expression with an open position available for "coindexed unselective binding." The structural requirements of Chamorro realize this predicative expression by a gap-creating strategy operating on a clause, producing a structure [$_{NP}$ NP [$_{S'}$ Comp [$_S$ ... EC ...]]] (where EC = empty category). As Chung notes, the path between the NP and the EC has the properties of one created by a process like question formation, that is, by movement. Since the local environment of the EC, and several other properties, are those of relativization constructions, something special must be happening here. Whatever its explanation, the standard form of the NP in the coda in English is also in some sense special, illustrated for instance by the difference between *There is a sick man* and *There is a man sick*. The prenominal adjective restricts the set of properties interpreting the NP and does not function as the predicate of a coda. The postnominal adjective leads to conjunction of properties. The form of the predicate in Chamorro E-sentences has the effect of excluding the standard attributive reading. The mixture of properties may arise from a process similar to the one operating in English purpose clauses (Chomsky 1981). The EC is created by moving an empty operator to Comp, accounting for properties of the path, and the result constitutes a predicate of the NP, coindexing the reference markers. The relative-like properties can be attributed to the lack of a lexical operator in Comp; that is, the item determining the value of the EC is an NP in head position, as in relatives.

These suggestions may sketch the outline of a comprehensive account of DEs in the various languages investigated in this book, while maintaining a sound universal foundation. Not only do the contributors present new substantive linguistic insights on the important topic of (in)definiteness; they also raise and perhaps resolve a number of foundational issues. If the research reported here should result in novel theoretical developments, we hope that this success will promote renewed and fruitful cooperation between the syntactic and semantic perspectives on natural language.

Note

1. These considerations do not exclude the possibility that one might find a sentential frame that appears to be ambiguous between having the force of an E-sentence and having the force of a declarative. In fact, even *there be NP* sentences in English could be said to be ambiguous, given a notion of structural identity that is sufficiently loose. However, given the distinction between locational and expletive *there,* the frames involved will be distinguished, as it is generally agreed they should be. Similarly, one might find a language in which what appears to be one and the same position relative to the verb is ambiguous with regard to whether it satisfies the conditions for counting as a canonical subject position or not. It is quite conceivable that in such a case the resolution of the ambiguity depends on a property of the structure that is by itself fairly abstract, such as the relation between inflection and verb (the *ci*-construction in Italian discussed in Belletti 1985 may constitute such a case). In order for such a situation to arise, a number of independent parameters must all be set in a specific way. Consequently, one may expect such cases to be quite rare, an expectation that agrees with the findings of Clark (1978).

Chapter 2

| Where Does the Definiteness Restriction Apply? Evidence from the Definiteness of Variables | Irene Heim |

Milsark's (1977) well-known *definiteness restriction* (DR) prohibits certain NPs—his *strong* class, including in particular the definites—from occurring as the postcopular subjects of *there*-insertion sentences. Although I do not offer an explanation for the DR here, if my observations are correct, they narrow down the range of plausible candidates for such an explanation. I make the following claims: (1) A peculiarity of *there*-insertion sentences that at first seems to be independent of the DR—namely, the confinement of the postcopular subject to narrowest-scope readings—can be explained as a special case of it. (2) The distribution of *wh*-traces in *there*-insertion sentences can be deduced from the DR as well, given independently motivated assumptions about the semantic interpretation of the *Wh*-Movement constructions in question. (3) Points 1 and 2 rely on, and thereby indirectly support, the assumption that the DR applies on whichever level of representation determines semantic interpretation most directly, rather than on a more "surfacey" syntactic level.

Milsark introduced the terms *weak* and *strong* as labels for two complementary distributional classes of NPs, roughly those that can and those that cannot appear in the postcopular subject position of *there be*-sentences. I will use the terms in the same way. Though it is certainly conceivable that these distributional classes are not natural semantic classes, there is a widespread inclination to think that they should be and hence to try to make them somehow definable in terms of concepts to be provided by an appropriate semantic theory for natural language. In fact, several (slightly different) definitions of weakness within truth-conditional semantics have already been suggested, including one explicitly stated in Barwise and Cooper 1981 and one implicit in Milsark 1977, both of which are conceptually simple and succeed in picking out the intended distributional class quite accurately.[1] It is surely significant in one way or another if the line betweek weak and strong can be drawn by a simple semantic definition, yet it is legitimate to wonder just what is accomplished by such a definition. What is it supposed to help explain? Does it, for instance, contribute anything toward an explanation of the DR?

The main motivation for those who have worked on such semantic definitions has been precisely this: to deduce with the help of that definition the deviance of *there be*-sentences with strong subjects. The two major lines of explanation that have emerged from such efforts, due to Milsark and to Barwise and Cooper, are quite different from each other, but both are attempts to reduce the DR to some common type of semantic deviance: vacuous quantification in one case, triviality in the other.[2] Surely, if such attempts succeed, that is one good reason to be interested in semantic definitions of weakness and strength.

Even if they do not succeed, however, and if indeed it remains largely obscure just what explains the DR, a hypothesis to the effect that the relevant distinction is a semantic one still need not be entirely without empirical consequence. It will influence our expectations concerning the level of analysis at which such an explanation will eventually be found. Everything else being equal, we expect it to be a semantic level rather than a syntactic one that is only indirectly related to semantic interpretation. It is this expectation that the present chapter provides evidence for.

2.1 Variables as Strong NPs

Given that the NP position after *there be* must be occupied by a weak NP, will it ever permit a bound variable? As far as overt bound variable pronouns are concerned, the answer is no.

(1) *Few people admitted that there had been them at the party

(2) *No perfect relationship is such that there is it

(Notice that (2) ought to mean just what *There is no perfect relationship* means.) These are completely hopeless, and one suspects this to be so for the same reason for which any definite pronoun whatsoever is prohibited after *there be,* regardless of what interpretation it receives. If we consider the semantics of individual variables as essentially analogous to that of names, except that the former depend on a variable assignment and the latter do not, their distributional similarity will not be surprising. Every known semantic characterization of the strong-weak distinction that characterizes names as strong automatically classifies individual variables as strong too, provided of course that it is relativized appropriately to a variable assignment so that it can apply to variables at all.[3] The prohibition in (3) thus seems natural.

(3) *There be x,* when *x* is an individual variable.

We have already seen that (3) is borne out when *x* is an overt bound variable pronoun. Let us now see whether other elements that have been analyzed as variables also bear out this prohibition.[4]

First, we must clarify at what level of representation (3) is supposed to apply. This is crucial because there are many cases where one may want to say that an NP position is occupied by a variable at one level of representation but by something else at another. Consider for example a *wh*-question like *Who did you see?* One may want to say that *who* is an operator of some kind (perhaps an existential quantifier, as in Karttunen 1977), but its trace is a variable—in other words, that the object position of *see* contains a nonvariable at D-Structure and a variable at S-Structure. Or consider sentences involving quantifiers, such as *Someone likes everyone.* Here the object position contains a nonvariable at both D-Structure and S-Structure, but some authors (see, for example, Montague 1974; May 1977) have assumed that it may, or even must, contain a variable at LF or some analogous level.[5] As far as the reading where *everyone* has narrower scope is concerned, there are diverging views on whether a variable or the quantifier itself appears in the object position at LF. But all investigators agree that a variable must appear there when *everyone* has widest scope. In these and similar cases it will obviously make a difference on what level (3) is hypothesized to apply.

Before we look at the empirical facts, let us consider the issue from the point of view of prima facie plausibility. Recall that (3) is a plausible hypothesis in the first place only to the extent that it follows as a corollary from the general prohibition against strong NPs that is imposed by the DR. According to the working hypothesis of this chapter, that prohibition is a "semantic" one in the sense that it singles out as prohibited a class of NPs with certain semantic properties. It is therefore most plausible, though admittedly not completely necessary, that it applies at the level that is most directly subject to semantic interpretation. In other words, everything else being equal we would expect (3) to hold at

LF rather than at D-Structure or S-Structure. Before we explore the empirical consequences of this assumption, let it be noted that alternative assumptions are conceivable and have been coherently advocated. For instance, Safir (1982, 1983b) assumes that the distinctive semantic property of strong as opposed to weak NPs is strictly correlated with a property that is relevant only at S-Structure: all and only the weak NPs are exempt from the binding theory, and it is this property that accounts for the distributional law under consideration. This puts an entirely different perspective on the status of (3). Supposing that variables are like strong NPs and unlike weak NPs in being subject to the binding theory at S-Structure, on Safir's analysis (3) should hold at S-Structure and have no relevance at LF. This is indeed what Safir assumes. But since his further assumptions conspire to ensure that no empty category after *there be* will count as a variable in the first place, this original assumption cannot be submitted to direct empirical evidence. It does, however, commit Safir's analysis to the expectation that the DR will never discriminate among examples that are essentially alike at S-Structure and have diverging properties only at LF, an expectation that appears to be falsified by the data I now turn to.

2.2 Absence of Wide-Scope Readings

One prediction that I will try to derive from the hypothesis that (3) holds at LF is the absence of wide-scope readings for the NPs in *there be*-sentences. Milsark noted that the (b)-sentences in (4) and (5) fail to exhibit the scope ambiguities of the corresponding (a)-sentences.

(4) a. Ralph believes that someone is spying on him
    b. Ralph believes that there is someone spying on him

(5) a. Someone must be in John's house
    b. There must be someone in John's house

Only narrow scope with respect to the propositional attitude verb or the modal is possible in the *there*-insertion variants, whereas either wide or narrow scope is possible in their (a)-counterparts. This phenomenon has been discussed by Williams (1984), who makes it follow from the assumption that *there* is what he calls a *scope marker*. If the alternative account sketched here is correct, it is more attractive than Williams's insofar as it reduces the wide-scope prohibition to the independently needed prohibition against strong NPs and makes unnecessary the stipulation that *there* is a scope marker. (Notice that it would not be easy for a child to learn that *there* is a scope marker, if this is simply an idiosyncratic property of this element. The child would seem to require evidence that a certain reading is absent, which is the sort of negative evidence that it is implausible that children make use of; see, for example, Baker 1979.)

Let us assume, contra May (1977) but with Montague (1974) and Williams (1984), that quantifying NPs may, at least sometimes, be interpreted in place and that this will correspond to narrowest-scope readings. (More accurately, it will correspond to readings where the NP in question has scope at most over what it c-commands in surface structure.) This option corresponds to an LF representation where the NP is in its S-Structure position. If, however, an NP is to have wider scope than another (non-c-commanded) element in the sentence, we assume that it must be moved and have its place filled by a variable at LF. The two potential readings of (5b), of which only one in fact appears, would thus have to have the LF representations given in (6a) and (6b).

(6) a. There must be someone in John's house
    b. Someone *x:* there must be *x* in John's house

Provided that (3) holds at LF, it will correctly rule out (6b), whereas (6a) should be acceptable since *someone* qualifies as weak.

A similar explanation may be applicable to an observation that Jackendoff (1977) attributes to Lakoff (1970): only the first of the following two sentences permits *few children* to take widest scope (what May (1977) would call the *inversely linked* reading) and thereby license *any*.

(7) a. Fathers of few children have any fun
    b. *Fathers with few children have any fun

Jackendoff hypothesizes that the contrast is due to a structural difference—namely, to the fact that *of few children* in (7a) is a complement and hence sister to N, whereas *with few children* in (7b) is a modifier and hence sister to N'. For all I know, this structural difference may well exist. But it is not clear, as Jackendoff admits, why it would have the observed effect on scope possibilities. At least this would not follow from any independently established structural constraints on quantifier scope. Besides, it is suspicious that the effect cannot be replicated with prepositions other than *with*. Consider, for instance, an example involving *in*.

(8) Someone in every city voted for Debs

May (1977) cites this example to illustrate an inversely linked reading. Under Jackendoff's assumption, this would imply that *in every city* can be construed as a complement rather than a modifier, which is not very plausible, either by his semantic criterion or by his distributional criterion. (Notice, for example, that such *in*-PPs may not precede other complements: **members in Fargo of the Democratic Party*.)

I would like to suggest instead that the absence of a wide-scope reading for the object of *with* in (7b) is related to another fact: that the *with* of possession, which is arguably the *with* found in this example, combines with weak NPs more acceptably than with strong ones.

(9) a house with many/no/27/*all the/*most windows

The exact nature of this cooccurrence restriction is unfortunately obscured by various complicating factors. For one thing, the prohibition against strong NPs mysteriously vanishes when the head is itself definite (compare *Here is the house with the five windows*). And even if we restrict our attention to indefinite heads, the prohibition seems to pertain only to certain readings for strong NPs after *with;* for instance, *a house with those windows,* strange though it is under an attempted interpretation where *those windows* demonstratively refers to a group of windows, is perfectly acceptable in the sense of 'a house with windows of that kind'. Pending a clearer picture of what is going on here, suppose the generalization is indeed that possessional *with* (under certain conditions at least) selects for a weak NP. Then we expect it to do so at LF. And this should entail as a special case that *with* must not be followed by a variable at LF, as it would have to for a wide-scope reading to arise. Another pair of Jackendoff's examples is also consistent with this suggestion.

(10) Arguments with few people yield any satisfaction

(11) ?*Arguments with few premises yield any satisfaction

Again, the *with*-PP in (10) may be a complement and the one in (11) a modifier, as Jackendoff supposes. But there is also another, and perhaps more relevant, difference—namely, that (11) involves a possession sense of *with,* whereas (10) does not. (Compare *This argument has three premises* to **This argument has three people*.) Here, too, the contrast in scope possibilities appears to correlate with a general contrast in the acceptability of strong NPs.

(12) ??Since this premise is not very well established, we should be skeptical of any arguments with it

(13) Since this guy has been known to get violent, we should stay clear of any arguments with him

2.3 Wh-Traces in Questions

I now turn to examples involving the traces of Wh-Movement in questions, relative clauses, and comparatives, all of which have frequently been regarded as variables. Starting with questions, let us consider the following judgments from Safir (1982).

(14) How many soldiers were there in the infirmary/drunk?

(15) ??Which one of the two men was there in the room/*drunk?

(16) ??Which actors were there in the room/*laughing?

(17) ?Who was there in the room when you got home?

It is not hard to describe in superficial terms what seems to be going on: the acceptability of such sentences depends on the "definiteness" of the moved wh-phrase. How many appears to be a weak determiner, just like its noninterrogative counterpart so many, and which seems to be strong, just like that. Who has often been analyzed as paraphrasing 'which person' or 'which persons', which would lead us to expect that (17) should be as questionable as (15) and (16). That it is in fact acceptable to some degree suggests that who can also be used with a slightly different meaning, perhaps paraphrasing something like 'what persons'. Clearly, what must be analyzed as something other than 'which thing(s)', given the full acceptability of (18).

(18) What is there in Austin?

The distinction between which and what has been described in terms of "definite" versus "indefinite" by more than one previous author (for example, see Katz and Postal 1964; Kuroda 1969; Stockwell, Schachter, and Partee 1973). But it is one thing to apply these labels and quite another to make sense of them in the context of an explanation that actually subsumes the data in (14)–(18) under a general prohibition against NPs of a certain semantic class. The problem is not merely that the wh-phrases appear in the wrong place at S-Structure, and therefore presumably in the wrong place at LF, for the DR to "see" them. Even if we base the analysis on a premovement representation where they are still in place, this will help us little unless we simultaneously make up some unconventional variety of interrogative semantics. (Under Karttunen's (1977) widely accepted treatment of questions, for instance, *which*-phrases are existential quantifiers, hence unfortunately weak, and should therefore be acceptable according to the DR.) If we want to make sense of the superficial generalization that our data suggest, then, we seem to need at least two potentially dubious assumptions: (i) that *wh*-phrases do not necessarily have scope over the S' whose Comp they move to; and (ii) that the interrogative determiners and pronouns *which, what, how many,* and so forth, have semantic properties by which they qualify heterogeneously as weak and strong. Would there be any independent support for these two assumptions?

Before addressing this question, a brief digression into interrogative semantics is in order. Following Karttunen (1977), I assume roughly the following analysis for a simple *which*-question like (19).

(19) Which woman do you blame *t*?

The trace *t* is interpreted as a variable, so the constituent *you blame t* denotes a proposition relative to any given variable assignment *g*, namely, the proposition that you blame $g(t)$. To this is applied an abstract question operator ?, and the result, *?you blame t,* denotes a set of propositions, either the unit set that contains the proposition that you blame $g(t)$, if the latter is true, or else the empty set. *Which woman* denotes the same thing as *a woman,* namely, the set of all properties that at least one woman has. This is now quantified into *?you blame t* in such a way that the result, (19), denotes a new set of propositions, namely, the set {*p:* there is a woman *x* such that *p* is true and *p* is the proposition that you blame *x*}. According to this analysis, *wh*-phrases are obligatorily quantified in. And that requirement makes good sense and should not be relaxed: if we first interpreted *you blame which woman,* giving *which woman* narrow scope, and then applied to that the question operator, we would predict a reading equivalent to *Do you blame any woman?*, which (19) does not have.

Karttunen (1977) did not discuss *how many*-questions, but in later unpublished work (whose results are reported most accessibly in Cooper 1983b), he addresses the general issue of interpreting questions involving so-called pied-piping, that is, questions where the moved phrase includes more than just the *wh*-word. Reiterating a point repeatedly made by Chomsky (for example, in Chomsky 1977), he notes that in pied-piping cases quantifying the moved phrase into the sentence whose Comp it has moved to gives rise to unwelcome readings. For instance, it would falsely predict that *Whose dog died?* calls for an answer like *Fido,* instead of one like *John's dog.* For present purposes, the issue is best illustrated with an example like (20).

(20) How many women do you blame *t*?

The problem here is that we do not want (20) to denote anything like the set {*p:* there is a degree *d* and there are *d*-many women *x* such that *p* is true and *p* is the proposition that you blame *x*}. If it denoted that set, (20) would be predicted to have answers like *I blame my sisters,* which intuitively is at best an indirect answer, insofar as the listener can be relied on to know how many sisters I have. The general consensus of those who have noticed this problem, from Chomsky to Cooper, is that such sentences are interpreted as if all of the *wh*-phrase except for the *wh*-operator itself were in its D-Structure position.[6] For instance, under Karttunen's approach the correct reading for (20) would result if *how*—which he would presumably interpret as equivalent to 'to some degree'—were quantified into ?*you blame x-many women.* There is thus independent evidence that the semantic analyses of *how many N*-questions involve narrow-scope occurrences of *x-many N.* This brings us an important step closer to our goal of explaining the contrast between (14) and (for example) (15) and (16); for *x-many,* despite the definiteness of the variable *x,* will certainly qualify as weak by any semantic definition, just like *that many* or, for that matter, *three.*

Still, our problem is not solved: what we would seem to be predicting from our current perspective is that *Wh*-Movement from the position after *there be* can be grammatical, but only when pied-piping is involved, that is, when the *wh*-operator does not exhaust the whole *wh*-phrase. This will not help in predicting either the grammaticality of (18) or the less than full ungrammaticality of (17).

Concerning (18), Cooper (1983b) provides a relevant observation. He notes that *what*-questions in dialogues like *What do you need?—A hammer* are not restricted to specific readings, as would be predicted if the semantic object of *need* had to be a variable, given Montague's treatment of specific-nonspecific ambiguities. He further notes that the same is not true for *Who do you need?—A psychiatrist,* which forces a specific reading, though, confusingly, this is less so for *Who do you need to see?—A psychiatrist.* Even in the absence of any explanation, the parallel with (18) and (17), including the ambivalent status of *who,* is encouraging.

Is there any way of treating *Wh-*Movement of *what* as some sort of pied-piping in disguise, that is, as movement of an NP that properly contains a variable bound by the interrogative operator but that as a whole is interpreted in its premovement position? I will suggest that *what* should be analyzed roughly as though it were 'something of what kind'. A *what-*question could then be analyzed as involving a narrow-scope occurrence of 'something of kind x', with x a variable bound by the interrogative operator in Comp. 'Something of kind x' is of course transparently indefinite, despite the definiteness of the kind-variable it contains, and this would explain its ability to follow *there be* in LF.

In spelling out this suggestion more explicitly, I will appropriate for my purposes a semantic analysis that Carlson (1977a) has proposed for the word *such.* This makes sense insofar as it can be argued that *what* is the interrogative counterpart of *such.* Of course, the analogy is far from complete. For one thing, *such* in modern English can only appear in front of a common noun, never as a complete N' or NP by itself. The closest noninterrogative counterpart of (18) that is actually expressible in English would be something like (21).

(21) There are/is such stuff/such things/such a thing in Austin

Actually, both the distribution of *such* and the distribution of *what* in English appear to be subject to various quite idiosyncratic restrictions that interact with and obscure their essential semantic properties and the parallels between them. This does not affect the legitimacy of my contention that Carlson's semantics for *such* is adequate for *what,* but it certainly makes it harder to give compelling arguments. I hope to make it at least plausible that the resulting interpretation is consistent with English speakers' intuitions about the meaning of *what.* First, however, I will briefly review some of the facts about *such* that provide the background of Carlson's analysis, pointing out some parallels between *such* and *what* along the way.

In line with previous authors (Bolinger 1972; Bresnan 1973), Carlson distinguishes between an "extent" reading and an "identifier" reading of *such.* The extent reading is only available when *such* precedes an adjective or a gradable noun, whereas the identifier reading is possible regardless of environment. An ambiguous example with two different disambiguating continuations is Bresnan's *Hilda is such a scholar (that all her work is impeccable/as you were talking of just now).* An analogous ambiguity can be observed in *what:* for instance, in *Betty didn't know what scholars they were* (Greg Carlson, personal communication). Here the choice between the two readings appears to correlate with the distinction between exclamatives and interrogatives. Exclamatives (*What scholars they are!, What a scholar she is!*) show the extent reading, interrogatives (*What movies/What music do you like?*) the identifier reading. *What a* is altogether limited to exclamatives and hence to the extent reading. (This curious defectiveness of the interrogative use of determiner *what* forces a speaker to resort to different locutions to express interrogative variants of many *such*-sentences—for instance, *How much of a scholar is she?* rather than **What a scholar is she?*) The reading of *what,* and correspondingly of *such,* that is exclusively relevant at the moment is the identifier reading. This is also the one that Carlson concentrates on in his analysis of *such.*

Basically, Carlson treats *such* as a modifier that means 'of that kind' or 'of kind *x*', where the variable *x* may be understood as referring to some contextually salient kind, or to a kind introduced in immediately preceding discourse. For instance, *every such bird* means 'every bird of that kind', *such people* means 'people of that kind' (with whatever reading the latter bare plural may have), and *such a scholar* means 'a scholar of that kind' (where the inverted order *such a* instead of *a such* is due to some superficial reordering process). He offers good reasons for this analysis as opposed to the obvious alternative of treating *such* simply as a semantically unrestricted pro-modifier. For one thing, *such* cannot be interpreted as standing for a modifier that does not pick out a subset of the modified common noun (*future teachers . . . ??such teachers*). Furthermore, *such Ns* resists being interpreted as standing for a closed set of individuals that do not constitute a kind (*people in the next room . . . ??such people*).

Putting the essence of Carlson's analysis in slightly more technical terms, we can say that the N' *such bird* denotes the set of things that realize the kind *x*, where *x* is presupposed to be a subkind of the birds. If we leave out the subkind presupposition, the result is an interpretation that will suit *such* used as an N' by itself, to the extent that such a use exists. The processes by which N's of the form *such* (*N*) can be completed to full NPs are the usual ones (though, curiously, the definite determiners are prohibited here, as in Carlson's *the such men), including the option of forming a determinerless NP (provided that the N is mass or plural), which has generic and indefinite (that is, existential) uses.

Interrogative *what* can be treated just like *such*, except that earlier remarks about the interpretation of the kind-variable x need to be qualified. Instead of referring to a contextually salient or previously mentioned kind, it will here be a bound variable, bound by an interrogative operator in Comp, which is, under Karttunen's analysis, an existential quantifier with scope over the question. For instance, (18) will denote the set of propositions {p: there is a kind x such that p is true and p is the proposition that there are (is) things (a thing/stuff) of kind x in Austin}. We may note that Cooper's problem with the nonspecific reading of *What do you need?* is thereby solved; this sentence will denote the set {p: there is a kind x such that p is true and p is the proposition that you need things (a thing/stuff) of kind x}. A potentially problematic feature of this analysis of *what* is that it assigns *what* (N) primarily to the type of N's (that is, predicates) and lets it become an NP only by whatever operations make an existential indefinite NP out of *such N* or any other N'. Why, then, should it be the case that identifier-*what*, unlike identifier-*such*, is never preceded by any other determiner and may not even be followed by *a?* (*What a*-exclamatives are not a counterexample to this generalization, since they involve the extent reading, which we are not concerned with here.) I cannot explain this any more than the prohibition against definite determiners before *such*.

As for *who*, we might say that it can mean either 'which person(s)' or the interrogative counterpart of 'such (a) person(s)', but the latter option is only marginally available. This would roughly make sense of the judgments that Safir and Cooper report.

To complete the picture, I should briefly comment on the behavior of questions involving *whose*. For semantic reasons exactly analogous to those mentioned in connection with *how many* (see again Cooper 1983b), a question like *Whose drink did you spill?* must be taken to involve a narrow-scope occurrence of x's *drink* (or, marginally, something amounting to 'such a person's drink'). This will count as a strong NP for whatever reason *that woman's drink* counts as strong, a welcome prediction in view of the following judgment.

(22) *Whose drink is there t left on the table?

I should mention as well that even interrogative phrases of the form *which N* have been argued to act as though everything but the *which* itself was interpreted in place. Engdahl (1980) has spelled out a treatment along such lines (for details of its motivation, see the dissertation itself). Recall that in the case of *which*-NPs, Karttunen's original analysis, under which the entire *wh*-phrase had wide scope and a mere (individual) variable occupied the trace position, made the right predictions for the *there*-insertion facts in question here. Luckily, though, so does Engdahl's analysis. Roughly speaking, she interprets *Which women came?* as 'For which function *W* is it true that everything in the extension of *W*(women) came?' (*W* ranges over functions that map sets of individuals into subsets thereof, so *W*(women) is a subset of the women.) Notice that what is interpreted in the place of the trace here is in effect a universally quantified NP ('everything in the set *W*(women)') and will hence qualify as strong. This is all that matters here.[7]

What I have said about *what* and *which* seems to put me into agreement with the above-mentioned traditional proposals to classify *which*-NPs as "definite" and *what*-NPs as "indefinite." However, it is not prima facie obvious that any of the symptoms of "definiteness" on which such proposals have been based are actually predicted by my treatment of *which*. Kuroda (1969), for instance, cites as evidence for the definiteness of *which*-NPs as opposed to *what*-NPs the contrast in *You may read* Syntactic Structures *or* La Nausée.—*Which*/??*What do you want to read?* To me, this example suggests that *which*-NPs are inherently partitives; in other words, *which (N)* is interpreted as equivalent to *which of them (of the Ns)*, whereas *what (N)* never means **what of them (of the Ns)*. One can hardly take for granted that this follows from *which* and *what* being strong and weak, respectively; after all, both strong and weak determiners can head partitives and nonpartitives in other cases, such as *how many of us, all applicants* (as opposed to *all the applicants*). It may, however, follow at least partially from the suggestion that *what* introduces a kind-variable. Observe the general unacceptability of partitives with kind-denoting heads.

(23) *Big ones of my turtles/*This kind of my turtles withstand(s) freezing temperatures

As Carlson (1977a) points out, restrictive modifiers that limit the extension of the common noun phrase to a closed, contextually definite set are intrinsically incompatible with kind-readings.

2.4 *Wh-*Traces in Comparatives

Carlson (1977b) notes that it is generally acceptable to have a gap after *there be* in *than-* and *as*-clauses.

(24) There are more women in high school than there are in college

(25) There aren't as many women in college as there are in high school

Every semantic analysis of comparatives that I am aware of assumes that the comparative clause in (24) (and analogously in (25)) looks like (26) or perhaps (27) on the level of representation to which semantic interpretation applies.

(26) . . . than there are x women in college

(27) . . . than there are x-many women in college

(See, for example, Cresswell 1976.) This implies that the position of the *wh-*trace after *there be* corresponds semantically to a narrow-scope NP that is weak (see the analogous case of *how many*-questions discussed earlier). To my knowledge, none of those semanticists tried to interpret such sentences under the assumption that the trace was simply an individual variable. (They mostly took it for granted that there was good syntactic evidence for deriving (24) by a deletion transformation from (26) or (27).) So we cannot claim that they had independent semantic evidence for their choice, as we could in the analogous case of pied-piped questions. Let us still make a brief effort to look for such evidence.

Following Cresswell (1976) and others, let us assume that at least those comparative clauses that are superficially complete up to a missing degree determiner are semantically degree descriptions; that is, they denote degrees.[8] So *(than) the door is wide* denotes the degree max$d$[the door is d-wide], and *(as) you saw lizards* denotes max$d$[you saw d-many lizards]. As for the comparative suffix *-er,* it essentially expresses a relation between two degrees. For instance, in the interpretation of a sentence like *The desk is higher than the door is wide,* *-er* may be taken to relate the (maximal) degree to which the door is wide and the (maximal) degree to which the desk is high.

Now if this semantics for *-er* is to extend in the most straightforward way to cases involving comparative clauses with an NP gap, those too should be descriptions of degrees. Suppose instead that *(than) I own* were interpreted as something like 'the x such that I own x' or '$^{\wedge}x$: I own x', with an individual (or set) variable x. This would be a description or predicate of things, not a description of degrees. To be sure, there is a uniquely determined degree description that can be recovered from every thing predicate F, namely the description 'the cardinality of F'. But this would not yield the correct degree in most cases. It would predict that in a sentence like *You caught more lizards than I own* the number of lizards that you caught is being compared with the number of all my possessions, whereas in fact it is being compared solely with the number of *lizards* that I own. To avoid this inadequacy, we would have to make *-er* a slightly more complicated sort of operator that first combines with a thing predicate and makes another operator, which then combines with another thing predicate (the one supplied by the N') to finally make a degree description that picks out the cardinality of the intersection of the extensions of the two thing predicates. But this move not only complicates matters; it fails to account for certain facts. (My reasoning here is inspired by Carlson 1977b.) For instance, it would seem to imply, contrary to the facts, that (28) permits only a "specific" reading for the object of *need* and that (29) precludes an idiomatic reading.

(28) I always have more paper clips than I need t

(29) We made more headway in one week than they made t in a whole year

The problem vanishes as soon as we revert to what semanticists have generally assumed: that the interpretation of comparative clauses with NP gaps involves narrow-scope occurrences of indefinite NPs of the form $x(-many/-much)$ N' in the trace position. We may thus conclude that such assumptions were not just a result of insufficient motivation to pursue alternatives but are in fact required by the demands of an optimally simple and adequate assignment of truth-conditions. The data in question here concerning *there*-insertion can be explained by this assumption and thus provide another bit of indirect support for it. Needless to say, the implications of such an analysis for a theory of how semantics and syntax fit together remain quite unclear. Bresnan's (1973) account of the deletion and extraposition rules that would be needed to relate the surface structures to the semantically relevant structures remains the only worked-out proposal.

2.5 *Wh*-Traces in Relative Clauses

Consider once again data from Safir 1982.

(30) ??The men/Many men who there were in the room were eating guavas

(31) *The men/Many men, all of whom there were in the back room, ate guavas

(32) ??Schools of fish which/∅/that there were in the river died suddenly

(33) The very few books that/∅/which there were on his shelves were all mysteries

(34) Every single man that/∅/who there was in the castle was ready to fight for his life[9]

(35) All the men that/∅/?which there were in the garrison sallied forth en masse to meet the enemy

(36) All of the men that there were in the room suddenly began eating guavas

Since the facts are rather bewildering here, it is unsurprising that Safir's discussion of them remains more or less inconclusive. He first considers the hypothesis that the definiteness of the *head noun* is the decisive factor for the grammaticality of these examples, dismissing it because of the indefinite variants of (30)–(32) on the one hand and because of (33)–(36) on the other. Then he considers another hypothesis: that it is the definiteness of the *relative operator* that matters. He notes that this hypothesis would imply that the relative operator need not agree in definiteness with the head, which he finds implausible, because in other features (he cites number as an example) transparently obligatory agreement obtains between head noun and relative operator. For this reason, which I do not find compelling (especially since he attempts no alternative explanation), he dismisses the second hypothesis as well.

A more encouraging attempt to make sense of the distribution of gaps after *there be* in relative clauses has been made by Carlson (1977b). To be fair to Safir, it must be noted that Carlson starts from slightly different judgments: according to him, (33), (34), and (35) are acceptable with *that* and zero complementizers (as they are for Safir) but not unacceptable with the *wh*-forms. As far as I can tell, though, this difference in judgments is minor compared to the generalizations that appear to hold for both authors' dialects and that Carlson's analysis predicts.

Carlson argues that the customary distinction between appositive and restrictive relative clauses should be replaced by a three-way distinction among appositive, restrictive, and "amount" relatives. The third group has usually been subsumed under the restrictive relatives, and its diverging syntactic and semantic properties have been neglected. Carlson notes, among others, the following differences between restrictive and amount relatives: (a) Only amount relatives permit relativization of the position after *there be*. (b) Only amount relatives permit antecedent-contained VP deletion. (c) Only restrictive relatives permit *wh*-relative pronouns; amount relatives must have *that* or zero complementizers. (d) Amount relatives are compatible only with a limited class of determiners on their heads, which includes *the*, *every*, *all*, free choice *any*, and nondemonstrative *that* but excludes all cardinality words, the zero determiner, *most*, *each*, demonstratives, and possessives.

As noted, there appears to be dialectal variation with respect to (c). In Safir's dialect *wh*-pronouns are acceptable in at least some amount relatives. Otherwise, Safir's data are consistent with Carlson's claims; specifically they seem to bear out the correlation between (a) and (d). The examples Safir judges fully grammatical contain the head determiners *the very few (books), every single (man), all the (men),* and *(all of) the (men).* Of the examples he assigns * or ??, one involves appositive relatives, one the zero determiner, and one *many (men);* only the first variant of (30)—*the men who there were,* which he assigns ??— does not quite fit in. Note, however, that this example involves *who* rather than *that* or a zero Comp. Could it be that the dialect difference with respect to Carlson's criterion (c) is not that much of a difference after all? I tentatively conclude that Carlson's claim that only amount relatives permit relativization of the postcopular subject of *there*-sentences carries over to Safir's dialect, even though there may be some differences in the way amount relatives can be realized, and I proceed to Carlson's semantic analysis of amount relatives and how it explains the *there*-insertion data.

As indicated by his choice of terminology, Carlson maintains that the semantics of amount relatives crucially involves talking about amounts (in my terminology, degrees) and is in that respect much like the semantics of comparative clauses. Although Carlson does not give an explicit semantics in his paper, his informal discussion is precise enough to make it in essential respects predictable. Concerning (37), he points out that it does not mean (38) but rather is equivalent to (39).

(37) Marv put everything he could in his pocket

(38) Every x (Marv could put x in his pocket $\rightarrow$ Marv put x in his pocket)

(39) Marv put as many things as he could in his pocket

Similarly suggestive, I might add, is the fact that sentences like (40) permit a reading where only identity of amounts, not identity of substances, is required for their truth.

(40) It will take us the rest of our lives to drink the champagne that they spilled that evening

Carlson concludes from observations such as these that amount relatives, like comparative clauses, are degree descriptions; for instance, the amount relative in (37) appears to denote max$d$[Marv could put d-many things in his pocket]. His proposal further implies that this degree description combines with the licensing head determiner (here, *every*) so as to form a complex cardinality word equivalent to 'as many . . . as he could (put things in his pockets)'. Exactly how *every* must be interpreted to accomplish this is not quite clear from his paper. Be that as it may, treating the amount relative as essentially a degree description appears to be a step in the right direction, whatever its exact contribution to the meaning of the containing NP.

If this is borne out, it supports a line of reasoning analogous to the one applied earlier to comparative clauses: the relevant degree description is easily determined on the basis of a logical form that contains a narrow-scope occurrence of something like *x-many Ns* or *x Ns* in the trace position, whereas it is not directly recoverable if the trace corresponds to a variable ranging over individuals. The acceptability of *there*-insertion falls out, once again, given that *x-many Ns* is a weak NP and that the prohibition against strong NPs applies at the same level (LF or whatever it is) at which the trace position supposedly contains such an NP.

It remains to be shown how *there*-insertion is in fact excluded in restrictive and appositive relatives. Here (as in the case of interrogative *which*-NPs considered earlier), we can arrive at the desired prediction in either one of two ways. We can claim that the trace of restrictive and appositive relativization is for semantic purposes an individual variable, presumably bound by the relative pronoun interpreted as a property abstraction operator. Or we can assume that in the semantically relevant structure the relative pronoun itself occupies the trace position and that this pronoun is an individual variable or a referential anaphoric definite. Perhaps the first view is correct for restrictives and the second for appositives. In any event, both are semantically feasible and conform to syntactic analyses that have been widely entertained. We may leave the choice open. All that matters here is that the element that is interpreted in the trace position is a strong NP in either case.

2.6 Conclusion

The facts we have considered here fall far short of suggesting any particular explanation for the DR. But they do not tell us one thing about it: it seems to apply at a level of analysis where scope ambiguities have been disambiguated and where *Wh*-Moved material has been restored to the position in which it is semantically interpreted. We may assume otherwise, but only at the cost of losing an explanation for the scope and *Wh*-Movement options of postcopular subjects that purports to derive them entirely from the DR and independently motivated assumptions concerning the representations that feed semantic interpretation. I hasten to concede that some of that independent motivation is highly tentative for the time being, and a much deeper understanding of the semantics of interrogative pronouns, comparatives, and relativization may be needed to assess it. But it should also be noted that most of the present facts are not, to my knowledge, covered by any competing explanation at all, and certainly not by one that requires fewer stipulations.

Notes

I am grateful to Alice ter Meulen and Eric Reuland for providing me with the incentive for the work reported here, and to Barbara Levergood and Greg Carlson for interesting constructive and critical comments on prefinal versions.

1. See also Doron 1983 and Keenan's discussion in chapter 12.

2. Details aside, Barwise and Cooper define a weak determiner as one for which *Det As are As* is contingent. For example, *every* and *neither* are strong, because *Every man is a man* is tautological and *Neither man is a man* is contradictory. But *three* and *no* are weak, because *Three men are men* is true if there are at least three men and false if there are fewer than three, and *No man is a man* is true if there are no men and false otherwise. Given their interpretation of *there are NP* as equivalent to "NP are in the universe of discourse,"

Barwise and Cooper can then deduce that any *there be*-sentence with a strong subject is tautological or contradictory, which they consider a sufficient reason for judging it deviant. There are several reasons to question the validity of this explanation, in particular its failure to account for contrasts in acceptability between truth-conditionally equivalent paraphrases such as *There is no perfect relationship* and **No perfect relationship is such that there is it*.

Milsark defines strong NPs as those that contain a quantifier and weak ones as those that do not. This definition presupposes a nonquantificational analysis of weak determiners that construes them as cardinality predicates (which appears to be advisable for other reasons; see, for example, Stechow 1980); it also presupposes a quantificational treatment of the definite article and a treatment of names and definite pronouns as implicit definite descriptions. *There be*, according to Milsark, is inherently an existential quantifier that must quantify the postcopular NP and is therefore in complementary distribution with any quantifiers already inherent in the latter. A problem with this attempt to explain the DR is that *there be*-sentences with monotone decreasing NPs (such as *no kisses, few hugs*) cannot be analyzed in terms of a widest-scope existential quantifier (again see Stechow 1980).

3. In Barwise and Cooper 1981 bound variable pronouns are literally analyzed as definite descriptions (p. 174), so they are obviously regarded as strong. An alternative might be to rephrase slightly Barwise and Cooper's definition of weakness so that it applies to NPs rather than Dets, defining a weak NP as one for which *NP are entities* is contingent. This would not make any substantive difference in the way the definition applies but would make it possible to assess the strength of variables without analyzing them as definite descriptions. Clearly, *x is an entity* is tautological under any given variable assignment, so *x* qualifies as strong.

As for Milsark's definition, it will designate variables as strong provided that they are analyzed as definite descriptions; but recall from note 2 that this proviso applies with proper names and deictic pronouns as well.

Notice, incidentally, that we are only talking about *individual* variables here. If we were to take into consideration variables of higher types—for instance, variables ranging over second-order properties (see Montague 1974)—these would not qualify as uniformly strong by any reasonable semantic definition of strength that has been or might be proposed.

4. An anonymous reviewer observes that the present formulation of (3) is blatantly inadequate when combined with the analysis of indefinites "as variables" that I put forward in Heim 1982. If indefinites are basically just variables, then (3) rules out every good *there be*-sentence!

A closer look at the source of this inconsistency shows that at least part of the problem is due to an assumption that is neither essential nor unique to Heim 1982—namely, the assumption that indefinites are never in situ in LF, but obligatorily undergo Quantifier Raising (QR; the "NP-Prefixing" of Heim 1982), leaving behind an individual variable. Clearly, such an assumption immediately renders (3) untenable, regardless of whether the QRed indefinite is given a standard quantificational or a variable analysis. If I were to rewrite this chapter in the framework of Heim 1982, the first step toward consistency would therefore be to refine the construal and interpretive system of that study in such a way as to permit genuine narrowest-scope representations for NPs with descriptive content. I would have to make NP-Prefixing optional and provide appropriate interpretive rules for LF representations with full NPs in situ by providing higher-type (that is, term-type) denotations for NPs: for example, $\{P: \text{cat}(x_7)\ \&\ P(x_7)\}$ for *a cat*$_7$. (The truth-conditions of sentences with indefinites remain unaffected by this.) With this revision of Heim 1982, (3) will no longer rule out indefinites after *there be*, provided they are construed with narrowest scope.

However, if the conclusions of this chapter are to carry over in full, I must also ensure that (3) continues to be a corollary of a natural semantically based formulation of the DR in general. I thus need a characterization of weak versus strong NPs that will correctly draw the line between the term-type interpretations of definites (including bound variable pronouns and traces of QR) on the one hand and indefinites on the other, even though both are alike in containing free individual variables. Definition (i) is a first try at such a characterization: an attempt to synthesize Barwise and Cooper's definition with the "familiarity theory" of definiteness from Heim 1982. (There are probably other possibilities, and formulation (i) almost certainly contains inadequacies that I have overlooked, but I hope that it will provide a basis that can later be improved upon.)

(i) NP is strong iff F entails $F + NP\ exist$ for every file F that conforms to the felicity conditions imposed by NP.

The pertinent definition of entailment between files is given in (ii).

(ii) F entails F' iff for every a_N and w such that a_N is in $\text{Sat}_w(F)$, there is a b_N that agrees on $\text{Dom}(F)$ with a_N such that b_N is in $\text{Sat}_w(F')$.

Suppose, for example, that NP is an indefinite (say, *a cat*$_7$), with the term-type denotation indicated above, so that *NP exist* amounts to $cat(x_7)$. By the Novelty/Familiarity Condition, this NP is only felicitous with respect to files F whose domain excludes 7. Will an arbitrary such F entail $F + cat(x_7)$? No, because there may be no cats at all. On the other hand, if NP is definite, the Novelty/Familiarity Condition will ensure that its index is already in $\text{Dom}(F)$ (and that F entails its descriptive content, if any); therefore, the pertinent entailment will always hold. (For NPs that do not contain free variables, the definition should reduce to Barwise and Cooper's.)

In the remainder of this chapter I will continue to assume the standard quantificational analysis of indefinites. I believe that my conclusions can be transposed into the alternative theory of Heim 1982 by spelling out the hints in this note, but an explicit demonstration of this will have to await another occasion.

5. Similar constructs in other theoretical frameworks that play essentially the role of the logical forms of Government-Binding (GB) Theory are for instance the analysis trees of Montague Grammar and the composition structures proposed by Ladusaw (1983). I will take the liberty of employing GB terminology (more or less) throughout this chapter, even where I appropriate ideas from authors who would not want to express themselves that way. It should be clear

that the issues I am concerned with arise independently of any assumptions specific to GB Theory.

6. Disagreement has merely concerned the question of how this should be accomplished, whether (for instance) by applying semantic interpretation on the D-Structure level, by positing reconstruction rules in LF, or by employing Cooper-storage devices in surface structure interpretation.

7. Engdahl has proposed somewhat different analyses in later work (Engdahl 1982), and still other variants of the idea that some part of the *Wh*-Moved *which*-NP is interpreted in the trace position are conceivable. It remains to be seen whether the best-motivated analysis on independent grounds will indeed posit a strong NP in the trace position.

8. The term *degree* is used here so as to include cardinalities and amounts as special cases. Examples of degrees are thus not only the degree to which Texas is large or the degree to which Hilda is a scholar, but also the degree to which my jazz records are many (which corresponds to the cardinality of the set of my jazz records) and the degree to which the loneliness I have endured is much (which corresponds to an amount).

The notation "max$d$[... d ...]" stands for 'the maximal degree d that satisfies ... d ...'.

9. Safir's original example reads *Every single man that/∅/who was there* . . . ; I have changed the order on the assumption that he intended *there was*.

Chapter 3

| Indefiniteness and Predication | James Higginbotham |

In this chapter I will consider several domains in which some distinction between *definite* and *indefinite* expressions, prototypically NPs, plays a prominent role in sentential syntax and conditions on interpretation. In these domains definite NPs are either disallowed or, if permitted, carry semantic implications that are not borne by indefinites; these phenomena are the *definiteness effects* (DEs) of modern syntactic literature. Those to be considered, and typical data from each, are as follows.

(i) Predicate nominals of the sort in (1).

(1) John is a/*every lawyer from Pittsburgh

(ii) Contexts of *there*-insertion, as in (2).

(2) There are some/*most books on the table

(iii) Scopal independence. Sentence (3) admits both the expected quantificational interpretation, represented by (4), and an interpretation in which the quantifiers are independent (neither falling within the scope of the other), paraphraseable as in (5).

(3) Several men danced with many women (at the party)

(4) [several x: man(x)] [many y: woman(y)] x danced with y

(5) At the party, some collection composed of several men, and another collection composed of many women, are such that dancing went on between them

Sentence (6), however, admits only the properly (individually) quantificational interpretation shown in (7); nothing corresponding to (5) is available.

(6) Several men danced with most women (at the party)

(7) [several x: man(x)] [most y: woman(y)] x danced with y

There is a distinction, then, between definite *most women* and indefinite *many women,* in that only the latter admits scopal independence. Similarly, it seems to me, NPs whose specifiers are *few* and *every* do not admit scopal independence, although all of the ordinary indefinites (specified by *some,* number-words, and so forth) do.

(iv) Support of unbound ("donkey-sentence") anaphora, as in (8) and (9).

(8) If I see [a few donkeys], I'll kick them

(9) *If I see [few donkeys], I'll kick them

(v) Accessibility to cleft and pseudocleft constructions, as in the contrasts shown in (10) and (11),

(10) What you drank was [lots of/*little] water

(11) Was it [an/*every] Irish poem John recited?

where what is excluded in (11) is the interpretation 'Did John recite every Irish poem (or did he recite something else)?' as explained more fully below.

To these five domains one might add a sixth, or even a seventh, namely, (vi) the availability in the case of indefinites of "specific" interpretations and, perhaps correlatively, (vii) the attenuation of weak crossover effects for pronominals with indefinite antecedents.[1] It appears to me that, insofar as the latter phenomena are grammatically controlled at all, they have an exclusively illocutionary character and belong, to use Fregean terminology, to a theory of *force* rather than to a theory of *sense.* Toward the end of the discussion I will endeavor to explain why I think that this is so.

What, if anything, do these DEs have in common? I will argue that they arise from an interaction between factors involving the variety of meanings permitted to a quantificational specifier or determiner and conditions on the form and interpretation of syntactic structures, especially conditions on *predication,* as explained later. If this thesis is correct, then there is no one DE; at the same time the several types afford a window through which to view a number of syntactic and semantic processes affecting even simple sentences in fairly intricate ways.

The major portion of my analytical discussion will be devoted to predicate nominals and *there*-insertion. However, even for those phenomena that I cannot consider in depth here, I will try to make the case for distinguishing the DEs into their different varieties.

Throughout this chapter I will consider almost exclusively simple nominals of the form NP = Spec – N′, where Spec(ifier) is a single word, as in the examples considered so far. This restriction is necessary both because of space limitations and because the internal structure of complex nominals, such as partitives, is not, in my view, well enough understood at present. If the proposals given here have some substance, then it may be possible to extend the analysis to the more complex cases.

For syntactic background, I will assume the outlines of the theory developed in Chomsky 1981, and specifically the linguistic levels of S-Structure and LF as understood there. I also assume general principles of adjunction (reflected semantically as scope assignment) at LF, along the lines of Higginbotham 1983a,b and references cited there, and the application of semantic theory to structures at LF as suggested in Higginbotham 1985. I turn now to a discussion of predicate nominals, the first of the five domains just mentioned.

3.1 Predicate Nominals

We owe to Edwin Williams the idea that the relation of *predication* plays a critical role in conditions on grammaticality. I understand predication as a formal binary relation on points (nodes) of phrase markers. Unlike Williams (1980), I envisage no special notation for it; however, the relation is a part of the syntactic structure to which it applies.

Predicate nominals are predicates and thus participate in the predication relation: the relevant question is why they must be indefinite. But the very existence of predicate nominals ought to be seen as something of a puzzle. NPs are the prototype of arguments—why are they capable of occurring as predicates at all? The answer to the latter question, I believe, will point the way to an answer to the question of indefiniteness.

I will use the terms *saturated* and *unsaturated,* in conscious imitation of Frege (1891), to mark a distinction between phrases that denote (or purport to denote) objects and those that have one or more open places, into which objects are to go. As noted in Rothstein 1983, we might expect the principles in (12) and (13) to be true.

(12) All arguments are saturated.

(13) All predicates are unsaturated.[2]

NPs are saturated, so they can be arguments. And it may be said, as for instance in Higginbotham 1983a, that the role of the determiner or Spec of NP is to saturate it, by binding the open position in N′. With this understanding, the phrase *a lawyer* counts as saturated as it occurs in (14).

(14) A lawyer is at the door

Thus, restricted quantifiers are included among the saturated expressions. Representing the open position in *lawyer* by a numeral enclosed in angled brackets, and representing the saturation of this position in the subject NP by marking that position with a star, *, the internal constitution of (14) is as shown in (15).

(15) $[_{\text{NP}}$ a $[_{\text{N}'}$ lawyer, $\langle 1 \rangle], \langle 1^* \rangle]$

The predicate of (14) also contains an open position, filled in S by the subject NP under predication. Fully annotated, the sentence has the S-Structure representation shown in (16).

(16) $[_{\text{S}}[_{\text{NP}}$ a $[_{\text{N}'}$ lawyer, $\langle 1 \rangle], \langle 1^* \rangle]$ [is at the door $\langle 1 \rangle], \langle 1^* \rangle]$

At LF the subject NP is adjoined to S, giving (17).

(17) $[_{\text{S}}[_{\text{NP}}$ a lawyer] $[_{\text{S}}$ *t* [is at the door]]]

For further details, see Higginbotham 1985 and the references cited there.

According to this interpretation of phrases like *a lawyer,* predicate nominals are impossible, contrary to fact. In (18),

(18) John is [a lawyer]
     ↑_____|

where the arrow shows predication, the predicate nominal must be unsaturated; but it cannot be unsaturated, since the N′ *lawyer* has but one open place, and that should be bound by the indefinite article, as in (15).

A contradiction has been deduced from a family of premises. The one to give up, I think, is that determiners are invariably binders of open positions. Suppose that the indefinite article in (18) is interpreted instead essentially as an adjective is interpreted. Then, I will argue, *a lawyer* will come out as (19).

(19) a(x) & lawyer(x)[3]

Finally, suppose that *a* means *one* — in other words, that it is a predicate true of each individual thing, or thing that is not a plurality. The whole of (19) is then predicated of the subject in, say, *John is a lawyer,* whose truth-conditions are then what they should be.

My proposal has been swiftly stated and deserves some examination before we proceed. In Higginbotham 1985 I argue that adjectival modification should be understood as *identifying* positions in the thematic structures of the modifying adjective and the modified noun. For instance, it seems to me that, assuming that *brown* and *cow* both have open positions in them, we should regard *brown cow* as formed along the lines of (20),

(20) [[brown,$\langle 1 \rangle$] [cow,$\langle 1 \rangle$],$\langle 1 \rangle$]
         └──────────┘

where the connecting line shows identification of positions. The identification is part of the syntactic structure, and the whole phrase *brown cow* therefore has, like its nominal head, a single open position. Modification is interpreted as conjunction, so that (20) will apply truly to the things that are brown and cows. Applying this doctrine to NP = [$_{Spec}$ X] [$_{N'}$ Y] results in structures like (21),

(21) [[$_{Spec}$ X,$\langle 1 \rangle$] [$_{N'}$ Y,$\langle 1 \rangle$],$\langle 1 \rangle$]
         └──────────┘

of which (19) is an instance, using the convenient notation of variables.

The view just sketched rescues (18) as a grammatical sentence, and given my stipulation about the adjectival interpretation of the indefinite article, it is moreover interpretively correct. The article appears only as a kind of grace note: it cannot fail to be true of the reference of a singular subject. At the same time the syntax of predicate nominals is just the autonomous syntax of NPs, so that a Spec is required: in English we cannot say **John is lawyer.*[4] Sentences like (22) are brought into the scheme as follows.

(22) They are [[three] friends of mine]
      ↑_____|

The predicate is interpreted as in (23),

(23) three(X) & friends of mine(X)

where *three* as a predicate is true of three-member collections, and of
nothing else. If it and the head *friends of mine* are both true of the
plurality denoted by *they*, then (22) is true.[5] The old philosophical
chestnut (24) will then be construed as showing predication by a numeral in an NP with no overt head.

(24) The apostles are twelve[6]

If the standard indefinites are taken as adjectives, then we gain an
appropriate understanding both of the possibility and of the interpretation of the predicate nominals in which they figure. Of course, the adjectival meanings of these expressions must be closely related to their
interpretations as quantifiers. The restriction of predicate nominals to
indefinites can then be seen as stemming from the absence of adjectival
interpretations for the definites. Let us say that a quantifier Q is *of
adjectival character* if the truth-value of the instances of (25)

(25) Q A are B

depends only on how many things are both A and B. There are several
equivalent ways to characterize this property. For instance, adopting
the standard algebraic picture in which restricted quantifiers over a
domain D are interpreted as functions from ordered pairs of subsets of
D to truth-values, we can say that a quantifier q over D is of adjectival
character if, for some function f from subsets of D to truth-values,
$q(X,Y) = f(X \cap Y)$, for every pair X and Y of subsets of D; or, more
simply, we might note that a quantifier is of adjectival character if and
only if it is *symmetric*, in the sense that Q A *are* B is always equivalent
to Q B *are* A.

If Q is of adjectival character, let us say that a *threshold* for Q is a
number n such that, if n things are A and B, then (25) is true. Then my
earlier remarks about the interpretation of the indefinite article and
number-words as adjectives may be generalized as (26).

(26) Interpret Q adjectivally as true of just those pluralities of
      threshold size.

The classic definites, including *every* and *most,* are not of adjectival character: they give no expressions that apply to single pluralities, since they essentially *relate A* and *B* in the frame (25). So these are excluded from being the specifiers of predicate nominals.

We have arrived at a view about the DE in predicate nominals. A number of particular questions concerning individual lexical items remain; but I will turn instead to some points about identity and predication that will both help to conclude this aspect of the discussion and prepare for other issues concerning the distinction between definite and indefinite.[7]

Nominals following *be* need not be predicative: there are identity statements. In these the copula behaves like other two-place predicates, combining with the following NP to form a VP that is then predicated of the subject. We are led, then, to locate the distinction between identity and predication in the optionality of assigning the relation of predication to the predicate nominal. Thus, sentences like *John is the man* have two different syntactic structures, namely, (27) and (28).

(27) John is [the man]

(28) John [is the man]

The difference between them is not, or need not be, structural in the classic sense; rather, they differ in that in one case a certain relation is incorporated into the constituent structure and in the other case it is not. Of course, in the extended sense of "structure" assumed here, which allows linguistic relations as well as constituency, we may say that the sentence is structurally ambiguous or, better, that it is a case of sentential homonymy.

In the case of (27) the copula is present for purely syntactic reasons, but in (28) it is significant, expressing identity. Hence, we derive the familiar fact that definite descriptions in complements that lack a copula must have a "predicative" rather than a referential interpretation.

(29) I consider [John [the man (for the job)]]

(30) *I consider [John [the man over there]]

Definite descriptions can be either predicative or referential, so that both (27) and (28) are grammatical. Since the relation of predication is itself optional, distinctions among NPs are to be traced to their lexical peculiarities. Names, and still more pronouns, are nonpredicative. Indefinite descriptions are predicative, as we have seen. Are they also referential? In (31), where predication has not been assigned, we should get the interpretation shown in (32).

(31) John is [a lawyer]

(32) [an x: lawyer(x)] John is ($=$) x

The interpretation is reasonable; but a powerful argument against the grammaticality of (31) is that (33) cannot be interpreted as in (34).

(33) John is not a lawyer

(34) For some lawyer x John is not x

(I owe this argument to Emmon Bach, from a lecture at City University of New York, 1977.)

Suppose then that nominals following *be* must be predicates, except when they are singular terms (names, pronouns, or definite descriptions). Interesting questions then arise about the status of moved and unmoved *wh*-expressions and about the status of traces. Traces of *wh*-expressions are variables and can be expected to behave like pronouns. But the trace t can itself be a predicate nominal, in view of (35) and other examples.

(35) What is John t?
       (John is) a lawyer

If t is predicative, then its antecedent, a quantificational or *wh*-expression, must in some sense range over the interpretations of predicates. In this way, we can account for Williams's (1984) observation that, where predicate positions themselves are quantified over, predicate nominals with *every* are allowed.

(36) John is [everything I respect]
       ⌞_____⌟

Now consider question-answer pairs where the *wh*-expression ranges over individuals, as in (37).

(37) [Which one] is John t?
       (John is) that one

If these examples show absence of predication between t and *John* in (37), then, on the assumption that predication applies blindly at

S-Structure to postcopular nominals other than singular terms, we should expect (38) and the like to be strange, at least when "echoic" interpretations are excluded.

(38) Which woman said the (best) movie was [which one]?

The reason is that the phrase *which one* must at S-Structure be a predicate, whereas its semantic role will be to range over individuals, as it does in (37). I think that this prediction is correct. If so, we see in English a combination of circumstances that will force *Wh*-Movement of postcopular phrases of the form *which F*. We expect (39) to be more acceptable than (38), as indeed it seems to be.

(39) Which one did which woman say the best movie was *t*?

By contrast, a *wh*-phrase that ranges over the interpretations of predicates will not have to undergo *Wh*-Movement. It is predicted, therefore, that (40) is worse than (41).

(40) Who knows whether John was [which man]?

(41) Who knows whether John was [where]?

I will consider further the properties of quantificational predicate nominals. With a grammar of quantification incorporating May's (1977) rule of Quantifier Raising (QR), the LF representation of (36) will be (42).

(42) [Everything I respect] John is *t*

The trace is bound by the quantifier, but it is not an argument of anything, being a predicate. The quantifier phrase itself is a reduced relative clause, so that its internal structure is as shown in (43).

(43) [Everything [*wh* [I respect *t*]]]

In (43) the trace *t is* an argument, namely, one of the arguments of *respect*. Let us call the trace in (43) *internal* and the one in (42) *external*. Then the full representation (44) is a case where the internal and external traces are not of the same kind: the external trace is predicative, and the internal trace is not.

(44) [Everything [*wh* [I respect *t*]]] John is *t'*

It seems that this situation is allowed only because the head, *thing*, of the quantifier *everything* is just a dummy, inserted for reasons of formal grammar. One cannot replace it by a substantive, *property* or *virtue* for example. When there is a true substantival head and a predicative external trace, then a *clash* occurs, as in (45).

(45) *[A lawyer (whom) I respect] John is *t*

To exemplify the ungrammaticality of (45), we may contrast (46) with (47), where in the former case but not in the latter the second assertion gives an instance on the basis of which the first is made.

(46) John is something I respect—he's honest

(47) John is a lawyer I respect—he's honest

Intuitively, the second clause in (47) gives a reason why I respect John, and not what it is that I respect about him. These facts are to be expected if the principle (12) is correct in prohibiting unsaturated arguments.

Postcopular coordinating conjunctions show a kind of "across-the-board" effect, in that the mixing of predicative and nonpredicative expressions is not allowed.

(48) *He is stupid and John

Accepting the judgment of Sag et al. (1984) that coordinating conjunctions may mix categories, as in (49),

(49) John is [$_A$ stupid] and [$_{NP}$ a liar]

the ungrammaticality of (48) supports use of the predication relation. As Howard Lasnik has pointed out to me, its ungrammaticality might be derived from a requirement of *univocity* on the copula *be:* it must be interpreted in whatever weak manner is characteristic of it in predication, because of the adjective, and also in the strong sense of identity, because of the singular term *John*. It is plausible to suppose that double duty of this kind for a single occurrence of a lexical item is not permitted, a condition that would be wanted independently to rule out utterances like *He took offense and coffee.*[8]

3.2 *There*-Insertion

There-insertion produces a different dimension of the DE from that seen in predicate nominals. The requirement of indefiniteness in this case is completely local, that is, strictly determined by the nature of Spec (Milsark 1974; Safir 1982). Thus, (50) is grammatical, despite the "specificity" of the NP; and (51) is ungrammatical, although the quantifier ranges over predicates.

(50) There was a certain man I know in the garden; namely, John

(51) *There was everything I respect about John

(51) contrasts with (36). Similarly, (50) contrasts with (52).

(52) ??I consider John a certain man I know

The oddness of (52) is expected, given the contrast between (29) and (30), and the singular-term-like air of an NP with *a certain*. But then, the full acceptability of (50) underscores the local and formal character of the DE for *there*-insertion.

Safir (1982) relates the position of *there* to the postcopular NP by coindexing, positing at the same time that indefinites are exempt from binding conditions (at S-Structure). His analysis requires the latter assumption, because of the point of view that he adopts toward linguistic relations: that, unless there are special stipulations to the contrary, they all obey the same kinds of formal conditions. Safir's view is the opposite of the one assumed here, and also in Higginbotham 1983a,b, that distinct linguistic relations satisfy conditions of their own and that interactions between them must be stated within the theory. Nevertheless, I will incorporate a part of Safir's account in what follows.

We might conjecture that the relation between expletive *there* and the postcopular NP is the (formal) relation of subject to predicate and assume with Safir that this relation is involved in Case assignment, in the sense that Case is transmitted just when it is present. From these assumptions, Safir's basic results follow, without any stipulations about exemptions from binding conditions (predication is not the anaphor-antecedent relation that binding theory is about; so the question of binding conditions does not arise, on the view of linguistic relations adopted here). For the reasons given above, predicative NPs must be indefinite; hence, we get a DE. However, we do not get in this way either the purely formal, or the local, character of the effect. An excursus into the semantics of *there*-insertion sentences will lead to the formulation of a very different proposal, in which predication will ultimately play a significant but secondary role.

There-insertion sentences are a paradigm of existential statements: they "herald existence," in Quine's phrase. How do they get to mean what they do? The at first sight natural idea that *there is* is itself existential runs into serious questions when confronted with examples like (53) and (54).

(53) There are many horses

(54) There is no justice

In (53), if *there are* is quantificational, there is no open sentence for it to be construed with; and in (54) the speaker asserts, not the existence of something called "no justice," but the nonexistence of justice. If it happens that *there is* can be understood existentially in (50), that is because of the article *a,* not the expletive construction. Therefore, we can reject the idea that *there is* has anything existential about it.

A possibility that I considered in a footnote to Higginbotham 1982, and employed also in Higginbotham 1983a,b, is that, given that the positions of *there* and the NP are somehow related and that the rule QR of quantifier construal applies to the NP if it is quantificational, we derive at LF a structure in which the position of *there,* rather than the position from which the NP moved, is regarded as the variable bound by this quantifier (Robert May first pointed out this possibility to me, in 1978). In the case of (53), for instance, we would derive (55), interpreted as shown in (56).

(55) [No justice] [there is t]

(56) [No x: justice(x)] [x is]

The predicate *is* would be true of everything; hence, (55) would be true just in case nothing satisfied *justice*(x)—which gives the right meaning. On this proposal, the roles of *there* and the position of the NP would reverse between S-Structure and LF: the expletive would be significant at LF, as a variable is significant, and the postcopular position would be pleonastic at that level. However, even if no interpretive problems befall this proposal, in (54) or other cases, and although it garners some further empirical support from the history of English (seen in nowadays marginal cases such as *God is*), it fails to interact with the DE.

Another way of looking at the matter is to suggest that the NP following the copula in *there*-insertion itself functions as a sentence, the result of applying a binder Q to an open sentence represented by N'. The binder must in this case be unrestricted, or *absolute,* since its usual restriction, the N', no longer serves that function. The other material in S, except for tense or modals supported by inflection or auxiliary, is inert. In this case, (54), ignoring tense, is in effect (57).

(57) [No x] justice(x)

This hypothesis will give our examples the same interpretation they receive under the "existential *there*" hypothesis (when that will work) or under the hypothesis that *is* is a predicate. For example, (56) and (57) will be equivalent; and the simplest cases, such as (58), come out indifferently, so far as meaning goes, as any of (59)–(61).

(58) There is a man in the garden

(59) [$\exists x$] man(x) & in the garden(x)

(60) [An x: man(x) & in the garden(x)] x is

(61) [An x] man(x) & in the garden(x)

More generally, pairs such as (62) and (63) will be equivalent whenever Q is of adjectival character.

(62) [Qx: $N'(x)$] x is

(63) [Qx] $N'(x)$

Therefore, for such Q the semantics will not go awry.

A quantifier whose role is always to relate *pairs* of open sentences, and so is not of adjectival character in the sense of section 3.1, might be conjectured to lack an unrestricted or absolute form. If so, then the absence of these quantifiers in *there*-insertion contexts will follow, and with it both the near-coincidence of the DEs for predicate nominals and for *there*-insertion and the principled distinctions between them.

Because of the initial plausibility of the hypotheses entertained and rejected above, my path to the present conclusion has been somewhat involved. Summarizing, I am now suggesting (a) that what is significant in a *there*-insertion sentence is what follows the copula, an NP that assumes in this case a sentential interpretation; (b) that this NP = Q – N' is interpreted as '[Qx] $N'(x)$', with Q absolute; and (c) that Q may be absolute if and only if it is of adjectival character. I will ultimately modify suggestions (a) and (b) as well, although in such a way that the consequences we may so far draw are preserved. Before presenting the modifications, I will review some of those consequences.

First, the hypothesis that the NP following *there is* is sentential in character implies that these NPs cannot be singular terms, hence that names and the like cannot appear in *there*-insertion contexts. Furthermore, by suggestion (c), definite descriptions, whether predicative or not, will be forbidden.

James Higginbotham 56

(64) *There is the man for the job

These consequences already cover part of the DE and explain its local character.

Second, the "bare NP" view of *there*-insertion, advanced by Jenkins (1975) and also advocated by Williams (1984), fits well with suggestions (a)–(c). It is because what follows *there is* is a bare NP that there is no subject-predicate relation, for instance, between *in the garden* and *a man* in (58). If there were, then quantifiers would not be forced to be absolute.

Third, Williams's point that *there* limits the scope of the postcopular NP, as illustrated by the absence of ambiguity in (65),

(65) There isn't a man in the garden

can be said to follow from my proposal, inasmuch as the NP is itself (interpreted as) what is negated or otherwise operated upon by modals or other inflectional elements. So *there* turns out to be a "scope marker," in Williams's phrase, not because of any properties of its own, but because of the thematic and interpretive properties of the constructions in which it appears. I count this consequence as appropriate, since it shows that the scheme adopted here can generalize to other languages, where the expletive subject, or the verb, or both are dissimilar to English (as in German *Es gibt*).

Fourth, the hypothesis that simple *there*-insertion sentences are interpreted as shown in (63) will help to explain semantic distinctions between pairs like (66) and (67).

(66) Many people I know are in the garden

(67) There are many people I know in the garden[9]

It seems that (66) can count as true even if I don't know many people, so long as a sufficient proportion of those that I do know are in the garden. But (67) cannot count as true under this circumstance: since I don't know many people, I don't in particular know many in the garden. The distinction follows, since in (67) the word *many* must have an absolute sense, derived from its adjectival interpretation as in *They are many* (see note 6). Now, *few* has a "proportional" meaning, roughly antonymic to *most,* as in (68).

(68) Few people I know are in the garden

The word *most* is barred from *there*-insertion contexts, as being inherently proportional ("more than half") rather than cardinal; hence, *few* in its "proportional" meaning is barred also. But *there*-insertion, it seems, involves a use of *few* as antonym of the absolute *many*.

(69) There are few people I know in the garden

Indeed, in the situation just described (68) may be false, but (69) is true if I merely know few people.

I turn now to the promised modifications. Thus far, I have ignored the fact that *there*-insertion, with attendant DEs, occurs in English with verbs other than the copula. One such class, the intransitives with so-called presentational interpretations such as *arrive, emerge,* and several others, unequivocally have the postverbal NP as subject.

(70) There arrived a man

(71) There emerged many locusts

The other class, which includes *appear* and *remain,* is, as I will explain, less clear in this regard. For verbs of neither class, evidently, can we regard the postverbal NP as carrying the burden of the sentence. Therefore, forcing this NP into the mold suitable for the interpretation of the context *there is* _____ can no longer be the whole story about the meanings of these sentences. Nevertheless, a further development of the suggestions so far presented will, I believe, show that the present analysis is not beyond extension to these cases.

In Higginbotham 1985 and elsewhere I have used the conception, due to Davidson (1967), of an event-place—or, as I will call it, an *E-position*—in verbs and other argument-taking phrases. Besides Davidson's applications, I have argued that exploitation of the E-position will explain certain properties of complement clauses; and I suppose in Higginbotham 1985 that E-positions are to be found not only in action verbs but also in statives. The objects over which the E-position ranges include both events and what were traditionally called *states of affairs;* and I will, as in the work cited, employ Barwise and Perry's useful term *situation* to cover both (Barwise and Perry 1983).

Still following Davidson, the E-position of the main verb is to be taken as existentially bound in simple sentences, and it is the subject of various adjuncts, such as instrumentals and certain adverbials. Finally, the tacit existential quantification over the E-position is interior to explicit quantifiers. To give an example making visible all of these devices, a sentence such as (72) will be interpreted as shown in (73), where e ranges over situations.

(72) John solved each problem without assistance

(73) [Each x: problem(x)] [$\exists e$] (solved(John,x,e) & without assistance(e))

For further details, see the references cited in the previous paragraph.

A noun, no less than a verb, may contain an E-position, and since some morphologically or syntactically derived nominals themselves range over situations, it is even demanded that they do so.[10] For an argument NP = Spec – N′, we can suppose that the E-position in N′ is bound, perhaps by existential closure as in the sentential cases, within NP. However, we may conjecture that the bare NP of *there*-insertion may contain an E-position as a free variable, so that (63) is replaced by (74).

(74) [Qx] N′(x,e)

If the variable e, free in NP, is bound through existential closure in S, the result is (75).

(75) [$\exists e$] [Qx] N′(x,e)

It is straightforward to verify that replacement of (63) by (75) in the semantics for *there*-insertion with a copular verb will not upset the conclusions already reached for the syntax and semantics of these sentences, including the desirable consequences I have listed. But now we may take a further step. Recall the hypothesis that *is* is not pleonastic in *there*-insertion but is instead a predicate true of everything. If this verb has a thematic grid $\langle 1 \rangle$, whose sole position is identified with the E-position in N′, then we obtain for a *there*-insertion VP the structure shown in (76).

(76) [$_{VP}$[be,$\langle 1 \rangle$] [$_{NP}$ Q [N′,$\langle 1,E \rangle$],$\langle 1^*,E \rangle$],$\langle E \rangle$]

The interpretation of this structure will be as shown in (77).

(77) is(e) & [Qx] N′(x,e)

Finally, assuming existential closure within S, we derive (78), which will be equivalent to (75).

(78) [∃e] is(e) & [Qx] N'(x,e)

In other words, for *there*-insertion sentences *there be Q N'* we obtain interpretations that can be paraphrased as shown in (79).

(79) A situation e is such that [Qx] N'(x,e)

The significance of the last construction is that it extends beyond the copula to take account of the verbs of the second class, those that admit *there*-insertion but need not be regarded as taking the postverbal constituent as their subject. Drawing this section to a close, I will illustrate this with the verb *remain*. What sorts of things may it apply to? Bodies, evidently; but also problems, empires, and other objects. All of these may "remain in place" through time, either in a literally spatial sense of *place* or in some extended sense. Situations remain, while other things change around them: Rome's ascendancy in Europe remained for many generations. Hence, for examples like (80), we are led to propose interpretations such as the one given in (81).

(80) There remained three men in the garden

(81) A situation e remained, such that [Qx] N'(x,e)

Notice in particular that this construction expresses the distinction between (80) and (82).

(82) Three men remained in the garden

In (82) the salient interpretation is that three men, such as Tom, Dick, and Harry, remained, the adjunct phrase *in the garden* saying where this happened; but in (80) it is sufficient that the situation "three men in the garden" persist, which might happen under successive replacements of men. Similarly, contrast (83) with (84).

(83) For several moves, there remained four pawns on the third rank

(84) For several moves, four pawns remained on the third rank

The further extension of these proposals to cases involving postverbal subjects (such as *There arrived a man*) must await another occasion. In the meantime the variety of phenomena involving *there*-insertion that can be explicated in terms of the view presented here gives some reason to pursue the proposed line of investigation.

3.3 Scopal Independence

The phenomenon of scopal independence is illustrated by (3) and by other examples given in Jackendoff 1972.

(85) I told [three of the stories] to [many of the men]

A simple suggestion for these cases, noted in passing at least as early as Van Lehn 1978, is to regard the quantificational NPs here as predicates of classes, so that (85) is interpreted as indicated in the rough paraphrase (86).

(86) For some X, a class comprising three of the stories, and for some Y, a class comprising many of the men, I told X to Y

Some account of such relations, as expressed by ordinary verbs, is wanted anyway for sentences like (87) and (88).

(87) I told these stories to those men

(88) These men danced with those women

(These are discussed for instance in Carlson 1980, Higginbotham 1981, and Schein 1984.)

We will assume that QR applies in sentences like (85), so that at LF we have the structure (89).

(89) [three of the stories] [many of the men] I told t to t'

Hence, the difference between, for instance, *three of the stories* interpreted as 'for three x such that x is a story' and *three of the stories* interpreted as shown in (89) might be taken as purely interpretive in character. However, it can also be seen as in part syntactic and to involve again the notion of predication as controlling the possibility of the unsaturatedness of NP, inasmuch as those quantifiers that can show scopal independence are also those that admit an interpretation as one-place predicates of classes.

3.4 Unbound Anaphora

Assuming the discussion thus far, we may now formulate a perspective on the fourth of the cases listed at the outset: the confinement of support for unbound, or "donkey-sentence," anaphora to indefinite antecedents. It has been clear since Kamp 1981 and Heim 1982 that the support of unbound anaphora by a quantifier has something to do with its existential character, so that of (8) and (9) (repeated here) only the former is grammatical.

(8) If I see [a few donkeys], I'll kick them

(9) *If I see [few donkeys], I'll kick them

More precisely, the supporters of unbound anaphora are generally of adjectival character, so that these will come at least very close to co-inciding with those quantifiers that are fitted out for predicative uses. The effects, however, have a different basis. Existentials are proper for unbound anaphora because it is with them that (as one says) indetermi-nate objects are introduced for later reference. What properties might we expect a quantifier Q to have, that it should be capable of behaving in this way? Following Kamp's suggestion that such quantifiers should be preserved under model extensions, I would propose as a sufficient condition for Q to be a supporter of unbound anaphora that it be both of adjectival character and monotone increasing in the sense of Barwise and Cooper (1981). Let us call such a quantifier *monotone adjectival*. It is straightforward to verify that if Q is monotone adjectival, then there is a cardinal α such that sentences of the form (90) are always equiva-lent to (91).

(90) Q A are B

(91) For at least α things x, $A(x)$ & $B(x)$

From the last suggestion, it follows that supporters of unbound anaphora will overlap almost to the point of coincidence with the Q admissible with *there*-insertion or predicate nominals. The difference in their bases implies that conditions on unbound anaphora should be strictly universal (as they in fact are, so far as I know).

3.5 Clefts

The last of the domains of the DE with which we began this discussion is that of the clefts and pseudoclefts. Here I will consider just the case of clefts, showing how the general analysis so far developed is to be applied. Question (11) (repeated here) shows the DE.

(11) Was it [an/*every] Irish poem John recited?

To see this effect as growing out of predication, together with the properties of the indefinite article and of *every* that make the former of adjectival character and the latter not, we must find something in the cleft to serve as subject. Clefts have the structure (92), where Clause(X) is a clausal constituent with an X gap.

(92) it – be – X – Clause(X)

Assume for concreteness that Clause(X) always arises from *Wh*-Movement, with a possibly silent operator O in the Comp position of the clause. Then Clause(X) always has the structure (93), where t is of type X, as shown.

(93) $[O [...t_X...]]$

I will suppose that this clause itself is the subject of predication, in effect a singular term, and that X is either predicated of it or else the other side of an identity statement, exactly as in the case of ordinary copular sentences. This stipulation will yield the facts in (11). That it is more than a stipulation is supported by the presuppositional peculiarities of clefts, as follows.

Notoriously, the sentences in (94) differ in their presuppositions from those in (95).

(94) John [solved/didn't solve] the problem

(95) It [was/wasn't] John who solved the problem

(95) but not (94) presupposes that somebody solved the problem. Now, if the constituent Clause(X) = [who [t solved the problem]] is a definite description, as in (96),

(96) (the x) (x solved the problem)

then the presuppositional effect of clefting is assimilated to the case of definite descriptions in subject position, as in (97).

(97) The person who solved the problem [was/wasn't] John

Whether this effect is semantic or pragmatic in nature we may set aside; the point is that if the constituent Clause(X) of a cleft is a definite description, then the presupposition that it is nonempty is the presupposition of the sentence.

Returning to the main theme, we can now take $X = $ *an Irish poem* as predicate in (11); and we must so take it, since that expression is not admitted as a nonpredicate in copular constructions, as shown by the behavior of simple predicate nominals. Similarly, if $X = $ *every Irish poem,* then the structure is ungrammatical.

Clefts are ambiguous, depending on focus. Under focal stress on *Irish* in (98)

(98) Was it an Irish poem that John recited?

the question is "Did John recite an Irish poem, or another kind of poem?" and the presupposition is that what he recited was a poem. Without the stress the question is "Did John recite an Irish poem, or something else?" and the presupposition is that he recited something of one sort or another. It seems that under focal stress the clefted constituent should be taken as just what is focused, the remainder traveling along as in pied-piping, since (99) is impossible.

(99) *Was it Irish that John recited a poem?

Under focal stress the cleft with *every* becomes grammatical.

(100) Was it every *Irish* poem that John recited?

Here the question is "Did John recite every Irish poem, or did he recite every poem of some other kind?" and the presupposition is that he recited every poem of some kind or another. Semantically, then, the predicate of the cleft is just *Irish,* and examples like (100) are not in conflict with the proposed analysis.

Clefted constructions are a species of copular constructions and therefore exhibit the distinction between *is* as expressing identity and *is* as mere carrier of verbal structure. Identity, I have suggested, is allowed only when the postcopular element (the constituent X in the case of clefts) is a name, definite description, or trace that does not itself come from a predicative position. The consequences of this suggestion, sketched inconclusively for the case of predicate nominals as in (37)– (39), are seen, I believe, to be correct for clefts. Consider (101).

(101) [Which ghost] was it *t* [(that) you saw]?

This question is grammatical, as expected, where the copula must express identity, and there is no predication. But the S-Structure representation shown in (102) is then predicted to give rise to no grammatical structure (where the expression *which ghost* is not echoic).

(102) It was [which ghost] [(that) you saw]?

For, if predication does not relate the NP to the clause, then (102) already violates the conditions on predicates at S-Structure; and if it does so relate them, then we derive at LF a structure like (101), but with a nonpredicative *t* as a predicate. The prediction, then, is that *wh*-nominals that range over individuals must have been displaced into Comp by S-Structure, as in (101) itself. Support for this position comes from examples like the following, among others.

(103) I know [when I saw which ghost]

(104) ?[Which ghost] do you know [when [it was *t* you saw *t'*]]?

(105) *I know [when [it was which ghost (that) I saw *t*]]

(106) Who knows [which ghost [it was *t* (that) you saw]]?

(107) ???Who knows [(that) [it was which ghost (that) you saw]]?

Finally, consider clefts where *X* is a quantificational or *wh*-expression that itself ranges over the interpretations of predicates, as in (108) and (109).

(108) It is [everything that I respect] that John is

(109) What is it *t* [that John is known for being]?

We should expect that unmoved (by S-Structure) *wh*-expressions are more acceptable in clefts if they sweep out predicate positions. It seems to me that this is correct, as shown in (110) and (111).

(110) [What/Which person] do you think [it is *t* [that John is believed to be]]?

(111) Who thinks [it is [?what/*which person] [that John is believed to be]]?

3.6 Concluding Remarks

The five domains of the DE listed at the outset have now been considered in some (though not full) detail. As noted, one might want to add to this list either the datum that only indefinites can be in some sense "specific" or the attenuation of weak crossover effects for those cases.

I should now like to offer my reasons for thinking that these data have an explanation of a different kind, within a theory of force rather than within a theory of sense.

Consider first of all the links that a full theory of language use ought to make between conditions of truth and falsehood of sentences and the assertive employment of them. The most fundamental link, no less fundamental for being pretheoretically open-ended, is that a person who utters as an assertion a sentence s, for which a correct grammar for that person's language has it that it means that so-and-so, represents himself, by so doing, as believing that so-and-so (see Davidson 1982). This link connects the *force* of assertion with the *sense* of a sentence. A person who asserts, for example, "I met a man," represents himself as believing that for some man x, he met x. Those investigators who have charted the specific use of indefinites have suggested that, although nonspecific cases are fully handled by taking them as existentially general, the specific uses involve something else. But now there is a problem: what more can the sentence *I met a man* mean than that for some man x, I met x? And if it cannot mean more than this, how can a person by asserting it represent himself as believing more?

In typical cases specific uses are said to involve a referent that the speaker "has in mind." But this condition seems much too strong. Suppose my friend George says to me, "I met with a certain student of mine today." Then I can report the encounter to a third party by saying, "George said that he met with a certain student of his today," and the "specificity" effect is felt, although *I* am in no position to say which student George met with. Perhaps the explanation of the specificity effect is to be sought in a link between assertion and belief that does not reflect itself in truth-conditions, or in meaning narrowly construed.[11]

Imagine a language in which specific and nonspecific indefinites were grammatically distinguished, by overt morphemes. In this language a person who asserted "I met a_1 man" would represent himself only as believing that there is some man or other that he met; but a person who asserted "I met a_2 man" would represent himself as believing that he met a man x such that he or somebody else could tell you more about x. But it does not follow that he *asserted* this second clause. It seems appropriate to regard assertion as but one way of representing oneself as believing something.

In English, where there appears to be only one formative a, we can well distinguish cases where we have the right to expect the speaker, or someone connected to the speaker, to provide an *instance c* such that

'*Fc* & *Gc*', where "An *F* is *G*" was asserted. It is to be expected that this phenomenon should occur with existentials, whose instances imply them—hence, that we should see here a DE. The attenuation of weak crossover—say, in (112)—

(112) His father hates [a (certain) boy I know]

is expected too; for we can have every right to expect that the reference of *his* should be the same as the promised instance.

I am aware that these remarks only commence the discussion. Still, I think that one should be impressed, in the case of *I met a man* and the like, by the difficulty, for those who suppose it is ambiguous, of saying just what this ambiguity is. If I am right in believing that specificity reveals itself in behavioral situations such as I have described, and in supposing that there might well be a human language with the formatives a_1 and a_2 as in my hypothetical example, then (a) there is no compelling reason to suppose that what is grammatically encoded, context-independently, in declarative sentences is infallibly reflected in the truth-conditions of those sentences, and (b) there is no compelling reason for cluttering the theory of truth with ambiguities whose explanation belongs to the theory of force rather than to the theory of sense.

In conclusion, it seems that many DEs may be seen as resulting from the interaction of conditions on binding and the construal of quantification and *wh*-expressions, together with conditions on predication. The restrictions on definite NPs, like the restrictions on passive, are not a unitary phenomenon.

Notes

This chapter is an elaboration of some of the material written up as an abstract for the Fifth Groningen Round Table. For discussions pertinent to the present work, I am particularly indebted to Andrew Barss, Noam Chomsky, Howard Lasnik, Peter Ludlow, Anna Szabolcsi, and Edwin Williams. Comments from the reviewers and editors for this volume have also been very helpful.

1. Weak crossover effects are attenuated in examples like (i).

(i) *His* father hates *a (certain) boy I know*

The papers at the Fifth Groningen Round Table added considerably to the already large amount of literature on the question of specific indefinites. An important source for me has been Fodor and Sag 1982.

2. See Rothstein 1983. The principle (13) must hold for all syntactic predicates that have the expected semantic interpretation. It is possible, I think, to derive (12), which figures as a premise in Rothstein 1983, from a certain generalization of Chomsky's (1981) θ-Criterion. Specifically, an unsaturated argument

would have an open position, which must be discharged in some way. If, by hypothesis, all discharge of thematic roles can take place only under government, and the unsaturated expression A is an argument of B in a structure such as (i),

(i) $B' = [...B...A...]$

then A cannot *also* govern a constituent through which its open position is discharged. For further discussion, see Higginbotham 1985.

3. To forestall misunderstanding, I may explain the relations between expressions like (19), of the sort used throughout this chapter to make clear what interpretations certain expressions of English are to have, and the expressions of English of which it is said that they show the interpretations. As in Higginbotham 1985, I assume that a necessary condition of giving an account of meaning for a natural language is that one characterize the notions of truth and reference in that language. Such characterization requires the proof, in the language of the theorist, or metalanguage, of certain *target equivalences,* of which Tarski's famous example (i) is an instance.

(i) *Snow is white* is true if, and only if, snow is white

In the simplest cases such equivalences will be *homophonous;* that is, the expressions that appear on their right-hand sides will be the very expressions whose names appear on the left, as in (i). However, homophony is not always a realizable or even reasonable ideal. In the case of predicative *a lawyer,* for example, we will prove (ii)

(ii) *A lawyer* is true of x if, and only if, a(x) & lawyer(x)

(where the *a* on the right-hand side is a neologism, with the meaning given in the text). This equivalence is not homophonous, since it contains variables and the logical constant '&', which shows how the interpretation of the predicate phrase depends upon the interpretation of its parts. Thus, the relation between (19) and the English phrase *a lawyer* of which it gives the interpretation is this: (19) is the expression that figures in the metalanguage as the target equivalence for *a lawyer* in a semantic theory for English.

More generally, when I write here or elsewhere that an expression A "is to be interpreted as shown in B" and then display B, I intend B as the target equivalence for A. Hence, in particular, B is not an LF representation (A is the representation).

What about the proofs of the target equivalences? I attempt none here, for the usual twin reasons that even the simplest are rather tedious, and there is a tendency, unless things are very carefully set up, for professional researchers to find the matter either quite obvious or else quite impenetrable, depending upon their backgrounds and interests. Here, moreover, I do not believe the proofs would further the discussion.

Finally, it may be asked why homophony is not a reasonable ideal, at least at this stage of inquiry. The reason is that, in order to carry out the proofs of target equivalences, we must be operating in a language for which a notion of proof is given to us. We cannot, therefore, assume that we have at our disposal a proper understanding of proof using the means of English itself—indeed, it is just by giving a theory of truth and reference for English that we may come eventually to understand what those means are.

4. There is some distinction in English between (i) and (ii),

(i) John is a lawyer

(ii) John is one lawyer

in that (ii) suggests that John is one lawyer among others. For this reason, it might be best to say that the article in (i) is inserted purely as a syntactic reflex and plays no semantic role at all.

5. Capital italic letters are used for variables ranging over pluralities. The semantics need not be viewed as two-sorted, however.

6. Similarly in (i) and (ii).

(i) Humble persons are few

(ii) They are many (in number)

The quantifiers in these examples have adjectival interpretations, *few* applying to contextually "small" pluralities and *many* to "large" ones. In contexts like (iii), however, they are intuitively not adjectival,

(iii) Few/Many A are B

speaking rather of the proportion of things that are B among the A. (Some examples are given in section 3.2.) Furthermore, neither *few* nor *many* occurs in predicate nominals with an overt head.

(iv) ??They are few/many lawyers

This curious distribution is not semantically governed, since (v) and the like are grammatical, where the addition of a head would be redundant.

(v) We met the lawyers, and they were few/many

   On the view that I have presented, a certain amount of elementary set theory is embedded even in very basic parts of English; at least this will be true if plural NPs are taken to refer to classes. Boolos (1983) suggests a different route, thinking of plural reference as higher-order and thus, for example, denying *the apostles* the status of a singular term in (24). Rather subtle questions of interpretation then arise, for instance for examples like (vi), related to those of Carlson (1980),

(vi) Any time you have [some ordinals], one of them is least

where it might be said that without higher-order reference we fail to capture the intended interpretation, because the class of all ordinals is not a set. See also Boolos (1983). The essentials of the present linguistic proposal, however, are preserved under Boolos's interpretation; I will therefore defer this and other questions that his considerations raise.

7. The word *some,* in construction with plurals, should apparently be taken as true of any plurality with at least two things in it, as in (i).

(i) They are some lawyers

For singulars, it is important in this context to distinguish *some* from the reduced form *sm*, a distinct English formative that occurs only with mass nouns.

(ii) He gave me sm water/*book

The form (iii) is grammatical and carries a kind of affective meaning,

(iii) John is some lawyer

to wit, 'What a lawyer John is!' or 'John is a mere lawyer (that's all I can tell you)'. This affect is available also in other uses of *some* (not *sm*).

(iv) He gave me some book for Christmas

 (v) I heard some/sm music yesterday

(I am grateful to a reviewer and the editors for urging me to consider these examples.)

8. It is not clear to me how the system of Sag et al. should be modified so as to distinguish (48) from (49).

9. This observation follows Milsark (1974).

10. Sproat (1985) discusses and analyzes a number of typical cases, as does Thomason (1985).

  I may also note that direct arguments for an E-position in nouns can be given, exactly paralleling Davidson's arguments in the case of action verbs. Two brief examples may be given here. First, nominal modifications such as *former,* as in *former president of France,* are easily extended even to ordinary nouns, such as *man, apple, cookie.* The obvious treatment of these cases (noticed independently by Larson (1983)) is to suppose that *former* is an indexical predicate true of events or situations prior to the time of speaking; if so, then we have a direct argument for an E-position in nouns. Second, parallel to Davidson's cases of pronominal anaphora we find examples like (i).

(i) John was once a philosopher, but fortunately it didn't last long (is to be forgiven him)

The reference of the pronominal is pretty clearly to *the situation of John's being a philosopher.* If the first clause of (i) makes indefinite reference to this situation, then we can understand this use of pronouns exactly as we understand the pronoun *she* as having an indefinite antecedent in (ii).

(ii) I spoke to a woman, but she didn't reply

The presumption, therefore, is in favor of an E-position in all of these constructions.

11. Fodor and Sag (1982) think of specific indefinites as used in expressing de re propositions; so "I met a man" might express, for some man x, the proposition that I met x. Allowing this way of speaking, it is *always* the case that, if I say truly, "I met a man," then some such proposition is true. It does not follow either that any such proposition is ever asserted or that none is ever asserted. Cases like the one given in the text, however, are problematic for Fodor and

Sag's view. In that case, by hypothesis, I believe no de re proposition such as (i),

(i) George said that he met with a today

for any person as value of a. So if specificity is always to show up in the proposition asserted, it must be allowed that I can assert (sincerely, and without linguistic error) a proposition that I do not believe. Inversely, if this view is rejected for (i), it becomes questionable whether it should be retained for the simple cases.

Chapter 4

What Explains the Definiteness Effect?

Kenneth J. Safir

The distribution of definiteness effects poses interesting methodological questions for linguistic theory, as it is not obvious what sort of explanation they should receive or how the right method of explanation should be distinguished from the inappropriate ones. These methodological issues will resound throughout my discussion, as the main concern of this chapter is to strive toward an explanation for the particular sort of definiteness effect illustrated in (1).

(1) a. There is a boy/someone/a strange book in the room
    b. *There is my sister/everyone/the strange book in the room

I will henceforth refer to the contrast in (1) as the *definiteness effect* (DE), although it should of course be kept in mind that it is one among many and, more importantly for our discussion, that this particular effect is found in a number of related constructions in other languages. These include the overlapping subclasses known as impersonal, existential, and presentational constructions.

My presentation is divided into two closely related parts. In the first part I address the central methodological issue of what sort of explanation, among the various possible types one can imagine, the DE ought to receive. In a theory-independent fashion, I will demonstrate that neither functional nor lexical semantic accounts based on special properties of the word *there* can possibly account even descriptively for the DE. Instead I will conclude, as I have argued in more detail elsewhere (Safir 1985), that at least a portion of any explanation of the distribution of the DE must be based on formal syntactic entities of a type naturally defined in current versions of the Government-Binding (GB) Theory of syntax proposed by Chomsky (1981).

In the second part of my discussion I propose a new approach to explaining the DE based on the conclusions of the first part and on a theory of NP predication developed within the context of GB Theory. From the theoretical perspective of GB Theory, this treatment of predication is controversial because it derives the effects of Principle C of the binding theory from NP predication and the θ-Criterion. The partial explanation of the DE that emerges from this approach will be shown to have significant advantages over earlier accounts.[1]

4.1 Methodology and Explanation

The DE has long intrigued linguists of many different stripes. Precisely because it is not a priori obvious what sort of account this phenomenon should receive, attempts have been made from a number of different perspectives, but I believe it is possible to classify all of them as appealing to one or more of the types of explanations listed in (2).

(2) *Typology of Explanation*
   a. Lexical semantic (for example, meaning of words)
   b. Pragmatics/discourse (for example, intersentential relations)
   c. Syntax/formal grammar (for example, structural relations within a sentence)

In order to clarify what I mean by this typology, it is perhaps useful to consider how these different sorts of explanation might be exemplified as they are applied to the different realms of phenomena wherein they are typically involved.

To begin, consider (3a).

(3) a. John killed the rock
   b. The rock was killed
   c. The rock$_i$ was killed e_i

Examples such as (3a) are considered odd because it is simply a fact about the meaning of the predicate *kill* that the patient of this action is something that can be deprived of animacy, whereas it is a fact about the meaning of *the rock* that it is generally not thought to be animate. This is what I mean by a lexical semantic account.

The fact that the same oddity of selectional restriction is preserved by the passive form in (3b) has received an account in terms of movement rules and traces as represented in (3c). The "thematic role" or

"θ-role" of the verb that is assigned normally to the object position subcategorized by *kill* is realized in subject position, and the trace in object position is presumed to facilitate this transfer. Insofar as this treatment appeals to syntactically defined entities to account for the phenomenon of the "displaced" selectional restriction in passive sentences, it is a formal syntactic treatment.

Of course, syntactically motivated accounts are routinely extended to bear on matters of interpretation, as in some cases of "missing readings" of sentences. In (4a), for example, the verb *visit* can be interpreted transitively or intransitively, but one of these interpretations disappears in (4b), which can only be interpreted transitively.

(4) a. Who do you want to visit?
    b. Who do you wanna visit?
    c. who$_i$ do you want [e]$_i$ to visit
    d. who$_i$ do you want to visit [e]$_i$

The permitted interpretation is the one that has the structure in (4d), whereas the example in (4b) is ungrammatical under the interpretation with the structure in (4c). This is explicable under the assumption that traces block contraction (5b), just as lexical items do (5c).[2]

(5) a. Who do you want [e] to sleep?
    b. *Who do you wanna sleep?
    c. *Do you wan' John 'na sleep?

Whereas there is no grammatical interpretation of (5b) because the verb *sleep* is only intransitive, the verb *visit* allows a grammatical output because the transitive structure in (4d) (and hence the transitive interpretation) is available. The point of these examples is that a phenomenon is susceptible to a syntactic analysis just in case independently motivated syntactic explanations can be extended to account for it in a revealing way. From this perspective, it is not methodologically unreasonable to view the DE in the same light.

Finally, we must consider another type of explanation based on properties of discourses. In one sense, "discourse" is simply the realm of phenomena to be found in units larger than a single sentence. For example, it is well known that an indefinite NP generally cannot be interpreted as anaphoric to an NP that precedes it in discourse, whereas a definite description typically can be anaphoric to a previously mentioned NP.

(6) a. An old man came in. The old fellow looked tired
    b. The old man came in. An old fellow looked tired

(7) a. The man who an old fellow saw liked the old fellow
    b. The man who the old fellow saw liked an old fellow

(6a) might involve only one old fellow; (6b) must involve two old fellows. As illustrated in (7), the same generalization that holds for intersentential relations holds for intrasentential relations (when intervening factors are controlled for, such as ensuring that one NP does not c-command the other). One plausible account of the contrasts in (6) and (7) is that indefinite NPs convey "new information" and therefore can never introduce old information by acting as NPs anaphoric to some previously mentioned antecedent. Such an account based on "given" versus "new" information ascribes a function to the use of definiteness versus indefiniteness and attempts to derive predictions about the distribution of these types of NPs on these grounds. This, then, is what I mean by at least one variety of a "discourse" explanation, namely, a "functional" explanation.[3]

4.1.1 The Question Restated

I am now in a position to restate the original question. Is the distribution of the DE in *there*-sentences in English a consequence of discourse/functional principles, of (word-based) semantics, or of principles of formal sentence grammar? What sort of evidence may be brought to bear on the choice among these alternatives? I will begin by exemplifying these various alternatives, drawing on cases from the relevant literature.

One widely known version of a lexical semantic account is that of Bolinger (1977). Bolinger proposes that the restrictions on the postverbal NP in *there*-sentences are to be attributed to the word *there*. For each new restriction on the postverbal NP that he describes, Bolinger adds a further provision about the word *there,* but all of them involve the idea that *there* has some extended locational meaning, where location is extended to existence, among other things.[4] According to Bolinger, *there*

'brings something into awareness' where 'brings into' is the contribution of the position of there and other locational adverbs, and 'awareness' is the contribution of there itself; specifically, awareness is [an] abstract location. . . . (p. 93)

It is this extended locational meaning that brings matters to attention, and this is why the construction has a presentational function. Insofar as Bolinger bases his account on the assumption that the whole effect is "about" the word *there,* this is a lexical semantic account, although Bolinger brings other matters to bear in his discussion.[5]

To represent the functional perspective, let us consider the analysis of Rando and Napoli (1978), who attempt to account for the DE by seeing it as a by-product of the discourse structure of topic and comment (see Kuno 1971 for an account along similar lines). As do many investigators with this perspective, Rando and Napoli assume that a definite NP can be anaphoric to a referent already introduced into the discourse, whereas an indefinite NP cannot be anaphoric to any earlier referent. Since the topic is what we are talking about, it is typically evoked by a definite NP, picking up earlier mention, whereas the comment, which adds new and presumably germane information about the topic, is typically introduced with an indefinite.

Rando and Napoli's main concern is the distribution of the list interpretation of *there*-sentences; by using their notion of "anaphoric," they attempt to explain the appearance of apparently definite NPs in *there*-contexts. In this regard, they point out a number of very interesting and challenging facts, but I am more interested in their assumptions about the construction in general. They are very succinct about these.

There Insertion, viewed functionally, is a transformation designed to provide a dummy theme or topic—definite in form (witness the *th* in *there*), in initial position—in a sentence which would otherwise have none. The comment is moved out of initial position, so that it may be more strongly emphasized or focused upon. The comment material, as expected, is usually required to be indefinite in form. (p. 308)

One issue that arises from this viewpoint is that the construction comes to have a certain form because of how it is used. That is to say, the word order is a function of how new information is presented and not of any properties of the formal syntax of English. It is simply assumed that postverbal position is the best place to focus things, perhaps because of stress, and that is why the word order is the way it is.

It is important to emphasize that from Rando and Napoli's perspective the properties they ascribe to the word *there* are crucial; otherwise, the idea of "comment" is ill defined as something that tells the hearer more about the "topic." Put another way, it is this "topic" quality of *there* that facilitates the claim that the postverbal NP should be new information or, in Rando and Napoli's sense of the term, "nonana-phoric." And this is why they suggest that the word *there* should be understood as definite, that is to say, potentially "anaphoric" to the topic under discussion. In this sense, then, Rando and Napoli's account resembles that of Bolinger, in that it depends crucially on special properties of *there*.[6]

Finally, a treatment that combines aspects of both the lexical semantic approach and a formal syntactic approach is that of Milsark (1974, 1977), which has often been assumed in generative accounts in recent years in one form or another (see, for example, Woisetschlaeger 1983; Williams 1984). Milsark proposes that the DE is the result of a semantic clash between existential quantification triggered by the formative *there* and any NP that fails to have an existential interpretation. NPs that fail to have an existential interpretation include proper names and universal quantifiers, among which Milsark includes definite descriptions. For example, the presence of *there* in (8) requires that a special rule apply, which in turn requires that the postverbal NP be compatible with an existential operator. The rule of interpretation is necessary to the analysis to make certain that the right construction is chosen (the verb *be* must be involved, and perhaps a marked class of additional predicates) and that the right NP is targeted, the output of the rule being something like the logical form in (8).

(8) There is a unicorn in the garden
     THERE BE NP . . . → $\exists x$ NPx & NPx is in the garden

It is possible to show that the interpretive rule in (8) must be highly complex if it is going to capture the range of constructions that permit the presence of the relevant phenomenon, as illustrated in (9).

(9) a. There have got to be some men in the room
     b. There seem to be some men in the room
     c. There exist several problems within this approach

But let us suppose that a simpler formulation were possible, such as that of Williams (1984), which simply states that *there* must have an indefinite NP in its scope, because *there* is an indefinite scope marker. Thus, with respect to the formal syntax of *there*-sentences, a syntactic relationship must hold between *there* and the postverbal NP, and this syntactic relationship has a semantic effect because of what *there* means.

Although there are a number of reasons for rejecting this approach on relatively technical grounds, the important point here is that Milsark's manner of explanation, as well as Williams's development of it, depends crucially on the word *there*.[7] Milsark's claim that there is a semantic clash between existential and universal quantification in this context has a certain independent appeal, and I will return to it later.

Function, structure, and lexical semantics play different sorts of roles in these accounts. How do we know which sort of explanation is on the right track? It is always attractive to extend the independently motivated principles of one domain to some new domain, and clearly each type of explanation has its proponents. All of these accounts, however, rely crucially on specific properties of *there*. If it is possible to show that the word *there* and its analogues in other languages do not necessarily preside over the effect, or appear when the effect is absent, then all of the above explanations fail. The lexical semantic account fails in principle if this is so. Moreover, the functional account must be made relevant to some property of this class of constructions, and if the key feature is not a lexical property of *there,* then it must be some structural property. Thus, if *there* plays no specific role as topic, then the functional account presupposes a structural syntactic account of the distribution of the DE.

4.1.2 The Definiteness Effect and the Impersonal Formative

Of course, the burden of any approach that assumes that *there* plays a crucial role in accounting for the DE is that in neighboring languages, where a similar effect is found, we would expect the presence of a similar lexical item. At first thought this might seem plausible, given *er* in Dutch and the *il* of French impersonal constructions. Yet I believe it is possible to show in these two languages, if not in English, that the impersonal formative does not play a role in the distribution of the DE. For reasons of space, I confine my demonstration to Dutch.[8]

Let us begin with a cursory look at the impersonal construction in Dutch, as exemplified in (10).

(10) a. . . . dat er door   de deur een/*het kind kwam
        that   through the door a/the   child came

   b. . . . dat er   door de storm een/*het huis   verwoest werd
        that there by   the storm a/the   house destroyed was

(11) a. [dat [$_S$[$_{NP}$ er] [$_{VP}$[$_{PP}$ door de deur] [een kind] kwam]]]

   b. [dat [$_S$[$_{NP}$ er] [$_{VP}$[$_{PP}$ door de storm] [een huis] verwoest werd]]]

I have embedded both of these examples to abstract away from the effects of Verb-Second in Dutch, and I assume further that Dutch is an SOV language where the verb and object are in a VP constituent (see Koster 1975 and Den Besten 1985 for discussion and references). The structures I assume for (10a) and (10b) are presented in (11). These examples show that when the structural subject position is occupied by *er,* the NP that evidences the DE is in VP; to pick a neutral term, we may call this the *NP-in-VP.* Now compare the impersonal passive in (10b) with the impersonal passive in (12a) and its structure in (12b).

(12) a. . . . dat er aan het kind gedacht werd

   b. [dat [$_S$[$_{NP}$ er] [$_{VP}$[$_{PP}$ aan   het kind] gedacht werd]]]
      that   there   about the child thought was

Notice that the DE disappears when the NP-in-VP is in a prepositional phrase. No topic-comment account would appear to predict this, nor any account based on stress. Moreover, if *er* requires existential interpretation parallel to *there* in Milsark's account, then clearly (12a) should be excluded. Why should a preposition have the effect of neutralizing the DE?

Before answering this question, let us ask another. If *er* is crucial to the presence of the DE, it does not necessarily mean that the effect is required every time that *er* appears. Suppose that the presence of *er* is just a necessary and not a sufficient condition to bring about the DE—a plausible retreat, perhaps. This view is refuted, however, by the existence of sentences like (13), reported by Perlmutter and Zaenen (1984) (first circulated in 1978), who note that in a dialect of Dutch they call South Dutch, the DE holds even when *er* is missing (where the dash indicates the apparently absent subject position).

(13) . . . dat ___ door   de deur een/*het kind kwam
       that   through the door a/the   child came

Examples such as (13) establish that *er* in Dutch is neither a necessary nor a sufficient condition for determining where the DE is likely to occur, and yet there is a clear sort of generalization here.

(14) The DE holds when the structural subject is nonthematic and the NP-in-VP is not in a PP.

Why should this generalization hold?

Now we are faced with a question that seems to have a formal syntactic character. A lexical semantic account of the impersonal formative is out of the question, except insofar as we must say that the subject, whether it is *er* or empty, is nonthematic. No formal scope marker account is motivated, such as Williams's version of Milsark's treatment, since there is no scope marker in the South Dutch examples cited by Perlmutter and Zaenen. It is clear that only the formal syntactic approach is likely to make sense of the generalization in (14).

Before going further, I would like to stress that the foregoing demonstration is not an argument confined to Dutch, although it is particularly easy to argue that the impersonal formative is neither a necessary nor a sufficient condition in Dutch. For French it may be shown that the impersonal formative is not a sufficient condition to bring about the DE, and for Portuguese it may be shown that it is not a necessary condition. See Safir 1985, where these matters are discussed in detail.

4.1.3 A Formal Syntactic Account

Let us assume that (14) is close to the right generalization. Why should PPs make a difference? Why should the structural subject be nonthematic? And why should (14) have to do with the DE? In this section I will try to answer the first two questions and reformulate the third.

I must begin by presenting a few assumptions about syntactic theory drawn essentially from Chomsky 1981, which I will simplify considerably to avoid unnecessary discussion. First, I assume the Case theory developed by Rouveret and Vergnaud (1980) and Chomsky (1980a) as stated in (15) and (16).[9]

(15) *Rules for Case Assignment*
   a. NP is Nominative if governed by Infl+tns.
   b. NP is Accusative if governed by V+transitive.
   c. NP is Oblique if governed by P or certain marked verbs.

(16) *Case Filter*
   *NP if NP is lexical and it has no Case (S-Structure).

Abstract Case is assigned by the rules in (15). For purposes of this discussion, we may simply assume *government* to mean "is a sister to," although this is a gross simplification.[10] The Case Filter is independently motivated, in that it accounts for the phenomena in (17).

(17) a. (For)* John to leave would be unfortunate
   b. the destruction (of)* the city

Case theory predicts that the subject of an infinitive is generally a Caseless position; hence, a lexical NP only appears as the subject of an infinitive if there is some other Case assigner available—as in (17a), where *John* can receive Case from the prepositional complementizer *for*. Assuming that nouns do not assign Case, the preposition *of* must be inserted in nominals in English, since the Case Filter will rule out *the destruction the city*. Many other sorts of examples could be adduced, but I am not interested here in the Case Filter per se, other than to explain why it is perceived to have explanatory force.

The Case Filter is also assumed to force movement in passive sentences, since it is assumed that passive verbs do not assign Case. This means that the object of a passive verb in D-Structure (for example, the NP bearing the patient thematic role in (18a) and (19)) must move to the subject position where it can receive Nominative Case. In a language where such Case marking is overt, such as German, the difference in Case marking on the logical object is easily observed, as in (18); it can even be seen in English with respect to pronouns, as in (19).

(18) a. Der   Hund wurde getötet
       the+Nom dog   was   killed

   b. Der   Mann hat den   Hund getötet
      the+Nom man   has the+Acc dog   killed

(19) He/*Him was killed

Another important notion of GB Theory involves the distribution of thematic roles, or θ-roles. Consider the examples in (20).

(20) a. John is fortunate that Mary left
    b. *These solutions are obvious that Mary left

Intuitively, (20b) is ungrammatical because only one θ-role is associated with *obvious* and the sentence contains more than one argument, whereas *fortunate* in (20a) is a two-place predicate and thus has enough θ-roles to match the syntactic arguments. Now consider a verb like *kill*, which is a two-place predicate and hence also assigns two θ-roles.

(21) Harry killed

The sentence in (21) is at best elliptical, but it certainly does not have the interpretation that Harry killed himself (both θ-roles assigned to

Harry). It is as if there are not enough syntactic arguments to go around. The right generalization appears to be that the relationship between θ-roles and syntactic arguments is one to one. This idea is more precisely instantiated in the θ-Criterion.

(22) *θ-Criterion* (Chomsky 1981)
     Every argument must be assigned a θ-role.
     Every θ-role must be assigned to an argument.
     Theorem: A chain can have only one argument.
     (argument = full NP, clause, pronoun, or reflexive)

Speaking formally now, *kill* assigns two θ-roles, one to object position and one to subject position. These positions are thus called *θ-positions* for the verb *kill*. A syntactic argument is assigned a θ-role if it is in a θ-position or related to one.

   Let us reconsider the passive construction in this light. I assume with Chomsky (1981) that passive verbs are formed in the lexicon from active ones by a word formation rule that removes the subject θ-role— that is to say, the structural subject position of a passive verb is not a θ-position, and the passive verb only assigns a θ-role to its object. As we have already assumed, the other property of passive verbs is that they do not assign Case. A passive derivation appears in (23) and my assumptions about the passive in (24).

(23) a. [*e*] was killed Bill   (D-Structure)
     b. Bill$_i$ was killed e_i (S-Structure)

(24) *Passive* (Chomsky 1981)
     In the lexicon: (a) dethematize (delink the agent θ-role from the subject position) and (b) mark the verb (morphologically).
     Move α: moves object to subject position optionally.
     Case Filter: makes sure D-Structure object has Case at S-Structure.
     θ-chain: links θ-role to argument in subject position.

The argument associated with the object position is only related to that position, however, by indexing. In this way the S-Structure subject inherits its θ-role by virtue of being in a *θ-chain* with the object position. The notion "θ-chain" is informally defined in (25) (a slightly more formal definition would allow for θ-chains containing more than two positions; see Safir 1985:25–26 for such a definition).

(25) Definition of θ-chain (informal): If X binds Y and only Y is a
θ-position, then X and Y are members of the same θ-chain.

These principles, the θ-Criterion and the Case Filter, are fairly standard
in GB Theory.

Now, again staying with the facts of Dutch, why should these notions
be relevant to the generalization concerning the distribution of the DE
in (14)? I assume that the same properties we have discussed for the
passive in English hold for the passive in Dutch, though of course word
order differs. For example, the passive verb *verwoest* assigns a θ-role to
the object position to which it does not assign Accusative Case. If this
is so, then the direct object of *verwoest* must move to subject position
to satisfy the Case Filter, as in the derivation in (26).

(26) a. Hij zei, dat vele   huizen door de storm verwoest werden
        he says that many houses by   the storm destroyed were

     b. D-Structure: [$_S$[e] [$_{VP}$[vele huizen] verwoest] [$_{Aux}$ werden]]

     c. S-Structure: [$_S$[vele huizen]$_i$ [$_{VP}$[e]$_i$ verwoest] [$_{Aux}$ werden]]

Once again, a θ-chain relates the subject position and the object position, so that *vele huizen* can receive its θ-role.[11]

If this is our account of the passive, however, we must now ask
questions about our treatment of impersonal passives with *er*. Given
the discussion so far, such sentences should be excluded, since the
D-Structure direct object does not move (*er* is in subject position) and
hence cannot be directly assigned Nominative Case. In order to account for this sort of example as well as a range of others in other
languages, Chomsky (1981) proposes that Case is inherited from subject position by virtue of coindexing. More specifically, I assume (27).

(27) Case may be inherited in a θ-chain.

With respect to examples like (10a–b), this means that *er* and the NP-
in-VP must be coindexed as in (28) in order to permit Case to be inherited; this may simply be accomplished by assuming that coindexing
is free between NPs, also a rough approximation of a standard
assumption.

(28) [$_S$[$_{NP}$ er]$_i$ [$_{VP}$[$_{NP}$ een huis]$_i$ verwoest werd]]

But if the subject position is to be in a θ-chain with the object position,
there must be only one argument in the chain and only one θ-role assigned to it; otherwise, the θ-Criterion is violated. This is only possible

if *er* is not an argument, a plausible claim I made earlier in stating the generalization in (14). My independent assumption about passives included the proviso that passives assign no subject θ-role.

By now it should appear an obvious move to identify the DE contexts with those constructions where an NP inherits Case from above. If this is correct, then the relationship between the fact that the subject must be nonthematic and the fact that the affected NP must be in VP follows directly from the requirements of θ-chain well-formedness, while the Case Filter ensures that the chain must be formed. Furthermore, the fact that the effect is neutralized when the NP-in-VP is in a PP (as in (12)) follows immediately, since the preposition can assign Case directly, and no θ-chain need be formed with the subject position. We may now replace the generalization in (14) with one based on entities defined by the theory of formal grammar.

(29) The distribution of the DE correlates with contexts of Case inheritance.

This proposal will immediately extend to unaccusative verbs, that is, those intransitive verbs discussed by Burzio (1981) and Perlmutter (1978) that take D-Structure object θ-positions and have derivations parallel to passive constructions. (An example is the Dutch verb *komen* 'come' in (10a).) Moreover, unlike proposals that rely on some special semantic property of the impersonal formatives, this proposal is in no way affected by the absence of an overt subject as in the South Dutch example (13) that minimally contrasts with (10a). This is because it is a formal property of a chain that matters, and not any particular word.

But what sort of account is this, after all? Although the correlation in (29) seems to make the right distinction in a striking way, why should it hold? Why should a semantic effect correlate with a syntactic property like Case inheritance?

Perhaps the answer lies in the sort of chain that is formed. Normally the argument of a θ-chain is the highest member of the chain. Only in the Case inheritance context does this generalization fail to hold. This is why I have called the downward Case inheritance chains *unbalanced* *θ-chains*. A peculiar property of chains of this type is that they seem to violate Principle C of Chomsky's (1981) binding theory, as stated in (30).

(30) *Principle C of the Binding Theory*
   Names must be free.
   ("Names" = quantified NPs, genitivized NPs, proper names)

Instead of ruling out just definite NPs in unbalanced chains, then, we would expect Principle C to rule out unbalanced θ-chains in general. This suggests that we can explain the DE if we can find some formal property of indefinite NPs that permits them to escape the effects of Principle C, whereas definite NPs must undergo Principle C and be excluded at S-Structure. If this is correct, then the crucial factor in predicting the distribution of the DE is not necessarily Case inheritance but rather the distribution of unbalanced θ-chains, as stated in (31), since only in such chains is Principle C apparently violated.

(31) The DE is found in unbalanced θ-chains.

It is one thing to demonstrate that the DE correlates with a syntactic entity, namely, the unbalanced θ-chain—any future account will have to begin by assuming this syntactic generalization or one that improves upon it—but it is another thing to say that there is a formal syntactic property that distinguishes definite NPs and indefinite NPs with respect to Principle C.[12] If some version of this view is correct, then the DE is entirely a reflex of the way formal properties of chains interact with a formal syntactic property that distinguishes indefinite NPs from definite ones.

Though the latter position is a more radical "pure syntactic" treatment than the one I will adopt, it serves to make another point. It may well be the case that constructions with unbalanced θ-chains are often used as presentationals introducing new entities into discourse, but this is not surprising if these constructions are precisely the ones in which indefinites are required independently by syntactic factors. Thus, to say that the function of indefinites determines the form of the construction, as Rando and Napoli suggest, would be to have the tail wag the dog.

4.2 Beyond the Distribution of the DE

We are now in a position to ask more fundamental questions. Assuming that the formation of an unbalanced chain is the key, we might ask why it is that only indefinite NPs appear to escape Principle C in unbalanced θ-chains. One way (perhaps not the best way) of trying to find an answer to this question is by attempting to discover some property of indefinite NPs that makes them formally different from definite NPs.

If we can indeed state this property formally, then the entire exis-tence and distribution of the DE should follow from it without further assumptions.

There are at least two accounts of what this property might be, one developed in Safir 1982 and 1985 and the other proposed in Reuland 1983. Both accounts assume that there is an independently characteriz-able class of NPs we may call "indefinite," as opposed to those that are "definite," and that the formal property in question makes the crucial distinction. My earlier account is not so explanatory in that it simply claims the formal property to be that indefinite NPs escape Principle C at S-Structure but not at LF (after QR has applied).

Reuland's suggestion is more interesting in that it exploits Heim's (1982) file change semantics with respect to the nature of the definite-indefinite distinction. Basically, the idea is that the index of an indefi-nite NP must be introduced for the first time in a discourse, whereas the index of a definite NP must have been introduced earlier in the dis-course. In an unbalanced θ-chain Reuland argues that the expletive NP will be treated as indefinite at S-Structure, where it bears no index and is thus free; that is to say, the expletive is technically indefinite. If at LF this expletive is coindexed with what I have called NP-in-VP, the NP-in-VP will have to be indefinite as well. Coindexing with a definite NP-in-VP, Reuland argues, would lead to a conflict, whereby the ex-pletive that was indefinite at S-Structure becomes definite at LF. This approach is not without some charm, since it relates a formal discourse property to a property of formal sentence grammar, but it is not obvi-ous why the indefinite NP-in-VP that is bound by a preceding indefinite expletive would not itself be excluded. In other words, it is not obvious that unbalanced θ-chains should exist at all on these assumptions.

It may well be that my objection to Reuland's approach is essentially a technical one that can be overcome by a plausible device. I suspect, however, that stating a formal syntactic property of indefinites as op-posed to definites may be the wrong way to capture the semantic effect typical of structures where unbalanced θ-chains are found. Rather, the semantic effect in question appears to be only partially about definite-ness and is in fact more closely related to the syntactic and semantic properties of a certain class of predications. Formal syntactic fac-tors will still make a crucial contribution to my treatment; to see how this is so, however, it is necessary to examine certain properties of predication.

4.2.1 NP Predicates

A number of formal properties of predicate nominals are reminiscent of properties I have described in unbalanced θ-chains, and in what follows I will exploit these formal similarities. I must admit at the outset, however, that my treatment of the DE in terms of a revised formal theory of predication will result in only a partial explanation for its nature. I will consider some of the new questions that emerge from my analysis in section 4.2.3.

First, however, it is necessary to set aside a misleading similarity between predicate nominals and lexical NPs in unbalanced θ-chains. It seems at first blush that some of the restrictions on predicate nominals recall the DE. Consider the examples in (32).

(32) a.   John seems a fool
     b.   ??John seems the fool
     c.   *John seems the president

I choose the verb *seems* in this set of examples because unlike the verb *be*, *seem* does not have an "identificational" reading; therefore, (32b) and (32c) are rejected in this context, whereas they would be acceptable with the verb *be*. Some small clause contexts give similar results, as with the verb *consider* and, for many speakers, the verb *believe*.

(33) a.   I believe/consider John a fool
     b.   I *believe/*?consider John the fool
     c.   I *believe/?consider John the president

The apparent DE found here is in fact distinguishable from the one found in the *there*-contexts discussed so far, in that superlatives can appear in small clause contexts but not in *there*-contexts; furthermore, specific NPs and cardinal NPs (such as *three men*) can appear in *there*-contexts but not as predicates in small clause contexts.

(34) a.   *Eve seems three women
     b.   There are three women in the room

(35) a.   Zack considers Erica the youngest child
     b.   *There is the youngest child in the room

Of course, I have not introduced the small clause predicate nominal contexts only to remark that they exhibit an unrelated effect; there is indeed a similarity between these constructions and the *there*-contexts that will turn out to be important. Nonetheless, the approach developed must also distinguish these restrictions on predicate nominals from the DE found in unbalanced θ-chains.

Now notice that the NP predicates in small clause contexts appear potentially problematic for two of the major grammatical principles I have discussed. First, if the verb *seem* does not assign any θ-role, or even if it assigns only one to some sort of small clause containing *John* and *a fool,* there are not enough θ-roles to go around for the two potential referring expressions. Second, if the predicate nominal and *John* are related by coindexing, which is after all a very plausible assumption, then Principle C should be violated. At least one of these problems is familiar, in that we are faced with an instance of a potential referring expression violating Principle C as in unbalanced θ-chains, as illustrated in (36).

(36) a. [John]$_i$ seems [a fool]$_i$
     b. I consider [John]$_i$ [a fool]$_i$

Obviously, the fact that the second NP is a predicate is what makes the difference here; hence, we must revise Principle C so that it does not apply to predicate nominals, as in (37).[13,14]

(37) *Predicate Principle*
     A potential referring expression (PRE) is a predicate or else free.

Thus, if a PRE is bound, then it must be a predicate. This way of looking at things may solve both of our problems at once. We know that referring expressions count as syntactic arguments; as such, they must bear θ-roles or violate the θ-Criterion. On the other hand, it seems reasonable to assume that if an NP is predicative, it is not necessarily an argument of anything; put another way, since predicate NPs are not required to bear θ-roles, it is no surprise that they can appear where arguments cannot.

If the Predicate Principle replaces Principle C, then when a PRE is bound, it will have to count as a predicate. Now consider a typical Principle C violation.

(38) *[John]$_i$ saw [a fool]$_i$

A fool is defined as a predicate, since it is A-bound, but this might be treated as a θ-Criterion violation, if in some sense (to be clarified) an element defined as a predicate cannot be an argument at the same time. Thus, in every case where Principle C was assumed to be violated, the end result would instead be a θ-Criterion violation, as in (38).[15,16]

It is necessary, however, to distinguish (38) from grammatical constructions with similar properties such as (39).

(39) John entered college a callow youth (and graduated a fool)

If *a callow youth* were to transmit a θ-role of its own to *John,* then we would expect (39) to be ungrammatical along with (38); in other words, *John* would have two θ-roles, one from *enter* and the other from the predicate nominal. It seems that we do not want adjunct θ-roles to create θ-Criterion violations when they transmit their adjunct θ-roles to their binders. Rather, it seems that we want to rule out (38) because the element defined as a predicate cannot also count as an argument because it is saturated by an argument itself.

The immediate relevance of this approach to the unbalanced chains discussed previously is that the lexical NP of the unbalanced chain, *a man* in (40), will be defined as a predicate by the Predicate Principle.

(40) There$_i$ is a man$_i$ sick

Now *there* is not in a θ-position. It is not an argument either, for lack of content, as I will assume. Therefore, even though *a man* is defined as a predicate, no θ-Criterion violation ensues, because *there* does not saturate the predicate *a man.* Moreover, the θ-chain that includes (*there,a man*) can satisfy the θ-role assigned by *sick* (as suggested to me by Eric Reuland, personal communication), even though *a man* is predicative. This is so because the head of the chain, *there,* is in an argument position, only lacking the semantic content necessary to qualify as an argument, whereas *a man,* lower in the chain, is a nonargument only functionally, while possessing the content to qualify as an argument. The chain as a whole thus has both the content and the functional characteristics of an argument and hence qualifies to bear a θ-role. The assumption concerning the effect of chain formation underlying this analysis is quite similar to what is assumed anyway for chains formed under NP-movement, where the requirement that an argument chain have both Case and a θ-role is also caused to be met by different members.

It would appear, however, that the predicate *a man* ends up having no argument. Predicates of this type will be those subject to the DE (see section 4.2.3), while both kinds of NP predicates—those in standard predicate nominal contexts and those in unbalanced chains—are no longer anomalies with respect to Principle C.

If binding by an A-position makes the bindee a predicate, then an immediate question arises with respect to lexical anaphors, as remarked in note 16. After all, if a bound PRE is a predicate, why should a reflexive be different? At issue, then, are sentences like (41), where if *himself* is defined as a predicate by the Predicate Principle, then the object θ-role should be unsatisfied by any argument and the θ-Criterion should be violated.

(41) John$_i$ saw himself$_i$

Of course, the Predicate Principle, just like Principle C, is stipulated to apply to all NPs except pronouns and anaphors; the Predicate Principle is thus no more stipulative in this regard, but it seems reasonable to ask for some independent evidence that lexical anaphors cannot be defined as predicates.

I believe that such evidence is available. Consider how *himself* acts if it appears in a position normally occupied by an adjunct predicate NP.

(42) a. Murray ate the cake himself
     b. Murray eats that sort of cake himself
     c. Murray saw to it himself

All of the interpretations in (42) are adverbial. Under the preferred interpretations, (42a) means that Murray ate the cake alone (no one else helped him eat it), (42b) means that Murray too, in addition to whoever else might have been mentioned (in the discourse), eats that sort of cake, and (42c) means that Murray saw to it personally (he gave it his personal attention). None of the reflexives in (42) has the meaning that Murray did something while being in the state of being himself. The latter interpretation superficially seems possible in an equative construction, however.

(43) John is himself again

The equative construction is notorious for permitting names to be predicated of any appropriate NP in a context where they are plausibly bound, as in *He is John* and *John is Smith's murderer*. The meaning of (43), however, is that John has regained his old personality or his health, so only by providing an idiomatic predicative reading can the reflexive be well formed. The latter reading is also marginally possible in an adjunct position, but only if helped along by *again*.

(44) ?John returned from the hospital himself *(again)

In fact, I do not believe that *John is himself* can be a grammatical identity statement about John (meaning 'John is in fact John'). This is plausibly due to the fact that an anaphor is inherently without content—its content is determined by its antecedent—and hence cannot be a predicate.[17] Thus, it seems that it is impossible to construe the reflexive as a predicate even where a PRE can normally be so construed; the exclusion of reflexives as possible predicates therefore appears well justified, at least under nonidiomatic interpretation. Perhaps the adverbial readings indicate that the reflexive is actually more like an adjunct argument (for instance, a manner adverbial), rather than an adjunct predicate. Of course, *each other* has no such idiomatic interpretations and is completely excluded in all of the environments corresponding to (42)–(44).

(45) a. *The men are each other again
     b. *The men ate the cake each other
     c. *The men eat that sort of cake each other
     d. *The men saw to it each other

Thus, it appears that lexical anaphors simply cannot act as predicates, even where PREs otherwise can. This supports the formulation of the Predicate Principle as more general than Principle C of the binding theory, since it also accounts for the distribution of NP predicates.

The account of NP predicates sketched here is far from complete, but it does suggest that the right direction to pursue is one that treats the NP-in-VP of unbalanced θ-chains as a type of predicate. Besides solving the formal problem with respect to Principle C in terms that apply to other predicate nominals, it provides a clear means of distinguishing pure DE contexts from other predicate nominal contexts, in that the other predicate nominal contexts always involve predication of a selected argument by a pure predicate NP. The definitions that result in this treatment of predicates already seem well motivated in light of the problems encountered by Principle C, but it is worthwhile to examine an independent reason for deriving Principle C from the Predicate Principle and the θ-Criterion.

4.2.2 NP Predication and Strong Crossover

In Chomsky 1981 and 1982a and in Safir 1984a it is argued that variables are contextually defined as locally $\bar{\text{A}}$-bound elements in A-positions. For our purposes, $\bar{\text{A}}$-positions include Comp, and A-positions include only subject, object, and indirect object positions. Thus, the variable bound by a *wh*-word can only be the element that is locally bound (that is, there is no intervening binder) by the *wh*-word in Comp, as in (46).

(46) $[_{Comp}$ Who$_i]$ $[_S$ did you see $[e]_i]$?

"Strong crossover" results when the locality of binding is violated.

(47) Who$_i$ [did he$_i$ see $[e]_i]$?

In (47) *he* locally binds the trace of *who;* therefore, *he* and not the trace is defined as a variable. It works out that if the trace cannot be defined as a variable, then it will be defined as an anaphor and excluded because an empty category anaphor cannot count as a syntactic argument (for *see*) to satisfy the θ-Criterion. (This derivation is attributed by Chomsky (1982) to Dominique Sportiche.)

By contrast, if variables are defined, not contextually, but by intrinsic features, as has been suggested by Brody (1984), then one might treat them as "names" (as in Chomsky 1976) and exclude them whenever they are A-bound, in effect using Principle C. Notice, however, that since we derive Principle C from the Predicate Principle, these proposals turn out to amount to the same thing: strong crossover violates the θ-Criterion.

These remarks suggest an answer to a reasonable objection I have thus far ignored. Suppose one were to say that NP predicates simply have the property of not bearing indices (predication being achieved by some sort of convention that does not require indexing). It would then follow that they could not be bound and that we would not expect them to count as bound names with respect to Principle C. If this is so, then there is no motivation for altering Principle C in any way, since predicative NPs, it might be claimed, simply fall outside its purview. We must therefore ask if there is any evidence that predicative NPs must bear indices. With this in mind, consider (48).

(48) [What sort of a fool]$_i$ do you consider John (to be) $[e]_i$?

It seems clear that *what sort of a fool* is an NP and that this NP must be related back to its position of origin, as is true of any instance of movement, especially one regulated by the Projection Principle, which requires that θ-assignment must operate the same way at every level (Chomsky 1981).[18] Thus, it seems that indices must be allowed to appear on predicative NPs.[19]

The persistent critic might still reply, however, that though predicative NPs have indices, there is no reason to suppose that Principle C deals with anything but arguments, so that example (48) is irrelevant. This would miss the point, however, since the Predicate Principle *predicts* that what has been called Principle C does not affect NP predicates, regardless of the indices they bear.

These considerations may be extended to a potential strong crossover violation in (48), as indicated by (49).

(49) [What sort of a fool]$_i$ do you consider John$_i$ (to be) [e]$_i$?

(49) is excluded under any approach that defines variables contextually as locally $\overline{\text{A}}$-bound elements, since *John* locally A-binds the trace and the sentence should be excluded. Under a theory that says, however, that variables are intrinsically defined as such (and are perhaps subject to a condition that requires that they be $\overline{\text{A}}$-bound), either by intrinsic features or by their absence (perhaps this is what the $\overline{\text{A}}$-binder is required to provide), we might treat the trace as a variable. Such a theory, however, if it is to capture the strong crossover facts, will then have to say that variables cannot normally be A-bound; in other words, they fall under Principle C. Thus, (49) should be excluded as a Principle C violation.

This is no longer a problem for a theory that employs the Predicate Principle instead of Principle C, since the A-bound variable in (49) is licensed by the (nonlocal) $\overline{\text{A}}$-binder (*what sort of a fool*) (assuming now, with Brody, that the variable is intrinsically designated as such) and defined as a predicate by the (local) A-binder (*John*). Thus, (49) is correctly treated as well formed. In true strong crossover configurations, as in (47), the variable will still be defined as a predicate with respect to *he* and thus could not count as an argument with respect to *see*. The result is a violation of the θ-Criterion, as argued earlier.

4.2.3 Bare Predicates

Now let us return in somewhat more detail to the structure of a typical *there*-sentence, as in (50).

(50) [There]$_i$ is [[a child]$_i$ sleeping]

Since the predicative verb *be* does not assign Case, *a child* must be coindexed with *there,* creating the unbalanced chain.[20] The chain consisting of (*there, a child*) must count as satisfying the θ-role assigned by *sleeping;* at the same time *a child* is also defined as a predicate by the Predicate Principle. The latter predication appears to be empty, however, since it does not assign a θ-role to an argument. It is not obvious, however, how we should interpret predicates without arguments, or, as I shall call them, *bare* predicates, since a predicate is generally thought to be relative to something predicated of.

The natural thing to do, then, is to consider what happens to other bare predicates. One such example is available in Germanic languages, namely, the impersonal passive of intransitive verbs, as in (51).

(51) Er sagte, daß getanzt wurde
    he said   that danced was
    'He said that there was dancing'

Clearly, these impersonal intransitive passives have the interpretation that a certain event took place, in short, an existential assertion about an event. It seems that the natural language interpretation of a bare predicate is as an existential "event" assertion about the denotation of the predicate.[21] But then it is no surprise that with a few exceptions, the typical limitation on unbalanced θ-chains is that they require an existential interpretation (which recalls, of course, the intuition behind Milsark's account).

Of course, it should be kept in mind that the impersonal in (51) has no apparent argument at all, whereas the existential in (50) involves two bare predicates, one of them formed by the unbalanced chain (*a child*), the other by the whole VP *is a child sleeping*. The first predicate should have the default interpretation, namely, that there is an event involving a child, and the second predicate should be interpreted to mean that there is a "(child-)sleeping event."[22] Of course, we do not expect that the DE should apply with the same force where predicate nominals are predicated of selected arguments, rather than the default "event" argument as suggested in the case of bare predicates. Presumably, any theory that attempts to capture the DE by appealing to predicatehood of NPs will require some such distinction.[23]

If this line of reasoning is correct, then the DE should follow as a property of unbalanced θ-chains, given the event interpretation assigned to bare predicates. This result requires appeal only to the Predicate Principle and the θ-Criterion, as well as the assumption that predicates act differently from arguments in some fairly specific ways. What this approach does not explain is why it is the event argument that "satisfies" the bare predicate, and not some other adjunct argument. This question I leave unanswered.

To summarize, a number of formal syntactic properties interact to predict the distribution of the Definiteness Effect. In particular, the DE is found wherever an unbalanced θ-chain is formed, a situation that arises when required by independently motivated constraints such as the Case Filter, which requires Case inheritance in certain contexts. No semantic generalization can make the same prediction. Two questions then remain: Why do unbalanced θ-chains appear to violate Principle C? and Why does the DE distinguish definite as opposed to indefinite NPs in unbalanced chains? To answer the first question, I have reformulated Principle C as the Predicate Principle, and I have proposed that the NP-in-VP is contextually defined as a bare predicate in addition to being an argument. As a step toward answering the second question, I have proposed that a bare predicate becomes a predication of the existence of what is denoted by the predicate, perhaps by exploiting an "event" argument place. A predication of existence is likely to heavily favor indefinites for the NP-in-VP. In addition, this approach extends beyond the cases where the DE is induced by unbalanced chains, since it also applies to the interpretation of "existential sentences" that contain neither argument NPs nor a θ-chain.

Notes

I would like to thank the participants of the Fifth Groningen Round Table, whose discussion and commentary were invaluable to me. I am especially grateful to Eric Reuland and Alice ter Meulen for making it possible for me to participate, and to Reuland in particular for useful substantive suggestions.

1. Although the discussion of section 4.1 is more oriented toward the comparison of methodologies than those I have published elsewhere, readers familiar with Safir 1982 and Safir 1985 may wish to skip directly to section 4.2, where I present new proposals.

2. The particular account of this phenomenon in terms of traces has been controversial; see Chomsky and Lasnik 1977, Jaeggli 1980b, Pullum and Postal 1979, Postal and Pullum 1982, Bouchard 1982, Milsark and Safir 1983, Aoun and Lightfoot 1984, and references cited in those works. All of the accounts mentioned acknowledge the syntactic character of the phenomenon, however, and I believe all of these authors would extend the account to explain the missing interpretation of (4b); therefore, it does not matter which account turns out to be the correct one insofar as the point in the text is concerned.

3. There are other ways of stating this idea that are not "functional" in this sense. Once again I am not really interested at this point in whether this is the correct account of the contrasts in (6) and (7); rather, I am interested in the sort of explanation that has been proposed. It may well be that a lexical semantic account of this phenomenon, for example, which relies on some property of the meaning of the definite-indefinite distinction, may underlie these functions, but I set this possibility aside for the time being, so that I may return to the main issues I want to address.

4. The purported relationship between locative and existential sentences has often been remarked upon. See Clark 1978 for some references concerning the source of this idea. In the Greenbergian spirit, Clark cites a wide range of languages where DE-like phenomena are found.

5. Bolinger's account is not limited to the semantic contribution of *there;* he also appeals to differences in the discourse function of *there*-sentences as opposed to "presentational sentences" without *there,* such as (i) as opposed to (ii).

(i) Across the street is a grocery

(ii) Across the street there is a grocery

After showing that there are discourse contexts where (i) is favored over (ii), Bolinger concludes that *there* must have meaning because (i) and (ii) are used differently. This argument only holds if (i) and (ii) have the same syntactic analysis, however. If they do not, then the structural differences may dictate the difference in discourse usage, and the absence or presence of *there* may simply be a further reflex of the structural distinction. I have argued elsewhere for independent reasons that these structures do differ (in the appendix of Safir 1985), but I set this discussion aside, since the main force of Bolinger's account is his claim about locational meaning of the word *there* in these constructions.

6. Many problems with this account of topic and comment arise immediately in garden-variety sentences like *A boy owns a dog* (where it is not clear what should count as topic or comment) and *The boy owns the dog* (see Chafe 1976). These sentences alone serve to define the kinds of problems that must be addressed by any such account, but I will set them aside and focus instead on the claim that *there* plays a special role in the DE by providing a dummy topic.

7. See Safir 1985 for a critique of Milsark 1974 and 1977 and Safir 1984b for a critique of Williams 1984.

8. Also for reasons of space, I will not discuss other accounts of the impersonal construction in Dutch; but see Safir 1985:chap. 4 for more extensive discussion and references, including a critique of Kirsner's (1979) functional account.

9. I am speaking here of abstract Case and its morphological reflexes in languages that inflect for Case. I do not use the word *case* in the sense of Fillmore (1968), who means something like "semantic role." This technical use of the word *Case* as abstract Case is always capitalized.

10. For discussion of the notion "government" in GB Theory, see especially Aoun and Sportiche 1982 and Chomsky 1981. The exact formulation of this notion will not concern us here.

11. See Safir 1985 for evidence that passive must be allowed to involve movement in German and Dutch.

12. The claim that the distribution of the DE correlates with that of unbalanced θ-chains has been disputed by a number of scholars, including Pollock (1984), Torrego (1983), and do Nascimento (1984). At least some of these criticisms are addressed in Safir 1985:chap. 8 and in Safir 1984b. Several of these scholars point out that there are lexically specific constructions such as the *es gibt-*

construction in German and the *haber*-construction in Spanish (for an extensive study, see Suñer 1983 in which it seems that the NP-in-VP can be assigned Accusative Case, and yet the DE still holds. If this is true, then it follows that no unbalanced θ-chain is required by the Case Filter, since there is no need for Case inheritance. This is only problematic if it can be shown that there is no other independent factor that forces unbalanced θ-chain formation independent of Case inheritance. Reuland (1983) defends the unbalanced chain theory along these lines, arguing that the formation of unbalanced chains is due, not to the Case Filter, but rather to a principle that requires nonthematic subjects to be coindexed with something in VP at LF. So far as I know, the criticisms of Torrego, Pollock, and do Nascimento do not apply to Reuland's approach (but see Safir 1985). I am still inclined, however, to stick to the Case account of chain formation, since it seems to me that the constructions that are problematic are in fact quite idiomatic and language-specific and that the general account should not treat a predicate like *es gibt* as though it were the general case. The lexical specificity of these predicates could be expressed in that they select A-binder subjects at D-Structure (as in the similar case of the possessive idiom pronouns discussed in Safir 1985:chap. 2). It is enough to say, however, that if either Reuland's account of chain formation is correct, or mine is, then we can still ask the relevant questions in roughly the same way.

13. The term *potential referring expression* is probably not a good one, in that I am treating quantified NPs as PREs as well. I am concerned here with the potential of a nonanaphoric nonpronominal NP to count as an argument with respect to the θ-Criterion. See note 16.

14. A small clause (SC) containing two NPs presumably has the structure $[_{SC} NP^a\ NP^b]$, in which NP^a and NP^b are mutually c-commanding. Nevertheless, it must be assumed that only the right-hand NP is the predicate in English; otherwise, both NPs are defined as predicates. Other approaches must make the same assumption. Rothstein (1983), for example, encodes this (language-specific) statement into her rule of predicate linking, and presumably a treatment such as that of Williams (1980, 1981) will also require it.

15. In Safir 1985:chap. 3 I note that predicative NPs do not appear to require abstract Case either—a further respect, I argue, in which the distributions of predicative NPs and argument NPs diverge. Eric Reuland (personal communication) suggests that this difference between predicates and arguments might be exploited to determine the distribution of predicates if we go a step further and say that a predicate *must* not bear Case. Thus, a Case-marked position cannot contain a predicate, which rules out examples like (38). Though such an approach has some appeal, it is clear that predicate nominals can bear Case in some languages. Problems also arise with the German *es gibt* construction, since there could be no predicate involved (*geben* assigns Accusative Case) yet the DE appears, as discussed in note 12.

16. One must keep in mind here the sorts of elements that are not PREs, such as pronouns, reflexives, and reciprocals. I will return to this issue shortly.

17. As for pronouns, it appears that a sentence like *John is him/he* may be an instance of disjoint reference overcome by the equative meaning of *be*. If the approach in the text is pushed, this would mean that the anaphoric interpretation of *he/him* is impossible for the same reason that lexical anaphors are ruled out: they have no semantic content that can be predicated; hence, they cannot be predicates under this interpretation. Thus, where *he* is anaphoric to *John* in *John thinks he's crazy*, the Predicate Principle does not apply.

18. This solves a problem for the theory I proposed in Safir 1985, in which it was not possible to define the empty category in (i) as a variable.

(i) [How many men]$_i$ will there$_i$ [be [e]$_i$ in the room]?

This example will be treated exactly like (48) and is grammatical for the same reasons.

19. I am assuming also that there is only one kind of indexing in grammatical theory, as required by the Unity of Indexing Hypothesis proposed in Safir 1985.

20. On the distinction between predicative *be* and identificational *be*, see Safir 1985:chap. 4.

21. On the "event" argument place, see Davidson 1967. It is reasonable to assume that the event argument place would be a nonselected argument, as all adjunct arguments are. For related discussion of the role of event interpretations in nominals, see Higginbotham 1985 and Sproat 1985.

22. This default event interpretation should be available whenever specific semantic limitations on the predicate in question do not intervene. For example, a semantic restriction might be invoked to explicate contrasts like *There arrived/*left an old man*, since it is well known that predicates expressing motion "away" in some sense are much less acceptable in existential constructions. For an interesting account of semantic restrictions on the existential constructions in Hungarian, see Szabolcsi 1984.

23. This way of characterizing the problem does not require a syntactic definition of the class of indefinite as opposed to definite NPs. This appears to be an advantage in light of the "exceptions" to the DE pointed out by Woisetschlaeger (1983) such as *There was the smell of pot in the room*. Such examples suggest that there can be no successful syntactic definition of the class of NPs that count as definite with respect to the DE. That such a syntactic definition is not required by this approach is an advantage over the accounts proposed in Reuland 1983 and Safir 1982 and 1985.

Chapter 5
Wh-in-Situ: Movement and Unselective Binding

David Pesetsky

The hypothesis that a syntactic level of Logical Form (LF) intervenes between S-Structure and semantic interpretation has been widely discussed and, by some, assumed. In this chapter I use the phenomenon of *wh-in-situ* to argue for the existence of this syntactic level.

A *wh-in-situ* is a *wh*-phrase that has not undergone *Wh*-Movement by S-Structure—that is, it has not visibly moved to Comp. In English *wh*-in-situ are found exclusively in multiple interrogations, as in (1a), whose S-Structure representation is given in (1b): the *wh*-phrase *what* in (1a) is an instance of *wh*-in-situ.[1]

(1) a. Who read what?

    b. $[_{S'}[_{Comp} who] [_S e_i \text{ read } what]]$

I will argue that *certain* *wh*-in-situ that are unmoved at S-Structure actually undergo *Wh*-Movement in the mapping from S-Structure to LF. In turn I argue for LF as a level by showing that a clustering of properties characterizes the proposed LF representations—the normal argument for a level of representation. The hypothesis of *Wh*-Movement at LF is of course not new. What is new here is the word *certain*, which will be crucial to the discussion to follow. Although some scope properties and other observations have long suggested *Wh*-Movement at LF, other facts have tended to dilute the case for such LF movement.

In this chapter I will show that the case for LF movement is actually quite strong. It is simply necessary to distinguish *two* types of *wh*-in-situ in terms related to discourse. One type moves, and the other does not. This distinction has identical consequences in a strikingly wide variety of languages, of which I consider English, Japanese, and Polish here. The distinction is especially interesting, I believe, because both types of *wh*-in-situ display scope ambiguities. This leads me to characterize the distinction in a manner very close to and inspired by Heim's (1982) distinction between indefinites and quantifiers.

5.1 Scope and Movement
5.1.1 Multiple Questions in English
A felicitous answer to (1a) involves a set of ordered pairs of people and things read, for example, *Bill read the dictionary; Harry read the encyclopedia; etc.* The *what* is thus "paired" with the *who*. *Wh*-in-situ in multiple interrogation are interesting because pairings of this sort may be taken to reveal *scope* ambiguities, as discussed first by Baker (1970). We can see this in (2).

(2) *Who* knows *where* we bought *what?*

Sentence (2) shows two *wh*-phrases in Comp (*who* and *where*) and one *wh*-in-situ (*what*). The sentence is ambiguous: *what* may be "paired with" either the *wh* in the lower Comp or the *wh* in the higher Comp. If the *wh*-in-situ is paired with the *wh* in the lower Comp, a felicitous answer must be of the form seen in (3a). If the *wh*-in-situ is paired with the *wh* in the higher Comp, a felicitous answer must be of the form seen in (3b).

(3) a. *John* knows where we bought what (for instance, he knows that we bought the book in Amsterdam, the record in Groningen, etc.)

    b. *John* knows where we bought the *book* (for instance, in Amsterdam); *Mary* knows where we bought the *record* (for instance, in Groningen); etc.

Let us take the pairings in the answers to reflect pairings of *wh*-phrases in the interpretation of the questions.

I will discuss two prominent accounts of these ambiguities. The first is due to Baker.[2] Baker proposed to represent the scope of *wh*-phrases, both moved and in situ, by coindexing the *wh*-phrase with the Q morpheme found in the Comp of interrogative clauses.[3] For Baker, sentence (1) might be represented as in (4).

(4) *Baker-style representation*
    $[[_{\text{Comp}} \ Q_{i,j} \ who_i] \ e_i \ \text{read} \ what_j]$

The ambiguity in (2) will result from the two coindexing possibilities for *what*. The narrow-scope interpretation reflected in (3a) results from coindexing with the lower Q, as shown in (5a); the wide-scope interpretation reflected in (3b) results from coindexing with the higher Q, as shown in (5b).

(5) a. $[[_{Comp} Q_j \; who_j] \; e_j$ knows $[[_{Comp} Q_{i,k} \; where_k]$ we bought $what_i \; e_k]]$

  b. $[[_{Comp} Q_{i,j} \; who_j] \; e_j$ knows $[[_{Comp} Q_k \; where_k]$ we bought $what_i \; e_k]]$

The second proposal for assigning scope to *wh*-in-situ stems from Chomsky (1976) and has been developed by Kayne (1979), Jaeggli (1980a, 1982), Aoun, Hornstein, and Sportiche (1981), Huang (1981), and others. In this proposal *wh*-in-situ undergo the familiar rule of *Wh*-Movement at the syntactic level of LF. Thus, all *wh*-words are in Comp at LF—both those that were already moved at S-Structure and those that were moved at LF. The scope of a *wh*-phrase is determined by which Comp the phrase finds itself in. In Chomsky's analysis (1) might be represented as in (6).

(6) $[[_{Comp} \; what_j \; who_i] \; e_i$ read $e_j]$

The narrow-scope reading of (2) results from LF movement of the *wh*-in-situ to the lower Comp; the wide-scope reading, from movement to the higher Comp. (7a) and (7b) show these LF representations.

(7) a. $[[_{Comp} \; who_j] \; e_j$ knows $[[_{Comp} \; what_i \; where_k]$ we bought $e_i \; e_k]]$

  b. $[[_{Comp} \; what_i \; who_j] \; e_j$ knows $[[_{Comp} \; where_k]$ we bought $e_i \; e_k]]$

Chomsky's proposal follows from the general theory of grammar if the theory contains the principle in (8), and if the statement in (9) is also true.

(8) Every quantifier (operator) occupies an $\overline{A}$-position (nonargument position) at LF.

(9) *Wh*-phrases are quantifiers (operators).

There has not been much debate about the two analyses of *wh*-in-situ. Indeed, it might seem that the choice between the two proposals, Baker's and Chomsky's, is not an empirical issue. After all, if our only task is to assign scope to a *wh*-in-situ, it is easy to assign the appropriate scope using either Baker's or Chomsky's representations. To the extent to which the two analyses have been compared (see, for instance, Huang 1981:fn. 24), the main question has been which analysis to use and which not to use. I will argue, however, that the choice *is* an empirical issue. Not only is it an empirical issue, but both analyses are correct, in their own ways. Each analysis is correct for a particular interpretation of *wh*-in-situ, and each type of representation is correctly associated with a different group of properties.

5.1.2 Indefinites

My analysis is inspired by the discussion of indefinites by Heim (1982), who develops ideas of Lewis (1975). Heim argues that although indefinite NPs show scope ambiguities of the familiar sort, indefinites are not quantifiers. She notes that the quantificational character of an indefinite depends on what quantifiers or adverbs of quantification happen to be in the neighborhood. Thus, (10a–d) have the paraphrases with real quantifiers found in (11a–d) ((10) and (11) from Heim 1982: 123, 127).

(10) a. If a man owns a donkey, he always beats it
    b. In most cases, if a table has lasted for fifty years, it will last for another fifty
    c. Sometimes, if a cat falls from the fifth floor, it survives
    d. If a person falls from the fifth floor, he or she will very rarely survive

(11) a. For every man and every donkey such that the former owns the latter, he beats it
    b. Most tables that have lasted for fifty years last for another fifty
    c. Some cats that fall from the fifth floor survive
    d. Very few people that fall from the fifth floor survive

From data like these, Heim concludes that indefinites "simply have no quantificational force of their own at all, but are rather like variables, which may get bound by whatever quantifier is there to bind them" (p. 127). The binders, like *always* in (10a), are thus *unselective,* in Lewis's sense: they may bind more than one variable. An intermediate representation of (10a) may thus be given as in (12).

(12) [always$_{i,j}$ [if a man$_i$ owns a donkey$_j$, he$_i$ beats it$_j$]]

By straightforward syntactic operations, *always* ends up binding variables in the position of the indefinites, where the domain of quantification is restricted by the predicates *is a man* and *is a donkey.* Note that I am simplifying Heim's treatment here for my purposes. I return to Heim's treatment of "novel indefinites," as in *A man is here to see you,* in the final section of the chapter.

Heim contrasts this treatment of indefinites with a more traditional view of indefinites as quantifiers—the tradition stemming from Russell.

Translated into generative linguistic terms, this view proposes that indefinites, like other quantifiers, move to an $\bar{\text{A}}$-position (typically ad-
joining to S) at the level of LF and treat the syntactic trace left by
movement as the variable they bind. The outcome of these syntactic
manipulations readily translates into standard logical notation (see May
1977).

(13) [a man$_i$ [a donkey$_j$ [if e_i owns e_j, he$_i$ always beats it$_j$]]]

Besides the previous argument, why else might one favor either
Heim's or Russell's type of analysis? One might examine whether indefinites show familiar island constraints on syntactic binding. Indeed,
scope assignment for indefinites does *not* obey these normal restrictions on extraction operations. For example, the indefinite in (14) may
take scope over the *if*-clause. If this indefinite receives scope by extraction, as in (15a), we cannot easily explain why it disobeys the island
condition that prevents just such extraction in the *wh*-question (15b)
and the topicalization structure (15c).

(14) If John comes upon a donkey, Mary always tries to hide it

(15) a. [a donkey$_i$ [if John comes upon e_i, Mary tries to hide it$_i$]]
      b. *What donkey$_i$, if John comes upon e_i, does Mary try to hide
          it$_i$?
      c. *This donkey$_i$, if John comes upon e_i, Mary tries to hide it$_i$

Since indefinites do not obey this and other island conditions on extraction, we have another argument that they are not assigned scope by
extraction.

It should now be clear why I have juxtaposed the *wh*-in-situ discussion with the debate over indefinites. The distinction between
Baker's and Chomsky's analyses of *wh*-in-situ is almost the same as the
distinction between Heim's and Russell's analyses of indefinites. In
fact, Baker's Q is simply an unselective binder in Lewis's and Heim's
sense. Though Baker did not have indefinites in mind, his syntactic
mechanism of Q-indexing clearly anticipates and parallels Lewis's and
Heim's analysis of adverbs of quantification and indefinites.

I have noted the temptation to treat Baker's and Chomsky's analyses
as rivals. The debate between Lewis's and Heim's approach and Russell's approach has had a different character. Although indefinite NPs
may involve unselective binding, there is little question about whether
English has quantifiers that involve some version (liberally construed)

of an extraction operation. Lewis's and Heim's analysis thus distinguishes real quantifiers from unselectively bound elements, while arguing that both exist.

One reason for this distinction is that there are scope phenomena that do obey island conditions. *Every*, for example, cannot take scope outside the *if*-clause in (16).

(16) *If John comes upon every donkey at the zoo, Mary tries to hide it

This is readily explained if *every* is interpreted after an extraction takes place.

(17) [every donkey$_i$ [if John comes upon e_i, Mary always tries to hide it$_i$]]

An NP with *every*, unlike an indefinite, does take scope as a result of extraction, and familiar island phenomena thus obtain.

In this chapter I demonstrate that some *wh*-in-situ are treated according to Baker's proposal: without movement but with unselective binding, like indefinites. Other *wh*-in-situ are treated according to Chomsky's proposal: with movement at the level of LF, like real quantifiers. This distinction can be motivated only by the sort of evidence I cited earlier in the discussion of indefinites and quantifiers: does a particular usage of *wh*-in-situ show the properties that are diagnostic of movement?

Considerations of this sort constitute perhaps the only possible kind of argument for a syntactic level of LF derived from S-Structure by movement operations. Movement is a relation between two positions α and β such that

(18) a. α c-commands β.
   b. α lacks an independent thematic role.
   c. The distance between α and β is governed by a cluster of island conditions (of the sort I have discussed).

In the proposed analysis of quantifiers and in Chomsky's proposal for *wh*-in-situ, (18a) and (18b) are trivially satisfied. (18c) is the interesting case. Are *wh*-in-situ ever subject to the sort of island conditions that are diagnostic of movement? My answer will be "Yes, sometimes."

This answer, if correct, is of some general interest. When one argues that some *wh*-in-situ do undergo movement and others do not, one makes a rather strong case for the existence of LF. LF is a level of interpretation intermediate between S-Structure and semantics whose *syn-*

tactic properties are important. I argue for LF, not by showing its "usefulness" to semantic interpretation, since, as has been frequently noted, a semantics could interpret S-Structure representations without LF. Nor do I argue for LF because I want a "disambiguated level." (Indeed, May 1985 argues that not all scope ambiguities are resolved at LF.) I argue for LF by showing that certain aspects of semantic interpretation display *the characteristic properties of movement rules*. In response to this observation, I give the output of visible syntactic movement and the output of certain scope assignments parallel representations.

In this chapter I thus argue that LF is more than a solution to the problem of assigning scope. Both unselective binding and extraction assign scope, yet only the extraction operation is expected to show all three movement properties seen in (18).[4] Previous work on *wh*-in-situ failed to distinguish the two types of scope assignment for *wh*-in-situ. The case for LF movement was correspondingly weaker: not all instances of scope assignment to *wh*-in-situ showed the diagnostics of movement. Making the distinction clarifies the issue: the scope assignment that really depends on movement does show the expected clustering of movement properties. Given that a *clustering* of syntactic properties characteristic of movement holds of one of these methods of scope assignment, we have identified a syntactic level: LF.

5.2 Superiority Effects as a Diagnostic for Movement
5.2.1 Nested Dependencies
Chomsky (1973) noted that a *Superiority Condition* applies to multiple interrogations in English. His condition was a constraint on movement at S-Structure, but we can for convenience restate it as a condition on S-Structure representations.

(19) *Superiority Condition*
In a multiple interrogation, where a *wh*-phrase is in Comp and another is in situ, the S-Structure trace of the phrase in Comp must c-command the S-Structure position of the *wh*-in-situ.

The Superiority Condition makes the correct distinctions in examples like (20) and (21).

(20) a. *Who$_i$* did you persuade e_i to read *what?*
 b. ??*What$_j$* did you persuade *who(m)* to read e_j?

(21) a. Mary asked [*who$_i$* [e_i read *what*]]?
 b. *Mary asked [*what$_j$* [*who* read e_j]]?

In the (a)-examples the trace of the *wh* in Comp correctly c-commands the S-Structure position of the *wh*-in-situ. In the (b)-examples the trace of *wh* in Comp does not c-command the *wh*-in-situ—just the opposite, in fact.[5] Hence the contrasts.

If embedded as is in the grammar, the Superiority Condition is quite odd. One might expect considerations of scope to require the *wh*-in-situ to bear some c-command relation to the *wh* in Comp, but it is hard to understand why the *wh*-in-situ should have to bear some particular relation to the *trace* of the *wh* in Comp. I think we can make sense of the Superiority Condition if we assume a version of Chomsky's analysis of *wh*-in-situ. In particular, if *wh*-in-situ does move at LF, we may explain Superiority effects as the result of a condition familiar from S-Structure *Wh*-Movement.

Structures like (22a) and (23a) are often taken to be somewhat unacceptable, since they violate the *Wh*-Island Condition. Nonetheless, it has frequently been observed that they are more acceptable, or more interpretable, than their counterparts (22b) and (23b) (see, among other works, Kuno and Robinson 1972; Bordelois 1974; Fodor 1978; Pesetsky 1982, forthcoming).

(22) a. ?*What book$_j$* don't you know *who$_i$* to persuade e_i to read e_j?

b. **Who$_i$* don't you know *what book$_j$* to persuade e_i to read e_j?

(23) a. ?This is one book *which$_j$* I do know *who$_i$* to talk to e_i about e_j

b. *John is one guy *who$_i$* I do know *what book$_j$* to talk to e_i about e_j

The lines drawn between each *wh* in Comp and its trace suggest the source of the problem. In the (a)-examples the *wh*-trace dependencies are *nested*, whereas in the (b)-examples they cross. The (b)-examples may be ruled out by some version of a *Nested Dependency Condition*.

(24) *Nested Dependency Condition*
   If two *wh*-trace dependencies overlap, one must contain the other.

The Nested Dependency Condition is a condition on *movement*. We can see this in some examples from Chomsky 1976.

(25) a. *What books$_i$* have *those men$_j$* written e_i about *each other$_j$?*

   b. I told *them$_i$* [*what books$_j$* [PRO$_i$ to read e_j]]

Where the Nested Dependency Condition appears to be violated in the relation between two positions, it turns out that this relation does not meet the criteria for movement outlined in (18).[6]

Now let us return to the multiple interrogations in (20) and (21). Suppose they do receive a Chomsky-style interpretation at LF. If we simply stipulate that *wh*-in-situ moves to a position slightly to the left of the Comp with which it is interpreted, the Superiority Condition is explained. For our purposes, we will accomplish this stipulation by assuming that LF movement of *wh*-in-situ adjoins the *wh* to S' (as first proposed by Jaeggli (1980a, 1982); the utility of this assumption in the present context was suggested to me by Edwin Williams, personal communication), instead of moving it into Comp.[7] (26a–b) and (27a–b) show the LF representations for (20a–b) and (21a–b), respectively, if this stipulation is correct.

(26) a. [$_{S'}$ *what$_j$* [$_{S'}$ *who$_i$* [$_S$ you persuade e_i to read e_j]]]

   b. ??[$_{S'}$ *who$_i$* [$_{S'}$ *what$_j$* [$_S$ you persuade e_i to read e_j]]]

(27) a. . . . [$_{S'}$ *what$_j$* [$_{S'}$ *who$_i$* [$_S$ e_i read e_j]]]

   b. *. . . [$_{S'}$ *who$_i$* [$_{S'}$ *what$_j$* [$_S$ e_i read e_j]]]

Whenever Superiority effects show up, a Chomsky-style LF representation violates the Nested Dependency Condition. Given the bizarre nature of the Superiority Condition, it is encouraging that we can derive its effects from the Nested Dependency Condition. In turn, if the Nested Dependency Condition is a condition on movement, then Nested Dependency effects will diagnose movement. Since *wh*-in-situ show Nested Dependency effects, we have a strong argument for LF movement of *wh*-in-situ—an argument for a Chomsky-style analysis.

5.2.2 Absence of Expected Superiority Effects

The preceding discussion is interesting because it is not entirely true. In a number of cases expected Superiority effects do not show up.[8]

(28) a. *Which man$_i$* did you persuade e_i to read *which book?*

   b. *Which book$_j$* did you persuade *which man* to read e_j?

(29) a. Mary asked *which man$_i$* e_i read *which book*

   b. Mary asked *which book$_j$* *which man* read e_j

I have claimed that Superiority effects show up when LF movement of *wh*-in-situ runs afoul of the Nested Dependency Condition. The obvious explanation for the lack of Superiority effects in (28a–b) and (29a–b) is that *which*-phrases in situ, unlike *who* or *what*, do not undergo LF movement.

The situation becomes even more interesting when we note that *which*-phrases show the same scope ambiguities as other *wh*-phrases. (30) is as ambiguous as (2); indeed, many speakers seem to find the ambiguity even sharper with *which*-phrases than with *who* or *what*.

(30) *Which man* knows *where which woman* will live?

If this discussion is correct, *which*-phrases in situ require a method of scope assignment that does not involve LF movement—for example, a Baker-style representation, with unselective binding by Q. The scope of a *which*-phrase may be determined by the Comp that contains its index after Baker-style binding has taken place. No Superiority effects are expected to show up because no movement takes place. (29b), for example, will have a representation after Baker-style binding like (31) (compare (27b)).

(31) ... $[_{S'}[_{Comp} \; Q_{i,j} \; which \; man_i] \; [_S \; e_i \; read \; which \; book_j]]$

Nonetheless, we cannot allow *wh*-in-situ to choose freely between Baker-style and Chomsky-style analyses. Clearly, *who* and *what* in (20a–b) and (21a–b) must receive a Chomsky-style analysis, or we will not ever expect to find Superiority effects.

A number of proposals come to mind. For example, it might be relevant that *which* is a specifier inside an NP, whereas *who* and *what* are heads of their NPs. (See Fiengo 1980 and Guéron and May 1984 for suggestions of this type.) Yet it seems that Superiority effects remain with other *wh*-specifiers.

(32) a. I need to know *how many people$_i$* e_i voted for *whom*
b. *I need to know *who(m)$_j$* *how many people* voted for e_j

Given (32), it seems equally unlikely that "heaviness" of the *vh*-phrase is at stake.

I wish to suggest that the crucial difference between a *which*-phrase and the *normal* occurrence of *who* or *what* is found in discourse. (See Katz and Postal 1964:94 for similar discussion, as well as Kuroda 1969.) Roughly, *which*-phrases are *discourse-linked (D-linked)*, whereas *who* and *what* are normally not D-linked. When a speaker asks a question like *Which book did you read?*, the range of felicitous answers is limited by a set of books both speaker and hearer have in mind. If the hearer is ignorant of the context assumed by the speaker, a *which*-question sounds odd.[9] Similarly, in a multiple *which*-question like *Which man read which book?* the speaker assumes that both speaker and hearer have a set of men and a set of books in mind, and that the members of ordered man-book pairs in a felicitous answer will be drawn from the sets established in the discourse. No such requirement is imposed on *wh*-phrases like *who, what,* or *how many books.* These phrases may be *non-D-linked.* If a speaker asks *How many angels fit on the head of a pin?*, there is no presumption that either speaker or hearer has a particular set or quantity of angels in mind.

If D-linking does govern the possibility of a Baker-style interpretation for *wh*-in-situ, we might then modify (9) as follows.

(33) Non-D-linked *wh*-phrases are quantifiers and adjoin to S'.

This adjunction is obligatory at LF, because of principle (8), which requires every quantifier to appear in an $\bar{\text{A}}$-position at LF.

The statement in (33), I will argue, is a principle of the grammar, from which the facts just observed follow. I will assume that both Baker-style and Chomsky-style treatments of *wh*-in-situ are allowed by Universal Grammar. Principles (33) and (8) together exclude a Baker-style treatment for non-D-linked *wh*-phrases. By contrast, suppose the following statement is true.

(34) D-linked *wh*-phrases are not quantifiers.[10]

It follows that D-linked *wh*-phrases are able to receive a Baker-style interpretation, without movement. As a result, they escape the Nested Dependency Condition and therefore fail to exhibit Superiority effects.[11]

If the absence of Superiority effects with *which*-phrases is truly due to D-linking and principle (33), we might expect Superiority effects to disappear even with *who, what,* and *how many books,* if we can force these *wh*-phrases to be D-linked. Speakers differ on this question. Bolinger (1978) attempts to argue against the very existence of syntactic Superiority effects on the basis of examples like (35a) (his (73)). Crucially, the context he establishes implies D-linking of *what* and *who.* I agree with his judgment in this case (though not with his overly sweeping conclusions), particularly if all the *wh*-phrases are given extremely heavy stress. Another example, perhaps easier to accept, is (35b).

(35) a. I know what just about everybody was asked to do, but *what* did *who* (actually) do?

b. I know that we need to install transistor A, transistor B, and transistor C, and I know that these three holes are for transistors, but I'll be damned if I can figure out from the instructions *where what* goes!

Even (32b) can be deemed acceptable in the proper context, particularly if we know that the voters fall into certain groups, how many are in each group, and who the candidates are, but simply do not know who each group voted for. Nonetheless, judgments on these examples, like all judgments swayed by context, are quite delicate. If the facts are as I suggest, then it seems correct to associate the Baker-style interpretation with D-linking.[12]

I thus formulate and support the hypothesis that some *wh*-in-situ move at LF, and others do not. The moved *wh* show a diagnostic for movement: Nested Dependency effects. The unmoved *wh* fail to show this diagnostic. I claim that *wh* must move at LF only if it is non-D-linked. D-linked *wh* do not have to move. Even if they do not move, however, they take scope, thanks to the binding mechanism proposed by Baker.

5.3 Move *Wh* in a Language without *Wh*-Movement

The discussion so far immediately raises the question of languages like Japanese. In this section I will show that my distinction indeed extends to Japanese and explains a pattern of island conditions and island violations that restores a missing argument for LF.[13] In languages like Japanese no *Wh*-Movement to Comp occurs at S-Structure. All *wh*-phrases are in situ, even in embedded questions. An overt Q morpheme—here, *ka* or *no*—marks the scope of *wh*.

(36) a. Mary-wa John-ni nani-o ageta-no?
Mary-Top John-Dat what-Acc gave-Q
'What did Mary give to John?'

b. Mary-wa [s' John-ga nani-o katta-ka] sitte-iru
Mary-Top John-Nom what-Acc bought-Q know
'I know what John bought'

c. Mary-wa [s' John-ga nani-o yonda to] itta-no?
Mary-Top John-Nom what-Acc read that said-Q
'What did Mary say that John read?'

The previous discussion of English immediately raises interesting questions about such languages. Following Huang's (1981, 1982) "Chomsky-style" analysis of similar phenomena in Chinese, Lasnik and Saito (1984) propose that *Wh*-Movement to Comp does apply in Japanese, much as in English. For them, the salient difference between Japanese and English questions is simply the absence of *Wh*-Movement at S-Structure: all *Wh*-Movement takes place at LF. (36a), for example, would have an LF representation in which *Wh*-Movement took place (to a right-hand Comp), as in (37).

(37) [$_{S'}$[$_S$ Mary-wa John-ni e_i ageta] [$_{Comp}$ -no *nani-o$_i$*]]

Lasnik and Saito's proposal has a troubling aspect, however. The proposed LF movement appears not to show an important diagnostic of movement—namely, the cluster of effects sometimes captured by the Subjacency Condition (as noted at least since Kuno 1973). (They do argue, again following Huang, that the proposed movement obeys at least one of the diagnostics for movement—namely, a version of Chomsky's (1981) Empty Category Principle. I will remark briefly on this argument in note 31.) In particular, the proposed movement violates the Complex NP Constraint and the constraint on extracting from adjuncts. We see these constraints for English in the ungrammatical sentences of (38) and their grammatical Japanese translations in (39).[14]

(38) a. *$What_i$ did Mary meet [$_{NP}$ the man [$_{S'}$ who gave e_i to John]]?
     b. ?*$What_i$ did Mary leave before John read e_i?

(39) a. Mary-wa [$_{NP}$[$_{S'}$ John-ni   nani-o   ageta] hito-ni]   atta-no?
         Mary-Top   John-Dat what-Acc gave   man-Dat met-Q

     b. Mary-wa [John-ga   nani-o   yomu mae-ni] dekaketa-no?
         Mary-Nom John-Nom what-Acc read   before left-Q

From facts like these, Huang (1982) as well as Lasnik and Saito conclude that Subjacency does not apply at LF. This conclusion is perfectly plausible but nonetheless disappointing. Given that island phenomena of this sort are one of the principal diagnostic tests for movement, it becomes harder to argue convincingly that the derivation of LF really does involve movement. A potential argument for LF movement thus seems to be missing.

The discussion in the preceding section suggests a different approach. Suppose Subjacency *does* hold at LF. We should investigate whether the apparent absence of Subjacency effects in sentences like

(39a–b) is connected to the discourse status of the *wh*-phrases in question. Perhaps Subjacency appears to be violated only when the *wh*-in-situ does not have to move at LF. This approach can be investigated with two experiments:

1. Force an occurrence of *wh*-in-situ to be aggressively non-D-linked. If the proposed hypotheses are correct, such a *wh*-in-situ *must* undergo LF movement. If Subjacency holds at LF, then Subjacency effects should show up.

2. In apparent Subjacency violations like (39a–b), show that the *wh*-in-situ must be D-linked, hence allowed to receive scope without movement.

I perform these experiments in the following subsections. I show that the first experiment turns out exactly as predicted by the theory. The second does not. In this case, however, work by Choe (1984) and Nishigauchi (1984) suggests an independent explanation, which, in fact, ends up reinforcing my hypothesis about the LF distinction between D-linked and non-D-linked *wh*-in-situ.

5.3.1 Forcing a Non-D-Linked Reading

Phrases like *what the hell* are good candidates for "aggressively non-D-linked" *wh*-phrases. Roughly speaking, the whole point of uttering a question like *What the hell did you read that in?* is to express surprise in the answer. The appropriate answer is presumed not to figure in previous discourse.[15] Note the sharp contrast between the colloquial (40a) and the impossible (40b).

(40) a. What the hell book did you read that in?
     b. *Which the hell book did you read that in?

(40b) can be ruled out by the conflict between aggressively D-linked *which* and aggressively non-D-linked *the hell*.

Japanese *ittai* seems to have the same function as English *the hell*.[16] Not surprisingly in a head-final language, *ittai* precedes the *wh*-phrase with which it is interpreted.[17]

(41) Mary-wa John-ni *ittai* *nani-o* ageta-no?
     Mary-Top John-Dat the-hell what-Acc gave-Q
     'What the hell did Mary give to John?'

(42) establishes that *wh*-phrases with *ittai* may take scope outside their clause and also that *ittai* is not limited to root environments.[18]

(42) Mary-wa [s' John-ga *ittai*   *nani-o*   yonda to] itta-no?
     Mary-Top   John-Nom the-hell what-Acc read   that said-Q
     'What the hell did Mary say that John read?'

I have hypothesized (a) that Subjacency *does* hold of LF movement and (b) that *ittai* forces a non-D-linked interpretation for *wh*-in-situ. This entails, by (8) and (33), that *ittai wh*-phrases must move at LF and that Subjacency effects should be detected. In fact, they are. (43a–b) differs from (39a–b) only in that the *wh*-phrase *nani* 'what' has been replaced with *ittai nani* 'what the hell'. Nonetheless, the result appears to be quite ungrammatical.[19]

(43) a. *Mary-wa [NP[S' John-ni *ittai nani-o* ageta] hito-ni] atta-no?

     b. *Mary-wa [John-ga *ittai nani-o* yomu mae-ni] dekaketa-no?

These examples thus provide evidence both for Subjacency at LF and for the connection drawn in the previous section between obligatory LF movement and discourse. I will have further comments on *ittai* in the next subsections.[20]

5.3.2 Subjacency Violations and D-Linked *Wh*-Phrases

The first experiment—forcing a *wh*-phrase to be non-D-linked—has succeeded: the expected Subjacency effects appeared. My hypotheses also predict that Subjacency effects should disappear with *wh*-in-situ only when the *wh*-in-situ is D-linked. At first sight, this prediction appears to be false. A sentence like (39a) or (39b) may be freely used in Japanese even when the *wh*-phrase is non-D-linked. Important work by Choe (1984) and Nishigauchi (1984), however, helps to save the hypotheses.[21] This work shows that even examples like (39a–b), when examined more carefully, show Subjacency effects. I will demonstrate in turn that *these* Subjacency effects do indeed depend on discourse.

Choe and Nishigauchi take into account not only the grammaticality of various *wh*-questions in Japanese and Korean, but also the felicity of various answers to these questions. My examples will be from Japanese. The following are natural discourses in Japanese; that is, the answer corresponds in a natural way to the *wh*-phrase in the question.

(44) Q: Mary-wa John-ni *nani-o* ageta-no?
'What did Mary give to John?'

A: Konpyuutaa desu
computer   Cop
'It's a computer'

(45) Q: John-wa *nani-o* yonda-no?
'What did John read?'

A: "Sensoo to Heiwa" desu
War and Peace   Cop
'It's *War and Peace*'

Everything is much the same if the *wh*-phrase is in an embedded sentence.

(46) Q: Mary-wa [_{s'} John-ga   nani-o   yonda to] omotteiru-no?
Mary-Top   John-Nom what-Acc read   that think-Q
'What does Mary think that John read?'

A: "Sensoo to Heiwa" desu
'It's *War and Peace*'

When a *wh*-word is embedded in an island, however, an answer that simply corresponds to the *wh*-phrase is no longer felicitous for many or most speakers. Instead, a felicitous answer must recapitulate the entire island. Although speakers differ on the strength of these judgments, the data for most speakers seem to be as presented in the following examples, and I have not found speakers who present the opposite judgments.[22] The questions in (47)–(48) are the same sentences presented in (39a–b), respectively:

(47) Q: Mary-wa [_{NP}[_{s'} John-ni nani-o ageta] hito-ni] atta-no?
'What did Mary meet the man who gave to John?'

A1:   */??Konpyuutaa desu
'It's a computer'

A2:   [_{NP}[_{s'} Konpyuutaa-o ageta] hito] desu
computer-Acc gave   man Cop
'It's the man who gave a computer (to him)'

(48) Q: Mary-wa [John-ga nani-o yomu mae-ni] dekaketa-no?
            'What did Mary leave before John read?'

     A1: *"Sensoo to Heiwa" desu
            'It's *War and Peace*'

     A2:   ["Sensoo to Heiwa"-o yomu mae]   desu
            War and Peace-Acc   read   before Cop
            'It's before (he) read *War and Peace*'

As both Choe and Nishigauchi note, these facts immediately suggest pied-piping. Suppose that the following principle holds in Japanese.

(49) *Felicity Principle*
     A felicitous answer to a *wh*-question consists of a phrase
     structurally identical to the *wh*-phrase whose index is
     immediately dominated by the Comp of the question at LF.[23]

Let us now consider the consequences if Subjacency does apply at LF and if the *wh*-phrases in (47) and (48) receive a Chomsky-style movement analysis. Although *Wh*-Movement cannot move the *wh*-phrase out of the complex NP in (47) and out of the adjunct in (48), nothing a priori prevents pied-piping of the entire complex NP or adjunct.[24] If pied-piping applies, (47) and (48) have the LF representations in (50) and (51), respectively.

(50) Mary-wa e_i atta- [$_{Comp}$ no [$_{NP}$[$_{S'}$ John-ni nani-o ageta] hito-ni]$_i$]

(51) Mary-wa e_i dekaketa- [$_{Comp}$ no [John-ga nani-o yomu mae-ni]]

The Felicity Principle correctly predicts the pattern of answers.[25]

If Choe and Nishigauchi are correct, examples that have been presented as Subjacency violations in Japanese are not Subjacency violations at all. Thus, the second experiment—to show that D-linking and only D-linking allows Subjacency violations—has not failed; rather, it has not begun.

First, however, we need to deal with a problem created by Choe's and Nishigauchi's analysis. The examples with *ittai* and the examples just considered really make the same point: non-D-linked *wh*-phrases must move at LF, and this movement obeys Subjacency. Nonetheless, they make the point in contradictory ways. In the case of *ittai* we saw Subjacency effects by looking for grammaticality judgments on *wh*-questions;* in the cases just considered we saw the effects only by looking at the *answers* to the questions. This was because of the pied-piping option. If a *wh*-word in an island may pied-pipe the whole island with it, the only possible way to detect Subjacency is through the answers, thanks to the Felicity Principle. But why then did we detect Subjacency effects in *ittai questions?*

Clearly, the examples with *ittai* must prohibit LF pied-piping for some reason. Note, however, that this prohibition is not a *deus ex machina,* since a similar prohibition is visible at S-Structure in English *the hell* phrases.

(52) a.   Pictures of whom cost the most at the sale?
     b.   *Pictures of who the hell cost the most at the sale?

(53) a.   I wonder what the hell he's talking about
     b.   *I wonder about what the hell he's talking

The examples in (53) might be due to a style clash between the relatively formal pied-piping and *the hell.* Those in (52), however, cannot be due to such a clash. Since pied-piping is obligatory here, the pied-piping in (52a) does not seem at all formal.[26] Furthermore, *what on earth* works much the same as *what the hell,* in that it disallows pied-piping; but it is not incompatible with the relatively formal register necessary to allow pied-piping in (53).[27]

Putting this problem aside, I return to the question of whether Subjacency effects do indeed disappear when *wh*-in-situ is D-linked. The relevant case is (54). Strikingly, my hypothesis is confirmed: Subjacency effects do indeed disappear. Compare (54) with (47).

(54) Q: (Context: IBM-to, Apple-to, Fuzituu-to, Matusita-no
           naka-de . . .)
           'Among IBM, Apple, Fujitsu, and Panasonic
           (National) . . .'
           Mary-wa [$_{NP}$[$_{S'}$ John-ni *dono konpyuutaa-o* ageta] hito-ni
           atta-no?
           '*Which computer* did Mary meet the man who gave to John?'

     A1:   IBM-no   konpyuutaa desu
           IBM-Gen computer   Cop
           'It's the IBM computer'

     A2:   [$_{NP}$[$_{S'}$ IBM-no   konpyuutaa-o ageta] hito] desu
               IBM-Gen computer-Acc gave   man Cop
           'It's the man who gave the IBM computer (to him)'

The acceptability of the first answer is unexpected if all *wh*-in-situ must move at LF and if, as I have argued, Subjacency does hold at

LF.[28] If *dono konpyuutaa* does not have to move, since it is D-linked, then Subjacency is irrelevant, and the acceptability of the first answer is predicted. The question in (54) need not have the Chomsky-style representation in (50). Rather, it has the Baker-style representation in (55).

(55) Mary-wa [$_{NP}$[$_{S'}$ John-ni *dono konpyuutaa-o$_i$* ageta] hito-ni] atta-no$_i$?

Why should the "pied-piping" second answer also be possible? Two possibilities present themselves. First, a movement option might be available even for D-linked *wh*-phrases. Second, the same percolation of the *wh*-feature that is necessary to allow pied-piping in movement cases might allow Baker-style Q indexing to apply optionally to the full NP, as in (56).

(56) Mary-wa [$_{NP}$[$_{S'}$ *John-ni dono konpyuutaa-o ageta*] *hito-ni*]$_j$ atta-no$_j$?

Since Comp now contains the index, not of *dono konpyuutaa,* but rather of the whole complex NP, the Felicity Principle will yield the second answer in (54). There are various ways to distinguish the two proposals, involving complex NPs embedded in other complex NPs. I will not attempt an investigation here.

5.3.3 Results
Summarizing, I believe that this section has achieved two goals. First, my central hypothesis concerning the interaction between D-linking and LF movement has been strongly confirmed by evidence from Japanese. Second, this hypothesis has provided a formerly missing argument for movement at LF—an argument from Subjacency. I showed first that non-D-linked *wh*-phrases do indeed obey Subjacency. In the case of *ittai*-phrases, which prohibit pied-piping, I demonstrated Subjacency effects simply by examining *wh*-questions. In other cases I followed Choe and Nishigauchi in examining the pattern of felicitous answers. Once a *wh*-phrase is D-linked, however, the evidence for Subjacency disappears, lending further credence to the idea that D-linked *wh*-in-situ are assigned scope by a mechanism like Baker's, without movement.[29]

Finally, I should like to emphasize a methodological point. If my discussion is correct, then work that deals with *wh*-in-situ in particular must take extraordinary care in drawing conclusions based on data.

Simple inspection of a grammatical utterance in which a *wh*-in-situ appears to take scope out of an island, for example, cannot be used in and of itself as a basis for conclusions about the status of islands at LF or about the existence of LF. One must carefully investigate at least the discourse status of the *wh*-phrases and the possibility of a pied-piping analysis.[30]

5.4 East European

Some of the most striking evidence for the discourse distinction (called to my attention by Jae Choe, personal communication) concerns the East European *Sprachbund* that exists with respect to multiple interrogation. The range of phenomena I will discuss comes from Polish. For most speakers, the same facts hold in Romanian, and Petr Sgall (personal communication) suggests that they may also hold in Czech. I do not have specific information on the other languages of this group.

Lasnik and Saito (1984) discuss sentences like (57a–b) from Polish. The judgment they cite is given in parentheses.

(57) a. Zastanawiam się [kto co   przyniesie]
         I-wonder   who what will-bring
         'I wonder who will bring what'

   b. (*)Zastanawiam się kto przyniesie co

They claim that in Polish multiple interrogations like (57a–b) all the *wh*-phrases that are interpreted together are fronted at S-Structure to an Ā-position. We will not be concerned here with the nature of this position—whether Comp or an adjunction site (see Toman 1981 for some discussion). Based on the contrast between (57a) and (57b), Lasnik and Saito formulate the following generalization for Polish (a particular setting of a general parameter).

(58) In Polish every *wh* must be in an Ā-position at S-Structure.
     (p. 239)

   The kind of movement seen in (57a) is exactly what is proposed for LF in the Chomsky-style analysis of *wh*-in-situ. Polish (and the other languages of the *Sprachbund*) is interesting because, with respect to *wh*, at least, it seems to wear its LF on its sleeve. I will suggest that this is truer than has been realized.

   In particular, there is more to the data than Lasnik and Saito's discussion suggests. In her original discussion of multiple interrogation in

Polish, Wachowicz (1974) notes that examples like (57b) are not actually ungrammatical. She considers examples like (59),

(59) W końcu, kto robi co?
     finally   who does what

and notes that they are actually acceptable in a very particular context. By now the reader may guess what that context is:

> [Such] questions are somewhat different from echo questions. We can call them clarifying questions. The speaker could ask [(59)] in the following situation. There are various tasks, and several people to be assigned for them. Proposals have been made how to pair up people and tasks, but no fixed plan has been set up yet. The speaker of [(59)] is confused by the proposals, and wants to have a fixed plan. (Wachowicz 1974:159)

This observation appears to hold quite generally: all non-D-linked *wh*-phrases move to an $\overline{\text{A}}$-position at S-Structure, but D-linked *wh*-phrases may stay in situ. The (b)-sentences of (60)–(62) all have the special usage described by Wachowicz.[31]

(60) a. Kto kogo zabił?
        who whom killed

     b. Kto zabił kogo?

(61) a. Kogo kiedy Maria zabiła?
        whom where Maria killed

     b. Kogo Maria zabiła kiedy?

(62) a. Kogo jak Maria zabiła?
        whom how Maria killed

     b. Kogo Maria zabiła jak?

Polish and the other languages of its group thus show on the surface what I have hypothesized for the LF representations of English and Japanese.[32] We can handle the details in a number of ways. One possibility is to claim that the following statements hold in Polish.

(63) a. More than one *wh* may undergo *Wh*-Movement in a single clause.
     b. There is no LF *Wh*-Movement.[33]

We might speculate briefly on how (63b) might find its place in a learnable system of core grammars. The answer might be that (63b) is the unmarked case, given the existence of languages like Italian that lack multiple interrogation entirely.[34] In any case, if true, the distinctions drawn here between D-linked and non-D-linked *wh*-in-situ are certainly parts of Universal Grammar, not learned from experience by the child.[35]

5.5 D-Linking

English, Japanese, and East European thus all provide evidence that non-D-linked *wh*-phrases are assigned scope by movement at the level of LF, whereas D-linked *wh*-phrases are assigned scope without movement. The next question is why movement versus nonmovement should correlate with D-linking. In particular, I have argued that the scope of D-linked *wh*-phrases is assigned by unselective binding, much as scope is assigned to indefinite NPs in Heim's system. Yet indefinites and D-linked *wh*-phrases may seem strange bedfellows.

In this section I will not solve this problem, but I will speculate briefly on the direction a possible solution might take. The key here is Heim's treatment of indefinite NPs, like *a man* in the sentence *Suddenly, a man appeared.* Heim proposes that an existential quantifier is introduced by a general rule of *Existential Closure,* which then proceeds to unselectively bind the indefinite. Importantly, the indefinite must also be interpreted as "novel" in the discourse. Heim later combines these requirements, assimilating Existential Closure to a more general phenomenon in which variables may be bound by "file cards" in a discourse representation. Uttering a novel indefinite creates a new entry in the filing system. Pronouns also exist, which have the discourse properties of indefinites except that they are not novel but are instead bound by an already existing entry, as in (64a–b).

(64) a. A man walked into the room. *He* was wearing a fur coat
  b. Some men walked into the room. *They* were wearing fur coats

The scope of the "file card" may vary, affecting the interpretation both of the indefinite and of a "familiar" pronoun that may return the indefinite (see Partee 1973 on such de dicto pronouns).

(65) a. John claimed Bill believed that I'd eaten a pizza. Mary even claimed that Bill believed it had anchovies. But in fact I ate chicken that night
  b. John claimed Bill believed that I'd eaten a pizza. Mary even claimed that Bill believed it had anchovies. But in fact Bill believed that I'd eaten chicken.

Which-phrases unselectively bound by Q seem to function pronominally in exactly this way: they are "familiar" rather than novel, returning old entries in the filing system of discourse. In this they contrast with the normal use of phrases such as *who* and *what*, but they act much like pronouns. (66) displays this contrast. In (66b) it is natural, almost obligatory, to assume that the question is asking for a choice among the men who entered the room. In (66c) considerations of textual connectedness make this assumption possible but much less natural.[36]

(66) a. Some men entered the room. Mary talked to them
     b. Some men entered the room. Which (ones) did Mary talk to?
     c. Some men entered the room. Who did Mary talk to?

We can thus say that *which*-phrases do have the properties of indefinite NPs but that they are familiar rather than novel.

The phenomenon of "accommodation" discussed by Heim can then explain the use of *which*-phrases in "quiz show" contexts (see note 9).

(67) For 100 dollars, which German author wrote *Faust?*

The discourse need not contain any mention of *Faust* or of Goethe. Both the quizmaster and the contestants may be equally ignorant of the answer. The question thus violates various felicity conditions on the use of "familiar" NPs like *which:* there is no preexisting file entry applicable to the situation. Under these circumstances quizmaster and contestants "[add] to the file enough information to remedy the infelicity" (Heim 1982:372), for instance, *A German author wrote Faust.*[37]

There is thus a natural connection between *which*-phrases and one instance of unselective binding—namely, the discourse binding seen with pronouns. The connection between this discourse binding and the interpretation of questions, however, remains to be drawn.

5.6 Finishing Touches

One salient detail remains to be taken care of. If D-linked *wh*-phrases do not have to undergo movement to satisfy (8), why are they required to move in English examples like (68)?

(68) a. I wonder which book you read
     b. *I wonder you read which book

Evidently, although no property intrinsic to *which*-phrases forces them to move, there is some property intrinsic to an interrogative Comp in English that forces this Comp to be occupied by a *wh*-phrase at S-Structure. Recall that nothing *prevents* a D-linked *wh*-phrase from moving to Comp (but see note 32). Therefore, if moving *which book* to an interrogative Comp at S-Structure is the only way to satisfy the requirements of this Comp, then it must so move.

Borrowing a leaf from Lasnik's (1981) discussion of why Affix Hopping is obligatory, I suggest that the requirement is essentially morphological: the Q morpheme must be supported by some appropriate adjacent phrase. Suppose the candidates are Infl or a *wh*-phrase.

(69) The Q morpheme must cliticize to a *wh*-phrase or Infl. (S-Structure)

In English Infl is not adjacent to Comp. Hence, *Wh*-Movement moves *wh* to Comp at S-Structure (unless Comp already contains a *wh*-phrase like *whether*), and cliticization takes place.[38] In Japanese, however, Infl and Comp are adjacent in clause-final position; hence, cliticization takes place without *Wh*-Movement.[39]

5.7 Conclusions

Once we separate the properties of D-linked *wh*-phrases from those of non-D-linked *wh*-phrases, we see that scope assignment to non-D-linked *wh*-phrases has essentially all the properties of syntactic movement.[40] I take this to be a strong argument for the level of Logical Form, since levels are motivated by just such a clustering of properties. Additionally, we see that what is paramount in exploring Logical Form are its properties as a *syntactic* level on the road to interpretation, not one or another arbitrarily assigned semantic property like disambiguation of scope.

It is also interesting to notice that the S-Structure treatment of *wh*-phrases in English, Japanese, and Polish essentially exhausts the spectrum of variation among languages, if we exclude mixed languages that optionally move *wh* or optionally move more than one. Yet despite the surface variety, the LF treatment of *wh*-in-situ in these languages appears to be the same. This is as expected, since the LF properties enunciated here are not plausibly learned by children from experience but must belong to Universal Grammar.

Finally, the interaction of discourse factors with other syntactic properties is intricate and difficult to decipher, as has long been recognized. Heim's (1982) study (along with parallel studies by Kamp and others) took an important step in working out certain areas of interaction that are amenable to linguistic inquiry. This chapter has attempted to link Heim's results to the study of *Wh*-Movement in Logical Form— a link, if correct, of some importance.

Notes

This chapter owes its existence to a discussion with Eric Reuland and to suggestions contributed by Jae Choe. Thanks to Nobuko Hasegawa, Junko Itô, Yoshihisa Kitagawa, Bożena Rozwadowska, Donca Steriade, and Ileana Comorovski for invaluable factual information and theoretical discussion, and to Guglielmo Cinque, Richard Kayne, and Eric Reuland for useful written comments on an earlier version (December 1984). I am also grateful to an unusually large number of colleagues—Emmon Bach, Steve Berman, Noam Chomsky, Alice Davison, James Higginbotham, Hajime Hoji, Janis Melvold, Mario Montalbetti, Taisuke Nishigauchi, Barbara Partee, Luigi Rizzi, Mats Rooth, Mamoru Saito, Barry Schein, Tim Stowell, and Karina Wilkinson—as well as to audiences at the Fifth Groningen Round Table and elsewhere for useful suggestions.

1. I will generally ignore echo questions, like *You saw WHO?*, except for a few miscellaneous remarks.

2. See also Katz and Postal 1964:sect. 4.2.4. A version of Baker's proposal has been revived in Van Riemsdijk and Williams 1981.

3. The difference between Katz and Postal's 1964 *Q* morpheme and the [+WH] feature introduced by Chomsky and Lasnik (1977) is essentially terminological. I will assume a Q morpheme in "Baker-style" representations, as well as anachronistic traces and Comp.

4. Elements that are unselectively bound are thus distinct from *any*, if the analysis in Aoun, Hornstein, and Sportiche 1981 and Hornstein 1984 is correct (but see Kurata 1986), and from *wh*-in-situ in echo questions (see Hendrick and Rochemont 1982), which are treated like names and, if they can be said to have scope at all, have obligatory widest scope.

5. The contrast between (20b) and (21b) may be due to the fact that (21b) also violates the Empty Category Principle (ECP) at LF. See Kayne 1979 and subsequent work, as well as Kayne 1983:fn. 13 and May 1985.

6. In Pesetsky 1982 I argued that certain movements—namely, movement to an A-position (argument position)—are also not subject to the Nested Dependency Condition. This might not be so, as I discuss in Pesetsky, forthcoming.

7. Strictly speaking, to derive a hierarchical condition like Superiority, we need a hierarchical, not linear, version of the Nested Dependency Condition. Elsewhere (Pesetsky 1982, forthcoming) I argue for exactly such a Nested

Dependency Condition: a hierarchical nesting constraint based on paths in a phrase marker, which I call the *Path Containment Condition*. Although there are empirical differences between the linear and hierarchical theories that are relevant to the Superiority Condition, they do not affect the main points of this chapter. On the other hand, if the Path Containment Condition is wrong, and a linear approach is correct, then (as Gert Webelhuth, personal communication, has pointed out) we do not need to assume adjunction to S' to derive the Superiority Condition. Movement to a left-hand position in Comp, as in (6), will work as well.

8. The examples in (29) appear to have been noted first by Chomsky (1980a), who attributes the observation to Richard Kayne. See also Koster 1978. Kayne (1983, loc. cit.) tentatively denies any grammaticality contrast here and in similar cases involving the ECP. To my ears, ECP contrasts exist between *who, what,* and so forth, and *which N'* along the lines of the Superiority contrasts cited in the text.

(i) ??Tell me what proves that who is innocent

(ii) Tell me which piece of evidence proves that which person is innocent

9. Of course, the set of books need not actually have been verbally specified in an utterance, as long as both speaker and hearer make the same assumptions about context. This is the phenomenon of "accommodation" discussed by Heim. Thus, if Mary is looking at a shelf full of books, John might sneak up behind her and ask *Which book are you planning to steal?*, without any preceding utterances. An apparent exception to my proposed generalization about *which*-phrases occurs in "quiz show" contexts, to which I return in a later section.

10. For a similar distinction motivated by Romance clitics, see Cinque 1985 and references cited therein.

11. Note that I have not said whether or not D-linked *wh*-phrases *may* optionally be moved in a multiple interrogation. So far it is only clear that they *need not* be moved. I return to this question in note 32.

12. Kuno and Robinson (1972) argue that all *wh*-in-situ obey a clausemate condition, effectively excluding the wide-scope interpretation for example (2). Hankamer (1974) disagrees, claiming that the wide-scope reading does indeed exist. He notes, however, (footnote 3) that the wide-scope reading is only available for *wh*-phrases that are, in my terms, D-linked—including D-linked *who* and *what*. My judgments do not coincide with Hankamer's here. Nonetheless his judgments are interesting, since they suggest that for some speakers LF movement is clause-bound, wide scope being possible only when assigned without movement. There is a clear parallel to widely accepted judgments on quantifier scope (not my own).

13. Kuno and Masunaga (1985) have offered a rejoinder to my arguments from Japanese as they appear in an earlier version of this chapter. I reply to their discussion in Pesetsky 1985. Nishigauchi (1985, 1986) also provides very relevant further discussion and debate.

14. The adjuncts in Japanese seem to be complex NPs; hence, there may be no real distinction between Complex NP Constraint effects and adjunct effects.

15. Roger Higgins (personal communication) brings up the question of the exclamative use of *the hell*. If John starts to leave the room and I say *Where the hell do you think you're going!*, I may know perfectly well that John is heading home. Nonetheless, we might still want to say that *where the hell* is non-D-linked, since *home* is in fact not a destination under previous discussion and there is no "accommodation" here. (See note 9.)

16. Speakers of Korean differ on whether Korean *todeche*, used much like *ittai*, acts like *ittai* with respect to the facts in question.

17. As Junko Itô (personal communication) points out, it is vital to distinguish this use of *ittai* from its use as a sentence adverb, meaning roughly 'in general'. The speakers with whom I worked had little difficulty in disambiguating the uses, which is essential if the effects discussed in the text are to be observed.

18. If *ittai* has such limitations, then the examples that follow tell us nothing about Subjacency. Nishigauchi (1985) claims that the acceptability of sentences like (42) is indeed "low" for him, but other informants do not share this intuition, or at worst find a marked contrast between (42) and (43b).

19. Complex NPs where the embedded S' is not a relative clause—for example, of the *fact that* type—show weaker Subjacency effects, exactly as with English S-Structure movement.

(i) ??What did Mary remember the fact that John read?

(ii) ??Mary-wa [$_{NP}$[$_{S'}$ John-ga *ittai nani-o* yonda] koto-o]
Mary-Top John-Nom the-hell what-Acc read fact-Acc
wasureteiru-no?
remembered-Q

20. Kitagawa (1984) points out some other relevant facts concerning *ittai*. Japanese has generally been taken not to have visible Superiority effects, plausibly because it cannot easily be seen in a multiple interrogation which of a set of *wh*-phrases has moved first. Nonetheless, contrasts of the following sort suggest Superiority (where *dare-ga* receives a non-D-linked interpretation).

(i) a. [Ittai dare-ga] nani-o tukamaeta-no?
the-hell who-Nom what-Acc caught-Q

b. ??Dare-ga [ittai nani-o] tukamaeta-no?
who-Nom the-hell what-Acc caught-Q

Clever construction of examples with center embedding shows that the contrast does involve c-command, and not some left-to-right restriction on *ittai*. Kitagawa notes that if we make the assumption that the *ittai*-phrase *must move to Comp first*, before the other *wh*-phrase does, then (ia–b) will be analogous to familiar English contrasts like *Who caught what?* versus **What did who catch?* In (ib) the object has moved to Comp first; in (ia) the subject has done so. Finally, the assumption that *ittai*-phrases must move to Comp first is not so shocking once we examine the English contrast in (ii) and the French examples in (iii) from Richard Kayne (personal communication; see Kayne 1972:97). Unlike English, French normally allows matrix *wh*-phrases to remain in situ even with the nonecho interpretation.

(ii) a.   Who the hell caught what?
     b.   *Who caught what the hell?

(iii) a.   Où (diable) est-il allé?
          'Where (the devil) did he go?'
      b.   Il est allé où (*diable)?

Why *ittai*-phrases must move to Comp first is a mystery to me. It is striking that elements that move to Comp first in Japanese are those that must move at S-Structure in English and French. The elements that move first to Comp seem to act as the "sorting key" for the answer, as suggested by Kuno (1982). Thus, *Which book did which man read, in alphabetical order?* invites a set of pairs alphabetized by book titles, whereas *Which man read which book, in alphabetical order?* invites a set of pairs alphabetized by men's names. The distinction between S-Structure movement and LF movement in languages like English might actually be a distinction between elements that serve as a sorting key, moving as soon as possible to fulfill that function, and those that can wait. The notion "sorting key" seems obviously related to the syntactic notion "head of Comp" in the sense of Lasnik and Saito.

21. Choe and Nishigauchi reached similar conclusions independently, Choe for Korean as well as Japanese. These results were also anticipated in Lee 1982 and in an early draft of Huang 1981. Also see Kayne 1983: sect.3.2.

22. Except Kuno and Masunaga (1985) in certain cases; see Pesetsky 1985.

23. I say *whose index is immediately dominated* rather than *which is immediately dominated* to allow Baker-style analyses of the type to be motivated shortly.

24. Once again, as in note 19, *fact that* complex NPs show weaker Subjacency effects than do complex NPs with relative clauses; thus, although recapitulating the whole island gives a more felicitous answer to example (ii) in note 19, the "simple" answer seems to be only weakly bad here (as noted by Nobuko Hasegawa, personal communication).

(i)   A1: ?"Sensoo to Heiwa" desu
           'It's *War and Peace*'

      A2: [$_{NP}$[$_{S'}$ "Sensoo to Heiwa"-o yonda] koto] desu
           'It's the fact that (he) read *War and Peace*'

25. Interestingly, the starred answers in (47) and (48) apparently improve for some speakers if the copula is omitted, in colloquial speech. Perhaps with the copula omitted the answers are no longer full sentences and are thus not governed by grammatical principles like the Felicity Principle. In a related observation, James Yoon (personal communication) suggests that the starred answers improve in Korean if the more formal copula *ipnita* (= Japanese *desu*) is replaced with the more colloquial *yo*. Something along these lines might also explain why English does not show similar effects: to the (stilted) question *Pictures of whom do you like the most?*, the answers *Mary* and *Pictures of Mary*

seem equally acceptable to me. English lacks a normal answering pattern with anything like the copula seen in Japanese or Korean.

26. Guglielmo Cinque (personal communication) observes that pied-piping is also generally ruled out with *wh diavolo* phrases in Italian, as in English, except where a single preposition is pied-piped as in (53b). If this is related in some way to the obligatoriness of P pied-piping in Italian, then we have an unexplained difference between English and Italian.

27. Why should there be a prohibition on pied-piping with *ittai* or *the hell?* An answer for Japanese may be found in an observation by Nishigauchi (1985). If pied-piping were possible in an example like (43a), such an example would be grammatical because the pied-piping convention allows the whole island to be treated as a *wh*-phrase and moved. Suppose that *ittai* must be attached to the *wh-phrase* that actually undergoes movement. Then if *ittai* attaches to *nani-o*, *nani-o* must be the *wh*-phrase that undergoes LF movement. Since that movement violates Subjacency, (43a) is ungrammatical. On the other hand, if *ittai* is attached to the whole island that contains *nani-o*, then that island should count as a *wh*-phrase, pied-piping should be possible, and the sentence should be grammatical. Nishigauchi observes that this is the case. Thus, (i) seems to be much better than (43a).

(i) Mary-wa ittai [$_{NP}$[$_{S'}$ John-ni nani-o ageta] hito-ni] atta-no?

Thus, pied-piping might not really be forbidden with *ittai*. Rather, *ittai* simply must attach to the *wh*-phrase that moves. When pied-piping is the only way to satisfy Subjacency, then *ittai* must be attached to the entire *wh*-phrase.

On the other hand, it seems to be somewhat unclear whether *ittai* in (i) is interpreted with the *wh*-phrase or has the interpretation "in general" mentioned in note 17. (This is Hoji's (1985:393, ex. (7)) claim about a similar example.) One other ground for caution might be the absence of examples like (i) with English *the hell: *Whose pictures the hell. . . . If Nishigauchi's suggestion is correct, it somewhat undercuts the claim that the island properties of *ittai* are solely due to "aggressive non-D-linking," though other properties of *ittai* continue to point in that direction (see note 20, note 28, and elsewhere). On the other hand, the *ittai* data would provide striking evidence in favor of LF pied-piping and would continue to contribute an argument for my central claim: although pied-piping saves non-D-linked *wh*-words from Subjacency violations at LF, D-linked *wh*-words do not need to be saved, since they do not move.

28. Nishigauchi (1984) gives an example with *dono* that, he claims, still requires a "pied-piping" answer. I am told, however, that *dono*, unlike English *which*, is not always D-linked. Setting up an explicit context as I have in (54) is crucial to forcing a D-linked reading and getting the results as shown. A related fact may be the possibility, noted by Hajime Hoji (personal communication), of *ittai dono konpyuutaa;* compare English *which the hell* in (40). *Ittai dono konpyuutaa* acts like other *ittai*-phrases with respect to Subjacency.

29. Hoji (1984) presents a number of additional, very interesting arguments from Japanese in favor of the distinction I have drawn. He notes, for example, that although the overt pronoun *kare* cannot normally be used as a bound vari-

able, it may be "bound" or "corefer" with a *dono*-phrase, *if* that phrase is interpreted as D-linked.

(i) *Dare$_i$-ga [kare$_i$-no haha] -o   semeta-no?
who-Nom he-Gen mother-Acc criticized-Q
'Who$_i$ criticized his$_i$ mother?'

(ii) Dono hito$_i$-ga   [kare$_i$-no haha] -o   semeta-no?
which man-Nom he-Gen mother-Acc criticized-Q
'Which man$_i$ criticized his$_i$ mother?'

What is more, weak crossover effects, which Hoji and Saito (1983) take to diagnose movement, disappear with D-linked *dono* phrases.

(iii) *[$_{S'}$ Mary-ga [sono hito$_i$]-o semeta koto]-ga *dare$_i$*-o odorokaseta-no?
Lit.: 'The fact that Mary criticized that person$_i$ surprised whom$_i$?'

(iv) [$_{S'}$ Mary-ga [sono hito$_i$]-o semeta koto]-ga *dono hito$_i$*-o odorokaseta-no?
Lit.: 'The fact that Mary criticized that person$_i$ surprised which man$_i$?'

Choe (1984) also demonstrates an argument from weak crossover for pied-piping at LF, which I will not detail here. This argument is criticized by Nishigauchi (1985, 1986); Nishigauchi's criticisms are answered by Hasegawa (in press).

30. Koster (1984), for example, concludes that the phenomenon of "Global Harmony" that holds of S-Structure movement does not hold of LF movement. His conclusions may indeed be correct, but many of his Dutch examples involve arguably D-linked *which* (*welk*) phrases, and pied-piping might even be an option for others.

31. Intriguingly, *dlaczego* 'why' may *not* remain in situ, whereas *zjakiego powodu* 'for what reason' may.

(i) Kogo dlaczego Maria zabiła?
whom why   Maria killed

(ii) *Kogo Maria zabiła dlaczego?

(iii) Kogo Maria zabiła zjakiego powodu?
whom Maria killed for-what reason

What seems to be at stake is that it is cross-linguistically extremely difficult to D-link the word that means *why*. This has an obvious relation to the facts concerning *why* discussed by Huang (1981, 1982) and by Lasnik and Saito (1983). In particular, they note (I simplify) that in Chinese and Japanese *why* cannot take scope out of an island. Yoshihisa Kitagawa (personal communication) reports that if one can force a D-linked reading for *why* in Japanese—an extremely difficult task—this scope restriction disappears. As an additional element for the explanation of the properties of *why*, note that it thoroughly resists pied-piping, closing the loophole available to other *wh*-words.

(iv) ?People who live where are the most likely to suffer from allergies?

(v) *People who left why are the most likely to succeed?

Thus, the properties of *why* might be due to Subjacency, as originally suggested by Huang (1981), and not to the ECP, as suggested by Huang (1982) and by Lasnik and Saito.

32. Polish in fact provides an opportunity to ask a question we could not answer before (see note 11). Granted that movement of D-linked *wh*-phrases is not obligatory in multiple interrogations, is it an option? Wachowicz (1974:n. 161) gives a relevant example that suggests that it is not an option: "Polish sentences containing two instances of the interrogative word 'which' sound better if only one of them has been fronted, e.g. *która dziewczyna zauważyła który błąd* 'which girl noticed which error'." Perhaps one must be fronted to satisfy the syntactic requirements discussed in section 5.6, but no other may be fronted, in accordance with some kind of "Move only when necessary" principle; see Chomsky 1986. One native speaker of Polish, at least, does not find fronting of both *which*-phrases so bad, but speakers of Romanian in general do find fronting bad in this case.

33. Except perhaps for movement of a single *wh* to a matrix Comp, as in Lasnik and Saito's example (72); though it is not clear that this example is really acceptable except as an echo question.

34. At least one Italian speaker suggests that multiple interrogation is sometimes marginally possible (as in *Chi ha detto che cosa?* 'Who said what?') when the *wh*-in-situ is D-linked, as (63) plus the other hypotheses advanced here would predict. On the other hand, Guglielmo Cinque notes (personal communication) that such expressions are not productive as true multiple interrogations and may be confined to newspaper style.

35. Nonetheless, there may be languages that do not allow even D-linked *wh*-in-situ to remain unmoved at LF; these languages might lack Q-indexing. An example is Kikuyu, as pointed out by Victoria Bergvall (personal communication). Bergvall (1984) notes that *wh*-in-situ is possible in Kikuyu much as in Japanese, although an S-Structure movement option is available. *All wh*-in-situ, no matter what the context, show clear Complex NP Constraint effects, much like Japanese *ittai wh*-phrases. This suggests that (1) the pied-piping option is missing in Kikuyu, and (2) Q indexing is also missing. Learnability considerations make one hope that this pattern is somehow related to the full optionality of S-Structure *Wh*-Movement in Kikuyu, which has both English and Japanese question types, but I have no insight to offer.

36. Compare also . . . *what men did Mary talk to?*, which acts like *who*, in my judgment. Also, Jerry Morgan (personal communication) correctly notes that many quantifiers appear to act like *which:* for example, *Some men entered the room. All were wearing suits.* This could indeed argue that *all* does not undergo LF movement; for example, in dialects like my own in which quantification is not clause-bound, *all* does not show ECP effects. Alternatively, *all* could be a genuine moving quantifier, yet one containing a restricting term (compare *all of the men*) that is D-linked. See Kuno 1982 for some discussion of related issues.

Also notice that in many cases the appropriate antecedent for *which* is less an indefinite than an NP with "wide-scope *or*." As discussed by Partee and Rooth

(1982), such NPs have a number of properties in common with indefinites, including insensitivity to islands (*pace* Larson 1985).

(i) Bill was telling me that he'd recently arrested Mary, who owned either a dog that barked too much or a cat that destroyed furniture. I forget which it was

(ii) John was talking about Bill, who he evidently considered either dishonest or dumb. I forget which it was

37. This information may also sometimes be expressed overtly; for instance, compare the (a)- and (b)-continuations in (i). The (b)-continuation does not naturally continue to ask about the assassin, as the (a)-continuation does.

(i) For 100 points and a chance at the jackpot:
  In 1963 a man shot Kennedy in Dallas.
  a. Which man then ran to a movie theater to hide?
  b. Who then ran to a movie theater to hide?

38. Dominique Sportiche (personal communication) points out that this might entail the absence of S-Structure movement in questions like *Who left?*, yielding essentially the Generalized Phrase Structure Grammar S-Structure representation for such questions, defended recently by Chung and McCloskey (1983) (see discussion in Chomsky 1985). I am personally doubtful about the facts claimed in that article, but the theoretical consequence is worth noting.

39. This does not explain why S-Structure *Wh*-Movement *must not* take place in Japanese (a general property of SOV languages), but it does explain why it is not obligatory.

40. One possible exception might be the Coordinate Structure Constraint, if Kuno and Masunaga (1985:ex. (14)) are correct; compare the opposite conclusions based on English in Pesetsky 1985:chap. 4.

Chapter 6

Specifier and Operator Binding

Tanya Reinhart

One of the contexts where the weak-strong distinction of Barwise and Cooper (1981) plays a role is that of donkey-anaphora, where only NPs with weak determiners can serve as antecedents. Extending Heim's (1982) analysis, a characteristic property of such NPs is that the variables in the sets they define can be bound, under certain conditions, by other operators, or determiners. As we shall see, this property surfaces in other contexts as well. The first part of this chapter addresses the interpretation of such NPs, focusing on the conditions that allow their binding, the semantics of the weak-strong distinction, and its relations to the interpretation of anaphora in donkey-contexts.

The next problem, which cannot be handled by the semantic analysis alone, is that generally the binding of variables obeys S-Structure conditions that still appear to be violated in donkey-contexts. Furthermore, donkey-anaphora itself obeys S-Structure restrictions that cannot be explained at Logical Form (LF). I argue that, in fact, donkey-anaphora obeys the standard conditions on binding at S-Structure, once certain implicit assumptions of the syntactic analysis of binding are made explicit. In approaches assuming LF, there is a certain discrepancy between S-Structure and LF binding: whereas at S-Structure syntactic binding is viewed as a relation between pronouns and NPs (that is, a relation between referential indices only), at LF the binder of the pronoun-variable is the determiner-operator, rather than the NP. In the standard cases this discrepancy has no empirical consequences, but the cases where a determiner of one NP binds a variable in another (weak) NP cannot be handled by referential indices. If the notion of operator binding is incorporated into the syntax (as specifier binding), this problem is resolved.

6.1 Background: Donkey-Sentences

The so-called donkey-sentences pose well-known problems both for the semantic theory of scope and for the syntactic theory of binding.

(1) a. If Max owns a donkey$_i$, he hates it$_i$
    b. If a man owns a donkey$_i$, he hates it$_i$

(2) Every man who owns a donkey$_i$ hates it$_i$

The pronoun in these sentences can be anaphoric to *a donkey*, and it is clear that this is bound anaphora rather than just pragmatic coreference, since the choice of value for the pronoun varies with the choice of value for *a donkey*. The semantic problem is that under a standard interpretation of such sentences, as in (3), the pronoun is not even in the scope of the quantifier that appears to bind it.

(3) a. If ($\exists x$(donkey(x) & Max owns x)) then (Max hates x)
    b. $\forall x$(man(x) & $\exists y$(donkey(y) & x owns y)) (x hates y)

(4) $\forall \langle x,y \rangle$(man($x$) & donkey($y$) & x owns y) (x hates y)

The peculiar property of these sentences is that an alternative scope analysis exists, as in (4), which seems equivalent both to (3b) and to the existential analysis of (1b). In this analysis the bound pronoun is in the scope of its binder, as required. However, if one wants to adopt this analysis for (1) and (2), the crucial issue is how it is derived from their S-Structure, since it appears to require operations that violate all known restrictions on semantic interpretation or LF formation rules.

The syntactic problem of binding posed by these sentences is that they violate the linguistic condition on bound-variable anaphora, which requires that the antecedent c-command the pronoun at S-Structure. For instance, anaphora is not possible in sentences like (5a) and (6).

(5) a. *His$_i$ friends voted for every candidate$_i$
    b. $\forall x$(candidate(x)) (x's friends voted for x)

(6) *We voted for each candidate$_i$ since the chairman recommended him$_i$/(although the chairman objected to him$_i$)

(7) Someone voted for every candidate

(8) We voted for every candidate since someone recommended it

It is crucial to observe here that the syntactic problem of binding is independent of the semantic problem. The well-known problem with the distribution of bound anaphora is that it does not follow from logical considerations of scope. It is generally believed that in structures of the type (5) and (6), the quantified antecedent may have scope over the whole sentence. For instance, in sentences (7) and (8), with the same structure, *someone* may be interpreted as being in the scope of *every candidate*. Nevertheless, a pronoun in the same position cannot be bound by *every candidate*. In other words, an LF representation like (5b) cannot be blocked for (5a) by scope considerations. For this reason, it is essential that the syntactic restrictions be met at S-Structure independently of (or prior to) the assignment of scope. (This is argued in detail in Reinhart 1983.) This means that even if the interpretive procedures that assign the donkey-sentences in (1)–(2) the scope analysis in (4) are defined, this analysis still violates the syntactic restriction and the sentences should have been filtered out, for the same reason that (5) is uninterpretable even though it has a corresponding well-formed LF representation. We may note, also, that some proposals have been made within the Government-Binding (GB) framework to capture the relevant binding conditions on variables with syntactic restrictions on LF representations, such as the Bijection Principle of Koopman and Sportiche (1981) or the Parallelism Principle of Safir (1984a). However, these conditions are in essence equivalent to the S-Structure condition and the LF representation in (4) violates these conditions as well.

6.2 Weak Determiners and the Interpretation of Donkey-Sentences
6.2.1 Bound Weak NPs
Donkey-anaphora is sensitive to the weak-strong distinction of Barwise and Cooper (1981). (For brevity I will use the terms *weak NP* and *strong NP* to designate NPs with weak/cardinal and strong/noncardinal determiners, respectively.) Only weak NPs such as the indefinites in the previous examples can bind a pronoun outside their apparent scope. When an antecedent in the same position is universally quantified, as in (9), no anaphora is possible, in conformity with both the binding and the scope conditions. The same is illustrated for plural strong NPs in (10).

(9) a. *If Max owns every donkey$_i$, he hates it$_i$
   b. *A man who owns every donkey$_i$ hates it$_i$

(10) *Every critic who fell asleep during $\left\{\begin{array}{l}\text{most}\\ \text{all but two}\\ \text{at least twenty percent of the}\end{array}\right\}$ pieces$_i$ wrote enthusiastic reviews about them$_i$

(11) *Their* readers expect *all critics* to be boring

(12) *Most pieces* were rejected by the public. *They* were too long

It should be remembered that in the case of plural quantified NPs a plural pronoun can always refer to the set fixed by the NP or, alternatively, to the common noun set (the set of all pieces in (10)). Such interpretation is not subject to the binding conditions of the grammar. For example, unlike what happens in (5), anaphora is permitted in (11), as well as across sentences in cases like (12). If anaphora seems possible for some speakers in (10), it is only under one of these interpretations. However, the only interpretation we are considering here is the one in which the strong NP is in the scope of *every critic* (that is, the choice of a set of pieces varies with the choice of a critic).

Weak plural NPs, on the other hand, can bind a pronoun in a donkey-context when they are in the scope of another operator, that is, under the dependent interpretation illustrated in (13).

(13) Every vampire who invited $\left\{\begin{array}{l}\left\{\begin{array}{l}\text{two}\\ \text{several}\\ \text{less than five}\\ \text{many}\\ \text{between ten and thirteen}\end{array}\right\}\text{ guests}\\ \text{as many guests as you can imagine}\end{array}\right\}$ for dinner was through with them by midnight

The clue for explaining this restriction on the possible antecedents for donkey-anaphora lies in the semantic analysis of weak NPs. This line of analysis is proposed for the indefinite cases of (1) and (2) by Heim (1982) and Kamp (1981). Heim's point of departure is that the indefinite article is not a quantifier; hence, indefinite NPs are not quantified. Rather, they are interpreted as open formulae containing a variable that needs to be bound by some operator (for example, $man(x)$ for *a man*). The different interpretations of indefinites follow from the selection of the operator. In the standard cases the operator is assumed to be an abstract "discourse" operator, introducing entities into the discourse. However, under certain conditions it can be bound by an available universal (or other) operator in the sentence. This analysis addresses only indefinite singular NPs. However, a growing contention in the analysis of weak determiners is that they are interpreted, not as operators, but as cardinality markers for the sets defined by their NPs. In sections 6.2.5 and 6.2.6 I will examine the extensions needed to account for the binding of plural weak NPs.

One way to phrase this approach, once extended to all weak NPs, is that since such NPs are open, in a sense to which I will return, they can "borrow" an operator to bind the variable they contain. This may be another determiner, or a sentential operator, like the conditional operator. In English this parasitic attachment of weak NPs to external operators is witnessed mainly in donkey-contexts. However, a much more direct and striking manifestation of this phenomenon is provided by the headless relatives of Lakhota, analyzed by Williamson in chapter 7. Lakhota's relative NPs do not contain an N head (or, as Williamson phrases it, their head is internal to the relative clause). Thus, an NP like *the quilt that Mary made* is expressed with the structure shown in (14).[1]

(14) a.

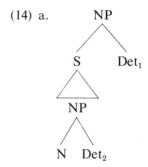

b. [$_{NP}$[$_S$ Mary [owįža wą] kağe] ki] he   ophewathų
      Mary quilt   a   make the that I-buy
   'I bought the quilt that Mary made.'

(15) [[hokšila yamni kuža pi] ki/iyuha]
      boys   three sick 3Pl the/all
   'the/all three boys that were sick'

(16) a. *[[hokšila iyuha kuža pi] ki] . . .
         boys   all   sick 3Pl the

    b. *[[hokšila ota ȟca wachi pi] ki/cha] . . .
          boys   most   dance 3Pl the/Ind

The crucial point is that the NP corresponding to the internal head must be weak, even if the relative NP as a whole is strong. In other words, the only way to obtain a strong relative NP is to use a strong determiner in the higher Det_1 position and a weak determiner in the internal Det_2 position. This is illustrated with a singular indefinite internal Det in (14b) and with a plural cardinal Det in (15). As we see in (16), if the internal determiner is strong, the NP is uninterpretable.

Note that the availability of this option of relative clause formation is what we should expect if weak NPs (and only weak NPs) can be attached to a higher determiner or be bound by another operator.

The interpretation of the relative NP in Lakhota is determined, as with all NPs, by its (top) determiner. However, since there is no common N head in such constructions, the set restricted by the determiner must be identified inside the relative clause, where only full NPs can be generated. Since weak NPs are open, they can provide the relevant set for the selection of subsets by the determiner, or can be bound by it, if it is an operator. The interpretation of (15), for example, is therefore identical to that of the English NP *all three boys who were sick*.[2]

Returning to donkey-contexts, under Heim's (1982) analysis, the LF structure derived for them resembles, in the case of relative clauses, that of Lakhota, with the external operator-determiner binding an internal weak NP. However, since that same determiner already binds its own N'' complement, we obtain pair quantification; that is, the LF structure (4) is derived for (2), both repeated in (17). (I will return to the details of Heim's derivations of this LF structure shortly.)

(17) a. Every man who owns a donkey$_i$ hates it$_i$
   b. $\forall \langle x,y \rangle$ (man(x) & donkey(y) & x owns y) (x hates y)

6.2.2 Operator Binding of Pronouns

In the LF structure (17b) the pronoun is appropriately bound, so there is no semantic problem of binding. However, under such an analysis, the anaphora relation in (17a), and in donkey-sentences in general, cannot be viewed as a relation between NPs. The apparent antecedent cannot bind the pronoun-variable in any logical sense since it does not contain an operator that can do so. The NP *a donkey* is not, then, an antecedent to the pronoun in the standard use of this term; rather, the variable in this NP and the pronoun are bound by the same operator. In fact, this result is not radically different from the other cases of anaphora with quantified NPs. In an analysis assuming standard LF and operator binding, as in (18b), the LF representation for (18a), what actually binds the pronoun is the determiner *every* rather than the NP *every man*.

(18) a. Every man$_i$ kissed his$_i$ dog
    b. $\forall x$ (man(x)) (x kissed x's dog)

However, since the determiner here is contained in its NP, it is easy to refer to this case, informally, as NP anaphora, and to capture it in the syntax by coindexing the pronoun and the NP as in (18a) (which is the relation of syntactic binding in the GB framework). What is specific to the donkey-cases is that the binding operator is not contained in the NP in which it binds a variable. Therefore, the convenient appeal to NP syntactic binding is not available. The semantic notion of binding, however, is the same in (17) and (18), and the problem here is only that the operator binding assumed in such framework at LF is not reflected in the system of S-Structure syntactic binding, where only NPs are assumed as binders. In section 6.3 I will argue later that operators, which syntactically are S- or NP-specifiers, are binders at S-Structure.

6.2.3 Where Weak NPs Can Be Bound
So far we have assumed that weak NPs can be bound by an operator when they occur in its scope. In fact, the context allowing this is more restricted. Let us look again at the two cases of bound weak NPs of Lakhota and English relative clauses. To make their similarity clearer, the Lakhota NP is given in English words and word order.

(19) Lakhota   English
    a. "every man who came"   every woman who likes a man
    b.

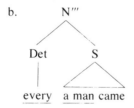

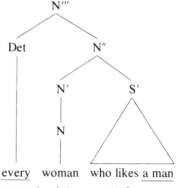

    c. every x (man(x) & x came) (. . .)   every $\langle y,x \rangle$ (woman(y) & man(x) & y likes x) (. . .)

The relevant relation here is that between *every* and *a man*, and it is precisely the same in both structures: in the S-Structure representation (19b) the determiner *every* c-commands this NP; in the logical analysis (19c) *man(x)* is in the restrictive term of the operator, *every*. It is only under these conditions that weak NPs can be bound (and, in effect, Heim's (1982) LF derivation allows them to be bound only under these conditions). We will see in section 6.2.4 that in the other donkey-context, that of conditionals (as in (1)), the conditional operator c-commands the weak NP and, under Heim's analysis, this NP is in its restrictive term in LF. In fact, as we shall see, these are not two separate conditions, since the restrictive term of an operator is always defined by the nodes it c-commands at S-Structure. In section 6.3.5 I will argue that donkey-type anaphora shows up also with certain sentential adverbs (like *always* and *often*), where there is no motivation for assuming any restrictive term at LF. The S-Structure c-command restriction, however, still holds. The actual condition, then, is that the weak NP be c-commanded by a specifier-operator at S-Structure. But since such c-command relations are lost at LF (where the quantifier c-commands the whole sentence), I assume here temporarily, following Heim, the restrictive-term requirement at LF.

This restriction on the contexts allowing the binding of weak NPs contrasts with Haïk's (1984) analysis that allows donkey-anaphora whenever both weak NP and the pronoun are in the scope of another, quantified, NP (which c-commands the pronoun). Let us, therefore, check it further.

(20) *Every woman thought [$_S$ that she'd already met *some man*] when she saw *him*

(21) a. Every man who brought *three bottles* put them in the refrigerator
      b. *Every man who brought *them* put *three bottles* in the refrigerator
      c. *If someone brought *them*, he put *three bottles* in the refrigerator

In (20) both the weak NP and the pronoun are in the scope of *every*, but *some man* is not c-commanded by it. (It is c-commanded by the QNP *every woman*, but not by its determiner.) It is consequently also not in the restrictive term of *every* at LF. If the condition on the binding of weak NPs were determined by scope alone, binding should have been permitted here. However, the bound donkey-type interpretation where the choice of value for the pronoun varies with the choice for *some man* is not available here. In donkey-type structures Haïk's analysis cannot distinguish between (21a), the standard donkey-sentence, and (21b–c), where the weak *three bottles* is still in the scope of the relevant operator but is not in its restrictive term. The problem cannot be reduced to pragmatic factors, like the unavailability of backward anaphora with indefinites, since backward anaphora is possible in donkey-contexts, as in (22a) (see also note 6).

(22) a. To show her *his* love, every knight who courted *a lady* sent her roses

b. *To show *her* his love, every knight sent roses to *a lady*/ courted *a lady* patiently

(23) *Every man assumed that jokes about *a lady in the party* annoyed *her*

The only difference between (22a) and (22b) is, again, the relation of *every* and *a lady*. In both sentences *a lady* can be in the quantifier's scope; however, only in (22a) is it c-commanded by the quantifier. Since *every* can also bind the pronoun, donkey-interpretation is obtained. In (22b), where *a lady* neither c-commands the pronoun nor is bound by the quantifier *every*, anaphora is impossible (the specific or wide-scope interpretation of the indefinite should of course be ignored in judging this example). In any case, no pragmatic factors could explain the lack of forward anaphora in (20), and (23) illustrates another case where the indefinite precedes the pronoun and can clearly be in the scope of *every man*, and yet where no binding can be obtained.[3]

An apparent counterexample found both in Evans 1980 and in Haïk 1984 to my claim that donkey-type anaphora is possible only when the "antecedent" is c-commanded by another specifier is the case of VP-conjunction, as in (24a), which they consider a donkey-type example.

(24) a. Every villager owns *some sheep* and feeds *them* at night (Evans 1980:ex. (39))

b. Lucie read *each book* and wrote a review about *it*

c. Felix kissed *every woman* and invited *her* to dance

This is not a case of donkey-anaphora, however, but a case of straightforward bound anaphora, since the antecedent *some sheep* does in fact c-command the pronoun. Given either the definition of c-command in (for example) Reinhart 1983 or its statement in terms of maximal projections in Aoun and Sportiche 1981, the relevant node for c-command here is the top VP (the maximal VP projection). That this is just a case of bound anaphora is witnessed by the fact that all quantifiers can bind pronouns from this position, as in (24b–c).

6.2.4 Heim's LF Derivation
We can turn now to the actual way the LF structure in (17b) is derived from the S-Structure representation (17a), or (1b), proposed by Heim (1982).

Following May (1977), Heim assumes LF formation rules similar to those assumed in the GB framework, the difference being only that unlike QR, Heim's rule of NP Raising *adjoins* to S any NP, regardless of its interpretation (excluding pronouns). This move, I believe, is correct even independently of the given problem. This operation is restricted syntactically, as assumed for QR. We may refer to it as *NP Raising* (NPR). The next rule applies specifically to determiners or operators, *attaching* them (out of the raised NP) to the dominating S. It may be called *Operator Raising* (OR). These are essentially standard LF procedures, but for convenience I illustrate them in (25). (For ease of presentation I have written some variables in already at this stage. The binding of variables is obtained in Heim's analysis by an explicit index translation system, which I will not discuss.)

(25) Every man who buys a car worships it

a. NPR $\Rightarrow$ [$_{NP}$ Every man who$_1$ e_1 buys a car]$_1$ [$_S$ e_1 worships it]

b. NPR $\Rightarrow$ [Every man who$_1$ [a car]$_2$ [$_S$ e_1 buys e_2]]$_1$ [e_1 worships it]

c. OR $\Rightarrow$

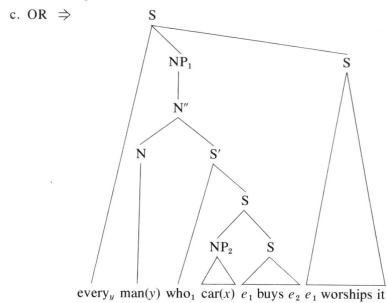

every$_y$ man(y) who$_1$ car(x) e_1 buys e_2 e_1 worships it

The way the raising rules are defined, the highest S always dominates three constituents if a quantifier is present. The second of these is defined by Heim as the restrictive term of a quantifier, and the third as its nuclear scope.

Although that much is assumed independently of the donkey-problem, the next LF procedure is specific to the binding of indefinite (or weak) NPs. In (25c) an open indefinite ($car(x)$) occurs in the restrictive term of a quantifier (*every*). Under these conditions the indefinite can be bound by *every*. The binding is obtained by a specific index-copying procedure. Extending Heim's procedure for indefinites (Heim 1982:146) to weak NPs in general, we may state it as follows.

(26) Copy the index of every weak NP as a selection index onto the lowest LF c-commanding quantifier, if the weak NP is in the restrictive term of the quantifier.

(In Heim's analysis the restrictive-term condition need not be mentioned in (26), since she also assumes existential closure of indefinites in the nuclear scope. Thus, if an indefinite is not in the restrictive term, it is not open, and (26) cannot apply to it. However, these details are not crucial for the present discussion.) Applied to (25c), the procedure (26) yields the indexing in (27a) for *every,* with two operator (selection) indices. With these indices, *every* can bind the pronoun *it* (assuming that both *a car* and *it* receive the same index, in a free indexing system). When all the variables are translated, the LF structure obtained is (27b), which we have been assuming in the discussion.

(27) a. every$_{y,x}$ . . .
   b. every $\langle y,x \rangle$ (man(y) & car(x) & y buys x) (y worships x)

Since (25) is restricted to "weak" (that is, open) NPs, it captures one set of distribution facts discussed in section 6.2.1; that is, it allows only weak "antecedents" in donkey-contexts. The restrictive-term clause captures the distribution facts discussed in section 6.2.3. In Heim's analysis, capturing the second set of facts depends crucially on the details of the LF formation rules (which nodes are *adjoined* to S and which are *attached*), since these details allow the restrictive term to be defined as the second daughter of S. In section 6.3 I will argue that the binding of weak NPs (like the binding of pronouns) takes place at S-Structure, so these details are not in fact crucial for the problem under consideration.

Turning now to conditionals, the question is what binds the indefinite, since there seems to be no overt operator in these sentences. Heim argues that conditionals contain an abstract sentential operator that she labels the *invisible necessity operator* and writes as □. The LF structure of (28a) is then (28b).

(28) a. If a man_1 owns a $donkey_2$, he_1 hates it_2

b.

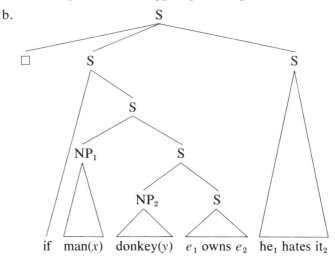

if   man(*x*)   donkey(*y*) e_1 owns e_2 he_1 hates it_2

The *if*-clause, as the second term, is the restrictive term of the necessity operator. It contains two weak NPs whose indices (*x* and *y*) are copied by (26) as operator indices into this operator. In its interpretation this operator is similar (though not precisely equivalent) to the universal operator. Hence, we derive here again something like the universal quantification over pairs, as in (27b). If the pronouns in the second clause are coindexed with *a man* and *a donkey*, they are translated as the same variables; hence, they end up bound (by the necessity operator).

6.2.5 The Interpretation of the Derived LF Structures

Now, what is the precise interpretation of the LF structures derived by the proposed analysis? In the case of the LF structure derived for (25), not much more seems to be needed concerning the interpretation of the formula. Under any interpretation, it appears to capture correctly the truth-condition of the sentence. The questions that arise, however, are (1) how the binding of plural cardinal NPs is to be interpreted (since we extended the analysis to all weak NPs) and (2) precisely what the source of the universal force of weak NPs in donkey-contexts is, given that this force is also maintained when the binding determiner is not a universal, as in (29).

(29) a. $\left\{ \begin{matrix} \text{Most men} \\ \text{Almost every man} \end{matrix} \right\}$ who bought a car$_2$ worshiped it$_2$

b. $\left\{ \begin{matrix} \text{most} \\ \text{almost every} \end{matrix} \right\}$ $\langle x,y \rangle$ (man(x) & car(y) & x bought y)
(x worshiped y)

A pair interpretation, as in (29b), does not give the right truth-conditions here. (This has been pointed out by Heim, Kempson (1984), and others.) If there are ten car-buying men, one of whom bought fifty cars and worshiped all of them and nine of whom bought one car each and neglected to worship it, then (29b) is true, since most man-car pairs enter the worship relation; but the original sentence (29a) is false under these conditions. What the sentence means, in fact, is that most car-buying men worshiped all the cars they bought. In other words, the indefinite still has a universal force here, which cannot originate in the determiner that binds it (as it could in (25)). I address these questions in detail in Reinhart 1986; here I will only summarize the analysis.

An emerging agreement in studies of weak NPs is that they are interpreted as sets with the determiner as a cardinality marker for the set. (This was originally proposed by Bartsch (1973) and (informally) Milsark (1974) and was independently developed by (for example) Scha (1981), Keenan (see chapter 12), Higginbotham (see chapter 3), Cormack (1985), and Löbner (1984).) The question, however, is how these sets are defined, that is, which are the sets whose cardinality is determined by the weak determiner. I argue that these sets are defined by the whole clause containing the weak NP and not by the NP itself. As we will see (section 6.2.6), this analysis follows from the semantic properties of weak NPs. This part of the analysis is similar to that proposed independently by Cormack (1985), though the analyses differ in details and in subsequent predictions concerning sentences like (29a). To illustrate: Rather than the common analysis in (30b) for the NP *two vampires* in (30a), I assume the analysis (30c). (X is the maximal set of individuals z with the vampire property and the appearing property, and its cardinality is equal to or greater than 2.)

(30) a. At least two vampires appeared
b. $X \subseteq \{z \,|\, \text{vampire}(z)\}$ & $|X| \geq 2$
c. $X = \{z \,|\, \text{vampire}(z)$ & z appeared$\}$ & $|X| \geq 2$

The set in (30c) is defined as a maximal set, and this is what enables weak NPs to receive a universal force in contexts of anaphora. Note, first, that this apparent universal force is found not only in donkey-type anaphora but also in discourse anaphora, as observed by Evans (1980).

(31) a. Two vampires appeared, and Lucie chased them away
     b. Lucie has at least fifteen dogs, and Felix takes care of them

The pronoun in such sentences refers to a set established in the previous sentence (as a discourse referent). It is clear, however, that in (31a) it refers, not to just any set of (at least) two vampires, but to all the vampires argued to have appeared in the first clause. Similarly, in (31b) Felix takes care of all of Lucie's dogs.[4]

These facts will follow, if an analysis like (30c) is assumed. The pronouns here (labeled by Evans *E-type pronouns*) are standard set pronouns, and as such they refer to the sets defined by their antecedents. Since this is the maximal set defined on the clause, the universal entailment is obtained. In case the clause contains another quantified NP, as in *Every neighbor has a dog*, the set defined for the weak NP contains a variable bound by that quantifier: $\{z \mid \text{dog}(z)$ and x has $z\}$. For this reason a pronoun can refer to this set only if it is in the scope of the operator that binds the variable in it. In other words, such sets are not available for discourse anaphora, as in *Every neighbor has a dog and I feed it.*

This analysis provides the answer to the two questions posed earlier: If a weak NP is bound by another quantifier, as in the donkey-contexts, the quantifier index is a set variable. This is obviously so, regardless of whether the NP is plural or singular, the difference being only one of cardinality.

(32) a. (Almost) every man who buys a car_2 worships it_2
     b. (almost every) $\langle x,y \rangle$ (man(x) & a car(y) & x buys y) (x worships y)
     c. (a car(y) & x buys y) $\Rightarrow Y = \{z \mid \text{car}(z)$ & x buys $z\}$ & $|Y| \geq 1$
     d. (almost) every $\langle x,Y \rangle$ (man(x) & $Y = \{z \mid \text{car}(z)$ & x buys $z\}$ & $|Y| \geq 1$) (x worships Y)

(33) a. Most vampires_2 who invited more than three guests_2 for dinner were through with them_2 by midnight
     b. most $\langle x,Y \rangle$ (vampire(x) & $Y = \{z \mid \text{guest}(z)$ & x invited z for dinner$\}$ & $|Y| > 3$) (x was through with Y by midnight)

(32b) is just the indexed LF structure derived for (32a) by Heim's LF rules. What the indices on the quantifier mean is determined by the interpretation of the arguments they bind. First, the clause containing *a car* is interpreted as in (32c). (That this is a clause at LF can be checked in its derivation tree (25c).) *Y,* then, is a set variable, and all other occurrences of *y* in the formula are replaced with the same set variable, including the pronoun (for more details on the pronoun interpretation, see Reinhart 1986). The final analysis is given in (32d): For (almost) every pair consisting of a man *x* and the set of cars he buys *Y,* it is true that the man *x* worships the cars in the set *Y.* (33) illustrates the same procedures with plural NPs.

This analysis also handles the problems with quantifiers like *most* and *almost every:* *Y* denotes the (maximal) set of cars bought by *x,* and the quantifier selects almost every pair of an individual *x* and a set *Y* (defined on *x*). If, as in the previous story, a given individual bought fifty cars, $\langle x, Y \rangle$ in this case still denotes only one pair consisting of one man and a set of fifty cars. The universal entailment observed there (that almost every man worships all the cars he buys), and in donkey-contexts in general, then follows from the set interpretation of the weak NP, and not from the operator that binds it.

6.2.6 The Weak-Strong Distinction

The clausal set analysis of weak NPs as in (30c) has been motivated so far by problems of anaphora. However, it is based on more general assumptions on the difference between weak and strong determiners, which I will outline briefly. (This section is based in part on work in progress conducted with Shalom Lappin and Stanley Peters.)

Barwise and Cooper (1981) show that there are three (equivalent) properties that are characteristic of only weak determiners, although they do not follow from their definition of *weak* (as not-strong, where a determiner is positive strong if the common noun set is necessarily a member of the NP denotation). These properties are *intersectivity, symmetry,* and a property that Keenan labels *existentiality* (see chapter 12). The definitions of the properties and examples of each are as follows (*N* stands for the category N' denoting the common noun set, *D* for Determiners, *x* for any set (property), and *E* for the set of all entities in the model).

D is *intersective* if for all N, X,
$X \in ||D(N)||$ iff $X \in ||D(N \cap X)||$

Two cats sneezed	$\equiv$ Two cats that sneezed sneezed
{sneezers} $\in$ ||two {cats}||	{sneezers} $\in$ ||two {sneezing cats}||
Every cat sneezed	$\not\equiv$ Every cat that sneezed sneezed

D is *existential* if for all N, X,
$X \in ||D(N)||$ iff $E \in ||D(N \cap X)||$

Two cats sneezed	$\equiv$ Two cats that sneezed exist
	$E \in$ ||two {sneezing cats}||
Every cat sneezed	$\not\equiv$ Every cat that sneezed exists

D is *symmetric* if for all N, X,
$X \in ||D(N)||$ iff $N \in ||D(X)||$

Two cats sneezed	$\equiv$ Two things that sneezed are cats
	{cats} $\in$ ||two {sneezers}||
Every cat sneezed	$\not\equiv$ Every thing that sneezed is a cat

Although Barwise and Cooper note that the intuitions concerning whether the weak determiners *many* and *few* meet these definitions are not clear, I will take these properties to be the defining properties of weak determiners, with the hope that future research can explain the (pragmatic?) peculiarities of *many* and *few*. This confirms Keenan's arguments in chapter 12 that the distribution of determiners in linguistic contexts follows from these properties (his "existentiality") rather than from Barwise and Cooper's definition of *not-strong*. For example, the "trivial" cardinal determiners *zero or more* and *less than zero* are acceptable in the contexts allowing weak NPs, such as *there*-sentences, donkey-anaphora, and the contexts to be explored shortly in (35). Such determiners will be defined as strong by Barwise and Cooper's analysis, but if *weak* is defined by the properties just considered, they are weak.

It is now easy to see that the clausal set analysis I have assumed for weak determiners follows directly from their intersectivity, or existentiality. This can be illustrated with the analysis of the NP in (30a), repeated in (34a).

(34) a. At least two vampires appeared
     b. $E \in ||$two$(\{$vampires$\} \cap \{$appearers$\}))||$
     c. $||$two {appearing vampires}$|| = \{X| \; |X \cap \{$appearing vampires$\}$
        $| \geq 2\}$
     d. $\exists(Y)(Y = \{(z)|$vampire(z) & z appeared$\}$ & $|Y| \geq 2)$

Since *two* is existential, one of the semantic representations of (34a) is (34b). The analysis of the NP denotation in (34b), using the notation of Barwise and Cooper, is (34c). (34d) is the analysis of this sentence assumed in (30c), using the notation of logical operators (operating on set variables); it is equivalent to (34b).

The clausal analysis assumed here is therefore always available for weak NPs, but it is impossible for strong NPs, which are not existential. (Note also that the quantification in (34d) is unrestricted, as permitted only with symmetric (weak) NPs.)

In more intuitive terms, the difference in the set analyses of weak and strong NPs assumed here reflects some basic differences in the processing, or the assessment, of sentences with the two types of determiners. In effect, weak determiners are processed as restricting the intersection of all sets mentioned in the clause (much like the unrestrictive sentence operators to be discussed in section 6.3.5). As an illustration for how this differs from the processing of strong determiners, we may note that a sentence like *Many students disappeared* is true if the intersection of the set of students and the set of individuals who disappeared contains many individuals, whereas *Most students disappeared* is true if this intersection contains most students, and not most individuals. (This difference follows from symmetry and existentiality: for symmetric determiners it holds that $E \in \|D\ (N{\cap}X)\|$ iff $N{\cap}X \in \|D\ (E)\|$.) In other words, to know if the first sentence is true, we need to know only how many students disappeared; to know if the second is true, we also need to know how many students there are. In procedural terms of assessment, the symmetry property means that it does not matter if we assess by checking the set of all disappearing individuals whom we know to see if they include students (and how many), or if we check the set of students to see if any of them disappeared (and if so, how many). In the strong determiner case, on the other hand, the procedure must involve searching the whole set of students and checking how many of them disappeared.

This means, then, that in the strong cases the determiner must first select subsets of the common noun set as a prerequisite for checking the intersection set, whereas no such prerequisite holds for weak determiners. This also correlates with Barwise and Cooper's description of strong NPs as "hard to use improperly" or De Jong and Verkuyl's (1985) analysis of them as "proper" (or presupposing existence of members of the common noun set): if the common noun set is empty, the search for a truth-value cannot continue (or truth is assigned by default), whereas in the weak determiner case, truth can still be assessed by checking the predicate set.

As further evidence both for the semantic properties assumed here to define weak NPs and for their processing counterpart, we may consider another context sensitive to the weak-strong distinction. Extraposition from NP is possible from "weak" NPs, as in the derivation of (35b) from (35a), but not from strong NPs, as in (35c). (The same is true for extraposition of relative clauses.)

(35) a. $\left\{ \begin{array}{l} \text{Many/two/zero or more} \\ \text{Most/all/half of the} \end{array} \right\}$ reviews about this book have appeared already

    b. Many reviews have appeared already about this book

    c. *Most reviews have appeared already about this book

    d. $E \in \|$many $(\{\text{reviews}\} \cap \{\text{things which appeared}\} \cap \{\text{things about this book}\})\|$

    e. $|\{x|\ \text{review}(x)\ \&\ \text{appeared}(x)\ \&\ \text{about this book}(x)\}| = $ many

This widely acknowledged fact is currently a mystery, but it would follow from the analysis proposed here: by intersectivity and existentiality, the weak determiners of (35a) allow the analysis in (35d), or, in the notation of this chapter, they define the set in (35e) (where the cardinality of the set including things that are reviews, that have appeared, and that are about this book is *many*). Therefore, the order and the constituent structure of the set expressions do not matter: (35a) and (35b) receive precisely the same semantic analysis. The strong determiners do not allow it, which is why (35c) has no interpretation (or at least it cannot receive the same interpretation as (35a)). In processing terms, since strong NPs operate on the NP, at the stage of S-Structure interpretation the full NP is no longer available and the determiner in (35c) can select only subsets for the set of reviews (and not of reviews about this book). In the weak case, (35b), the determiner restricts directly the intersection of all sets defined for the clause.

It remains to determine the precise sense in which weak NPs are "open" and hence can be "bound," whereas strong NPs are "closed." In the framework of this chapter this is captured by assuming the traditional logical operators that bind the set variables defined by weak NPs; since, unlike strong NPs, weak NPs do not contain an inherent operator, they end up bound either by an existential or by an operator corresponding to another determiner. It is to be hoped, however, that the analysis need not depend so crucially on the assumption of logical operators. Although I have no formal answer to this question, the processing counterpart of the weak-strong distinction seems suggestive here. As we have seen, although in the processing of strong NPs there is no way to avoid a full NP interpretation (that is, computing all subsets of the NP denotations), a weak NP is interpreted, at the NP level, only as an unrestricted common noun set. The relation of such syntactic NPs with c-commanding determiners outside them is thus semantically identical to the relation of a syntactic common noun with its determiner: namely, the external determiner can select subsets of this set, which is what I have referred to as the "binding" of the variable in the weak NP. Possibly the fact that weak NPs are not interpreted as full NPs correlates with a syntactic distinction between weak and strong NPs: Lyons (1984) argues that although strong determiners occupy the N'''-specifier position, weak determiners occupy only the N'' position (that is, all lexical nodes of a weak NP are contained in N'' rather than in N''').

6.3 Specifier Binding and the Syntactic Analysis of Donkey-Anaphora
6.3.1 The Remaining Problem of Binding
The syntactic problem posed by donkey-sentences is not, however, solved by the above analysis (as acknowledged by Heim). Essentially, it is not sufficient that the pronoun is in the scope of a given operator at LF; it must also be bound by its antecedent at S-Structure. The donkey-sentences still violate this condition, under any of its existing formulations.[5]

If we give up the binding restrictions assumed here to accommodate the donkey-sentences, we are back to the question of what prevents bound anaphora in, say, (5), repeated in (36).

(36) a. *His$_i$ friends voted for every candidate$_i$

b.

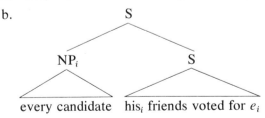

(Standard LF procedures can assign the LF structure (36b) to the sentence. In this LF structure the pronoun is in the scope of the quantifier, which may in principle bind both *his$_i$* and *e$_i$*.)[6]

Precisely the same problem arises directly in the donkey-anaphora cases. If the binding of the pronoun takes place at LF, there is no way to distinguish at this level between (37a) and (37b).

(37) a. Every knight who courted a lady$_i$ visited her$_i$ mother

b. *Her$_i$ mother visited every knight who courted a lady$_i$

In (37b) QR operations may raise the quantified NP, in which case the pronoun is in its scope, and if the index of the indefinite is copied into *every*, a pair-quantification LF structure is inappropriately derived.

More generally, Haïk (1984) has observed that donkey-anaphora obeys a restriction very similar to the general restriction on bound pronouns: for such anaphora to be possible, the quantified NP that contains the antecedent (or has it in its scope, in Haïk's terms) must c-command the pronoun at S-Structure. Let us consider more examples for this.

(38) a. To show *her* his love, every knight who courted *a lady* fought some dragons

b. *To show *her* his love, Felix fought every knight who courted *a lady*

(39) a. Every woman who has *a cat* hates me, because I am allergic to *it*

b. *I hate every woman who has *a cat*, because I am allergic to *it*

c. *Lucie fell in love with every knight who came on *a white horse*, although *it* didn't smell so good

(40) *The rumor about every woman who had *a friend* at the party upset *him*

In all these examples the weak antecedent is contained in a quantified NP; that is, it is in the restrictive term of another quantifier, which, as we have seen, is a requirement for donkey-type anaphora. The only difference between the (a)-sentences of (38) and (39) and all other sentences here is in the relation of the quantified NP containing the antecedent and the pronoun. In the first cases it c-commands the pronoun; in the others it does not.

This structural information is, again, unavailable at LF, where after QR (NPR) the quantified NP c-commands the pronouns equally in all these sentences.

This means, then, that for the proposed semantic analysis to work, the binding of the variables in the donkey-sentences must be captured at S-Structure, the problem being that at this level binding appears to be impossible. I turn now to an S-Structure analysis of binding that can resolve this mystery.

6.3.2 Specifier Binding

The semantic solution to the indefinite (donkey-) puzzle enables us to state the question of syntactic binding somewhat differently. What leads to the binding problem is the assumption that NPs are syntactically bound only by other NPs. Consequently, the only type of syntactic binding assumed in the grammar is that of referential indices. Under these assumptions, the weak NP obviously cannot bind the pronoun in the donkey-sentences. However, the essence of the semantic analysis of the previous sections has been that the weak NP is *not* in fact an antecedent in such examples. Rather, anaphora is obtained in these cases because the weak NP and the pronoun are both bound by the same operator, which is external to the weak NP. More generally, in the cases where a determiner binds a variable in another NP as in both the donkey-contexts and the Lakhota relative clauses, this binding cannot be captured by referential indices. The binder here can only be some operator that corresponds, syntactically, to a specifier (either a determiner or a sentential operator that can be viewed as an S-specifier). If we extend our notions of syntactic binding to allow NPs to be syntactically bound by specifiers, this type of direct operator binding will no longer be a mystery. In fact, as we will see, within the interpretive (for instance, GB) framework, such an extension will only make explicit some assumptions that are already implicit. We will also see that once this move is taken, the binding in the donkey-cases turns out to obey the general S-Structure binding restriction. Let us first examine the mechanism needed for this notion of specifier binding.

I assume that each specifier receives a specifier index, marked with a slash (for instance, $every_{/i}$), to distinguish it from a referential index. Since this is a syntactic index, all specifiers will receive it. However, this index will be interpretable only if the specifier is interpreted as an operator (just as the referential index of a bound NP is interpretable only if it can be interpreted as a variable). Following the indexing conventions of the government theory of the GB framework (see, for instance, Kayne 1983), it is reasonable to assign the specifier the index of the head, or of the constituent whose specifier it is (which means also that possibly the indexing at issue is already assumed, independently, in the grammar). The index of *every man* is given in (41). In case a specifier is an NP, it has both a referential index and a specifier index, as in (42).

(41)

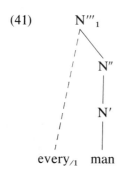

(42) a.

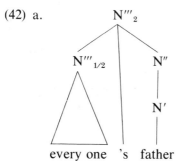

    b.

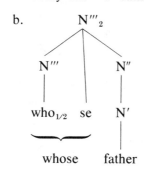

    c.

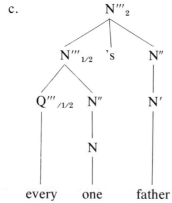

The specifier NP—for instance, *everyone's* in (42a)—is further analyzed, as in (42c): the specifier *every* of this NP has all the indices of its NP as specifier indices.

In fact, as we saw in (18), the new type of specifier index is implicitly assumed, anyway, by theories assuming standard translations of quantifiers at LF. Whereas the referential indices (R-INDEX) are translated as variable arguments, the specifier index is the operator index indicating which variables it binds. In this respect, introducing specifier indices in the syntax only makes the interpretive procedure more explicit: the translation of the indices into variables in (43a) yields (43b). After NPR (= QR) applies, yielding (43c), *every* with its operator index is extracted, yielding (43d).

(43) a. [Every$_{/1}$ man]$_1$ thinks he$_1$ is a genius
     b. [every x man]$_x$ thinks x is a genius
     c. [every x man]$_x$ [x thinks x is a genius]
     d. every x (man(x)) (x thinks x is a genius)

Furthermore, the system enables us to derive an LF representation for problematic NPs of the type illustrated in (42). Such NPs provide another instance of pair quantification (which we assumed earlier for the donkey-cases). This derivation, given in (44), is obtained since the *every* specifier in such cases has two operator indices (see the discussion of (42c)).

(44) a. [[Every$_{/1/2}$ man]$_{1/2}$'s father]$_2$ . . .
     b. [[every x,y man] $x(y)$'s father]$_y$
     c. [every x,y man]$_x$ [x's father]$_y$
     d. every $\langle x,y \rangle$ (man(x) & x's father (y)) . . .

At S-Structure the specifier NP *every man* also has a specifier index (/2). However, since this specifier does not correspond to an operator at LF, its operator index (marked with parentheses in (44b)) has no interpretation, and it is deleted. More generally, whenever a node has both a referential index and a specifier index, the latter is deleted at LF as uninterpretable.

6.3.3 The S-Structure Restriction on Binding

A few words are needed about the general theory of binding at S-Structure before we consider how the specifier binds the pronoun in the donkey-cases. In the GB framework, which I am assuming here (Chomsky 1981, 1982), all NPs are indexed freely, and the binding principles filter out inappropriate cases of coindexing. The theory distinguishes two types of coindexing relations, however, bound and unbound: a node α binds a coindexed node β iff α c-commands β at S-Structure. Unbound nodes are "free," which means that a free node is not necessarily uncoindexed—it may be coindexed with an NP that does not c-command it. For example, the pronoun may be coindexed with the full NP in all the following cases.

(45) a. Each gardener$_1$ talks to his$_1$ plants
     b. Max$_1$ talks to his$_1$ plants

(46) a. *His$_1$ friends voted for each candidate$_1$
     b. His$_1$ friends voted for Max$_1$

However, in (45) the coindexed pronoun is defined as bound, whereas in (46) the coindexing is unbound.

Although this is not explicitly assumed in the current framework, I have argued elsewhere (Reinhart 1983, 1985) that this distinction is sufficient to capture the distribution of bound variable anaphora.[7] A pronoun may be interpreted as a bound variable iff it is syntactically bound at S-Structure. Since the grammar currently allows unbound coindexing as well, we need the translation procedure for indices in (47), which translates only bound indices, leaving other indices uninterpreted. Its results are illustrated in (48) and (49).

(47) For any given node α, replace the index of α and all NPs that α binds at S-Structure with an identical variable index.

(48) a. [Each$_{/1}$ gardener]$_1$ talks to his$_1$ plants
     b. [each gardener]$_x$ talks to x's plants
     c. [each$_{/x}$ gardener]$_x$ talks to x's plants

(49) a. Max$_1$ talks to his$_1$ plants
     b. Max$_x$ talks to x's plants

Since pronouns and other anaphoric elements lack lexical content, their only content at LF is their index, so they are replaced by the variable. In the case of lexical NPs the variable is written as an index. If we incorporate specifier indices, these indices are translated as in (48c). If an NP that cannot be interpreted as anaphoric (that is, as containing a free variable) is syntactically bound, its translation as a variable by (47) will be uninterpretable (this situation may arise if Principle C of the binding theory of Chomsky 1981 is eliminated from the grammar).

Pronouns that are not syntactically bound cannot be translated by (47). For this reason, (47) does not apply to (46), which means that bound variable interpretation is not possible there. If the "antecedent" is a referential NP, as in (46b), pragmatic coreference is still possible, but if it is quantified, as in (46a), such pragmatic interpretation is unavailable and no anaphora reading is possible.

The further interpretation of the structures derived by (47) depends on other LF rules. If the antecedent's specifier is translated as an operator (as, for example, in (48)), it binds both variables. In other cases, such as (49), it depends on our theoretical assumptions whether the result is interpretable. I argue in Reinhart 1983 that a λ operator is construed to bind the variables in such cases.

The procedure (47) must apply before the LF QR operations, since the latter change the syntactic binding relations of the sentence. The QR operations, then, will not allow pronouns not already translated by (47) to be interpreted as variables. The result is that bound variable interpretation is possible only when the antecedent binds the pronoun at S-Structure, and it is not effected by scope.[8]

Although that much is assumed, independently, for the analysis of bound variable anaphora, a certain modification is required in order to allow for the specifier binding introduced in section 6.3.2. The specifier itself does not c-command anything outside its NP. However, its binding domain is identical to that of the NP. To capture this, the definition of binding stated in (50) is required.[9]

(50) A node α binds a node β iff α and β share an index and α either c-commands β or is the specifier of a node that c-commands β.

I should note that this definition is not required only for the cases of specifier binding in the donkey-sentences. In fact, it captures an anaphora problem acknowledged by all theories of bound anaphora— namely, that an NP that is in specifier position allows binding outside its NP. For example, the pronouns in (51) are bound, even though they are not c-commanded by their quantified antecedent.

(51) a. Every boy$_1$'s mother thinks he$_1$ is a genius
     b. Whose$_1$ mother did the rumor about him$_1$ worry?

(52) a. [[Every$_{/1/2}$ boy]$_{1/2}$'s mother]$_2$ thinks he$_1$ is a genius
     b. every $\langle x,y \rangle$ (boy(x) & x's mother(y)) (y thinks x is a genius)

The NP *every boy* in (51a) is the specifier of its NP. Hence, by (50) its coindexing with the pronoun is defined as binding, and the translation procedure (47) allows these two indices to be translated as identical variables. The translation of all other indices in (52a) as variables is unproblematic here, since each specifier c-commands its NP and hence binds it. This means that the coindexing in this sentence is interpreted as bound variable anaphora. Further LF rules like QR yield the final LF structure in (52b). The same procedures apply in (51b).

We may turn now to the donkey-cases.

6.3.4 The Binding in the Donkey-Cases

As we have seen, a characteristic property of weak NPs is that they can be "bound" by another operator in the sentence, if they meet the conditions described earlier. In Heim's analysis the LF index-copying procedure (26) copies the index of the weak NP into that operator in such cases. However, since variable binding must be captured at S-Structure, handling the donkey-cases requires that the same procedure apply at S-Structure.

Heim's procedures allow weak NPs to be bound only if they are in the restrictive term of the operator, which depends crucially on her LF construal rules. However, the same results follow directly from S-Structure relations: the restrictive term of an operator (if it has one) is its domain at S-Structure (that is, the nodes it c-commands). In other words, the restrictive domain of an operator is narrower than its binding domain (determined by (50)), and it is defined directly by c-command. (Given the system of specifier indexing, the restrictive domain is already marked, since it is the constituent the quantifier is coindexed with. For instance, in (54a) the restrictive term of the operator is the domain indexed 1. I will return to the conditionals directly.) All that needs to be specified is that a weak NP can be bound by a c-commanding specifier, and this is captured by the copying procedure (53), which applies at S-Structure before the index-translation procedure (47). (53) applies in exactly the same way to the Lakhota relatives in (19).

(53) Copy the index of an NP β_j into a c-commanding Q node, $Q_{/i}$, if β_j is free. (Resulting in $Q_{/i/j}$.)[10]

(Procedure (53) need not be restricted in the syntax to apply specifically to weak NPs. If an NP that is inherently quantified, or cannot be bound, is copied, the derivation will be filtered out at LF as uninterpretable, since two operators bind the same variable.)[11]

(54) a. [Every$_{/1}$ man who hates a donkey$_2$]$_1$ beats it$_2$

b.

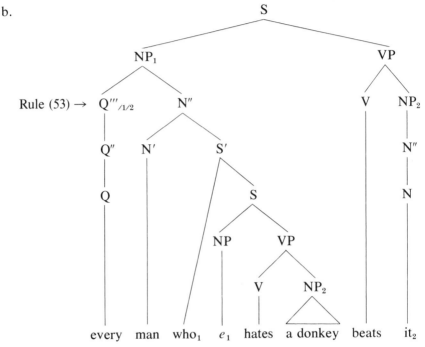

every   man   who$_1$ e_1 hates   a donkey   beats   it$_2$

c. [every$_{/x/y}$ man who x hates a donkey$_y$]$_x$ beats y

In a sentence like (54a) the Q *every* c-commands the donkey-NP. (For the structural analysis of relative clauses assumed here, see Jackendoff 1977.) Procedure (53) therefore applies, yielding the indexing in (54b). This structure captures the unique properties of the donkey-anaphora discussed earlier: the donkey-NP$_2$ does not bind the pronoun *it$_2$*, but they are both bound by the quantifier *every*, given the definition in (50). (*Every* c-commands the NP *a donkey* and is the specifier of an NP c-commanding the pronoun.) The translation procedure (47) can now apply, translating all indices 2 as identical variables, as in (54c). After subsequent interpretive procedures apply, we derive the pair-quantification analysis we assumed for such sentences. (The LF derivation of (54) is given in (69) in the summary.)

This means, then, that once (53) applies at S-Structure, donkey-type anaphora obeys the general binding constraints of the grammar; that is, the translation procedure for variables applies in a uniform way. The c-command restrictions on the type of anaphora observed in (37)–(40) (some of which are repeated following (57)) are captured in a straight-forward way.

(55) a. [Every$_{/1/2}$ woman who has a cat$_2$]$_1$ hates me because I am allergic to it$_2$

b.

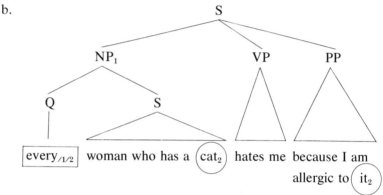

(56) a. *I hate [every$_{/1/2}$ woman who has a cat$_2$]$_1$ since I am allergic to it$_2$

b.

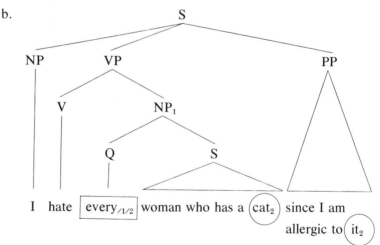

(57) *Her$_2$ mother visited [every$_{/1/2}$ knight who courted a lady$_2$]$_1$

The index-copying procedure (53) is permitted to apply in all these cases, since the *every* quantifier c-commands the weak NP$_2$. Hence, at this stage the quantifier has both indices. However, the difference between the trees of (55) and (56) lies in the relation of *every* to the pronoun. Given the definition (50), in (55b) *every* binds the pronoun (since its NP c-commands it). The translation procedure (47) can therefore apply and translate both *a cat* and *it* as bound by *every*, eventually yielding the bound variable interpretation. In (56b), on the other hand, the NP containing *every* does not c-command the pronoun; hence, *every* does not bind it. The translation procedure can only bind the NP *a cat* (which yields the correct interpretation for this NP); but it cannot translate the pronoun as a variable, so the coindexing here has no interpretation. Similarly, in (57) *every* does not bind the pronoun *her*, the indexing is untranslatable, and no bound anaphora interpretation is obtained.

6.3.5 Sentential Operators

In the case of relative clauses the specifier that binds the weak NP is a determiner. However, sentential operators can also serve as binders. We have already seen one such case, in the discussion of Heim's conditional operator, but this phenomenon is much larger. In fact, the type of anaphora examined here is not restricted to the traditional donkey-contexts. All sentential adverbial operators (described by Lewis (1975) as "adverbs of quantification") allow weak NPs to bind pronouns freely, as illustrated in the following examples.

(58) a. *Lucie kisses some guest$_i$ when he$_i$ talks about Hegel
     b. Always Lucie kisses some guest$_i$ when he$_i$ talks about Hegel
     c. Often Lucie kisses some guest$_i$ when he$_i$ talks about Hegel
     d. Lucie never kisses a/any guest$_i$ when he$_i$ talks about Hegel

(59) a. *Lucie throws some dress$_i$ away after she wears it$_i$ once
     b. Always Lucie throws some dress$_i$ away after she wears it$_i$ once

(60) a. *Always Lucie kisses each guest$_i$ when he$_i$ talks about Hegel
     b. *Lucie never kisses each guest$_i$ when he$_i$ talks about Hegel
     c. *Often Lucie throws each dress$_i$ away after she wears it$_i$ once

(61) a. Always/often my attempt to calm someone$_i$ down only makes him$_i$ more angry
     b. *Always/often my attempt to calm everyone$_i$ down only makes him$_i$ more angry

Here the antecedent does not c-command the pronoun; hence, standard (NP) binding is impossible, as illustrated by (58a) and (59a). However, when an adverbial operator is present, binding is permitted, as in (58b–d) and (59b). (Note that this is quantified anaphora, and not coreference, since the pronoun interpretation varies with the choice for the "antecedent.") Just as with the donkey-contexts, this type of binding is permitted only if the "antecedent" is weak. In (60), where the antecedent is strong, anaphora is impossible despite the presence of the operator; also compare (61a) with (61b).

The availability of anaphora in such contexts follows directly from the S-Structure analysis proposed here. In the S-Structure representation of such sentences the adverbial Q c-commands both the "antecedent" NP and the pronoun, as illustrated for (58b–c) in (62).

(62)

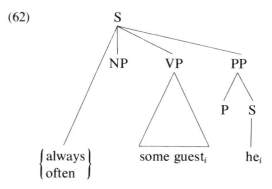

The index-copying procedure (53) then allows copying the index of *some guest* as an operator index on Q, which will then syntactically bind both NPs. Since the conditions for procedure (47) are met, the indices are translatable. (If the index of a strong NP is copied, the derivation is uninterpretable; see note 11.) The semantic interpretation of the binding here requires more study, since I believe, unlike Lewis (1975), that it involves quantification over times. However, the general principles are the same here as in the donkey-contexts, although no restrictive term is present at LF.

Turning now to the conditional contexts, we have seen that Heim (1982), following Lewis (1975), treats the (abstract) conditional operator in much the same way as the adverbial operators, assuming that it originates in the matrix S and not in the *if*-clause. The *if* itself functions in this analysis only as a marker for the restrictive term of the operator. A problem with this assumption is how to explain the difference in distribution between anaphora triggered by the adverbial operator and anaphora triggered by the conditional operator. In the case of "bare" conditionals anaphora is allowed only if the antecedent is in the *if*-clause, as in (63b), but not otherwise, as in (63a).

(63) a. *Lucie kisses *some guest* if *he* talks about Hegel
   b. If *some guest* talks about Hegel, Lucie kisses *him*

(64) $\left\{\begin{array}{l}\text{Always} \\ \text{Often}\end{array}\right\}$ Lucie kisses *some guest* if *he* talks about Hegel

In and of itself, this fact follows from Heim's analysis of the *if*-clause as the restrictive term of the conditional operator (since her copy rule (26) can apply in (63b) but not in (63a)). However, if another adverbial operator is added to (63a), as in (64), anaphora is permitted, although the *if*-clause is still analyzed as the restrictive term. More generally, if the conditional operator is identical in interpretation and scope to the adverbial operator, there is no obvious explanation for the fact that it cannot allow anaphora in the same way.

If the conditional operator instead originates in the *if*-clause, these facts will follow from the proposed S-Structure analysis, assuming, temporarily, an empty Q node in the S-Structure representation of the *if*-clause: in the adverbial cases, as in (64) (or (58)–(61)), the operator node c-commands the whole sentence, but in the conditional case it c-commands only the *if*-clause. Hence, the index-copying procedure (53) allows copying in (63b) but not in (63a); that is, the operator cannot bind a weak NP outside the *if*-clause.

The assumption that the conditional operator originates in the *if*-clause is motivated also by the fact that the conditional operator triggers negative polarity items, such as *anyone* in (65a).

(65) a. If anyone arrives, we'll have a party
   b. *If we have a party, anyone will come

Generally, the distribution of such items requires that the triggering operator c-command the item at S-Structure (this is, originally, Klima's (1964) analysis), and there is no obvious way to capture it at LF. (For example, after QR a sentence like *Any lady danced with no gentleman* is indistinguishable from *No gentleman danced with any lady.*) To capture the difference between (65a) and (65b), then, the relevant triggering operator must be in the *if*-clause, at S-Structure.

This analysis of the conditional operator stresses the similarity between conditionals and relative clauses: in both cases the indefinite antecedent can occur only in the "restrictive term" since only this part of the sentence is c-commanded by the operator at S-Structure. This would mean that the conditional operator is independent of the other adverbial operators, and (unlike what happens under Lewis's proposal) it is realized even if an adverbial operator is present. The problem of the interaction between this operator and other adverbial operators (which motivated Lewis's analysis) should be handled by whatever analysis handles similar interactions with universally quantified NPs, as in *Often every guest talks about Hegel* or *Sometimes every woman who likes a guest talks to him about Hegel*.

We should consider next the possibility that *if* itself occupies the sentential Q position of its clause—in other words, that *if* is an S′-specifier that is interpreted as the conditional operator (which would mean that (53) copies the NP index directly to this node). Although I will not elaborate on this, it is clear that *if* has a special categorial status. It obviously cannot be a sentential connective. For example, as noted by Emonds (1976), among others, gapping is prohibited in *if*-clauses, though permitted in, say, *but*-clauses. Moreover, *if* can be moved with its clause, as in (67), though such movement is impossible in the connective case with *but* in (66).

(66) a. I'll be late, but wait for me
     b. *But wait for me, I'll be late

(67) a. I'll come, if you wait for me
     b. If you wait for me, I'll come

It is also clear that *if* is not a preposition, since it cannot occur in the most standard P environments, preceding an NP (compare *before the lecture, after his arrival* to **if the lecture*). This, then, distinguishes *if*-clauses from PP clauses (such as *after I arrive*). The treatment of *if* as an S′-specifier therefore seems reasonable, and it can be analyzed as a quantified specifier, similar to the quantified specifier of an NP (the determiner).

Under this assumption, donkey-anaphora in conditionals is analogous to the case of relative clauses. (53) copies the index of (for example) *some guest* in (63b) into the c-commanding specifier Q node. This node does not itself c-command the pronoun, but, as a specifier of a c-commanding node (S′), it still binds it (if they are coindexed), under the definition of binding in (50). Hence, the translation of the pronoun by (47) as a variable bound by the operator is permitted.

6.3.6 Summary

For convenience, I summarize the definitions and the procedure assumed in this section for the syntactic analysis of donkey-sentences or, more generally, for the binding of variables. Procedures (47) and (68) are assumed independently in the grammar. (In defining the "QR" operations in (68), I follow Heim's analysis surveyed earlier.) I have also argued that the definition of binding in (50) is needed for other cases as well. The only procedure required specifically for the present problem (donkey-contexts, Lakhota relative clauses, and the contexts of adverbial operators) is (53). Furthermore, apart from the standard binding principles A and B, the procedures in the following list are the only ones I assume; that is, they cover everything needed in the grammar to capture the facts of anaphora and scope.

Summary of Definitions and Rules

Definition of Binding
(50) A node α binds a node β iff α and β share an index and α either c-commands β or is the specifier of a node that c-commands β.

Rules Mapping S-Structure onto LF (Ordered)
(53) *Index Copying*
Copy the index of an NP β_j into a c-commanding Q node $Q_{/i}$, if β_j is free.
(47) *Index Translation*
For any given node α, replace the index of α and all NPs that α binds at S-Structure with an identical variable index.
(68) *"QR" Operations*
a. NP Raising (NPR): Adjoin an NP to S.
b. Operator Raising (OR): Attach a quantifier node to S.

Derivation of LF Structure for Tree (54)
(69) a. Rule (53) $\rightarrow$ [Every$_{/1/2}$ man who t$_1$ hates a donkey$_2$]$_1$ beats it$_2$
b. Rule (47) $\rightarrow$ [every$_{/x/y}$ man who x hates a donkey$_y$]$_x$ [x beats y]
c. Rule (68a) $\rightarrow$ [every$_{/x/y}$ man who (a donkey$_y$ (x hates y))]$_x$ [x beats y]
d. Rule (68b) $\rightarrow$ every$_{/x/y}$ [man, a donkey$_y$ (x hates y)]$_x$ [x beats y]
e. Interpretation $\rightarrow$ every $\langle x, Y \rangle$ (man(x) & $Y = \{y|$donkey(y) & x hates $y\}$ & $|Y| \geq 1$) (x beats Y)

(69) illustrates the LF derivation of the donkey-sentence whose structure was given in (54). The general procedures derive (69d), which represents something like the logical syntax of the sentence. The interpretation of this formula in (69e) is determined by considerations specific to the set interpretation of weak NPs examined in sections 6.2.5 and 6.2.6.

Notes

This chapter owes much to extensive discussions with Ed Keenan, Remko Scha, and especially Irene Heim. Its first draft was written during a visit in the summer of 1984 to the Max-Planck-Institut für Psycholinguistik in Nijmegen, whose staff I also wish to thank.

1. Example (14b) is discussed by Williamson in chapter 7. The examples in (15) and (16) have been furnished by Janis Williamson (personal communication).

2. If the top determiner is weak, it provides the cardinality of the set defined by the internal NP and this NP is assumed to be bound by the general discourse operator.

3. The motivation for Haïk's analysis is that other types of apparently unbound anaphora with bound properties are possible in the environments just cited. Compare (22b), (21b), and (23) to (i)–(iii).

(i) To show her_2 his love, every $knight_1$ sent roses to his_1 $mistress_2$

(ii) Every man_1 who remembered to bring $them_2$ put his_1 $bottles_2$ in the refrigerator

(iii) Every man_1 assumed that jokes about his_1 $wife_2$ annoyed her_2

(NP$_2$ in these examples contains a pronoun bound by NP$_1$; hence, the pronoun with the same index behaves like a bound pronoun, although it is not c-commanded by NP$_2$.) Haïk's analysis allows correctly for anaphora in (i)–(iii) but cannot filter it out in the equivalent donkey-type cases.

Although I believe that Haïk's semantic analysis, which follows ideas of Evans (1980), is a promising direction, at present I do not see a way to avoid this problem in this framework. In examples like (20) Evans's description is clearly met; still, the pronoun cannot refer to the men satisfying *X had met some man*.

4. In principle, a plural discourse anaphor can refer backward to three different sets: some set selected for the NP itself, the intersection set of the NP and the predicate, or the common noun set (the last is possible independently of the determiner type). I am only arguing here that the first is excluded in the case of weak NPs.

Strong NPs also prefer the intersection interpretation, but the pronoun is more free in referring to any of these options, and it is often not clear which is intended. Compare (ia) and (ib), for example.

(i) a. Lucie adored many movies and Max hated them

b. Lucie adored $\left\{ \begin{array}{l} \text{almost all the} \\ \text{all but five} \end{array} \right\}$ movies and Max hated them

(ii) But luckily, they weren't all the same movies

In (ib), although it is likely that Max hated precisely the same movies that Lucie adored, it is not necessary, and in the appropriate context the pronoun can refer to any set of almost all movies. For instance, it is possible to continue (ib)—but not (ia)—with (ii). The mere availability of the intersection interpretation does not require the clausal set analysis, since it can be obtained by a pragmatic choice of reference in discourse. The crucial point is that in the weak cases it is the only option; hence, it must reflect semantic properties rather than pragmatic strategies.

5. For example, once the variables are written in tree (25c), it becomes clear that it also violates the Bijection Principle at LF: each operator ($\square\ x_i$) binds two occurrences of x_i, neither of which c-commands the other. Similarly, neither the Bijection nor the Parallelism Principle can distinguish between the LF structures of (37a) and (37b). If pair quantification is assumed at LF for such sentences, these principles should either allow both sentences or rule them both out (depending on the exact formulation of the principles). I should mention that under the analysis I propose directly, donkey-anaphora still violates these principles, although it does not violate the S-Structure condition on anaphora. This does not worry me, since I believe that the Bijection and Parallelism Principles are not correct in any case, and the restrictions on variable binding must be stated at S-Structure and not at LF (see note 8).

6. It may be suggested that backward anaphora with indefinite or quantified NPs is filtered out by discourse considerations, since (for example) they do not convey "old" information. However, as noted earlier, the problem is not restricted to backward anaphora. Furthermore, although it is true that backward anaphora in such cases is not easy to find, in the only empirical study of backward anaphora, Carden (1978) found numerous occurrences of it in the texts he considered. For example:

(i) In his$_1$ own way, however, each man$_1$ is petitioning for the same kind of administration (*New York Times,* 1/21/77).

(ii) "We are . . . lawyers who go into court to . . . return to her$_1$ classroom [a pregnant girl illegally suspended from school]"$_1$ (Advertisement, *Children Defence Fund* . . .).

In all these cases, however, the pronoun is syntactically bound by its antecedent, as required.

7. In the current framework the distinction obtained here seems superfluous. The definition of binding is needed, independently, for other binding phenomena, but in the case of pronouns the system makes no interpretive use of the distinction obtained. Instead, the same distinction is restated, in effect, at LF as the Bijection or Parallelism Principle. However, there is no principled reason why this should be so. (In fact, this concept of the bound anaphora procedures follows from traditional assumptions concerning the interpretation of pronouns that need to be revised in any event. For details, see Reinhart 1983, 1985.)

8. This result overlaps with, but is not precisely equivalent to, the results of the Bijection Principle. They differ in cases of *Wh*-Movement, illustrated in (i) and (ii).

(i)   Which paper$_1$ did you file e_1 without reading e_1?

(ii) *[Whose$_1$ mother]$_2$ did the rumor about her$_2$ worry e_2 (though she$_2$ denied it)?

(iii) [Whose$_1$ mother]$_2$ did the rumor about him$_1$ worry e_2 though he$_1$ denied it?

Here the *wh*-antecedent binds both anaphoric elements at S-Structure, so procedure (47) allows their translation as bound variables, whereas the Bijection Principle filters (i)–(iii) out as ungrammatical, since at LF one operator locally binds more than one argument. With respect to (i), the S-Structure analysis (based on (47)) seems to be correct, since parasitic gaps are increasingly viewed as grammatical, contrary to the predictions of the Bijection Principle. However, it fails with respect to (ii), where anaphora is as bad as in (46a). Although I cannot elaborate on this here, I believe that (ii) is filtered out by other principles of the binding theory. This hinges on the typology of anaphoric elements in the language—namely, on which elements can serve as Comp-bound anaphors. Pronouns cannot be Comp-bound in English (though they can be A-bound). In languages with genuine resumptive pronouns in *wh*-questions, sentences like (ii) have been found to be acceptable (see examples in Engdahl 1983). In any case, anaphora is possible in (iii), where the antecedent is *whose* rather than the moved element in Comp, although the operator corresponding to this node binds both pronouns, *him* and *he*. So the Bijection Principle cannot be the correct generalization here. (I return to the S-Structure analysis of (iii) in (51b).)

More generally, the anaphora phenomena examined in this chapter all violate the Bijection Principle, since they involve an operator locally binding more than one argument. They also violate the Parallelism Principle since the operator binds both an empty position and a pronoun. (See note 5.)

9. Assuming (50) necessitates a notational change in binding Conditions A, requiring that the anaphor and the antecedent have the same GC. (In **Ben's mother loves himself,* the NP is the GC of the antecedent but not of the anaphor.) Cf. Reinhart (1983).

10. The requirement that β be free in (53) guarantees that it cannot apply to cases like (ia–b).

(i) a. *Every patient$_1$ who told him$_2$ that a doctor$_2$ was lousy died mysteriously

  b. *If he$_1$ thinks a man$_1$ gets tired, he$_1$ takes a vacation

(ii) If those he$_1$ loves betray a man$_1$, he is in trouble

In (ia–b) the weak NP cannot be copied into the quantifier since it is not free—it is bound by the pronoun. This means that the accidental coindexing in these sentences will have no interpretation. In (ii), by contrast, where the weak NP is free, it can be copied to the Q operator, which would yield a bound interpretation for the pronoun.

11. For example, in deriving the interpretation for sentences such as (ia), the stage in (ib) is well-formed, but the final stage (ic) is filtered out, since two operators bind the same variable.

(i) a. *Every man who bought *every car* worshiped *it*

  b. [Every$_{/1/2}$ man who bought every car$_2$]$_1$ worshiped it$_2$

  c. *$\forall\langle x,y\rangle$ (man(x) & $\forall y$ (car(y) & x bought y)) (x worshiped y)

If a pronoun is copied into a quantifier, the derivation will be filtered out by the principle prohibiting unrestricted quantification in natural language. That is, (iib) is inappropriate for the same reason that (iii) is inappropriate.

(ii) a.   [Every$_{1/2}$ man]$_1$ who liked her$_2$ died

    b. *every $\langle x,y \rangle$ (man(x) & x likes y) x died

(iii) every x (x died)

If we assume all details of Heim's (1982) analysis, including existential closure, if an indefinite NP is copied while being also in the scope of another Q (both in the relative clause), then the derivation will be filtered out on the same grounds.

Chapter 7

An Indefiniteness Restriction for Relative Clauses in Lakhota

Janis S. Williamson

The relative clause construction in Lakhota (one of the Dakotan dialects spoken by the Sioux Indians in North America) is typologically unusual in that it contains *internal heads*. That is, unlike many well-studied languages where the lexical NP denoting the semantic class of the restricted noun is external to the relative clause, in Lakhota the head is internal to the relative clause. These two types are schematized in (1).

(1) a. *External*

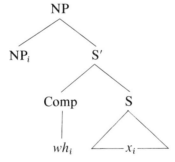

b. *Internal*

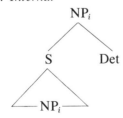

Though internal head relative clauses are not unknown in typological discussions, until now no systematic description of them has been undertaken. In Lakhota such an examination has revealed certain expected properties (such as unbounded dependencies between the internal head and elements in the clause containing the entire NP) but also a surprising and, to my knowledge, previously undocumented restriction: the internal head must be indefinite. In this chapter I will argue that this indefiniteness restriction can be derived from the interaction between the interpretation of relative clauses and the proper treatment of indefinites in general.

The current rules of interpretation of relative clauses (RCs) have been based on structure (1a): the RC forms a complex modifier expression that is either "predicated" of its coindexed NP (Chomsky 1982a) or substitutes for a free variable (Cooper 1975). These interpretations cannot be directly applied to a structure such as (1b). Previous studies of internal head RCs have either ignored the interpretive problem that this type of RC poses or assumed more abstract syntactic structures with empty elements resembling (1a). In neither approach has the indefiniteness restriction been considered.

My account will be based on the facts that (1) the indefinite NP is the head of the RC and (2) the indefinite NP is in a structurally internal position at S-Structure. The account makes crucial use of Heim's (1982) analysis of indefinites and may be seen as further independent support for the view that indefinites are not quantifier-operators. Though I have no explanation for the typological division of languages with respect to these types of relative clauses,[1] I will claim that all languages that have internal head RCs will have an indefiniteness restriction (that is, a "definiteness effect").

This chapter is organized as follows: In section 7.1 I discuss the structure of internal head RCs in Lakhota, motivating the coindexing relation between the internal head and the NP that contains it and providing a descriptive characterization of possible heads. In section 7.2 I examine more closely the LF properties of RCs, arguing for an unbounded dependency between the "in-situ" head and mother clause elements. The obligatory wide scope of the head over modifier clause is accounted for by an LF rule of Head Raising. In section 7.3 I address the indefiniteness restriction, arguing for an interpretation of RCs that builds on the analysis developed in the previous sections.

7.1 Lakhota Relative Clause Structure
7.1.1 Background
Lakhota can be characterized as a language of remarkably free word order, flat structure, rich and complex verbal morphology, and a limited number of movement rules. In Williamson 1984 I argue that Lakhota is "nonconfigurational" with respect to phrase structure rules. However, this property holds of *clause* structure. For, in the terminology used by Gil in chapter 10, Lakhota may be viewed as a language with "configurational" NP structure. It displays all of the typological characteristics that Gil claims hold of configurational NP structure, English being his canonical case. In this chapter I will assume the following phrase structure rules for clauses and NPs. (More complete discussion can be found in Williamson 1984.)

(2) $S \rightarrow X''^* \; V \; \text{Infl}$

$NP \rightarrow \begin{Bmatrix} N' \; \text{Det} \\ \text{pronoun} \end{Bmatrix}$

$N' \rightarrow (NP) \; N \; \text{Infl}$

7.1.2 Constituent Structure of Lakhota Relative Clauses
The basic structure of the relative clause construction is given in (3). It consists of a bare clause (simple or complex) followed by a determiner. The lexical NP denoting the semantic class of the restricted noun (that is, the head of the RC) is internal to the clause. An appositive demonstrative pronoun often follows this constituent.[2] This is the only RC strategy in Lakhota and is used for all NPs, regardless of grammatical relation.

(3)

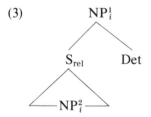

I begin with a brief description of each constituent in (3), introducing the terminology appropriate for such a structure. First, I will call NP_1, which expands as the relative clause, the *mother NP*. (I introduce this term in preference to, say, *matrix NP*, since a relative clause is obviously not restricted to matrix clauses.) The definiteness of the entire RC is determined by the determiner immediately dominated by this mother NP. This is illustrated in (4).

(4) a. [$_{NP_i}$[$_S$ Mary [owįža wą]$_i$ kaǧe] *ki*] he   ophewathų
       Mary quilt a   make the Dem I-buy
       'I bought the quilt that Mary made'

   b. [$_{NP_i}$[$_S$ Mary [owįža wą]$_i$ kaǧa] *cha*] he   ophewathų
       Mary quilt a   make Ind Dem I-buy
       'I bought a quilt that Mary made'

   c. [$_{NP_i}$[$_S$ Mary [owįža wą]$_i$ kaǧe] *k'ų*]   he   ophewathų
       Mary quilt a   make the-P Dem I-buy
       'I bought the (previously mentioned) quilt that Mary made'

I will discuss these determiners in greater detail when I consider their role in the interpretation of the RC.

The S_{rel} (the clause that "restricts" the head) expands by the usual expansion of S given in (2). Because of the free word order of major constituents in a Lakhota clause, the internal head may appear in any position within the clause.[3]

Finally, NP$_2$, which I will refer to as the *internal head,* specifies the semantic class of the restricted noun and is contained within the modifying RC (S_{rel}).[4] In calling NP$_2$ an internal head, I have identified the NP by its role in the interpretation of the RC and not by any phrase-structural identification of the head. Indeed, the usual X'-theory treatment of modifiers, such as Jackendoff 1977, where modifiers are uniformly of level 2, fail to identify the head.

7.1.3 Relative Clause Indexing

In the S-Structure form in (3) there must be one and only one NP in the S_{rel} identified as the head, indicated by coindexing. In this section I look more closely at this device.

Only indefinite NPs may be heads. If the RC does not have any indefinite NPs, the construction is uninterpretable and the sentence containing the RC is ungrammatical if no other interpretation is possible. Compare (4) with (5), where I have substituted the definite *owįža ki* 'the quilt' for the indefinite *owįža wa* 'a quilt'. The result is ungrammatical.

(5) *[$_{NP_i}$[$_S$ Mary [owįža ki]$_i$ kaǧe] *ki*] he   ophewathų
      Mary quilt the make the Dem I-buy

If the S_{rel} contains more than one indefinite NP, there is more than one potential head and the RC is ambiguous with respect to the head. Of course, some readings will be eliminated as semantically anomalous, but in many cases only context reduces the ambiguity. This is illustrated in (6).

(6) a. [$_{NP}$[$_S$[Wįyą   wą] [owįža wą] kaǧe] ki] he   ophewathų
       woman a   quilt   a   make the Dem I-buy
    i.   I bought the quilt that a woman made
    ii. #I bought the woman that made a quilt

    b. [$_{NP}$[$_S$[Wįyą   wą] [owįža wą] kaǧe] ki] he   kichi wowaglake
       woman a   quilt   a   make the Dem with I-talk
    i.   #I talked with the quilt that a woman made
    ii. I talked with the woman that made a quilt

The two possible readings of (6a) and (6b) can be disambiguated by indexed tree structures. For the readings in (i), the NP *owįža wą* will be coindexed with the mother NP; for the readings in (ii), the NP *wįyą wą* will be. In (5) there is no coindexing at all. Thus, the coindexing of the internal NP and the mother NP in (3) serves to identify (syntactically) the semantic head, and in fact characterizes the RC construction.

The facts illustrated in (5) and (6) have a parallel in languages with external heads. The ungrammaticality of (5) finds its parallel in the requirement that in external head RCs the S' must contain a position bound by the head NP, as shown by the ungrammaticality of (7a). The fact that an RC can have at most one head is shown by the ungrammaticality of (7b).

(7) a. *The woman that Mary made a quilt (for me) . . .
    b. *The boy and the girl who kissed whom . . .

Indexing rules for external head RCs involving deletion have been formulated so as to derive this "one and only one" binding relation between the external head and an empty category–resumptive pronoun (see McCloskey 1979). Such a coindexing rule would coindex an indefinite NP with a higher NP that contains it.[5]

Chomsky (1982) proposes that RC Indexing (predication) applies only at the level of LF. However, agreement phenomena provide evidence that the coindexing in (3) does have purely morphosyntactic justification, in addition to its disambiguating function.

Lakhota has agreement markers for all NP arguments of the verb. There are two sets of agreement markers, one that indicates agreement with subjects and another that indicates agreement with what can loosely be called "objects." (For details, see Williamson 1984.) Third person singular arguments have null person and number agreement, third person plural subjects are marked by an enclitic *pi* that follows the verb, and third person plural objects are marked by the prefix *wicha*.

(8) a. Wįyą   eya   cheya *pi*
       women some cry   Pl
       'Some women cried'

    b. Ed wįyą   eya wą+*wicha*+yąke
       Ed women some   +3Obj+see
       'Ed saw some women'

Agreement is interesting with respect to the RC construction because both the "mother" verb and the embedded S_{rel} show agreement with the internal head. This is illustrated in (9).

(9) a. [[Wįyą   eya   owįža ki   kaǧa *pi*] ki] hena cheya *pi*
        women some quilt the make Pl the those cry   Pl
        'The women who made the quilt cried'

    b. Ed [[wįyą   eya   owįža ki   kaǧa *pi*] ki] hena wą*wicha*yąke
       Ed   women some quilt the make Pl the those 3Obj+see
       'Ed saw the women who made the quilt'

These facts can be straightforwardly accounted for if the features of number and person are inherited by the mother NP from its coindexed head. Assuming that agreement is a Phonetic Form (PF) rule sensitive to S-Structure but blind to LF representations (which is the present Government-Binding Theory conception of these components), then these coindexing relations must be present at the level of S-Structure.[6]

Further justification for a rule of RC Indexing comes from the fact that the RC construction in Lakhota allows stacked RCs. Stacked RCs are in fact very common in Lakhota since adjective modifiers are quite limited. Stacking is achieved by the expansion of the internal head NP as an RC itself. This implies that RC Indexing (and its concomitant, Head Raising, in LF; see section 7.2) applies iteratively, in a bottom-to-top fashion. Some examples are given in (10). They will conform to the general schema given in (11).

(10) a. [[[wowapi wą]$_i$ Deloria owa cha]$_i$ blawa cha]$_i$ . . .
          book   a   Deloria write Ind   I-read Ind
          'a book that Deloria wrote that I have read . . .'

   b. [[[Ogle eya]$_i$ šapšapa cha]$_i$ agli   pi wachį ki]$_i$ lena e
          shirt some dirty   Ind take-home Pl I-want the these be
          'These are the shirts that are dirty that I want them to take
          home'

(11)   NP$_i$

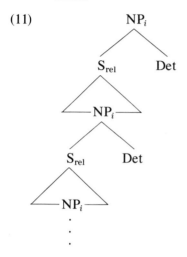

Again, in these examples the definiteness of the entire NP is determined
by the highest (and rightmost) mother NP determiner: *cha* in (10a) and
ki in (10b). Furthermore, the intermediate NP must be indefinite. If not,
the examples are ungrammatical, as (12a–b) illustrate. This is exactly
as expected, if recursion is mediated through the internal head. Thus,
the rule of RC Indexing must be allowed to apply iteratively.

(12) a. *[[[wowapi wą]$_i$ Deloria owa ki]$_i$ blawa cha]$_i$ . . .
           book   a   Deloria write the I-read Ind

    b. *[[[Ogle eya]$_i$ šapšapa ki]$_i$ agli   pi wachį ki]$_i$ lena e
           shirt some dirty   the take-home Pl I-want the these be

   Both the obligatory nature of RC Indexing and its iterative application distinguish it from other types of indexing. Later I will demonstrate that internal heads are different from ordinary quantifiers with
respect to scope interactions as well.

7.1.4 The Range of Indefinite Internal Heads

In this section I will briefly illustrate the range of NPs that may serve in Lakhota as internal heads and show that the notion of "indefinite" that characterizes the Lakhota RC construction corresponds to Milsark's (1974) broader class of "cardinality expressions." The significance of this characterization and its role in the analysis will be discussed in section 7.3.

Milsark distinguishes between two classes of expressions on the basis of the existential construction in English. "Cardinality expressions" (allowed in existentials) include the indefinite determiners *a* and *some*, the quantifiers *many* and *few*, and the cardinal numbers. In contrast, "quantified expressions" (ungrammatical in existentials) include the definite determiner *the*, demonstratives, proper names, definite pronouns, and the quantifiers *all, every, most,* and so forth.[7]

In Lakhota exactly these quantified expressions are excluded from the position of internal head: traditionally definite NPs, including NPs with the definite determiners *ki* 'the' and *k'ų* 'the aforementioned', proper names and definite pronouns (whether null or emphatic), and various universal quantifiers, including *iyuha* 'all, every', *iyohila* 'each', and *ota hca* 'most'. Some examples are given in (13).

(13) a. *[[Edwin$_i$ kuže] ki/cha]$_i$ he lel thi
        Edwin sick   the/Ind Dem here live
        (Edwin who is sick lives here)

    b. *[[(Miye)$_i$ makuže] ki/cha]$_i$ wichawota ki ekta mnį kte
        1Emp I-sick   the/Ind feast   the to   I-go Fut
        (The/A I who am sick will go to the feast)

    c. *[[Mila k'u$_i$ mų   he] ki/cha]$_i$ phe   šni
        knife the-P I-use Dur the/Ind sharp Neg
        (The aforementioned knife that I was using isn't sharp)

    d. *Ed [[šųkawakhą ota-hca$_i$ othehika   pi] ki/cha]$_i$ wichayuha
        Ed   horses   most   expensive Pl the/Ind own-them
        (Ed has most horses that are highly priced)

    e. *[[Wichaša iyuha$_i$ t'a pi] ki/cha]$_i$ Lakhota pi
        men   all   die Pl the/Ind Lakhota Pl
        (All men who died were Lakhota)

On the other hand, all of Milsark's cardinality expressions can serve as internal heads. Note that all of the grammatical examples given so far have had either the singular (*wą* 'a') or plural (*eya* 'some') realis indefinite determiner. There are also singular (*wążi*) and plural (*etą*) forms of an irrealis indefinite determiner that may mark internal heads: examples of these are discussed in section 7.2.3. In addition to these indefinite determiners, indefinite pronouns (such as *tuwa* 'someone, who', *taku* 'something, what'), expressions with certain quantifiers (such as *ota* 'many', *conala* 'few', and *tona* 'several, how many'), and cardinal numbers are all possible heads. Some examples are given in (14).

(14) a. [[Wichaša ota$_i$ t'a pi] ki]$_i$ hena Lakhota pi
        men   many die Pl the those Lakhota Pl
        'The many men who died were Lakhota'

    b. [[Leo taku$_i$ eye] ki]$_i$ he   hecetu wala
        Leo something say   the that be-that I-consider
        'I consider what Leo said to be that way'

    c. Ed [[šųkawakhą conala$_i$ othehika   pi] cha]$_i$ wichayuha
        Ed horses   few   expensive Pl Ind   own-them
        'Ed has few horses that are highly priced'

    d. [[Wakhąyeža nųp$_i$ iyotą wachi wophika pi] ki]$_i$ atkuku ki
        children   two best dance be-skillful Pl the father the
        slolwaye
        I-know
        'I know the father of the two children who know how to
        dance best'

A complete discussion of the range of RCs in Lakhota is beyond the scope of this chapter. But the correlation between cardinality expressions and internal heads established here is important in at least two respects. First, it should be clear that this restriction is not just some morphological quirk of Lakhota, a language with a particularly rich determiner system, but that it holds for a wide range of NP expressions in addition to determiners. This suggests that even for languages lacking definite and indefinite determiners, an indefiniteness restriction can be demonstrated. This restriction is expected to play a fundamental role in the proper analysis of internal head RCs. Second, this class of indefinites characterizes three distinct constructions: existentials (documented in many languages), internal head RCs, and the well-known "donkey-anaphora" sentences (see Heim 1982; also see Cormack and Kempson 1984 for an extension of Heim's analysis to this broader class of cardinality expressions). The explanation is thus expected to follow from some general property of indefinites, a property that can account for their role in these different constructions.

7.2 Internal Heads and Scope Phenomena

In spite of their unusual constituent structure, RCs in Lakhota display evidence typical of the more familiar RCs: in particular, there are various scope interactions that argue for an unbounded dependency between the internal head and the NP that contains it. In this respect, RCs parallel the question and cleft constructions in Lakhota, which also exhibit a binding relation across an unbounded context. Not surprisingly, the focused element in these constructions is also internal, that is, 'in situ' (see Williamson 1984 for discussion).

The agreement phenomenon used in section 7.1.3 to argue for coindexing at S-Structure can also be used to show that this obligatory relation holds across contexts of unbounded length (agreement is italicized; notice that in (15b) the agreement marking is phonetically null).

(15) a. [[Edwin [[[[wįyą   eya]$_i$ owįža ki kaǧa *pi*] ki]   ilukcha]
        Edwin   women some quilt   the make Pl Comp you-think
        keye] ki]$_i$ hena wą*wicha*blake
        say   the those I-see-them
        'I saw the women that Edwin said that you thought made the quilt'

    b. Wichota   wowapi wą Ø-yawa pi cha ob   wo?ųglaka pi
        many-people paper   a   read   Pl Ind with we-speak Pl
        ki he L.A. *Times* Ø-e
        the that L.A. *Times* be
        'The newspaper that we talk to many people who read (it) is the L.A. *Times*'

Similar constructions in other languages that involve movement rules over a seemingly unbounded context have provided evidence for Subjacency (Chomsky 1977; Rizzi 1983). Yet Lakhota RCs and questions freely violate Subjacency ((15b) illustrates this). One might wish to attribute this to the fact that no movement rule is involved, only indexing. However, there are more subtle interactions involving relative scope that argue that the head itself must have scope over the S$_{rel}$. These data are directly accounted for by a movement rule at LF. If this is the case, then the lack of Subjacency effects cannot be attributed to the lack of movement rules. Rather, this suggests that Subjacency does not hold at LF, a position I argue for in detail in Williamson 1984, based on questions in Lakhota. In the section that follows we will explore data that argue for a "head-movement" rule.

7.2.1 Indefinites, Negation, and Relative Clauses
A Lakhota indefinite NP in the scope of negation has a negative suffix -*ni* suffixed to its rightmost element (either a pronominal head or a determiner). In (16) I give a partial list of these plain and negated forms.

(16) tuwa 'someone', tuweni 'no one'; taku 'something', takuni 'nothing'; tohą 'sometime', tohąni 'never'; wą, wąži 'a', wąžini 'not a/any'; eya, etą 'some', etąni 'not some/any'

Normally these negative indefinite NPs must be c-commanded by the negative *šni* in the same clause. (I will not formalize this condition here, but note that my use of the term *scope* is not to be equated simply with *c-command*. Government is not involved, since negative indefinites may be objects of postpositions and possessors.) Compare (17a) and (18a), where the negative indefinites are in the same clause, with (17c) and (18c), where they are not. Note that these negative indefinite pronouns are ungrammatical in nonnegated contexts (compare the (b)-examples). Furthermore, simple indefinites in negated sentences have wide scope over the negation. These sentences are judged quite strange and require considerable context to be appropriate (compare the (d)-examples).

(17) a.   Tuweni u   pi šni
          no one come Pl Neg
          'No one came'

     b.   *Tuweni u   pi
          no one come Pl
          (No one came)

     c.   *[[Tuweni u   pi] ki]   imųge šni
          no one come Pl Comp I-ask Neg
          (I didn't ask if anyone came)

     d.   #Tuwa   u   pi šni
          someone come Pl Neg
          (Some people didn't come)

(18) a. Šųka wą́žini ophewathų šni
         dog not-a I-buy   Neg
         'I didn't buy a dog'

   b. *Šųka wą́žini ophewathų
         dog not-a I-buy
         (I didn't buy a dog)

   c. *[[Šųka wą́žini ophethų]] wakųze   šni
         dog not-a buy   I-pretend Neg
         (I didn't pretend to buy a dog)

   d. #Šųka wą ophewathų šni
         dog a I-buy   Neg
         (I didn't buy a certain dog)

How do these scope facts interact with RCs? When clauses containing these negative indefinite NPs are embedded into an RC structure, they are ungrammatical. In (19), (17a) and (18a) have been embedded into an RC.

(19) a. *[[Tuweni u   pi šni] ki/cha] hena iyokipi pi
           no one come Pl Neg Dets   those happy Pl
         (*Those such that not any came are happy)

   b. *[[Šųka wą́žini ophewathų šni] ki/cha] he   sape
         dog not-a I-buy   Neg Dets   that black
         (*The dog such that I didn't buy any is black)

Instead, the internal head must be a plain indefinite.

(20) a. [[Tuwa   (eya) u   pi šni] ki] hena iyokipi pi
           someone some come Pl Neg the those happy Pl
         'Those who didn't come are happy'

   b. [[Šųka wą ophewathų šni] ki] he   sape
         dog a I-buy   Neg the that black
         'The dog that I didn't buy is black'

The pattern of grammaticality in (19) and (20) is the reverse of what is expected of the embedded clause in isolation. In isolation, (17a) and (18a) are grammatical. But as relative clauses in (19), they are not. In isolation, (17d) and (18d) are at best highly marked. Yet when they are embedded S_{rel}'s in (20), the wide scope of the indefinite is perfectly grammatical.

In other words, negative indefinite pronouns under the scope of S_{rel} negation cannot be interpreted as heads. Rather, the internal head must have wide scope, that is, scope over the S_{rel} negation, which forces the use of the plain nonnegative indefinite. In fact, Lakhota is just like languages with external heads in this respect: in these languages the external head (and the relative pronoun) always have wide scope at S-Structure.

7.2.2 The Structure of Relative Clauses at LF
How is this distribution of grammaticality in Lakhota between indefinites and negation in simple clauses and their distribution in RCs to be explained? I propose that RCs in Lakhota undergo obligatory "head" movement (or "Head Raising") at LF, with the result that the head is Chomsky-adjoined to the S_{rel}. This rule must operate over an essential variable in the sense of Ross (1967). (Since Subjacency does not hold, we are not forced to claim that it is successive cyclic.) The LF structures of the ungrammatical (19b) and the grammatical (20b) are given in (19b′) and (20b′), respectively.

(19b′) *

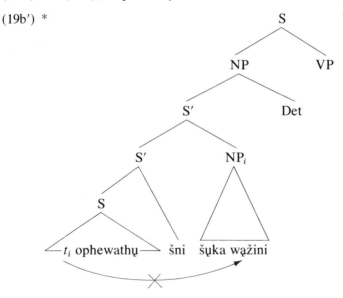

(20b′)

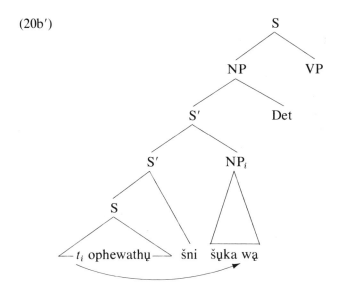

In (19b′), as a result of the attempt to raise the "head" in order to derive the RC, the negative indefinite is no longer c-commanded by a negative and is ruled out. Thus, it is now clear why indefinites under the scope of negation cannot be heads. These indefinites must be c-commanded by negatives at LF, a condition that would be violated if they were to undergo Head Raising.

Consider now (20b′), where again the internal head has been raised. Here the indefinite NP has wide scope over the relative clause negation, as indeed it should. Hence, the plain indefinites are perfectly grammatical in negated S_{rel} constructions.

It is possible, however, to have negative indefinite heads.

(21) [[Šųka wąžini ophewathų] cha] sape šni
       dog   not-a I-buy   Ind black Neg
     'No dog that I bought is black'

Here, *matrix* negation (or rather, "mother" clause negation) triggers the negation suffix -*ni* on the internal head. This, too, is expected, given the rule of Head Raising. Following Head Raising, the negative indefinite NP is within the scope of the negation.

7.2.3 Indefinites, Intensional Contexts, and Relative Clauses
Further evidence can be presented for this (narrow-scope) dependency between the head and elements in the clause containing the mother NP

and, conversely, the obligatory wide scope of the head over elements in the S_{rel}. As noted earlier, Lakhota has indefinite "realis" and "irrealis" determiners. Just as the negative indefinites must be in the scope of negation, so irrealis indefinites are only possible in the scope of certain lexically determined "irrealis" markers. Their properties in RCs provide a second argument of the same type as negative indefinites.

The contrast between realis and irrealis indefinites reflects most closely the distinction made in philosophy between extensional and intensional "referents": irrealis indefinites appear in the scope of intensional verbs (22a), imperatives (22b), and the irrealis mood marker *kte* (22c). In these examples the speaker has no particular apple, sticks, or book in mind (and, indeed, these objects may not even exist).

(22) a. Thaspą wąži wachį
       apple   a-Ir I-want
       'I want an apple'

   b. Chą etą   aku   we!
      sticks some-Ir bring-back Imp
      'Bring back some sticks!'

   c. [Wowapi wąži lawa   kte] iyececa
      book   a-Ir you-read Ir   be-proper
      'It is proper that you read a book/You should read a book'

In contrast, if the realis determiners had been used in (22), the speaker would have some particular apple, sticks, or book in mind.

Like the negative indefinites, irrealis indefinites may be internal heads if they are licensed by appropriate elements in the clause containing the mother NP.

(23) a. [[Thaspą wąži tąyą yužaža pi] cha] wachį
       apple   a-Ir well wash Pl Ind I-want
       'I want an apple that is well washed'

   b. [[Chą etą   spaye šni] cha] aku   we!
      sticks some-Ir wet   Neg Ind bring-back Imp
      'Bring back some sticks that aren't wet!'

   c. [[Wowapi wąži Deloria Jr. owa] cha] lawa   kte] iyececa
      book   a-Ir Deloria Jr. write Ind you-read Ir   be-proper
      'It is proper that you read a book that Deloria Jr. wrote'

(Note that in (23b) the irrealis head has scope over S_{rel} negation.)
Again, the instances of S_{rel} in these examples would all be ungrammatical in isolation. As simple realis declaratives, they do not contain any irrealis element that would sanction the irrealis determiner.

In order to capture the structural conditions concerning the relative scope of indefinites in simple clauses and as heads of RCs, we are forced to posit a derived level of LF where relative scope relations are represented. With the additional assumption that this level does not differ significantly among languages, we can further capture the strong parallels between languages such as English and Lakhota at this level, in spite of their obvious differences at S-Structure.[8]

7.3 The Interpretation of Internal Head Relative Clauses
7.3.1 The Minimalist Position
The constituent structure that I have been assuming and its derived LF structure represent a "minimalist" position. I have posited no empty nodes or nonbranching nodes. These structures are schematized in (24).

(24) a. S-Structure

b. LF

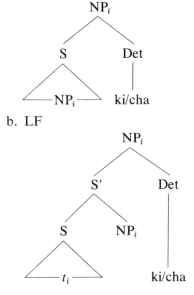

There is an obvious difference between these minimalist structures and the more familiar RC structures with external heads: the lack of an external head in (24) means that the coindexing holds between an NP and a higher NP that contains it. The problem that these structures present for the current rules of interpretation is clear: how can one speak of "predication" when there is no external head of which an open sentence may be predicated? Or, in terms more familiar in logic, how can the interpretation of S' in (24), which denotes a truth-value, be part of the interpretation of an NP?

Many previous studies on internal head RCs have assumed that the concept of "internal head" is incoherent and that rules of RC interpretation can only apply to distinct, coindexed NPs. In this spirit, more abstract structures such as (25a) and (25b) have been proposed.

(25) a.   NP   b.   NP

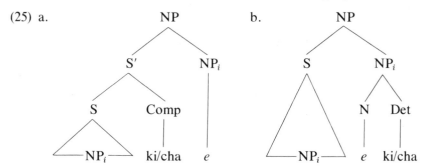

It is my opinion that there are no purely syntactic arguments that would help to decide among these alternatives.[9] Even the syntax of external head RCs (that is, Nom–S, NP–S, and even head raising analyses) has never been resolved, and rules of semantic interpretation have been formulated for both Nom–S and NP–S structures (Cooper 1975). Of course, given that the rules of interpretation for RCs are based on specific LF representations (via S-Structure representations), if it were impossible in principle to formulate a rule of RC interpretation on (24), we would be forced to reject the minimalist position.

For example, the minimalist position could be ruled out in principle if it were the case that the coindexing relation that characterizes the RC construction was interpreted as discourse *coreference*. Given that co-reference is a relation holding between two distinct expressions (that is, one cannot include the other), the minimalist structures in (24) would have to be rejected in favor of those in (25). This interpretation has never been seriously proposed for external head RCs, and it seems a priori quite unlikely that internal head RCs should involve a very different type of coindexing. In fact, there are insurmountable problems with such a literal interpretation of coindexing, but I will not go into the details here (see note 9). I will assume that the RC must be interpreted as the intersection of the set of things denoted by the head noun and the set of things denoted by the S_{rel}.

It may be possible to force the abstract structures in (25) in such a way that an appropriate interpretation is achieved. But positing empty nodes simply begs the issue that RCs in Lakhota raise: What is the proper interpretation of internal head RCs, and why must the head be indefinite? In the rest of the chapter, I will attempt to answer these questions, assuming that the minimalist constituent structure is correct. I will show that the indefiniteness restriction follows from the interaction between the interpretation of relative clauses and the characterization of indefinites.

7.3.2 The Indefiniteness Restriction

One might suppose that the indefiniteness restriction can be derived from the fact that the internal head raises in LF. One would thus be restating the problem as the question, Why is it that only indefinites raise in this construction?

First, let us rule out two possible approaches. The indefiniteness restriction cannot be attributed to some inherent (that is, lexical) property requiring "wide scope" of the indefinite NP. Although internal heads always have wide scope over the S_{rel}, they may have narrow scope with respect to mother clause elements. Examples (21) and (23) are of this type. Furthermore, one cannot attribute this restriction to the traditional distinction between quantifiers, on the one hand, and proper nouns and definite NPs, on the other. Universal quantifiers, which must also be allowed to raise to show relative scope distinctions, are excluded from this construction.

Let us approach the indefiniteness restriction from the point of view of the interpretation of RCs. Why does the semantic head correspond to an indefinite NP?

The basic intuition that I think will be behind any account of this restriction is that both simple declaratives containing an indefinite and RCs indicate the intersection of two sets. For example, *I bought a dog* is interpreted as shown in (26), whereas *dog that I bought* is simply interpreted as shown in (27).

(26) $\exists x \, (\text{Dog}(x) \, \& \, \text{Buy}(\text{I},x))$

(27) $(\text{Dog}(x) \, \& \, \text{Buy}(\text{I},x))$

The set denoted by the head in (27) corresponds to the set denoted by the indefinite in (26). Of course, a declarative is a proposition with a bound variable, whereas an RC is a propositional function with a free variable. This difference in interpretation between a sentence and an RC is not trivial. From this perspective, it will be impossible to capture the similarities. (And looking at languages with external head RCs, it would seem an accidental fact.) The LF of the RCs in (24) makes the nature of the problem clear: the mother NP expands as an S. The interpretation of the clause will be a proposition, denoting a truth-value. Assuming that rules of semantic interpretation are compositional, there is neither any way that a truth-value can combine with the denotation of a determiner to yield an NP denotation nor any way that the propositional function could be "reduced" to the propositional function that is needed.

These facts suggest that we reconsider the traditional view of indefinites as existential quantifiers. If indefinites did not always have quantificational force, the interpretation of declaratives and relative clauses could be the same.

Precisely this view of indefinites has been developed and defended by Heim (1982). Her arguments are based on completely independent grounds: the well-known problems that indefinites in donkey-sentences and conditionals present for anaphora. I will assume some familiarity with her analysis here. Relevant to the discussion is her claim that indefinite NPs are "quantifier-free" and in fact consist of the predicate and an essential free variable. For Heim, then, *I bought a dog* has the interpretation of (27), not (26). The quantifier force of indefinites in simple declaratives is determined by a rule of Existential Closure, applying at the level of texts, or within the scope of various operators.

Let us suppose that Heim's treatment of indefinite NPs is correct. Then the interpretation of the relative clause in Lakhota is straightforward: the S_{rel} is given the interpretation of a propositional function (as, indeed, all simple clauses have). At the level of the mother NP the RC is a complex predicate, subject to a repeated "predicate-free variable" interpretation if the mother determiner is not a quantifier, and open to Existential Closure should the appropriate operators be present in the mother clause.

Why are only indefinites possible heads in Lakhota? Universal quantifiers are excluded as heads because semantically such a quantifier is interpreted as a restrictive term with the conditional connective; for example, *I bought every dog* is interpreted as $\forall x(\text{Dog}(x) \rightarrow \text{Buy}(I,x))$.

No RC interpretation is possible. Why are definite NPs not possible heads? In Heim's analysis definites, like indefinites, are quantifier-free, consisting of a predicate and an essential free variable. The difference between the two is based on the given-new distinction. A definite is familiar (known) and presupposes the content of its predicate. I suggest that this property is at variance with the meaning of restrictive RCs, for if the head is already familiar to the hearer, further specification by the RC is, at best, unnecessary.

This discussion is only the barest outline of how the semantic interpretation should proceed, but the program should be clear. If this analysis can be maintained, and I think that something along these lines should be, it raises the broader issue of the relationship between LF and its model-theoretic interpretation. The LF structure of internal head RCs in Lakhota is different from the "received view" of the LF structure of external head RCs. Though it has often been claimed in the literature of Montague Grammar that different constructions within a single language may have the same semantic interpretation, it is not widely accepted that different languages may have different constructions for a given semantic interpretation. These facts should make us more cautious in our desire for a single analysis in Universal Grammar.

7.4 Conclusion

I conclude by summarizing the results of this investigation.

First, I have argued that RCs in Lakhota involve a rule of Head Raising at LF. This analysis is forced upon us by the special obligatory wide-scope properties that the internal head has vis-à-vis operators such as negation and irrealis mood in the S_{rel} and finds independent support in the narrow-scope properties of some heads vis-à-vis mother clause operators. The rule of Head Raising provides a unified analysis of scope phenomena in both simple clauses and RCs. Head Raising, however, does not provide any explanation for the indefiniteness effect. (This point is also made by Chung in chapter 8.)

Second, I have argued that the indefiniteness effect follows from the interpretation of RCs and Heim's analysis of indefinites. Though my discussion has been limited to Lakhota, I feel that all languages with internal head RCs will have this restriction. Although I have no account for the existence of the typological division, I would like to speculate on why such languages have the restriction. First, I have argued that RCs have *no* empty external heads or any other extra invisible structure. RCs are produced by the same phrase structure rules used for simple clauses. As a result, we expect them to be interpreted by the same rule that interprets clauses. And only clauses with indefinites can have the same interpretation as RCs. I suggest that if a language does not resort to a special phrase structure rule for RCs, then it must "make do" with the rules of interpretation in its inventory.

Third, I have demonstrated that the class of indefinite NPs characterized by this construction corresponds to Milsark's class of "cardinality expressions." This is now the third construction in Universal Grammar where this notion is relevant. The proper treatment of indefinites must explain why these different constructions have this same restriction. To the extent that the analysis presented here succeeds, it provides further support for Heim's analysis of indefinites as being quantifier-free.

Notes

I would like to thank the Lakhota speakers for their time, interest, and intuitions, especially Shirley Apple Murphy and Charlotte Standing Buffalo Ortiz. I would also like to thank the participants at the Fifth Groningen Round Table for their comments and encouragement when this chapter was originally presented as a paper at that conference, and Peter Cole, Robbie Ishihara, and Eduardo Raposo for their comments on an earlier draft.

1. There are other types of relative clauses as well. See Andrews 1975.

2. These pronouns are not special to the RC construction (they often follow simple NPs as well), nor are they obligatory. Nonreferring RCs and NPs are not followed by demonstrative pronouns (universally quantified expressions, irrealis indefinites, and so forth). These demonstrative pronouns are ungrammatical in intermediate levels of stacked RCs. For ease of exposition, they have been left untranslated.

3. Some speakers prefer the head in S-initial position.

4. I deliberately refrain from using the term *headless*, which has been used in two distinct senses. If *headless* is used to indicate a particular *syntactic* configuration where there is no external head, then both Lakhota RCs and some analyses of English free relatives can be said to be "headless." But if *headless* is meant to indicate a relative head that lacks a lexical common noun specifying the semantic class (free relatives), then Lakhota can also be said to be "headless," for Lakhota certainly has free relatives. Free relatives in Lakhota are simply those RCs whose internal heads are indefinite pronouns. Compare the RCs in (4) to (i).

(i) [$_{NP_i}$[$_S$ Mary [taku]$_i$ kağe] ki] ophewathų
       Mary something make the I-buy
    'I bought what Mary made'

This terminology becomes even more confusing in the context of Lakhota, since all free relatives optionally drop the indefinite pronoun. Thus, (i) has (ii) as an alternative.

(ii) [$_{NP_i}$[$_S$ Mary [e]$_i$ kaǧe] ki] ophewathu
         Mary   make the I-buy
     'I bought what Mary made'

5. Assuming random assignment of referential indices that are subject to filters excluding double assignment of indices, we may formulate the rule as follows.

(i) In a configuration of the form

where α = NP, β = S, and γ = Det, find a node label $\begin{matrix} NP \\ [+indef] \end{matrix}$ that is dominated by β and copy the numeral to the right of that node label to the right of α.

If an RC fails to share an index of an NP that it contains (for lack of any appropriate NPs or just as a result of failure to apply this rule), the rule of RC interpretation cannot apply and the phrase has no interpretation. Coindexing more than one head with the mother NP is excluded by Heim's (1982) Novelty Condition, which prevents two indefinite NPs from receiving the same index.

6. Van Riemsdijk and Williams (1981) propose a linear model, where various indexing rules deriving scope relations are formulated on NP-Structure, ultimately deriving S-Structure. This model is compatible with the facts of agreement just presented.

7. This is a simplification. I have ignored certain ambiguities and qualifications argued for by Milsark. For further discussion, see Milsark 1974 and Löbner 1984.

8. This level has been justified as the locus for various restrictions (for instance, certain versions of the Empty Category Principle) or the lack of them (for instance, the lack of Subjacency effects); see Huang 1982, Williamson 1984. But this view of LF conflicts with previous claims made in work based on simple quantifiers (May 1977) and is further complicated by evidence for some additional level of reconstruction to capture scope relations between quantifiers and constituent questions. As these interactions have only been investigated in a very preliminary way in Lakhota, I will not go into these issues, leaving the model of LF presented here open to further refinements.

9. Cole (1983) offers the most recent analysis that raises the issue of the relationship between syntax and the interpretation of RCs. Cole proposes that internal head RCs have the syntactic structure of (25a). His argument can be summarized as follows. He observes that the only languages that are attested to have internal head RCs are SOV languages. He proposes to derive this fact from two assumptions: (1) that the original "precedes and commands" formu-

lation of Principle C of the binding theory constrains coreference and (2) that RC indexing between the internal head (the "antecedent") and the external null head pronominal is another case of coreference. Since SOV languages typically have external heads to the right of the modifying S_{rel}, a null pronominal will never precede its antecedent and the structure is permitted.

One may wish to dispute the first assumption (although in Williamson 1984 I argue that Lakhota, unlike configurational languages, does require a "precedes" condition for pronominal coreference), and the second assumption cannot be maintained at all. The coindexing relation in RCs cannot be interpreted as discourse coreference. First, (25a) predicts that all RCs are definite, on the reasonable assumption that the definiteness of the external head determines the definiteness of the entire RC and that null pronominals are always definite. (25b), which avoids this particular problem, also predicts that all RCs are definite, however, since coreference between two indefinites is impossible. (This is formulated as the Novelty Condition in Heim 1982.) A more general objection can be made against a coreference approach: it has no explanation for the indefiniteness restriction on internal heads and indeed remains an obstacle for a literal coreference view, since coreference is a relation holding between two definite NPs.

Peter Cole has suggested (personal communication) that the coindexing in RCs may be viewed as coreference at S-Structure (hence, subject to the binding theory) but may be interpreted differently at LF. This modification of the theory seems quite unconstrained and could possibly have far-reaching implications.

Chapter 8

The Syntax of Chamorro Existential Sentences

Sandra Chung

> It is important to bear in mind that the study of one language may provide crucial evidence concerning the structure of some other language, if we continue to accept the plausible assumption that the capacity to acquire language, the subject matter of [Universal Grammar], is common across the species.
>
> Noam Chomsky, *Knowledge of Language: Its Nature, Origin, and Use*

Linguists who work on the syntax of non-Indo-European languages tend to view it as a kind of testing ground for syntactic theory. On this view, a theory succeeds to the extent that it can account for, say, western European languages as well as languages radically different from them on the surface. Though I certainly subscribe to this view, I think it has tended to have an odd consequence in practice: the study of exotic languages has most often contributed to the theory by *expanding* the class of analyses that the theory makes available. So, if the best analysis of some Dyirbal construction diverges sharply from the best analysis for Dutch, one's usual reaction is to try to parameterize the theory so that both possibilities are allowed.

A different, but equally valuable, exercise is to use exotic language facts to help illuminate a familiar phenomenon whose best analysis remains unclear. In the limiting case these facts may help to *restrict* the class of analyses provided by the theory. For instance, suppose the theory is vague about the analysis of some phenomenon, in part because the English facts could be dealt with in several ways. Then it makes sense to look to less familiar languages to see what evidence they provide. If the facts there point uniquely to one analysis, one might want to adjust the theory so that other possibilities are not allowed, with the result that the theory then dictates what the right analysis of English should be.

With this in mind, I am going to analyze a construction in Chamorro that is superficially similar to existential constructions in some western European languages. Existential sentences—and English *there*-insertion sentences in particular—have been the focus of some interest within the Extended Standard Theory (EST). Syntactically, debate has centered around the internal structure of these sentences, with various linguists advocating a rightward movement analysis (Milsark 1974), a small clause analysis (Stowell, 1981; Safir 1982; Reuland 1983), and the NP analysis, in which all the material to the right of the verb forms an NP (Jenkins 1972; Williams 1984). Semantically, various attempts have been made to derive the definiteness effect (DE) in existential sentences from more general principles.

My aims here are two. First, I will demonstrate that the facts of Chamorro existentials support the NP analysis as opposed to the small clause and rightward movement analyses (sections 8.2, 8.3). The strength of the Chamorro evidence indicates that the NP analysis may be a better candidate for the best analysis of existentials than some have supposed. Second, I will describe some characteristics of the relative clause in an existential sentence that appear to be related to the DE (section 8.4). The proper treatment of these characteristics may well complicate any attempt to make the DE fall out from general semantic principles, as I will try to suggest.

8.1 Background

Chamorro is a verb-initial language whose basic word order is VSO. It is also a pro-drop language that allows subjects, possessors, and NPs with several other grammatical functions to be null (Chung 1982b, 1984). Consider the examples in (1).[1]

(1) a. Mattu   i   taotao gi   petta
       Infl(s)-arrive the person Loc door
       'The man appeared in the doorway'

   b. Ha-sodda' si   Juan i   yommuk na patgun gi   me'nan
       Infl(3s)-find Unm Juan the fat   L child Loc front-L
       iya siha
       their-place
       'Juan found the fat child in front of his (lit. their) house'

   c. Ma-ñáchalik
       Infl(p)-laugh+Impf
       '(They) are laughing'

Despite the fact that its word order suggests a flat constituent structure, Chamorro acts for the purposes of many subtheories of Government-Binding (GB) Theory as though it were a fully configurational language—a patterning that I have discussed elsewhere. Here I simply assume that Chamorro sentences have associated with them an S-Structure representation that contains a VP (Chung 1983a,b).

It will be useful later to have catalogued the morphosyntactic differences between definite and indefinite NPs in this language. First, definite NPs contain the definite article *i,* whereas indefinite NPs lack an article.

(2) a. i ga'lagu
       the dog
       'the dog'

    b. ga'lagu
       dog
       'a dog'

Second, definite NPs are inflected for morphological case, whereas indefinite NPs are not. Thus, *kareta* 'car' is an oblique argument in both of the examples in (3), but it is accompanied by the oblique case marker only when it is definite. The case marker fuses with the definite article to produce the *ni* in (3a).

(3) a. Malägu'   yu' ni   kareta
       Infl(s)-want I   Obl car
       'I want (lit. am desirous of) the car'

    b. Malägu'   yu' kareta
       Infl(s)-want I   car
       'I want (lit. am desirous of) a car'

Finally, although there are important exceptions to this, indefinite NPs normally cannot serve as S-Structure subjects or direct objects.[2]

(4) a. *Mattu   taotao gi   petta
        Infl(s)-arrive person Loc door
        (A man appeared in the doorway)

    b. *Ha-sodda' si   Juan yommuk na patgun gi   me'nan
        Infl(3s)-find Unm Juan fat   L child   Loc front-L
        iya siha
        their-place
        (Juan found a fat child in front of his (lit. their) house)

Focusing on indefinites for the moment, we see that they are "bare" —
caseless and articleless—NPs with a restricted syntactic distribution.[3]

8.2 Existential Sentences

The existential construction in Chamorro is illustrated in (5).

(5) a. Guäha   buteya gi hälum kahun áis
Infl(s)-exist bottle inside   box   ice
'There's a bottle in the icebox'

     b. Hähassu   ha'   na   taya'   gäs
remember+Impf Emp Comp Infl(s)-not+exist gas
'Remember that there's no gas'

     c. Guäha   taotao mattu   gi   petta
Infl(s)-exist person Infl(s)-arrive Loc door
'There was a man (who) appeared in the doorway'

     d. Taya'   lahi t-um-aitai   i   lepblu
Infl(s)-not+exist boy Infl(*wh*)-read the book
'There was no boy (who) read the book'

This construction minimally consists of *guäha* 'exist' or *taya'* 'not
exist', followed by an NP. Semantically, it asserts the nonemptiness or
emptiness of the set defined by the NP, as can be seen most obviously
in (5a–b).

This section establishes three ways in which Chamorro existentials
resemble existential sentences in more familiar languages.

8.2.1 *Guäha* and *Taya'* Are Verbal Predicates

The meanings of *guäha* and *taya'* make it conceivable that these lexical
items might be NP-internal quantifiers parallel to *pälu* 'some', *käda*
'each', and the like. However, the NP in an existential sentence may
undergo *Wh*-Movement, and when it does *guäha* or *taya'* is left behind.

(6) Hafa guäha   gi hälum kahun áis?
what? Infl(s)-exist inside   box   ice
'What is there inside the icebox?'

Wh-Movement in Chamorro does not otherwise strand NP-internal
quantifiers, so it appears that *guäha* and *taya'* cannot be constituents of
that category.

(7) *Hayi un-chiku   pälu?
     who? Infl(2s)-kiss some
     (Who did you kiss some (of)?)

That *guäha* and *taya'* are instead verbal predicates is established by their inflectional properties. Predicates in Chamorro are distinguished by their ability to inflect for the imperfective aspect. The inflection is realized as reduplication of the primarily stressed CV.

(8) a. Ma-ñáchalik   i   taotao siha
        Infl(p)-laugh+Impf the person Pl
        'The people are laughing'

    b. P-um-ápatgun
       Infl(s)-child+Impf
       '(She) is becoming a child'

    c. Pälu/*päpalu   ha' siha taotao ma-ñáchalik
       some some+Impf Emp Pl   person Infl(p)-laugh+Impf
       'Some people are (still) laughing'

Like other predicates but unlike, say, the NP-internal quantifiers, *guäha* and *taya'* can inflect for the imperfective.

(9) a. Guäguaha   ha' taotao gi päpa'   lamäsa
        Infl(s)-exist+Impf Emp person underneath table
        'There's still someone underneath the table'

    b. Guäguaha   ha' siha taotao ma-ñáchalik
       Infl(s)-exist+Impf Emp Pl   person Infl(p)-laugh+Impf
       'There are still some people laughing'

Further, predicates of all types agree with their subjects in the realis mood, but only verbs and predicate adjectives exhibit agreement in the irrealis. In the irrealis sentences in (10) the agreement is realized as the third singular prefix *u-*.

(10) a. Pära u-fattu   agupa'
         will Infl(3s)-arrive tomorrow
         '(He) will arrive tomorrow'

     b. Pära u-malangu   si   nana-nmami
        will Infl(3s)-sick Unm mother-our
        'Our mother is going to be sick'

     c. Pära (*u-)agupa'   i   fandanggu
        will   Infl(3s)-tomorrow the wedding
        'The wedding will be tomorrow'

The fact that *guäha* and *taya'* agree with their subjects in the irrealis mood argues that they are either verbal or adjectival—that is, [+V] in the X′ system.

(11) a. Pära u-taya'   néngkanu' gi   tenda
       will Infl(3s)-not+exist food   Loc store
       'There isn't going to be any food in the store'

   b. Pära u-taya'   asuddä'-ta   man-maolik na taotao
      will Infl(3s)-not+exist meet-Infl(1p) Pl-nice   L person
      giya SF
      in   SF
      'There aren't going to be any nice people we meet in SF'
      (= We aren't going to meet any nice people in SF)

Although this much is straightforward, it turns out to be considerably harder to determine whether *guäha* and *taya'* are adjectives or verbs. Verbs and predicate adjectives in Chamorro have virtually the same inflectional properties, and it is not clear that their few differences follow from syntactic category alone. For instance, predicate adjectives inflect for the comparative, whereas verbs do not; *guäha* and *taya'* similarly lack a comparative form. But given that the comparative is restricted to scalar adjectives and existence is not a scalar notion, this inflectional gap is not particularly telling.

I therefore conclude only that *guäha* and *taya'* are [+V] predicates. This conclusion is enough to reveal one parallel between the Chamorro construction and English *there*-insertion: both contain an existential predicate.[4]

8.2.2 The NP Is an Oblique

The question of the grammatical function held by the NP in existential sentences like (5c–d) will be definitively settled in section 8.3. Still, in minimal existential sentences like the embedded clause of (5b), which consist only of *guäha* or *taya'* plus an NP, it would seem undeniable that the NP is an argument of the existential predicate. Limiting ourselves to these minimal sentences, we can broach the question of grammatical function.

Observe first that the NP in (5b) is indefinite; it lacks both an article and a case marker. This indefiniteness suggests that the NP is neither a subject nor a direct object at S-Structure—a conjecture that is supported by the agreement properties of the existential predicate.

Verbal predicates in Chamorro generally agree in person and/or number with their subjects, as shown in (12).

(12) a. Tristi   i   palao'an
       Infl(s)-sad the woman
       'The woman is sad'

   b. Man-tristi i   famalao'an
       Infl(p)-sad the women
       'The women are sad'

But the agreement displayed by *guäha* and *taya'* is always singular, regardless of whether the NP is singular or plural. The NP is thus not the subject of the existential predicate.

(13) a. Guäha   famalao'an man-malangu
       Infl(s)-exist women   Infl(p)-sick
       'There were some women sick'

   b. *Man-guäha famalao'an man-malangu
       Infl(p)-exist women   Infl(p)-sick
       (There were some women sick)

Further, agreement not only registers the features of the subject but also signals whether the verb is transitive or intransitive, that is, whether it has objective Case to assign. Consider the sentences in (14), which have third singular subjects. In (14a) the verb is transitive and agreement is realized as the third singular prefix *ha-*, whereas in (14b–c) the verb is intransitive and agreement has no overt realization.

(14) a. Ha-toktuk   si   Joaquin i   neni
       Infl(3s)-hug Unm Joaquin the baby
       'Joaquin hugged the baby'

   b. Machócho'chu'   si   Rita
       Infl(s)-work+Impf Unm Rita
       'Rita is working'

   c. T-in-ektuk   i   neni as   Joaquin
       Infl(s)-Pass-be+hugged the baby Obl Joaquin
       'The baby was hugged by Joaquin'

The agreement displayed by *guäha* and *taya'* is always that appropriate for intransitives, a fact that argues that the NP is not a direct object either.

(15) a. *Ha-taya'   lahi guini
        Infl(3s)-not+exist boy here
        (There is no boy here)

     b. Taya'   lahi guini
        Infl(s)-not+exist boy here
        'There is no boy here'

The idea that the NP is neither a subject nor a direct object leaves open the possibility that it is some other complement of the predicate. I will tentatively assume that it is an oblique complement, since nothing contradicts that assumption.

We can round out the picture of minimal existential sentences by assuming that their subject position is nonthematic and invariably null— presumably because it is occupied by a null expletive. The S-Structure form of these sentences can, in sum, be represented as shown in (16).

(16)

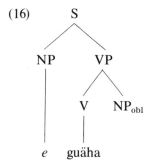

(In the configurational representation employed here, left-to-right order is irrelevant.) Such a structure is reminiscent of proposals that have been made for minimal existential sentences in English, German, Spanish, and other languages (see Reuland 1983 for a survey).

8.2.3 The Definiteness Effect
Given these observations, it should come as no surprise that the Chamorro existential construction displays a DE: the oblique NP cannot be definite, in the extended sense that this term has acquired in the literature on English *there*-insertion.

Not only true indefinites but also NPs quantified by *pälu* 'some', *bula* 'much', numerals, and the like, count as indefinite for the purposes of this restriction (see (5) and the examples in (17)).

(17) a. Guäha   pälu famalao'an man-malangu
     Infl(s)-exist some women   Infl(p)-sick
     'There were some women sick'

    b. Guäha   tres buteya gi hälum kahun áis
     Infl(s)-exist three bottle inside   box   ice
     'There are three bottles in the icebox'

On the other hand, true definites and universally quantified NPs count as definite.

(18) a. *Guäha   i   kätni gi hälum kahun áis
     Infl(s)-exist the meat inside   box   ice
     (There's the meat in the icebox)

    b. *Guäha   todu ha'   man-malangu
     Infl(s)-exist all   Emp Infl(p)-sick
     (There was everyone sick)

The dichotomy extends to S-Structure variables— more precisely, S-Structure gaps bound by an element in a nonargument position. (I will use the term *variable* in this sense throughout.) The S-Structure variables in constituent questions formed with *hafa* 'what?' or *kuantu* 'how many?' count as indefinite.

(19) a. Hafa guäha   gi hälum kahun áis?
     what? Infl(s)-exist inside   box   ice
     'What is there in the icebox?'

    b. . . . ma-tugi'   put   hafa   na klasin relihón
     Infl(s)-Pass-be+written about what? L   sort-L religion
     guäha . . .
     Infl(s)-exist
     '[Nothing] was written about what sort of religion there was
     . . .' (Cooreman 1982:21)

    c. Kuantu   na buteya guäha   gi hälum kahun áis?
     how-many? L bottle Infl(s)-exist inside   box   ice
     'How many bottles are there in the icebox?'

So do the S-Structure variables in amount relatives (Carlson 1977b).

(20) a. Hu-limosnannäihun todu i   guäha   na salape'-hu guätu
        Infl(1s)-donate   all   the Infl(s)-exist L money-my there
        gi Guma' Yu'us
        Loc house God
        'I donated all the money of mine that there was to the
        church'

    b. Ha-chuli'   todu i   halumtanu' ni   guäha . . .
        Infl(3s)-take all   the forest   Comp Infl(s)-exist
        '(They) took all the forest that there was . . .' (Cooreman
        1983:55)

But the S-Structure variables in questions formed with *manu* 'which?'
or *hayi* 'who?' count as definite.

(21) *Hayi guäha   gi   kusina?
      who? Infl(s)-exist Loc kitchen
      (Who is there in the kitchen?)

The same is true of the variables in restrictive relatives.[5]

(22) *Adyu i   litratu ni   guäha   gi   petta-mmu,
      that the picture Comp Infl(s)-exist Loc door-your
      parehu   yan i   guäha   gi   petta-kku
      Infl(s)-same with the Infl(s)-exist Loc door-my
      (The picture that there is on your door is the same as the (one)
      that there is on my door)

    The DE is firm in elicitation contexts, with speakers rejecting defi-
nites in this construction even in the special readings described by Milsark (1974). However, definites are occasionally found in narratives
when the list reading is present and/or the NP contains a demonstrative, such as *edyu* 'that (close to third person)'.

(23) a. Guäha   man-ma-ñúñuli'   néngkanu', gimin, yan
        Infl(s)-exist Infl(p)-AP-bring+Impf food   drink and
        guäha   lokkui' i   ma-ñúñuli'   guätu tinifuk
        Infl(s)-exist also   the Infl(s)-AP-bring+Impf there weaving
        'There were some who brought food, drink, and there were
        also the ones who brought woven stuff' (Cooreman 1983:21)

b. Guäha   guihi edyu i   ilek-ñiha   "Santa Ana" na
Infl(s)-exist there that   the say-Infl(3p) Santa Ana   L
floris
flower
'There was that flower they call "Santa Ana" ' (Cooreman
1983:6)

This concludes the introduction to Chamorro existentials. Although
the discussion so far has stressed their parallels to English *there*-
insertion constructions, in the next sections I explore some less familiar
syntactic territory.

8.3 The Syntax of Complex Existential Sentences

Alongside minimal existential sentences like the embedded clause of
(5b), Chamorro also has what can be called *complex* existentials—sentences in which the material surrounding the indefinite NP contains a
second predicate (which I will refer to as the *lower predicate*). Consider
(5c–d) and (24a–c).[6]

(24) a. Guäha   lahi ma-ma'nána'gui   guini
        Infl(s)-exist man Infl(s)-AP-teach+Impf here
        'There's a man teaching here'

    b. Taya'   guma' kumasón
       Infl(s)-not+exist house Infl(s)-aflame
       'There was no house (that) burned down'

    c. Taya'   impottantin taotao asuddä'-ña   si   Juan
       Infl(s)-not+exist important-L person meet-Infl(3s) Unm Juan
       'There were no important people Juan met'

This section examines the syntax of complex existential sentences,
with a view to showing that they fall squarely under the NP analysis of
such constructions proposed by Jenkins (1972) and Williams (1984).

8.3.1 Preliminaries
The EST literature offers three competing proposals for the syntax of
complex existentials, which can be summarized as follows.
    In the transformational analysis advocated by Milsark (1974) and oth-
ers complex existential sentences are derived from ordinary subject-
predicate structures via a transformation of *There*-Insertion. In English
this transformation involves rightward movement of the subject and

insertion of the expletive *there;* in Chamorro it would, at minimum, have to insert the existential predicate, as shown in (25).

(25) *Transformational Analysis (shown configurationally)*
   [$_S$ NP VP] → [$_S$ e [$_{VP}$ guäha NP VP]]

In contrast, in the small clause analysis advocated by Stowell (1981) and Safir (1982) (see also Stowell 1978) complex existentials are base-generated with the following internal structure: the existential predicate selects as its argument a small clause in which the indefinite NP serves as the subject of the lower predicate, as shown in (26).

(26) *Small Clause Analysis (shown configurationally)*
   [$_S$ e [$_{VP}$ guäha [$_S$ NP VP]]]

Finally, in the NP analysis developed by Jenkins (1972) and Williams (1984) complex existentials are also base-generated, but the argument selected by the existential predicate is an *NP* constituent—a relative clause that takes the indefinite NP as its head. On this view, all the material to the right of the existential predicate forms a single NP, as shown in (27).

(27) *NP Analysis (shown configurationally)*
   [$_S$ e [$_{VP}$ guäha [$_{NP}$ NP$_i$ [$_{S'}$ ... t_i ...]]]]

These three proposals differ from one another in the internal structure that they assign to complex existential sentences, as well as in their answers to the question of which predicate (if any) the indefinite NP is an argument of. Of particular relevance here, however, is the following: the NP analysis is the only proposal to claim that complex existential sentences contain a variable at S-Structure. This variable is produced by the relativization process, which in Chamorro is normally Controlled Pro Deletion (Chung 1982a; but see section 8.4).[7]

(28) *Controlled Pro Deletion*
   [$_{NP}$ NP$_i$ [$_{S'}$ ... [e] ...]] → [$_{NP}$ NP$_i$ [$_{S'}$ ... t_i ...]]

It should be emphasized that the choice between these proposals is not trivial in Chamorro. For one thing, Chamorro seems not to have any small clauses of the classical type (by which I mean small clause complements of *seem, want, consider*), so one cannot evaluate the small clause analysis by comparing complex existentials with small clauses elsewhere in the language. Further, although Chamorro does have relative clauses, there is an imperfect match between these and the constructions in (24): relative clauses with initial heads contain an overt complementizer (*ni* in (29)), whereas the existential sentences in (24) do not.

(29) [i   lähi [ni   ma-ma'nána'gui   guini]]
     the man Comp Infl(s)-AP-teach+Impf here
     'the man who is teaching here'

Nonetheless, I now demonstrate that there is substantial evidence supporting the NP analysis as opposed to the other two.

8.3.2 *Wh*-Agreement

To begin with, it can be shown that when the existential construction contains a lower predicate, it also contains a variable.

Chamorro has a special type of agreement that occurs only in constituent questions, relative clauses, and other so-called *Wh*-Movement constructions (see Chung 1982a). This agreement registers on the predicate the abstract Case of a variable dependent on it, as stated in (30).

(30) Wh-*Agreement*
     A predicate agrees in abstract Case with a variable dependent on it.

The effect of *Wh*-Agreement can be seen most easily by comparing a simplex sentence with the relative clauses that can be formed from it. In (31), for example, the verb *fa'gasi* 'wash' displays normal person-and-number agreement with its subject.

(31) Ha-fa'gasi   si   Antonio i   kareta ni   häpbun
     Infl(3s)-wash Unm Antonio the car   Obl soap
     'Antonio washed the car with the soap'

This same verb assumes different morphological forms in the relative clauses of (32)–(34), depending on the abstract Case borne by the variable in these examples. Thus, in (32) the variable is nominative and the verb exhibits nominative *Wh*-Agreement (the normal subject agreement here is replaced by -*um*-).

(32) [i   lähi [ni   f-um-a'gasi   *t* i   kareta ni   häpbun]]
     the boy Comp Infl(*wh*)-wash   the car   Obl soap
                    [+Nom]
     'the boy who washed the car with soap'

In (33) the variable is objective and the verb exhibits objective *Wh*-Agreement (it is optionally nominalized with *-in-*).

(33) [i   kareta [ni   fina'gase-nña si   Antonio *t* ni   häpbun]]
     the car   Comp wash-Infl(3s) Unm Antonio   Obl soap
                    [+Obj]
     'the car that Antonio washed with soap'

Finally, in (34) the variable is oblique and the verb exhibits oblique *Wh*-Agreement (it is nominalized, but without *-in-*).

(34) [i   häpbun [ni   fa'gase-nña si   Antonio ni   kareta *t*]]
     the soap   Comp wash-Infl(3s) Unm Antonio Obl car
                    [+Obl]
     'the soap that Antonio washed the car with'

The relevant fact is that *Wh*-Agreement is also found in complex existential sentences, where it surfaces on the lower predicate.

(35) a. Taya'   ha'   taotao ch-um-onnik
        Infl(s)-not+exist Emp person Infl(*wh*)-push
                             [+Nom]
        'There was no one (who) pushed (it)'

     b. Taya'   hugeti sinedda'-mami
        Infl(s)-not+exist toy   find-Infl(1p)
                             [+Obj]
        'There weren't any toys we found'

     c. Guäha   man-bihu na ramenta fa'maolik-mami ni
        Infl(s)-exist Pl-old   L tool   fix-Infl(1p)   Obl
                             [+Obl]

        kareta-nmami
        car-our
        'There were some old tools we fixed the car with'

The lower predicate exhibits nominative *Wh*-Agreement in (35a), objective *Wh*-Agreement in (35b), and oblique *Wh*-Agreement in (35c). The pattern of agreement is precisely the same as in the relative clauses of (32)–(34).

Assuming the *Wh*-Agreement rule (30), the appearance of agreement morphology in (35) argues that these existential sentences contain a variable dependent on the lower predicate. *Wh*-Agreement therefore supports the NP analysis, which is the only one of the analyses in section 8.3.1 to posit a variable in this sentence type.

We can push the conclusion further by scrutinizing the particular pattern of agreement in (35). Judging from the facts presented there, the variable bears an abstract Case that signals the grammatical function that we understand *the indefinite NP* to bear to the lower predicate in the interpretation of these sentences. Such an observation would make sense if the variable and the indefinite NP were coindexed. But this, of course, is exactly what the NP analysis predicts.

8.3.3 Animacy Hierarchy

More support for the idea that complex existential sentences contain a variable is provided by the following data.

As I have discussed elsewhere (Chung 1981, 1983b), Chamorro has several S-Structure filters that regulate the combinations of subject and direct object allowed in transitive clauses. One of these filters excludes clauses in which the direct object outranks the subject on an animacy hierarchy.

(36) a. *Surface Filter*
*{V [+Nom] [+Obj]}, if [+Obj] outranks [+Nom] on the animacy hierarchy.

    b. *Animacy Hierarchy*
Animate Pronoun > Animate NP > Inanimate NP

Filter (36) has the consequence that an (overt) pronoun may not be the direct object of a clause unless the subject is a pronoun as well. Thus, both of the examples in (37) have pronominal direct objects. (37a) is grammatical because its subject is a (null) pronoun, but (37b) is ungrammatical because its subject is a full NP.

(37) a. Hu-li'i'   hao [ ] nigap
     Infl(1s)-see you   yesterday
     'I saw you yesterday'

    b. *Ha-li'i'   hao si   Maria nigap
     Infl(3s)-see you Unm Maria yesterday
     (Maria saw you yesterday)

The relevant fact here is that null pronouns also count as pronouns for the purposes of the filter, as has been pointed out by Woolford (1986). This is the reason why (38a), with pronominal subject and direct object, is grammatical, but (38b–c), with a corresponding full NP subject, are not.

(38) a. Ha-kastiga   [ ] [ ]
         Infl(3s)-punish
         'She punished him'

   b. *Ha-kastiga   i   ma'estra [ ]
         Infl(3s)-punish the teacher
         (The teacher punished him) (But grammatical in the mean-
         ing 'He punished the teacher')

   c. *Anai in-telefón   si   Juan, ha-kuentútusi
         when Infl(1p)-telephone Unm Juan Infl(3s)-talk+to+Impf
         i   tian   Maria [ ]
         the aunt-L Maria
         (When we telephoned Juan, Maria's aunt was talking to him)
         (But grammatical in the meaning '. . . he was talking to
         Maria's aunt')

Examples (38b–c) only allow the interpretation in which the full NP is
the direct object and the null pronoun is the subject, an interpretation
consistent with the requirements of the filter.[8]

Crucially, although null pronouns count as pronouns for the purposes
of filter (36), variables evidently do not. Therefore, the *wh*-questions in
(39) are allowed to reach the surface, despite the fact that the direct
object is a variable and the subject is a full NP.

(39) a. Hayi ha-kastiga   i   ma'estra *t*?
         who? Infl(3s)-punish the teacher
         'Who did the teacher punish?'

   b. Hu-kariñu   [i   pätgun [ni   ha-kastiga   i
         Infl(1s)-comfort the child   Comp Infl(3s)-punish the
         tia-hu   *t*]]
         aunt-my
         'I comforted the child who my aunt punished'

This patterning follows naturally from the assumption that variables are
names rather than pronominals (see Chomsky 1981).

Consider now the complex existential sentences in (40), in which the
lower predicate is transitive but exhibits only one overt argument in
surface structure. If we follow the Projection Principle in assuming that
the lower predicate must have another argument associated with it in
the syntax, then we can ask what the character of that null argument is.

If it is pro, then it should count as a pronoun for filter (36), and the interpretation in which it is the direct object of the lower predicate, and the full NP is the subject, should be ruled out. On the other hand, if it is a variable, then an interpretation in which it is the direct object, and the full NP is the subject, should be possible.

In fact, as (40) shows, the null argument may serve as the direct object of the lower predicate.

(40) a. Taya'   ha-kastiga   si   Maria
         Infl(s)-not+exist Infl(3s)-punish Unm Maria
         'There was no one Maria punished'

    b. Guäha   ha-li'i'   si   Juan
         Infl(s)-exist Infl(3s)-see Unm Juan
         'There's someone Juan saw'

The fact that this combination of subject and direct object is allowed provides another argument that complex existential sentences contain a variable.

The conclusion to which these arguments lead is that complex existential sentences contain a variable-binding construction—specifically, a relative clause of the sort posited by the NP analysis. This conclusion is bolstered by three further parallels between relative clauses and complex existentials.

8.3.4 Islandhood

Relative clauses in Chamorro are islands, a fact that I will choose to attribute here to Kayne's (1981) Empty Category Principle (ECP) (see Chung 1983b and, on the inadequacy of a Subjacency account, Chung 1982a:n. 17). In particular, subconstituents of a relative clause cannot be moved outside of it by Wh-Movement.

(41) *Hayi siha na famagu'un un-rispeta   [edyu i   palao'an
       who? Pl   L   children   Infl(2s)-respect that the woman
       [ni   f-um-a'na'gui t]]?
        Comp Infl(wh)-teach
       (Which children do you respect the woman who taught?)

Significantly, complex existential sentences are also islands to Wh-Movement.

(42) a. *Hafa guäha   siha na famagu'un mu-li'i'   *t*?
        what? Infl(s)-exist Pl   L children   Infl(*wh*)-see
        (What were there some children (who) saw?)

   b. *Manu na kahun na   taya'   un-pu'luyi   *t*?
        which? L box   Comp Infl(s)-not+exist Infl(2s)-put+in
        (Which box was there nothing you put into?)

(42) demonstrates that dependents of the lower predicate cannot be moved by *Wh*-Movement to the left of the indefinite NP. (The indefinite NP in (42b) has a null head; see section 8.3.5.) The ungrammaticality of these examples has a natural account if we assume that complex existential sentences contain a relative clause.[9]

Admittedly, the picture becomes cloudier when we turn from *Wh*-Movement to the Topicalization constructions shown in (43). In such constructions a definite NP to the left of S is typically resumed by some sort of gap later.

(43) a. Si   Dolores, ha-lalatdi   siha i   famagu'un
        Unm Dolores Infl(3s)-scold Pl   the children
        'Dolores, (she) scolded the children'

   b. I   che'lu-hu palao'an, esta   sinku añus ni
        the sibling-my female   already five years Comp
        um-äsagua
        Infl(s)-married
        'My sister, it's been five years that (she's) been married'

Now a topic NP outside a relative clause ordinarily cannot be connected to a gap inside, as shown in (44).

(44) *Si   Maria, hu-hässu   [edyu na biahi [änai
        Unm Maria Infl(1s)-remember that L time Comp
        ha-sodda'   i   rilos-su]]
        Infl(3s)-find the watch-my
        (Maria, I remember that time when (she) found my watch)

A topic in an existential sentence *can*, however, be connected to a gap dependent on the lower predicate.

(45) a. Si   Larry, guäha   ha-na'hokka   ni   basula
        Unm Larry Infl(s)-exist Infl(3s)-make+take+out Obl trash
        'Larry, there's someone (he) made take the trash out'

b. Si   Dolores, esta   pa'gu taya'
Unm Dolores already now   Infl(s)-not+exist
ha-sangángani   ni minagahit
Infl(3s)-tell+Impf Obl truth
'Dolores, until now there's no one (she) has told the truth to'

Though I have nothing to say about the ungrammaticality of (44) (but see Kuno 1976), it is possible to motivate the apparent nonislandhood of complex existentials in (45) by appealing to the character of Topicalization. The actual requirement of this construction is not that the topic be resumed by a gap, but rather that some relation of pragmatic relevance hold between the topic and the S following it. Consider, for instance, (46).

(46) I   siminteyu, guäha   dos na lugát, gi   tiningo'-hu
the cemetery Infl(s)-exist two L place Loc knowledge-my
'(As for) the cemetery, there are two places (where people are buried), to my knowledge' (Cooreman 1983:8)

Examples like this one suggest that Topicalization differs from *Wh*-Movement in that it does not involve variable binding at S-Structure. The sentences in (43) merely contain a null pronoun that is identified with the topic NP by some sort of construal rule in Logical Form (see Chomsky 1977:81).

If we suppose that only variable-binding relations at S-Structure are sensitive to islands, then the islandhood of complex existential sentences remains exceptionless, despite the Topicalization facts just discussed. Interestingly, this description of the facts can be derived fairly automatically from Kayne's ECP, once one adopts the assumption (independently motivated in Chung 1983b) that this principle holds at S-Structure in Chamorro.

8.3.5 Position and Content of the Head NP
A more straightforward parallel between relative clauses and complex existential sentences in Chamorro is provided by some characteristics of the head NP.

The head NP in relative clauses can occupy several surface positions with respect to the embedded S', a fact that helps to determine the choice of the complementizer for the S'. Complementizer choice is also influenced by the properties of the *variable* within the relative clause, as we will see later (section 8.4.1). To simplify matters here, I consider only relative clauses whose variable is not a locative or temporal phrase.

In these relative clauses the head NP may either precede or follow the embedded S'. If the head precedes, the S' displays the complementizer *ni*.

(47) [i   lähi [ni   ti   machócho'chu'   *t* trabiha]]
     the boy Comp not Infl(s)-work+Impf   yet
     'the boy who is not working yet'

If the head follows, the *ni* complementizer does not appear, and the S' is optionally followed by the "linker" *na*, which serves generally to join prenominal modifiers to their heads.

(48) [i   [ti   machócho'chu'   *t* trabiha] na lahi]
     the not Infl(s)-work+Impf   yet   L boy
     'the boy who is not working yet'

The head NP also has the property that its own head N may be null. Head Ns of this type are semantically underspecified (corresponding to 'one, thing'), and they too have a role in determining the morphology of the S': relative clauses with null head Ns display neither the complementizer *ni* nor the linker *na*.

(49) [i   *e* [p-um-enta   *t* esti na guma']]
     the   Infl(*wh*)-paint this L house
   , 'the (one) who painted this house'

If we allow for the fact that the overt complementizer *ni* is absent (sections 8.3.1, 8.4.1), the indefinite NP in complex existential sentences presents the same picture. The indefinite NP may precede the lower predicate and its dependents, as in (50), or it may follow them, as in (51), in which case the linker *na* optionally appears.

(50) Taya'   hugeti sinedda'-mami
     Infl(s)-not+exist toy   find-Infl(1p)
     'There weren't any toys we found'

(51) Taya'   sinedda'-mami (na) hugeti
     Infl(s)-not+exist find-Infl(1p) L   toy
     'There weren't any toys we found'

The indefinite NP may have a head N that is phonetically null and semantically underspecified.

(52) Guäha   mu-na'nalalu' i   che'lu-hu lahi
     Infl(s)-exist Infl(*wh*)-anger the sibling-my male
     'There was someone (who) angered my brother'

These facts are, of course, consistent with the view that the indefinite NP is the head of a relative clause.

8.3.6 Category of the Variable

Finally, relative clauses and complex existential sentences place the same restrictions on the syntactic category of the variable.

The variable in a relative clause must be an NP. Thus, subjects, direct objects, and various adverbials and other obliques may be relativized, because all of these grammatical functions are instantiated via NPs.

(53) a. [i   taotao [ni   ch-um-iku   *t* si   Maria]]
        the person Comp Infl(*wh*)-kiss Unm Maria
        'the person who kissed Maria'

   b. [i   palao'an [ni   ma'a'ñao-ña si   Antonio *t*]]
      the woman   Comp afraid-Infl(3s) Unm Antonio
      'the woman who Antonio is afraid of'

   c. [i   gima' [änai s-um-ásaga   i   päli' *t*]]
      the house Comp Infl(s)-live+Impf the priest
      'the house where the priest is living'

The variable cannot be a PP, as the contrast between (54) and (55) shows.

(54) Hu-tugi'   i   kätta pära i   taotao
     Infl(1s)-write the letter to   the person
     'I wrote the letter to the person'

(55) *[i   taotao [ni/änai/pära   hayi hu-tugi'   i   kätta *t*]]
      the person Comp/Comp/to who? Infl(1s)-write the letter
      (the person to whom I wrote the letter)

The variable also cannot be an NP that is the object of a preposition, since Chamorro does not allow preposition stranding. This means that indirect objects, clauses, and other grammatical functions that can be instantiated only via PPs cannot be relativized at all.

In this respect, relative clauses differ from constituent questions, which allow both NPs and PPs to be variables.

(56) Ginin hayi na   un-chuli'   i   lepblu *t*?
   from who? Comp Infl(2s)-take the book
   'From whom did you get the book?'

As is to be expected, the variable in complex existential sentences
must be an NP.

(57) a. Guäha   palao'an mu-lalatdi   yu'
        Infl(s)-exist woman   Infl(*wh*)-scold me
        'There was a woman (who) scolded me'

     b. Taya'   ma'a'ñao-ña i   che'lu-hu palao'an
        Infl(s)-not+exist afraid-Infl(3s) the sibling-my female
        'There's no one my sister is afraid of'

     c. Taya'   siña na   um-ätuk   hao
        Infl(s)-not+exist can Comp Infl(s)-hide you
        'There's nowhere you can hide'

     d. *Guäha   taotao (na)   hu-chuli'   i   lepblu
        Infl(s)-exist person Comp Infl(1s)-take the book
        (There's a man from whom I got the book)

Further, the ban against stranding imposes the predicted paradigmatic
gap on indirect objects and other grammatical functions that are realized as PPs: these cannot have their indefiniteness syntactically encoded by the existential construction at all.

8.3.7 Conclusion
Summing up, the complex existential construction contains a relative
clause whose head is the indefinite NP. This conclusion follows from
the fact that complex existential sentences display five syntactic characteristics of relatives: *Wh*-Agreement is present; gaps respond to filter
(36) as though they were variables; the construction is an island; the
indefinite NP has the surface properties of the head of a relative; and
the variable must be an NP. It should be obvious that these characteristics cannot be accommodated naturally by an analysis that treats
complex existentials as small clauses or derives them via a *There*-
Insertion transformation. The Chamorro evidence argues directly and
substantially for the NP analysis of existential sentences.

This conclusion about Chamorro has consequences for syntactic
theory in general. At minimum, it can be viewed as a kind of confirma-
tion of the EST program, given that the present conception of EST
makes it virtually impossible to rule out the NP analysis for existentials

in *all* languages. Thus, even if one adopts the small clause analysis for *there*-insertion sentences in English, Chamorro fills a gap in the class of existential constructions allowed by Universal Grammar.

I would, however, like to take a more contentious position. When one considers the *practice* of exotic language analysis, the standard approach is to assume (until it is proven otherwise) that analyses proposed for familiar languages will also work for less familiar languages. Note that there is no necessity for this, given the well-known observation that syntactic form is not predictable from semantics.

Suppose that one were instead to assume—until it is proven otherwise—that syntactic analyses that are strongly motivated in some language should be assumed in languages where the facts are less clear. Then the Chamorro conclusions reached here might be taken to suggest the viability of the NP analysis for English, as well.

What is interesting about this suggestion is that it would cost relatively little to rule out the small clause analysis for existentials in English and—for that matter—all other languages. All that would be required is that syntactic theory include the stipulation that there are no small clauses. Such a stipulation would square nicely with the anomalous character of small clauses vis-à-vis X'-theory (for instance, according to Chomsky 1981:107, small clauses are not maximal projections and need not be projections of any head; see Williams 1983). In other words, it is conceivable that the ban against small clauses might fall out as a consequence of some more general set of principles governing the construction of phrase structure trees (*pace* Stowell 1981).

I should emphasize that I am not claiming that the NP analysis of existentials is correct for English just because it is correct for Chamorro. Ideally, every language should be dealt with on its own terms, within the limits that syntactic theory in general imposes. The analytic issue that I am addressing is, rather, how one proceeds in practice to deal with particular languages, given that many of the limits imposed by the theory are not known in advance. As far as this issue goes, there seems to me some value in taking seriously the idea that the study of exotic languages may tell us something about the languages we already know.

8.4 Parallels with *Wh*-Movement and the Definiteness Effect

The analysis just developed has so far had nothing to say about one notable Chamorro fact: the relative clause in an existential sentence virtually never displays the *ni* complementizer that is found in true relative clauses with initial heads.[10] This can be seen, for instance, in (58).

(58) a. Guäha   ma'estra siha ma-ñásaga   Yigu
       Infl(s)-exist teacher Pl   Infl(p)-live+Impf Yigo
       'There are some teachers living in Yigo'

   b. [i   ma'estra [ni   ma-ñásaga   Yigu]]
       the teacher   Comp Infl(p)-live+Impf Yigo
       'the teachers who are living in Yigo'

It turns out that the contrast between (58a) and (58b) is not an idiosyncratic one. Rather, in this and several other ways the relative clause in an existential sentence patterns less closely with true relative clauses than it does with constituent questions. Here I use this pattern to motivate a Head Raising analysis for the existential relative in (58a). I then attempt to draw out the consequences of the Head Raising analysis for any general explanation of the DE.

8.4.1 Complementizers

The absence of *ni* in existential relatives brings to mind a curious contrast between relative clauses and constituent questions. In both of these constructions the choice of complementizer is determined by whether or not the variable is adverbial. However, the particular complementizers allowed are different for relative clauses than they are for constituent questions—a fact that I will illustrate with reference to head-initial relative clauses.

When the variable of a relative clause is a subject, direct object, or nonadverbial oblique, the complementizer *ni* appears, as in (53a–b), (59a–b). But when the variable is adverbial—a locative or temporal phrase—the complementizer *änai* (*ni* in the Saipan dialect) is found, as in (53c), (59c).

(59) a. [i   palao'an [ni   ha-ye'lúlusi   si   Maria]]
       the woman   Comp Infl(3s)-jealous+of+Impf Unm Maria
       'the woman that Maria is jealous of'

   b. [i   taotao [ni   mahalang-hu]]
       the person Comp lonely-Infl(1s)
       'the person who I am lonely for'

c. [i   tiempu [änai   um-äsagua]]
   the time   Comp Infl(s)-marry
   'the time when (they) got married' (Cooreman 1982:8)

In contrast, when the variable of a constituent question is a subject, direct object, or nonadverbial oblique, there is no overt complementizer at all, as in (60a–b). And when the variable is adverbial—a locative or temporal phrase, or a PP—the complementizer that appears is *na* (*ni* in the Saipan dialect), as in (56) and (60c).

(60) a. Hayi ha-achaka   si   Juan?
        who? Infl(3s)-accuse Unm Juan
        'Who did Juan accuse?'

     b. In-tingu'   ha'   hayi mahalang-mu
        Infl(1p)-know Emp who? lonely-Infl(2s)
        'We know who you are lonely for'

     c. Ngai'an na   pära ufan-hanao i   bisita?
        when? Comp will Infl(3p)-go the visitor
        'When will the visitors leave?'

These differences in complementizer choice are fairly salient morphosyntactically. It is significant, then, that existential relatives like (58a) turn out to exhibit the same array of complementizers as do questions. When the variable in an existential relative is a subject, direct object, or nonadverbial oblique, no complementizer appears, as in (57c) and (61).

(61) Taya'   ni   unu pära gando-kku
     Infl(s)-not+exist not one will play-Infl(1s)
     'There's no one I can play with'

And when the variable is an adverbial, the complementizer that appears is *na* (*ni* in the Saipan dialect), as in (62).

(62) a. Guäha   na   man-malagu i   famagu'un
        Infl(s)-exist Comp Infl(p)-run the children
        'There were (times) when the children ran'

     b. Taya'   rasón na   pära un-taiguini
        Infl(s)-not+exist reason Comp will Infl(2s)-like+this
        'There's no reason why you should be like this'

Evidently, existential relatives pattern more closely with questions than they do with true relative clauses in their complementizer choice—an observation that raises the question of how far the parallelism between these two constructions extends. For an answer, I now turn to the facts of *Wh*-Agreement and stacking.

8.4.2 *Wh*-Agreement

A second difference between true relative clauses and constituent questions involves the workings of *Wh*-Agreement in long-distance structures—structures in which the variable is several clauses removed from its ultimate antecedent.

In long-distance relative clauses *Wh*-Agreement is typically found only on the predicate on which the variable depends. This is the most deeply embedded predicate in (63).

(63) [i   pätgun [ni   ma'a'ñao   si   Maria pära u-lalatdi   *t*]]
     the child   Comp Infl(s)-afraid Unm Maria will Infl(3s)-scold
                                                      [+Obj]
     'the child that Maria is afraid to scold'

In long-distance questions, however, *Wh*-Agreement appears on *every* predicate on the path between the variable and the moved *wh*-phrase. Compare (64a) with the ungrammatical (64b), in which *Wh*-Agreement occurs only on the most deeply embedded predicate.

(64) a.   Hayi ma'a'ñao-ña   si   Maria pära u-lalatdi   *t*?
          who? afraid-Infl(3s) Unm Maria will Infl(3s)-scold
          [+Obl]   [+Obj]
          'Who is Maria afraid to scold?'

     b.   *Hayi ma'a'ñao   si   Maria pära u-lalatdi   *t*?
          who? Infl(s)-afraid Unm Maria will Infl(3s)-scold
                                              [+Obj]
          (Who is Maria afraid to scold?)

In Chung 1982a I explained this contrast by proposing that different syntactic rules account for relative clauses than account for constituent questions. Relative clauses are derived via an unbounded rule of Controlled Pro Deletion, whereas constituent questions are derived via *Wh*-Movement, which observes Subjacency. Within this proposal, the *Wh*-Agreement found in long-distance relative clauses follows automatically from the original agreement rule (30). Consider (65).

(65)

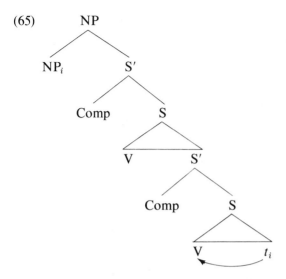

The pattern of *Wh*-Agreement in long-distance questions is also predicted, once some further (and relatively conservative) assumptions are made about the character of S'. In particular, suppose that abstract Case in Chamorro is assigned to S', Comp is the head of S', and maximal projections share Case features with their heads. Then intermediate traces in Comp will trigger *Wh*-Agreement on the next higher predicate, thereby producing the correct agreement pattern, as in (66).

(66)

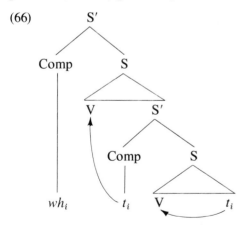

When we turn to existential relatives that involve relativization across a distance, we find the "question" pattern of *Wh*-Agreement: *Wh*-Agreement must occur on every predicate on the path between the variable and the indefinite NP.

(67) a. Taya'   ma'a'ñao-ña si   Carmen pära
         Infl(s)-not+exist afraid-Infl(3s) Unm Carmen will
                          [+Obl]
         u-kuentusi   *t*
         Infl(3s)-talk+to
         [+Obj]
         'There's no one Carmen is afraid to talk to'

   b. *Taya'   ma'a'ñao si   Carmen pära
        Infl(s)-not+exist Infl(s)-afraid Unm Carmen will
        u-kuentusi   *t*
        Infl(3s)-talk+to
        [+Obj]
        (There's no one Carmen is afraid to talk to)

Wh-Agreement, then, offers a second area in which existential relatives
pattern with questions as opposed to relative clauses.

8.4.3 Stacking

A third and final difference between relative clauses and constituent
questions involves whether or not these constructions can be stacked.

A stacked relative is a relative clause whose head NP is itself a relative clause. (68) gives a Chamorro example.

(68) [[Edyu na lepblu ni   hu-tätaitai]   ni
       that L book Comp Infl(1s)-read+Impf Comp
       um-istotba   siha], ti   munhayan   hu-taitai
       Infl(*wh*)-disturb them not Infl(s)-finish Infl(1s)-read
       '[[That book that I was reading] that disturbed them], I haven't
       finished reading'

Constituent questions may not be stacked, for the obvious reason that
it would be semantically incoherent for the questioned element of a
sentence to itself be a sentence that contained another questioned element. However, constituent questions do allow their questioned element to be a true relative clause with a *wh*-head. In (69) the S' of this
relative clause has been extraposed.

(69) Hafa bidáda-mu   [ni   um-istótotba   siha]?
     what? do+Impf-Infl(2s)   Comp Infl(*wh*)-disturb+Impf them
     'What were you doing [that was disturbing them]?'

Once again, existential relatives pattern with constituent questions, although the parallel here is perhaps more one of form than of substance. Existential relatives cannot be stacked, in the strict sense that it is ungrammatical for an existential relative to have an existential relative such as (58a) as its head.[11] In (70) the most deeply embedded existential relative is 'women Manuel took to the party'.

(70) *Taya'   [asuddä'-hu   [famalao'an kinenne'-ña si
      Infl(s)-not+exist   meet-Infl(1s) women   take-Infl(3s) Unm
      Manuel pära i   giput]]
      Manuel to   the party
      (There were [[no women Manuel took to the party] that I met]
      = I didn't meet any women Manuel took to the party)

However, an existential relative may have a true relative clause as its head, as long as the DE is met.

(71) a. Taya'   [asuddä'-hu   [famalao'an ni
        Infl(s)-not+exist   meet-Infl(1s) women   Comp
        kinenne'-ña si   Manuel pära i   giput]]
        take-Infl(3s) Unm Manuel to   the party
        'There were [[no women who Manuel took to the party] that
        I met] = I didn't meet any women Manuel took to the party'

     b. Taya'   ma'estra-ña ha-hässu   si   Julia
        Infl(s)-not+exist teacher-her   Infl(3s)-remember Unm Julia
        [ni   ha-rispeta]
        Comp Infl(3s)-respect
        'There's [[no teacher of hers that she respects] that Julia
        remembers] = Julia doesn't remember any teacher of hers
        that she respects'

8.4.4 Head Raising

In short, existential relatives pattern with constituent questions in three ways. They select the same complementizers as do questions; they have the same *Wh*-Agreement pattern in long-distance structures; and they cannot be stacked in the strict sense. Nonetheless, it seems clear that the embedded constituent in the existential construction is not an embedded question but rather a type of relative. Otherwise, it would be impossible to explain why the indefinite NP has the properties of the head of a relative (see section 8.3.5) or why the variable exhibits the same restrictions as variables in true relative clauses as opposed to *wh*-questions (see section 8.3.6). Rephrasing somewhat, the NP positions in the existential relative identify it as a kind of relative clause. But the path between these positions has the earmarks of a path produced by movement, not Controlled Pro Deletion.

There are several conceivable ways of describing this situation via the syntactic apparatus provided by EST. The one that I propose to pursue involves the claim that existential relatives are produced by Head Raising, in the sense of Vergnaud (1974), Carlson (1977b), and others.

Let us suppose that true relatives and existential relatives both have a phrase structure in which NP immediately dominates NP S'. A true relative clause, we can continue to assume, has a head position that is filled by a contentful NP at D-Structure; that NP is related to a gap position within S' by the unbounded rule of Controlled Pro Deletion (28). In contrast, an existential relative clause has a D-Structure configuration in which the head position is empty and the gap position is occupied by a contentful NP. This NP will undergo Head Raising in the syntax, moving first to Comp and ultimately to the position of the head.

(72)   NP

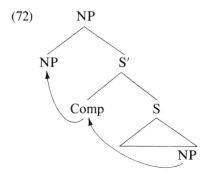

Such an analysis continues to account for the facts of existential sentences that were discussed in section 8.3. At the same time it can accommodate the parallels between existential relatives and constituent questions, as I will show.

First, the pattern of *Wh*-Agreement in existential relatives follows from the assumption that Head Raising observes Subjacency. Such an assumption forces traces to appear in every intermediate Comp on the path between the variable and the head NP, with the result that the correct agreement pattern is generated.

Complementizer choice can be handled in something of the same spirit. For instance, suppose we choose to implement the facts of

(59)–(62) by a set of surface filters that, among other things, relates the form of a complementizer to whether or not it shares its Comp with a phrasal category at S-Structure. Filters of this sort will be able to differentiate true relative clauses from questions and existential relatives, because only the latter have a syntactic representation in which phrasal categories (either overt or null) occur in Comp.[12]

Finally, the failure of existential relatives to stack can be related to the fact that Head Raising is not an option for all relative clauses. As I will discuss shortly, Head Raising is permitted only for those relatives that constitute the NP argument of an existential predicate. But since the most deeply embedded relatives in (70) and (71) do not meet this criterion, their failure to allow Head Raising comes as no surprise.

In short, the Head Raising analysis of existential relatives deals straightforwardly with all the facts that we have seen so far. This strikes me as reason enough to adopt it (though I am aware that other conceivable analyses could produce the same results).[13] Part of the appeal of this analysis is that it has parallels in other languages. Head Raising in Chamorro is essentially the syntactic counterpart of the LF Head Raising proposed by Williamson in chapter 7 for all relative clauses in Lakhota. It seems significant that Lakhota relative clauses exhibit a DE, as Williamson shows, and so in this way too are similar to the existential relatives of Chamorro.

8.4.5 Conclusion

In concluding this chapter, I would like to pursue one line of thought suggested by the analysis just proposed.

Perhaps the least satisfying aspect of the Head Raising analysis is that it appears not to provide any deep explanation of the properties of existential relatives. It seems arbitrary that Head Raising should be allowed in Chamorro for existential relatives but not for true relative clauses. The issue can be rephrased as a problem of overgeneration. Given that at least some relative clauses have D-Structure expansions in which the head position is empty and the variable position is filled, what is to prevent any other Chamorro relative clause from being expanded this way?

One might first conjecture that this question could be answered by appealing to the definiteness of the eventual head. On this view, an indefinite head would somehow force the Head Raising derivation, whereas a definite head would force a derivation via Controlled Pro Deletion. Such a view might make it possible to draw the desired parallel between existential relatives and constituent questions, given that *wh*-phrases have the semantics of existentially quantified NPs (Karttunen 1977; McCloskey 1979). However, this suggestion is frustrated by the fact that, outside the existential construction, *no* Chamorro relative clause permits the Head Raising option.[14]

We can see this most clearly from the character of true relative clauses with indefinite heads when they occur outside the existential sentence type. Such relative clauses, like other indefinite NPs, may bear one of several grammatical functions: they may serve as the oblique object of a psychological predicate, a verb of transfer, an antipassive verb, and so forth, or—somewhat exceptionally—the direct object of the verb *nisisita* 'need'. (Recall that indefinites have a restricted syntactic distribution.) Significantly, these relative clauses have none of the morphosyntactic earmarks of Head Raising. They display the *ni* complementizer when head-initial.

(73) a. Ti man-bisita   i   médiku [malangu [*(ni)
        not Infl(s)-AP-visit the doctor   sick   Comp
        in-tingu']]
        Infl(1p)-know
        'The doctor hasn't paid a visit to a patient who we know'

    b. Ha-nisisita si   Juan [kareta [*(ni)   siña ha-sugun]]
        Infl(3s)-need Unm Juan   car   Comp can Infl(3s)-drive
        'Juan needs a car that he can drive'

And they show the pattern of long-distance *Wh*-Agreement that we have attributed to Controlled Pro Deletion.

(74) In-nisisita   [lahi [ni   ti   ma'a'ñao   si   Carmen pära
     Infl(1p)-need man Comp not Infl(s)-afraid Unm Carmen will
     u-kuentusi   *t*]]
     Infl(3s)-talk+to
     [+Obj]
     'We need a man who Carmen is not afraid to talk to'

Evidently, the indefiniteness of the head per se does not determine the choice of the Head Raising option. It seems rather to be a global property of the existential predicates *guäha* and *taya* that their relative clause arguments are derived by Head Raising, whereas no other relative clauses allow this option.

In a previous version of this chapter I encoded this property as part of the lexical specification of *guäha* and *taya'*, in effect claiming that the choice of the Head Raising option is an arbitrary one. Though that may be so, it should be noted that such a claim is spiritually at odds with the attempts that have been made to derive all properties of existential sentences—both syntactic and semantic—from more general principles. A more satisfying approach would be to try to relate the Head Raising option to the other property that distinguishes existentials from all other Chamorro constructions—namely, the DE. For this to be so, however, the explanation of the DE must make reference not only to the relation between the existential predicate and its NP but also to the internal structure of that NP, and its relative clause portion in particular. It seems to me that such a state of affairs implies a treatment of the DE (and of existential relatives) more sophisticated than those that have been offered heretofore.

Notes

Thanks to the Chamorro speakers who contributed to this work, especially Priscilla Anderson-Cruz, Maria H. Borja, Agnes C. Tabor, and Francisco Tomokane. Thanks also to Ann Cooreman for permission to quote from her Chamorro texts, to Leslie Saxon for her suggestions, and to Jeanne Gibson, James McCloskey, Alan Timberlake, and Janis Williamson for listening to me worry about the analysis. The final version of this chapter was prepared while I was a Fellow at the Max-Planck-Institut für Psycholinguistik.

1. Chamorro is a western Austronesian language spoken in the Mariana Islands. The examples in this chapter are cited in an orthography that retains some characteristics of traditional Chamorro orthographies: specifically, *ch* = [t͡s], *y* = [d͡z], *ng* = [ŋ], ' = [ʔ], *ao* = [ɒw], and *ai* = [ay]. The following abbreviations appear in the morpheme-by-morpheme glosses.

AP	antipassive (prefix)	p	plural
Comp	complementizer	Pass	passive (infix or prefix)
Emp	emphatic	Pl	plural
Impf	imperfective (reduplication)	s	singular
Infl	inflection	Unm	unmarked case
L	linker	*wh*	*Wh*-Agreement (infix)
Loc	locative case	1	first person
Nom	nominative *Wh*-Agreement	2	second person
Obj	objective *Wh*-Agreement	3	third person
Obl	oblique case/*Wh*-Agreement		

2. The exceptions to this statement include the following.
   (a) Indefinite possessed NPs, such as *paine-kku* 'a comb of mine', may evidently occur as S-Structure direct objects of transitive verbs and as subjects (= D-Structure objects) of unaccusative verbs. However, the possibility remains that the S-Structure subjects and direct objects in this case are not the

(indefinite) possessed NPs but rather their (definite) possessors; if so, the "exception" would be only apparent. See Crain 1979 on Chamorro Possessor Ascension in Relational Grammar.

(b) For at least some speakers, indefinite NPs may serve as S-Structure direct objects in some opaque contexts, as in (i).

(i) Malägu' si Antonio na in-bisita man-maolik na Amerikanu
Infl(s)-want Unm Antonio Comp Infl(1p)-visit Infl(p)-good L American
'Antonio wants us to visit (some) nice Americans'

This makes it tempting to recast the statement in the text as "Referential indefinites cannot serve as S-Structure subjects or direct objects." Unfortunately, such a revision leads to wrong predictions in a number of cases where an indefinite clearly has a nonreferential reading but nonetheless cannot serve as a subject or direct object. As my understanding of the matter is incomplete, I simply leave it here.

3. NPs containing the cardinal quantifier *un* 'one' sometimes function semantically/pragmatically as though they were true indefinites: *un bihu* 'one old man, an old man'. However, such NPs pattern with other cardinally quantified NPs in their syntactic distribution, being able to occur, for instance, as S-Structure subjects or direct objects. I therefore do not consider them here.

4. One difference is that English *be* also occurs in copular sentences, the progressive, and the passive, whereas Chamorro *guäha* and *taya'* are found only in the existential construction. Chamorro has no (overt) copula; locative existential sentences with definite subjects employ the verb *gaigi* 'be'.

5. The observations about relative clauses are borne out by narrative texts (Cooreman 1983) and a traditional grammar (Costenoble 1940). The thirteen examples from these sources in which the NP of an existential construction is relativized are clearly identifiable as amount relatives rather than restrictive relatives.

6. Although I will not explicitly discuss sentences of the type (5a), it will become clear why I propose to analyze them as minimal existential sentences that contain an adverbial phrase immediately dominated either by VP or by the matrix S.

7. Although some relative clauses in Chamorro appear to be derived via *Wh*-Movement (see Chung 1982a), it will simplify matters to ignore this possibility here.

8. Further facts examined by Woolford reveal that null pronouns are actually located to the immediate right of overt pronouns on the animacy hierarchy, so that the hierarchy has the form Overt Animate Pronoun > Null Animate Pronoun > Animate NP > Inanimate NP. For present purposes, though, the version given in (36b) is adequate, if oversimplified.

In Chung 1984 I described the facts of (38) by positing a pragmatic strategy that forced a single unmarked NP associated with a transitive verb to be interpreted as the direct object. Since Woolford's account is superior to mine in a number of ways, however, I hereby adopt it.

9. Observe that, of the three analyses we are considering, only the NP analysis accounts for the ungrammaticality of (42). Both the transformational analysis and the small clause analysis predict that complex existential sentences will *not* be islands, as pointed out by Milsark (1974) and Safir (1984b:6).

10. On very rare occasions an existential relative with an initial head does exhibit the *ni* complementizer.

(i) Guäha   lapes-su   ni   ti   siña manggi'
    Infl(s)-exist pencil-my Comp not can Infl(s)-AP-write
    'There's a pencil of mine that doesn't write'

(ii) Guäha   tä'lu   otru   na kumpania guihi ni
    Infl(s)-exist again other L   company   there Comp
    man-ma-chócho'gui   i   katbón
    Infl(p)-Pass-make+Impf the charcoal
    'There was at that time another company where charcoal was being made' (Cooreman 1983:35)

The conditions governing the appearance of *ni* in (i) and (ii) are not very clear. However, the mere existence of such examples is enough to argue that the NP in the existential construction must be allowed to expand to a true relative clause.

11. For reasons unknown to me, in all cases where an existential relative has a true relative clause as its head, the S' of the true relative is the *final* constituent of the existential relative. (This situation can arise in two ways: either the existential relative is head-final, as in (71a), or else the most deeply embedded S' is extraposed, as in (71b).) This fact has no bearing on the issue at hand.

12. The question begged here is how to deal with the fact that complementizer choice is also determined by the syntactic category of the *variable*. I ignore this, in part because I do not know enough about complementizer choice in long-distance structures to give a precise description of the facts.

13. In particular, one could imagine that existential relatives are headed relative clauses in which there is obligatory *Wh*-Movement of an invisible relative pronoun. I do not adopt this alternative, in part because I believe it obscures the parallel between Chamorro and Lakhota that is mentioned in the text.

14. In fact, a few quantificational predicates, such as *bula* 'much', appear to allow relative clause arguments of the Head Raising type. But these predicates have an obvious semantic connection to the existential predicates, and they too appear to display a DE.

Chapter 9
Existential Sentences   C.-T. James Huang
in Chinese and
(In)definiteness

This chapter addresses four questions: What do existential sentences look like in Chinese? What is the structure of such sentences? Under what conditions do they exhibit the definiteness effect, requiring an indefinite but disallowing a definite argument? How is this distribution of the definiteness effect to be explained? These questions are taken up in turn in the four major sections that follow.

9.1 Kinds of Existential Sentences

In Chinese all existential sentences may be considered to involve a string having the general form depicted in (1).

(1) ... (NP) ... V ... NP ... (XP) ....
       1   2   3   4

Position 1 is the position of the subject, and position 3 that of the NP whose existence is being asserted. The phrase in position 4 is an expression of predication, generally a descriptive clause or phrase, semantically associated with the NP in position 3. Based on the different kinds of verbs involved, four kinds of existential sentences may be distinguished. These are (a) sentences with the existential verb *you* 'have', (b) those with a verb of appearance or disappearance, (c) those with a locative verb, and (d) those with a verb expressing the existence of an event or experience. Each type is illustrated in the paragraphs that follow.

   You-sentences are the closest counterparts to *there be*-sentences in English.

(2) You gui
    have ghost
    'There are ghosts (here)'

(3) You yige ren hen xihuan ni
    have one man very like   you
    'There is a man who likes you very much'

(4) Zhuo-shang you yiben shu
    table-top   have one book
    'On the table there is a book'

(5) Zhuo-shang you yiben shu hen youqu
    table-top   have one book very interesting
    'On the table there is a book very interesting'

As these examples illustrate, both positions 1 and 4 are optional. Position 1, if filled, may be filled with a locative NP, as in (4) and (5),[1] or it may be filled with an NP assuming the role of a possessor, as in (6).

(6) Wo you yiben shu hen youqu
    I   have one   book very interesting
    'I have a book (that is) very interesting'

The locative phrase need not always occupy the subject position. It may occur as a PP anywhere in the sentence.

(7) a. Zai zheli (wo) you yiben shu
       at here I   have one   book
       'I have a book here' (or 'There is a book here')

    b. Wo zai Taipei you yige pengyou hen youqian
       I   at Taipei have one friend   very rich
       'I have a very rich friend in Taipei'

    c. You yiben shu hen youqu   zai zhuo-shang
       have one book very interesting at table-top
       'There is a book very interesting on the table'

    d. You yiben shu zai zhuo-shang hen youqu
       have one book at table-top   very interesting
       'There is a book on the table very interesting'

Sentences of the second type involve verbs like *lai* 'come', *fasheng* 'happen', and *dao* 'arrive', which have to do with "coming into existence," or verbs like *si* 'die', *pao* 'escape', and *qu* 'go', which have to do with "going out of existence."

(8) Fasheng le   yijian chehuo
    happen Perf one   accident
    'An accident happened'

(9) Si   le   liangge ren
    die Perf two   men
    'Two men died'

Positions 2 and 4 may also be optionally filled, position 2 with a locative (or temporal) phrase and position 4 with a descriptive clause.

(10) a. Zuotian   fasheng le   yijian chehuo
        yesterday happen Perf one   accident
        'An accident happened yesterday'
        (Lit. 'Yesterday happened an accident')

     b. Zheli fasheng le   yijian chehuo hen kepa
        here happen Perf one   accident very terrible
        'A very terrible accident happened here'
        (Lit. 'Here happened an accident very terrible')

The third type of existential sentence is exemplified in (11) and (12).

(11) a. Chuang-shang tang-zhe yige bingren
        bed-top   lie-Dur   one patient
        'In the bed lies a patient'

     b. Shu-dixia   zhan-zhe   liangge xiaohai
        tree-bottom stand-Dur two   child
        'Below the tree stand two children'

(12) a. Fangjian-li fang-le xuduo xingli
        room-inside put-Perf many luggage
        'In the room are put many pieces of luggage'

     b. Qiang-shang gua-zhe   yiding maozi
        wall-top   hang-Dur one   hat
        'On the wall hangs a hat'

The verbs used in sentences of this type are locational verbs—transitive or intransitive verbs that subcategorize for a locative phrase. These include intransitives like *zhu* 'live', *zuo* 'sit', *tang* 'lie', *piao* 'float' and transitives like *fang* 'put', *gua* 'hang', and *xie* 'write'. Each of these verbs is usually suffixed with the durative aspect *-zhe*, as in (11a–b) and (12b). In the case of a transitive locational verb the perfective aspect *-le* is also acceptable, as in (12a).

Like the other two types of existential sentences illustrated in (2)–(10), a locative existential sentence may also optionally take a predication clause in position 4.

(13) Hebian   gui-zhe   liangge guniang zai xi   yifu
     river-side kneel-Dur two   lass   at wash clothes
     'By the river kneel two girls washing clothes'

(14) Qiang-shang gua-zhe   yifu hua   hen   haokan
     wall-top   hang-Dur   one picture very pretty
     'On the wall hangs a picture very pretty'

An important special feature of the third type of existential sentence is that the subject position must be filled with a lexical phrase. In each sentence of (11)–(14) this requirement is fulfilled with the locative phrase appearing in position 1 in the form of an NP without the preposition *zai* 'at'. If the initial position is not filled, the sentences are ill formed.

(15) a. *Tang-zhe yige bingren zai chuang-shang
        lie-Dur   one patient at bed-top

     b. *Zhan-zhe liangge xiaohai zai shu-dixia
        stand-Dur two   child   at tree-bottom

     c. *Gua-zhe   yiding maozi zai qiang-shang
        hang-Dur   one   hat   at wall-top

Furthermore, if the locative phrase appears in initial position in the form of a PP, the sentences are also unacceptable.

(16) a. ?*Zai chuang-shang tang-zhe   yige bingren
         at bed-top   lie-Dur   one patient

     b. ?*Zai shu-dixia   zhan-zhe   liangge xiaohai
         at tree-bottom stand-Dur two   child

     c. ?*Zai qiang-shang gua-zhe   yiding maozi
         at wall-top   hang-Dur   one   hat

The unacceptability of (16a–c) shows that the locative phrase must not only occur in preverbal position but also occupy the subject position. This is because only subjects must be filled by NPs. Other preverbal positions, such as the position of a topic or of an adjunct, may be filled by PPs.

(17) Zai jiali   wo xihuan gen didi   wan
    at   home I   like   with brother play
    'At home, I like to play with my brother'

(18) Wo zai jiali   changchang ma   ta
    I   at home often   scold he
    'I often scold him at home'

Note that under certain circumstances the following sentences may be
felt to be well formed, where the subject position is unfilled and the
verb is a transitive locative verb (with the suffix -le).

(19) a. e fang-le   xuduo xingli   zai fangjian-li
       put-Perf many luggage at room-inside
       'e put many pieces of luggage in the room'

    b. e zai fangjian-li   fang-le   xuduo xingli
       at   room-inside put-Perf many luggage
       'e put many pieces of luggage in the room'

(20) a. e gua-le   yiding maozi zai qiang-shang
       hang-Perf one   hat   at   wall-top
       'e hung a hat on the wall'

    b. e zai qiang-shang gua-le   yiding maozi
       at   wall-top   hang-Perf one   hat
       'e hung a hat on the wall'

However, these sentences are well formed only if an understood agent
is implied. In this respect, they differ from sentences like those in
(11)–(12), where no agent is implied. In other words, in the context of
an existential sentence like any of those in (11)–(12), but not in the
context of the sentences in (19)–(20), the D-Structure subject position
is dethematized; that is, the verb does not assign it a thematic role as a
lexical property. Thus, in (19)–(20) the empty subject is a "small pro"
in the sense of Chomsky (1982a), analogous to the empty subject of a
null-subject language like Italian. In each of the ill-formed examples in
(15), however, the empty subject is an expletive. The correct generalization is therefore that only the expletive subject position must be
filled with a lexical NP. Those with a D-Structure thematic subject are
not considered members of the third type of existential sentence.

The fourth type of existential sentence generally involves a verb with
the experiential suffix -guo, as in (21)–(22), or a verb with the perfective suffix -le, as in (23)–(24).[2]

(21) Wo jiao-guo   yige xuesheng hen congming
     I   teach-Exp one student   very clever
     'I have the experience of teaching a student who is very clever'

(22) Wo ai-guo   yige nuhai hen piaoliang
     I   love-Exp one girl   very pretty
     'I have the experience of falling in love with a girl who is very pretty'

(23) Wo xuan-le   yimen ke   hen nandong
     I   elect-Perf one   course very hard-to-understand
     'I took a course which was hard to understand'

(24) Ta song-le   yiben shu gei wo hen youqu
     he give-Perf one   book to I   very interesting
     'He gave a book to me that was very interesting'

This final class of sentences differs from the others in the following two ways. First, position 1 is always occupied by a D-Structure subject (agent in the examples given here), whereas verbs in the other types of sentences are generally "unaccusative" in the sense of Perlmutter (1978) (or "ergative" in the sense of Burzio (1981)), in that they do not have a D-Structure subject—with the single exception of *you* 'have', which may or may not have a D-Structure subject. Second, the verbs in this last type (though not those in the other three types) belong to an open class, in that any transitive verb, as long as it is suffixed with the experiential -*guo* or the perfective -*le,* may qualify as the verb of a sentence of this type. On the other hand, sentences of this type are similar to the other three types in two other ways. First, the verbs used all have to do with "existence" of some sort. A verb with the experiential suffix conveys the existence of an experience, and a verb in the perfective denotes the existence of an event. (Recall that the English perfective is *have;* also see (35).) Second, all four types of sentences may optionally contain a clause of predication in position 4. The examples in (21)–(24) all contain such a clause of predication. The following sentences show that the predication clause is optional.

(25) Wo jiao-guo   yige xuesheng
     I   teach-Exp one   student
     'I have the experience of teaching a student'

(26) Ta song-le   yiben shu   gei wo
     he give-Perf one   book to   I
     'He gave a book to me'

If the verb is not suffixed with *-guo* or *-le,* then often no expression of predication may appear.

(27) Ta meitian   jiao   yige xuesheng (*hen   congming)
     he every-day teach one   student   very clever
     'He teaches a student (*very clever) every day'

These two points of similarity—existentiality of the verb and the possible occurrence of XP—tie together our four types of sentences, to the exclusion of other sentence types.

9.2 The Structure of Existential Sentences

We have seen that existential sentences in Chinese have the linear form (NP) V NP (XP). Let us now consider the possible hierarchical structure of such sentences. The only thing that appears to be really worth discussing is the structural relationship of XP and the NP in position 3: Does the sequence NP – XP form a constituent? If so, what category is that constituent? The other aspects of the structure of an existential sentence appear to be relatively uncontroversial. For example, the NP in position 1 is the subject under the immediate domination of S but not VP. The sequence V – NP – (XP) is dominated by VP. That the XP, when it appears, is under VP but not immediately under S is assumed in all discussions of existential sentences in the literature that I am aware of and is further confirmed by the fact that in Chinese a sentential adjunct can only appear preverbally. I will further assume, without any comment, that the NP in position 3 is in object position in both D-Structure and S-Structure, regardless of whether the sentences are, in traditional terms, transitive or intransitive. That is, I assume that no "subject-inversion" whatsoever is involved in any of the sentences above. All intransitive existential verbs are unaccusative in the sense of Perlmutter (1978), and they are assumed to select, as a lexical property, only complements but no subjects. (A "pure intransitive" or "unergative" verb does not qualify as an existential verb since it does not subcategorize for an object: *Ku-le yige ren* '*There cried a man'.)

The question about the structural relationship of the object NP and the XP has been a point of controversy in recent discussions of *there be*-sentences in English. Three structures have been proposed for a sentence like (28), indicated in (29).

(28) There was a pig roasted

(29) a. There was [$_{NP}$ a pig roasted]
      b. There was [$_{SC}$ a pig roasted]
      c. There was [$_{NP}$ a pig] [$_{AP}$ roasted]

According to both (29a) and (29b), the sequence NP – XP is a constituent: in (29a) it is an NP (the "bare NP" analysis), and in (29b) it is a "small clause" in the sense of Williams (1975) (the clausal analysis). These two analyses differ with respect to whether NP or XP is the head of the constituent [NP XP]. According to (29c), NP and XP do not form a constituent but are both sisters of the verb (the "NP – XP" analysis). The "bare NP" analysis is championed by Williams (1984) and Jenkins (1975). The small clause analysis is proposed by Stowell (1981) and followed by many others (see, for instance, Safir 1982; Reuland 1983). The NP – XP analysis is assumed by Milsark (1974), among others. Let us consider these analyses with respect to existential sentences in Chinese.

The bare NP analysis claims that [NP XP] is a structure of postnominal modification, the XP being a postnominal modifier of the preceding NP. In English, nominal modifiers may often follow their heads. Therefore, as Williams (1984) puts it, a possible argument for the bare NP analysis is that it is not only possible to generate all *there be NP XP* strings with the structure *there be NP* but also quite impossible to prevent their generation in this manner. If we consider Chinese existential sentences, however, a completely different conclusion can be reached. This is because the internal structure of Chinese noun phrases is, as is well known, strictly head-final. Given this general rule, it would be impossible, within the bare NP analysis, to generate any existential sentence in which an XP appears in position 4. That is, within this analysis one must allow for an exception to the general word order rule. The question then arises why a postnominal modifier may occur only in the four kinds of constructions just illustrated, and only in position 4 of such constructions. For example, if not in position 4, a nominal modifier is always prenominal.[3]

(30) a. Ta bei yige [hen keqi de] ren pian le
         he by one   very polite Rel man cheat Perf
         'He was cheated by a very polite man'

     b. *Ta bei yige ren [hen keqi] pian le
          he by one   man very polite cheat Perf

(31) a. Wo ba liangge [hen congming de] ren pian le
         I   ba two   very clever   Rel man cheat Perf
         'I cheated two very clever men'

     b. *Wo ba liangge ren [hen congming] pian le
          I   ba two   man very clever   cheat Perf

This restriction on the distribution of the XP poses an important
problem for the bare NP analysis, since there appears to be no general
reason why the position of a given constituent should make a difference
with respect to the relative order of its head and modifier. No similar
problem arises, of course, within the NP – XP or the clausal analysis.
According to these analyses, the NP – XP sequence is either a nonconstituent or a clause, but not an NP. (30b) and (31b) are therefore ill
formed because such a sequence occurs in a position that must be filled
by one and only one NP constituent (as the object of a preposition) but
not by a nonconstituent or a clause, a requirement that is fulfilled in the
case of (30a) and (31a), respectively. But the NP – XP sequence is not
blocked from occupying positions 3 and 4 within a sentence, since the
XP may be considered to fill either the position of a verb phrase complement or that of a small clause subcategorized by the higher verb.

Another way in which both the NP – XP analysis and the clausal
analysis fare better than the bare NP analysis concerns the semantic
difference between a prenominal and a postnominal XP that can be
observed in (32) and (33).

(32) a. There is a flying plane
     b. There is a plane flying

(33) a. Zhuo-shang you yiben hen youqu   de shu
         table-top   have one   very interesting Rel book
         'On the table there is a very interesting book'

     b. Zhuo-shang you yiben shu hen youqu
         table-top   have one   book very interesting
         'On the table there is a book very interesting'

The phrases *flying* and *hen youqu* 'very interesting' each have a restrictive function when they appear prenominally, so that what is being asserted is specifically the existence of a flying plane (and not just a plane) in the case of (32a) and that of an interesting book (and not just a book) in the case of (33a). When they appear in position 4, however, the XPs have a descriptive but not a restrictive function. (32b) asserts merely the existence of a plane and goes on to give a description of the existing plane. Likewise, in (33b) the AP 'very interesting' is a continuative description of the existing book. In other words, a postnominal XP makes a comment about the preceding NP. If such an XP is to be represented as a postnominal modifier in accordance with the bare NP analysis, then it must be represented as a nonrestrictive modifier. However, this raises two problems. First, in English such XPs do not have the comma intonation characteristic of nonrestrictives. Second, in Chinese it is not clear why postnominal modifiers are possible only with nonrestrictives.[4] Within the NP – XP or the clausal analysis, these problems do not arise. According to these analyses, the XP is treated as a predicate. The relation that it has with the preceding NP is therefore that between subject and predicate, or between topic and comment.[5] And this is the correct interpretation of the XP.

Incidentally, the semantic difference between the (a)-examples and the (b)-examples of (32) and (33) is similar to that between (34a) and (34b).

(34) a. He ate the raw meat
     b. He ate the meat raw

Williams himself (1984:136) assumes that (34b), unlike (34a), has an NP – XP structure, thus accounting for the fact that *raw* is a modifier in (34a) but a predicate in (34b). But if the NP – XP sequence in an existential sentence is analyzed as a bare NP, then it is not clear how a similar distinction can be made.

In short, I have argued against the bare NP analysis on two grounds. First, the internal structure of NP in Chinese is strictly head-final. Second, whereas an NP with a prenominal modifier clearly has a structure of modification, an NP – XP sequence has a structure of predication.

As for the choice between the clausal analysis and the NP – XP analysis, it seems to me that both structures may be involved in the existential sentences discussed here. On the one hand, the clausal analysis appears to be implausible for the sentences belonging to the second, third, and fourth types. This is because, first, verbs like 'teach', 'sit', and 'die' in general subcategorize for an NP, but not for a clause, as their (D-Structure) object, and this makes them very different from verbs like 'consider', which take only clausal objects. Second, a clausal analysis of the NP – XP sequence would treat the XP as the head of the sequence. But, as we have seen, XP is optional. Within the NP – XP analysis, the optionality can be easily accounted for by the parenthesis notation in the subcategorization frame of each of these verbs. Within the clausal analysis, however, it would be necessary to set up two separate subcategorization frames for each of these verbs.

On the other hand, there appears to be some reason for postulating the clausal analysis as a *possible* structure for the *you*-sentences. More specifically, suppose that *you* 'have' is an Aux, and that the rule expanding S is S → NP Aux XP, as proposed by Williams (1984); that is, Aux may subcategorize for any category. Then the NP – XP sequence in a *you*-sentence is forced to be a clause, given that Aux can only be followed by one XP. (The bare NP analysis is excluded by our earlier considerations.)

There is some evidence for analyzing *you* as an auxiliary. For one thing, it is well known (since Wang 1965) that *you* alternates with *-le* in marking the perfective aspect (an instance of Aux).

(35) a. Wo pian-le   Zhangsan
        I   cheat-Asp Zhangsan
        'I have cheated Zhangsan'

     b. Wo mei you pian Zhangsan
        I   not have cheat Zhangsan
        'I have not cheated Zhangsan'

As suggested originally by Wang, this shows that the suffix *-le* is a suppletive allomorph of the Aux *you* that has undergone Affix Hopping. Given that *you* may be an Aux, it is plausible at least, though not necessary, to postulate that it is an Aux in existential sentences. The necessary assumption is that *you* as an Aux subcategorizes for both VP and clause, a possibility that is allowed by the rule S → NP Aux XP. It is even possible to assume that *you* subcategorizes for all categories (like *be* in English, following Williams). We have already seen that it can be followed by VP and NP.[6] For some speakers, it can also be followed by PP and AP.

(36) a. Ta mei you hen piaoliang
     she not have very pretty
     'She is not very pretty'

   b. Zhangsan you mei you zai nali?
      Zhangsan have not have at   there
      'Is Zhangsan over there?'

In the related language Amoy there is even clearer evidence that 'have' subcategorizes for XP.

(37) Gua wu   khi-kue a
     I   have go-Exp Part
     'I have been there'

(38) Li wu   kui-e   pingyiu?
     you have how-many friend
     'How many friends do you have?'

(39) I   wu   sui   bo?
     she have pretty not-have
     'Is she pretty or not?'

(40) I   wu   ti chhu bo?
     he have at home not-have
     'Is he at home or not?'

Given that *you* may subcategorize for NP, VP, AP, and PP, it is only natural to assume that it may also subcategorize for a clause, another instance of XP.[7]

Summarizing, I have argued that the NP – XP sequence is best analyzed, not as a structure of modification in accordance with the bare NP theory, but as a structure of predication in accordance with the NP – XP or the clausal theory. Furthermore, although the NP – XP theory appears to be more reasonable for sentences of the second, third, and fourth types, with *you*-sentences the clausal analysis appears to be plausible as well, though more evidence is needed to determine whether it is indeed the only correct analysis.

9.3 Distribution of the Definiteness Effect

It is well known that some existential sentences in Chinese, as in every other language, exhibit what Safir (1982) calls *definiteness effects*

(DEs), manifestations of the requirement that the NP in position 3 must be "indefinite."

(41) a. You yiben shu   zai zhuo-shang
        have one   book at   table-top
        'There is a book on the table'

    b. *You neiben shu   zai zhuo-shang
        have that   book at   table-top
        'There is that book on the table'

A proper semantic characterization of the definite versus indefinite distinction is beyond the scope of this chapter (see Milsark 1974, 1977; Barwise and Cooper 1981; Reuland 1983; and other chapters in this volume, especially chapter 12 by Keenan). For present purposes it suffices to say that "definites" include proper names, pronouns, NPs with a definite article or a demonstrative, bare NPs interpreted as generic or definite, universally quantified NPs, and NPs with quantifiers like 'most'. "Indefinites," on the other hand, include NPs with existential quantifiers and bare NPs interpreted as nongenerics.

The sentences in (41) already show that an NP with a definite determiner is disallowed in *you*-sentences. The following sentence shows that the same restriction applies to proper names, pronouns, universals, and 'most-NPs'.

(42) *You Lisi/ta/meige ren/daduoshu-de ren zai wuzi-li
      have Lisi/he/every man/most man   at   room-in
      '*There is/are Lisi/him/everybody/most people in the room'

In the context of a nonexistential sentence, or in a position other than position 3 of an existential sentence, a bare NP may be interpreted as generic or definite (and sometimes as nongeneric).

(43) Wo xihuan shu
     I   like   book
     'I like books'

(44) Wo mai-le   shu   le
     I   buy-Perf book Prt
     a. 'I bought a book/(some) books'
     b. 'I bought the book(s)'

(45) Ren si-le
     man die-Perf
     'The man died'

However, in position 3 of a *you*-sentence a bare NP has only the non-generic, nondefinite interpretation.

(46) You ren lai-le
have man come-Perf
'Someone came'

Moreover, in Chinese a possessive NP may be definite or indefinite in the context of (47) but only indefinite in (48).[8]

(47) Ta da-le   wo-de pengyou
he hit-Perf my   friend
'He hit (one/some of) my friends'

(48) You wo-de pengyou zai wuzi-li
have my   friend   at room-in
'There is/are a/some friend(s) of mine in the room'

Although these kinds of *you*-sentences exhibit a clear DE, it has also been a commonplace observation that not all existential sentences exhibit the same effects. The lack of a DE is observed not only in "list" contexts like (49) but also in other contexts such as (50) and (51).

(49) Who do we have here?
Well, there are the two students of yours, you, and me.

(50) Chuang-shang tang-zhe Zhangsan
bed-top   lie-Dur   Zhangsan
'In the bed lies Zhangsan'

(51) Tai-shang   zuo-zhe zhuxi-tuan
platform-top sit-Dur presidium
'On the platform sits the presidium'

As far as I know, there has been no clear description of where the DE occurs in Chinese existential sentences. In this section I attempt a systematic statement of its distribution.

There is a clear difference with respect to the distribution of the DE depending on whether or not a given existential sentence contains an expression of predication in position 4.[9] First of all, consider sentences in which the predication does not occur.

The DE is most often observed within a *you*-sentence. However, there is an asymmetry between *you*-sentences in which the subject position is lexically occupied and those in which it is not. In particular, in the examples in (52) and (53) the object of *you* can be definite or indefinite.

(52) a. Ni you-mei-you   yiben shu   zai zheli?
        you have-not-have one   book at here
        'Do you have a book here?'

     b. Ni you-mei-you   zheben shu zai zheli?
        you have-not-have this   book at here
        'Do you have (a copy of) this book here?'

(53) a. Zheli you-mei-you   yiben shu?
        here have-not-have one   book
        'Is there a book here?'

     b. Zheli you-mei-you   zheben shu?
        here have-not-have this   book
        'Is there (a copy of) this book here?'

In (52) position 1 is occupied by a D-Structure subject that has the thematic role of a possessor. In (53) the same position is occupied by a locative NP. Since no possessor is implied in (53), we may assume that the sentence does not have a D-Structure subject; that is, the subject position is an expletive position before the locative moves into it. The well-formedness of both (52) and (53) shows that, as long as the surface subject is filled with an NP, no DE obtains in a *you*-sentence.

Now, consider a *you*-sentence in which the subject position is not lexically occupied.

(54) a. You-mei-you   yiben shu   zai zheli?
        have-not-have one   book at here
        'Is there a book here?'

     b. *You-mei-you   zheben shu zai zheli?
        have-not-have this   book at here
        'Is there this book here?'

(54b) may be considered acceptable only in a context where an understood possessor is implied (that is, only when the empty subject is not an expletive but a pro with an independent thematic role—see (19)–(20)). In other words, (54) contrasts with (53), where no possessor is implied. Whereas (54a) may be used to ask the same question as (53a), (54b) may not be used to ask the same question as (53b). The relevant contrast shows that a DE obtains just in case a nonthematic subject position is lexically unoccupied on the surface.

Notice that although in some sentences (such as those in (52) and (53)) a definite NP may follow *you*, such an NP is only syntactically definite but not semantically so. Thus, a sentence like 'Do you have this book here?' does not ask the contradictory question whether you have *the* copy of the book I am holding in my hand. Rather, it asks whether you have another copy of the book. The relevant point being made here is that, although a *you*-sentence with a lexical subject allows an object that is syntactically definite but semantically indefinite, a *you*-sentence with an unoccupied nonthematic subject position cannot.

Turning now to sentences with an appearance or disappearance verb, we find that the DE obtains in the following examples.

(55) Lai-le   liangge ren/*Lisi/*ta/*neige ren/*meige ren le
     come-Perf two man/Lisi/he/that man/every man   Prt
     Lit. 'Came two men/*Lisi/*him/*that man/*everybody'

(56) Si-le   liangge ren/*Lisi/*ta/*neige ren/*meige ren le
     die-Perf two man/Lisi/he/that man/every man   Prt
     Lit. 'Died two men/*Lisi/*him/*that man/*everybody'

In each case a definite D-Structure object must be NP-Moved to the subject position.

(57) Lisi/ta/neige ren/meige ren lai-/si-le
     Lisi/he/that man/every man come-/die-Perf
     'Lisi/he/the man/everybody came/died'

Even if the surface subject position is filled, the DE still obtains; this is one way the (dis)appearance sentences differ from *you*-sentences.

(58) Zheli si-le   yige ren/*ta/*neige ren/*meige ren le
     here die-Perf one man/he/that man/every man   Prt

Another different property of (dis)appearance sentences is that the DE obtains only if the existential verb is in the main clause, as in (58), or in an assertive clause, as in (59).

(59) Lisi shuo (zheli) si-le   yige ren/*ta/*neige ren
     Lisi say   here die-Perf one man/he/that man
     'Lisi said that (here) died a man/*he/*the man'

If the existential verb is embedded in a nonassertive clause, such as an adjunct, the DE disappears.

(60) Suiran lai-le   Lisi/neige ren, keshi . . .
     though come-Perf Lisi/that man   but
     'Although Lisi/the man came, but . . .'

(61) Ruguo fasheng zhejian shiqing, jiu . . .
     if   happen this   matter then
     'If this thing happens, then . . .'

(62) Zicong zou-le Zhangsan yihou, jiu . . .
     since go-Perf Zhangsan after   then
     'Ever since Zhangsan left, . . .'

As for existential sentences of the third type, they exhibit no DE at all. This is true regardless of whether a given locational verb is in the main clause or an adjunct clause.

(63) a. Shu-dixia   zuo-zhe yige ren/Zhangsan/neige xiaohai
        tree-bottom sit-Dur one man/Zhangsan/that child
        'Under the tree sits a man/Zhangsan/the child'

     b. Zhuo-shang fang-le yiben/neiben ni   yao de shu
        table-top   put-Perf one/that   you want Rel book
        'On the table is put a/the book that you want'

     c. Qiang-shang gua-zhe   rili
        wall-top   hang-Dur calendar
        'On the wall hangs a/the calendar'

(64) a. Suiran wuzi-li zhu-zhe zhege jiahuo, . . .
        though room-in live-Dur this   fellow
        'Although in the room lives this fellow, . . .'

     b. Yinwei   limian tang-zhe neixie bingren, . . .
        because inside lie-Dur   those patient
        'Because inside (the room) lie those patients, . . .'

Finally, with sentences of the fourth type, the DE also does not obtain.

(65) a. Wo jiao-guo   yige xuesheng/ta/Lisi/neige ren
        I   teach-Exp one student/he/Lisi/that man
        'I have taught a student/him/Lisi/the man before'

     b. Wo mai-le   liangben/zheben/neiben shu
        I   buy-Perf two/this/that   book
        'I bought two/this/that book(s)'

(66) a. Suiran wo jiao-guo   yige/neige xuesheng, . . .
        though I   teach-Exp one/that   student
        'Although I have taught a/the student before, . . .'
     b. Zicong wo kan-le   liangben/zheben shu   yihou, . . .
        since I   read-Perf two/this   book after
        'Ever since I read two/this book(s), . . .'

We have seen the distribution of the DE in sentences that do not
contain a predication phrase in position 4. Let us now consider what
happens when they do contain such a phrase. Quite unlike the previous
cases, no definite NP may appear in any such sentence.

(67) You yige/*neige ren   hen youqian
     have one/that   man very rich
     'There is a/*the man very rich'

(68) Lai-le   yige ren/*ta/*neige ren hen yonggan
     come-Perf one man/he/that man   very bráve
     'There came a man/*he/*the man very brave'

(69) Di-shang zuo-zhe yige/*neige ren   hen congming[10]
     floor-top sit-Dur one/that   man very clever
     'On the floor sat a/*the man very clever'

(70) Wo ai-guo   yige nuhai/*Mali/*neige nuhai hen piaoliang
     I   love-Exp one girl/Mary/that girl   very pretty
     'I have been in love with a girl/*Mary/*that girl very pretty'

This restriction obtains without exception, regardless of whether or not
the subject is lexically filled, and whether the verb is in the main clause
or in an adjunct clause. Compare (71) with (52)–(53), (72) with (60)–
(62), (73) with (64), and (74) with (66).

(71) Wo you yiben/*zheben shu   hen youqu
     I   have one/this   book very interesting
     'I have a/*the book which is very interesting'

(72) Fasheng-le yijian/*neijian shiqing hen kepa   yihou, . . .
     happen-Perf one/that   matter very terrible after
     'After there happened a/*the thing which is terrible, . . .'

(73) Suiran zheli zhu-zhe yige/*neige ren   hen xiong, . . .
     though here live-Dur one/that   man very fierce
     'Although here lives a/*the man who is very fierce, . . .'

(74) Yinwei ni jiao-guo   yixie/*neixie xuesheng hen
     because you teach-Exp some/those   student   very
     congming, . . .
     clever
     'Because you have taught some/*those students who were very
     clever, . . .'

Summarizing, the distribution of the DE in Chinese existential sentences is as follows. When a predication phrase occurs in position 4, the
DE obtains without exception. In the absence of the predication the
DE is observed with *you*-sentences when an expletive subject is empty
and with (dis)appearance verbs when they appear in the main clause or
in an assertive clause, but not with locative existential sentences or
sentences of experiential existence, with *you*-sentences whose subject position is filled, or with (dis)appearance clauses in nonassertive
contexts.

9.4 On Deriving Definiteness Effects

Now that we have seen the distribution of the DE in existential sentences in Chinese, the next questions to be addressed are why such
sentences may exhibit the DE, and why the distribution of the DE is
precisely as it is.

There have been a number of approaches to the theory of the DE.
These are either syntactic, semantic, or pragmatic in nature—following the typology used by Safir in chapter 4—or a combination thereof.
A syntactic, and by now well-known, account is that of Safir (1982; see
also chapter 4) and Reuland (1983). According to this account, the
presence of the DE is closely tied to the fact that most existential sentences involve verbs that do not select D-Structure subjects. The essence of this theory is based on the generalization in (75).

(75) The DE is found in unbalanced θ-chains.

A θ-chain, as defined in Chomsky (1981), is a c-command chain (X,Y),
X c-commanding Y, where X is a nonthematic position and Y is a
thematic position. Typical examples of θ-chains are those established
when an argument is moved. A normal chain established in this way has
the form (NP,EC), where NP is a lexical phrase and EC is an empty
category. An unbalanced chain, on the other hand, is one of the form
(EC,NP). In each of the sentences (76) and (77) there is an unbalanced

chain if we assume that the NP in position 3 is coindexed with the subject position.

(76) EC_i you yiben shu_i zai zheli
      have one book at here
'There is a book here'

(77) EC_i fasheng-le   yijian $shiqing_i$ hen kepa
      happen-Perf one   matter very terrible
'There happened something terrible'

Since in an unbalanced chain the lexical NP is A-bound, if nothing else is said such a chain would be excluded by Principle C of the binding theory, which requires all R-expressions to be A-free. Safir's theory then postulates that indefinite NPs, but not definites, are exempt from Principle C—on the ground either that indefinites are less referential than definites (the "Indefinite NP Property" proposed in Safir 1982: 237) or that they are predicates in some sense in existential sentences (the "Predicate Principle" proposed by Safir in chapter 4). The result is, then, that when an unbalanced chain must be formed (for whatever reason), a sentence is well formed just in case the chain can escape Principle C. And this is the DE.

This approach appears to be quite plausible in view of some of the facts we have seen in Chinese. For one thing, we saw that, in the absence of a predication clause in position 4, the DE obtains only in existential sentences of the first two types but not in those of the third and fourth types. Consider sentences of the fourth type, in which the verb has a thematic subject. Obviously, in such sentences there can be no unbalanced chain connecting the subject with the NP in position 3—in fact, they cannot form a θ-chain at all, or the θ-Criterion would be violated. The absence of an unbalanced chain thus correctly predicts that no DE obtains in such sentences. The same applies to sentences of the third type. As noted earlier, an important property of locative existential sentences is that the subject position must be filled with a locative NP. The locative phrase cannot occur as a PP either postverbally or preverbally. It is not clear what forces the subject position to be filled, but it is clear that no unbalanced chain is present in such sentences, and again there is no DE. On the other hand, sentences of the first two types are clearly those in which an unbalanced chain may be formed, because the verbs do not select a D-Structure subject— except for *you*, which may or may not have a D-Structure subject—

and because their expletive subjects need not always be lexically filled. The fact that the first two types of sentences differ from the last two types thus comes as no surprise.

Another piece of support for the syntactic approach comes from the distribution of the DE in *you*-sentences. We have seen that a *you*-sentence exhibits the DE just in case an expletive subject position is left lexically unoccupied (see the discussion centering around (52)–(54)). If an expletive subject position is filled with a locative phrase, or if the subject of a *you*-sentence is not expletive (either filled with a lexical possessor NP or a pro), then the DE does not obtain. Obviously, in these cases no unbalanced chain can be involved, and the lack of the DE is correctly predicted. In the case of an unfilled expletive subject position it is plausible to assume that it always entails the existence of an unbalanced chain. The obligatory existence of such a chain may be forced by Case inheritance, as suggested by Safir (1982), or by a principle that requires an expletive subject to be coindexed with something in VP at LF, as suggested by Reuland (1983). In either case the existence of the DE is predicted. This syntactic explanation is particularly appealing, especially in view of the fact that what is prohibited in the DE context is not just an NP that is semantically interpreted as definite but one that cannot have a definite syntactic form. A semantic explanation would not be sufficient to make the necessary distinction.

We thus see that Safir's and Reuland's account receives some support from certain existential sentences in Chinese. It does not appear to be capable of deriving the full range of DE facts that we have observed, however. First, we have seen that within a (dis)appearance sentence the DE may obtain regardless of whether the subject position is occupied by a locative or temporal NP (see (55)–(59)). In the absence of an unbalanced chain in such sentences as (58), Safir's and Reuland's theory is too weak to account for the presence of the DE. Second, given that the DE disappears when a (dis)appearance sentence is embedded within an adverbial adjunct (see (60)–(62)), this theory also appears to be too strong in predicting a DE that actually does not occur even when the subject is unfilled. There appears to be no general reason why the difference between main and adverbial clauses should make a difference with respect to the presence of an unbalanced chain. Third, whenever a predication clause is present in position 4, the DE obtains in all sentences without exception, regardless of whether the subject is thematic or expletive, filled or empty, and therefore regardless of whether there is an unbalanced chain (see (67)–(74)). This last case suggests that, in addition to "Safir's generalization" (75), the generalization in (78) is operative.

(78) The DE is found in existential sentences with a clause of predication.

The three facts just mentioned apparently cannot be derived from Safir's and Reuland's theory. It seems, however, that they may be partially derived from a theory that is less syntactic in nature. Consider first the distribution of the DE when no predication is present. It seems that the four kinds of sentences differ with respect to the degree of existentiality inherent in the verbs involved. In particular, *you* appears to be purely existential in meaning. A (dis)appearance verb conveys existence primarily but also something else. A locative verb appears to convey primarily the location of a given object, though also its existence. Similarly, an experiential or perfective verb denotes primarily an action, and only secondarily the existence of an experience or event. More specifically, *you* is completely existential, a (dis)appearance verb is highly existential since the verb stem itself expresses existence, and a locative, experiential, or perfective verb is less so since the existentiality is associated only with its suffix.

If this is correct, then it makes sense to assume that whereas the DE obtains with *you* in most cases, it obtains with (dis)appearance verbs only when they appear in positions where an assertion of existence can be most easily made—that is, when the relevant NP is in focus, as in main or assertive clauses.[11] The DE does not obtain with locative, experiential, or perfective verbs since the existence component of the verb, being within a suffix, is too weak to make the verb sufficiently existential. The DE is found, then, only when a given sentence is "highly existential"—presumably because a definite NP is highly inappropriate with the semantics of existence. In the words of Barwise and Cooper (1981:183), a "strong" determiner will result in either tautology or contradiction.

A plausible account of the asymmetry between *you*-sentences and (dis)appearance sentences thus appears to be one that is lexical-semantic in nature—one that appeals to the semantic difference between *you* and other verb types.[12] If correct, however, this account would undermine the syntactic account regarding the absence of the DE in locative, experiential, and perfective sentences (where the subject is either filled or thematic), though the contrast between certain *you*-sentences (see (52)–(54)) appears to continue to resist a semantic account.[13]

Now consider generalization (78), when a predication clause does occur. (78) apparently has no similar explanation within the lexical-semantic approach, given that the DE obtains uniformly with verbs of all four types, in the presence of a predication. In fact, the possible occurrence of a predication probably has nothing to do with the inherent features of a verb. Although I have indicated that XP occurs most typically with an existential verb or one that contains some feature of existentiality (as in an experiential or perfective sentence), it is also possible to find sentences like (79)–(80), in which the verb appears to have nothing to do with existence.

(79) Wo hen xiang xuan yimen ke   tamen shuo hen youqu
     I   very hope elect one   course they say very interesting
     'I very much hope to elect a course, which they say is very interesting'

(80) Wo zheng zai kan yiben shu   hen youyisi
     I   right at read one   book very interesting
     'I am right now reading a book which is very interesting'

Furthermore, there is in fact a condition more strict than the DE on sentences with a predication clause. In addition to being indefinite, the NP in position 3 must contain a numeral quantifier (as in (79)–(80) and other previous examples) but cannot be a bare NP. Compare (81) and (82).

(81) a. Wo renshi yige nuren hen piaoliang
         I   know one woman very pretty
         'I know a woman who is very pretty'

     b. *Wo renshi nuren   hen piaoliang
         I   know woman very pretty

(82) a. Wo jiao-guo   yige xuesheng hen congming
         I   teach-Exp one student   very clever
         'I have taught a student who is very clever'

     b. *Wo jiao-guo   xuesheng hen congming
         I   teach-Exp student   very clever

The (b)-sentences are ill formed even if the object NP is interpreted as an indefinite nongeneric on a par with a bare plural in English. Clearly, this is not an instance of the DE, and it is not observed with sentences that exhibit a DE but contain no predication clause.

(83) a. Si-le   yige ren le
       die-Asp one man Asp
       'A man died'

    b. Si-le   ren le
       die-Asp man Asp
       'Someone/People died'

What (81) and (82) show is that they require the NP in position 3 to be *referential*. Together with the DE, this means that the NP must be *specific*, that is, referentially indefinite. The generalization is that these sentences exhibit a "specificity effect" (and not just a DE).

(84) In sentences with a predication clause in position 4 the NP in position 3 must be specific.

There is further evidence that this generalization is correct. It is well known that in Chinese a numerically quantified NP is generally specific. Thus, such an NP does not occur naturally in the scope of negation.[14]

(85) *Wo meiyou kanjian yige ren
    I   not   see   one man
    'I did not see a certain man'

Furthermore, a sentence with a clause of predication cannot occur as a question.

(86) *Ni shenme shihou jiao-guo   yige ren hen congming?
    you what   time   teach-Exp one man very clever
    '*When did you teach a certain man who is very clever?'

(87) *Shei renshi yige nuren hen piaoliang?
    who know one woman very pretty
    '*Who knows a certain woman who is very pretty?'

Questions like (86)–(87) are as odd as their English translations. Given the generalization (84), the object NP in each of (86)–(87) is necessarily specific—that is, an NP whose reference is known to the speaker but assumed by the speaker to be unknown to the addressee. The oddness of these questions thus follows—for the simple reason that the interrogator is not being cooperative in the sense of Grice (1975).

What, then, might be the explanation for generalization (84)? Notice that the syntactic account proposed by Safir and Reuland is not intended to deal with "specificity effects," and one need not regard (84) as a problem for their theory. However, it is possible to factor (84) into two parts: an indefiniteness requirement (the DE) and a referentiality requirement. In this case it is reasonable to hope to derive the indefiniteness requirement from whatever principle it is that derives the DE in general terms. It is unclear, however, how either the syntactic account described here or any account based on lexical semantics can provide an adequate explanation for both parts of (84). A functional-pragmatic account may be plausible in this case. Intuitively, the predication clause seems to exist solely for the purpose of elaborating on some NP being introduced into the discourse. Such an NP is necessarily indefinite (see Heim 1982). Furthermore, such an NP must be referential, inasmuch as the predication clause is a continuative description. (As in the case of a nonrestrictive relative clause, it is impossible to provide a continuative description of something that is entirely nonreferential.) Since the NP cannot be definite or nonreferential, it can only be specific. This intuitive remark, however, cannot stand as a real explanation for the "specificity effect." Unfortunately, I am not able to formulate in precise terms a better theory of definiteness and specificity effects, and I must leave the problems observed for future studies.

9.5 Conclusion

In this chapter I have provided a description of some general properties of existential sentences in Chinese and discussed, in a rather preliminary fashion, how some of these properties may be derived in a proper theory of grammar. I have argued that existential sentences cannot be properly analyzed along the lines of the bare NP theory, and I have suggested that most of them may be best analyzed along the lines of the NP – XP theory, though the clausal analysis may also be quite plausible for some of them. Regarding the distribution of the DE, I have shown that although some facts appear to support a syntactic account of the DE, others appear to resist such an account and favor instead an account that is either lexical-semantic or functional-pragmatic in nature. This discussion is inconclusive regarding which account might provide the right solution to the problem of explaining the DE. I hope to have at least given a fair survey of the problems involved that any adequate theory of the DE must be prepared to deal with.

Notes

For helpful discussions on the issues addressed here I am grateful to Yun-Hua Huang, Kuang Mei, Jeffrey Tung, Shou-Hsin Teng, Peter and Gaby Cole, the participants of the Fifth Groningen Round Table, and particularly Eric Reuland. Citation of the papers presented at the Round Table is based on the oral presentation or material circulated at or before the meeting.

1. The string *zhuo-shang* 'table-top' in (4)–(5) consists of the N 'table' followed by what Chao (1968) calls a "localizer." Li and Thompson (1981) have assumed that a "localizer" is a postposition. However, except for the way it is usually translated into English (as a preposition 'on'; see the translation of (4)–(5)), there appears to be no reason for this assumption. If *zhuo-shang* were a postpositional phrase, one would expect that it could, like a prepositional phrase, occur alone in adjunct position *and* could not occur as the object of a preposition. But *zhuo-shang*, and similar examples given later, cannot occur in adjunct positions alone, is usually preceded by the preposition *zai* 'at', and may occur in regular NP positions (for instance, as a subject) in a sentence. A more reasonable assumption is that it is an NP.

2. The first three types of existential sentences have been fairly well known among Chinese grammarians. For more detailed descriptions, see Fan 1963, Teng 1977, Mei 1972, Huang 1967 [1983], and Wang 1981. Li and Thompson (1981) consider the fourth type of sentence on a par with the other types, all of which they call "presentative sentences."

3. Sentences like the following are well formed, where the bracketed clause contains the relative clause marker *de*.

(i) Ta bei yige ren [hen youqian de] pian-le
    he by one man very rich   Rel cheat-Asp
    'He was cheated by a man, one who was very rich'

(ii) Ta kanjian-le neige xuesheng [dai   yanjing de]
     he see-Asp that student   wear glasses Rel
     'He saw the student, the one who had glasses on'

These bracketed clauses differ from the expressions of predication given in (30)–(31) in that each contains a relative clause marker and is obviously a relative clause modifier. Such a clause can occur with an NP in any NP position, unlike the predication clause discussed in the text. Although these clauses may look like postnominal modifiers, they do not constitute real evidence for postnominal modification, since they can be readily analyzed as prenominal modifiers of an appositive NP with an empty head following *de* (as in the case of a normal free relative).

4. Shou-Hsin Teng (personal communication) has suggested that the grammaticality of sentences like (i) provides a further argument against the bare NP analysis.

(i) Wo you yige pengyou ta hen congming
    I   have one friend   he very clever
    'I have a friend who is very clever'

It is well known that, in Chinese, relativization of a subject must use the gap strategy but not the resumptive pronoun strategy. If, according to the bare NP analysis, the descriptive clause *ta hen congming* 'he is very clever' were analyzed as a postnominal relative clause, then *ta* would be a resumptive pronoun, a situation that is otherwise impossible in normal cases of relativization.

5. Structures of predication are not limited to those in which the predicate literally forms a constituent with the NP that it predicates on. For example, Chomsky (1980a) assumes that a purposive clause is a predication on a main clause NP though the two do not form a constituent. In other words, both the clausal analysis and the NP – XP analysis are consistent with the view that the NP – XP sequence involves a structure of predication.

6. In case *you* 'have' is followed by NP alone, it may also be the main verb; indeed, it must be if it is itself suffixed with the perfective *-le*, as in *Ta you-le haizi* 'she have-Perf child' (that is, 'She is pregnant').

7. Williams (1984) argues that his bare NP theory (but not the NP – XP theory) is picked out as the only possible one by the independently motivated assumption that *be* is an Aux and that it subcategorizes for a single XP. But the bare NP theory cannot be argued for in this way, since in a sentence like *There arrived a man sick, arrived* is apparently not an Aux, though apparently Williams will also assume that *a man sick* is an NP.

8. The Chinese counterpart of both *my books* and *books of mine* is *wo de shu,* the same form as *my book.* Whereas *my books* is definite and *books of mine* indefinite in English (given *There are *my books/books of mine on the table*), *wo de shu* can be either definite or indefinite; hence the well-formedness of (48). This difference between English and Chinese possessives may involve a difference in what Gil calls the ''NP configurationality parameter'' between them (see chapter 10). In English genitives must occupy the same position as articles and demonstratives and may be assumed to be a kind of definite determiner. However, in Chinese genitives may cooccur with demonstratives in prenominal position: *wo de neiben shu* 'my that book (= that book of mine)'. Genitives in Chinese are therefore not determiners in any sense and may be assumed to have no definitizing function as determiners do. See the discussion in Lyons 1984.

9. Throughout, I have assumed that the locative PP sometimes following the NP in position 3 is *not* an instance of the expression of predication in position 4 but rather material intervening between positions 3 and 4.

10. In fact, sentences (69) and (70) are grammatical even when the NP in position 3 is definite—but only with an irrelevant meaning. Note the translation of (i) and (ii).

(i) Di-shang zuo-zhe neige ren   hen   congming
    floor-top sit-Dur that   man very clever
    'The man who sat on the floor is very clever'

(ii) Wo ai-guo   neige nuren   hen   piaoliang
     I   love-Exp that   woman very pretty
     'The woman I fell in love with before is very pretty'

In each case the sequence 'that man' or 'that woman' is taken to be the head of the subject of the entire sentence and the string preceding it is a relative clause modifying it. That is, 'that man' and 'that woman' are not in position 3; instead, each is the head of a relativized NP in position 1.

11. The following sentences provide further evidence that the DE obtains with (dis)appearance sentences only when the postverbal NP is in focus.

(i) Zeme hui fasheng zhejian chehuo ne?
   how   can happen this   accident Prt
   'How could this accident happen?'

(ii) Shenme shihou fasheng zhejian shi   de?
    what   time   happen this   matter Prt
    'When did this thing happen?'

Since the focus is on 'how' and 'when', no DE is observed here.

12. There is a point of similarity between this account and a suggestion made by Szabolcsi (1984). Szabolcsi shows that, in Hungarian, the DE associated with an existential sentence with a "particular-fashion verb" may be neutralized when something "extra" is added to the sentence, and she suggests that the "extra" has the effect of "highlighting" the nonexistential part of the sentence. In the present case verbs other than *you* express something more than existence, and this "extra" may neutralize the DE in certain contexts.

13. One may want to extend the lexical-semantic approach to cover even the DE facts regarding *you*-sentences. One possibility is to postulate that there are two distinct *you*'s, one expressing possession and the other existence. Recall that when *you* takes a possessor as subject, as in (52), it does not exhibit the DE. We may assume that this is because possessive *you* is not purely existential and is on a par with existential verbs of the third type, which also do not exhibit the DE. As for cases like (53), in which the subject position is filled with a locative NP but no genuine possessor is implied, we may postulate that the verb is still a possessive *you* taking a location as its possessor in some extended sense (compare *The table has a book on it*). If so, then the lack of the DE in (53) can be explained on a par with that in (52).

14. Since specific NPs are "positive polarity items," in sentences like (i) the object NP must be construed as having wide scope with respect to negation.

(i) John didn't see a certain man

Compare (i) with (85), which is ill formed. This contrast in grammaticality appears to stem from the fact that whereas in English the scope order of quantifiers and other logical elements may often be the inverse of their order in surface structure, this is in general impossible in Chinese (Huang 1982:chap. 3).

Chapter 10

Definiteness, Noun Phrase Configurationality, and the Count-Mass Distinction	David Gil

Most chapters in this volume deal either with the nature of the distinction between definite and indefinite NPs understood in a general sense or with various restrictions on the occurrence of definite or indefinite NPs within certain syntactically, semantically, or pragmatically motivated environments. This chapter, however, is concerned with a different aspect of (in)definiteness—namely, the morphosyntactic devices used by various languages to express the distinction between definite and indefinite NPs, understood in a narrower sense, as corresponding to the distinction expressed by the choice of the article in English (also see Heim 1982). As is evident from the chapters in this volume, languages vary considerably with respect to their strategies for marking (in)definiteness. Whereas in some languages, such as French and Lakhota (Williamson, chapter 7 of this volume), use of both definite and indefinite articles is obligatory, in other languages only the definite article is obligatory, the indefinite article being either optional, as in Hungarian (Szabolcsi 1984), or nonexistent, as in Chamorro (Chung, chapter 8). In still other languages, such as Chinese (Huang, chapter 9) and Japanese (Pesetsky, chapter 5), there are no definite or indefinite articles whatsoever: subject to various "definiteness effects," a bare noun may be construed as either definite or indefinite.

In this chapter I will be concerned with the status of such variation within grammatical theory. Specifically, I will show that whether or not a language has obligatory markings for definite and indefinite NPs is correlated with an array of other NP properties. Accordingly, I will argue that variation with respect to the morphosyntactic strategies for expressing (in)definiteness does not constitute an independent parameter within Universal Grammar but instead is a consequence of two more general parameters governing the structure of NPs in a language:

configurationality (Hale 1981; Chomsky 1981) and the count-mass distinction (Stein 1981; Gil 1982). However, since, as I will argue, one of these two covarying parameters, the count-mass distinction, lies partly outside of grammar, I will suggest that an adequate account of the morphosyntactic devices for marking (in)definiteness must have recourse not only to a theory of Universal Grammar but also to a broader theory concerned with the structure and modes of interaction of other mental faculties underlying language.

Before proceeding with the exposition, I should like to state briefly the methodological assumptions governing the discussion. Following Keenan (1978a,b, 1982, 1983) and Chomsky (1981, 1982a), I will assume that a major goal of linguistic theory is to construct a richly articulated Universal Grammar within which patterns of cross-linguistic variation in syntax and semantics may be reduced to a small number of independent parameters easily learnable by the child. (However, I will assume no particular model of formal semantics or generative grammar.) Moreover, following Chomsky (1975, 1980b, 1982b), I will assume that language is a joint product of several autonomous but interacting mental faculties: one, grammar, accounting for those structural properties unique to language, the remaining faculties accounting for properties shared by language and other domains of mental activity such as music and mathematical reasoning. Thus, for any given linguistic phenomenon, it is an empirical question whether it is most appropriately accounted for within grammatical theory or within a theory of some other mental faculty. For a more extensive defense of this point, see Lightfoot 1980 and Gil, to appear.

10.1 (In)definiteness Marking and the Noun Phrase Typology

Whether or not a language possesses an obligatory morphosyntactic strategy for marking (in)definiteness is one of several correlates of a language typology governing NP structure. Languages generally belong to one of two types that I will denote simply—in order not to prejudge the issues involved—as *Type A* and *Type B*. Table 10.1 presents some of the characteristic features of both language types.

I will argue that the NP typology is a joint product of the two covarying parameters of configurationality and the count-mass distinction. Specifically, Type A languages have configurational NPs and distinguish between count and mass nouns, whereas Type B languages have nonconfigurational NPs and do not distinguish between count and

Table 10.1
The noun phrase typology

Typological Correlate	Type A	Type B
1 Obligatory marking of (in)definiteness	+	−
2 Obligatory marking of nominal plurality	+	−
3 Obligatory marking of numeral classification	−	+
4 Existence of adnominal distributive numerals	−	+
5 Free NP-internal constituent order	−	+
6 Existence of stacked adnominal numeral constructions	−	+
7 Existence of hierarchic interpretations of stacked adjective constructions	+	−

mass nouns, instead treating all nouns as mass. I begin by illustrating the seven correlates and showing how each is a consequence of one of the covarying parameters. In order to illustrate the typology, I will contrast similar constructions in English, a Type A language, and Japanese, a Type B language.

The first correlate of the NP typology is the one that relates it to the theme of this volume: obligatory marking of (in)definiteness. Consider the following constructions.

(1) a. Sam read a/the book
    b. Susumu-ga   hon-o   yonda
       Susumu-Nom book-Acc read-Perf

In Type A languages, such as English, nouns are obligatorily marked as either definite or indefinite. Conversely, in Type B languages, such as Japanese, nouns may occur without overt morphosyntactic marking of (in)definiteness, as does *hon* in (1b); in such cases they may be construed as either definite or indefinite.

This typological correlate is a straightforward consequence of the configurationality parameter. In Type A languages the semantic distinction between definite and indefinite nouns is expressed in one of two ways: (a) as an opposition between an obligatory definite determiner and an obligatory indefinite determiner (for instance, for English singular count nouns such as *book* in (1a)); or (b) as an opposition between one obligatory determiner (definite or indefinite) and either an optional determiner or a "zero" marking (for the opposite (in)definiteness value) (for instance, for English plural count nouns such as *books* and mass nouns such as *water*). Hence, in Type A languages the distribution of bare nouns, such as *book,* is considerably more restricted than that of nouns in construction with articles, such as *a book, the book*. Accordingly, such expressions are commonly assigned different syntactic categories. Specifically, if a bare noun—or other nominal expression—is assigned category N^n (NP of bar level n), then the same expression in construction with a definite or indefinite determiner is assigned category N^{n+1}. However, in Type B languages nouns may occur without overt marking of (in)definiteness; hence, bare nouns, such as *hon,* enjoy roughly the same distribution as quantified nouns, such as *sansatu no hon* 'three books', nouns with demonstratives, such as *kono hon* 'this book', pronouns, such as *anata* 'you', and proper nouns, such as *Susumu.* Consequently, there is no reason not to assign bare nouns to the same syntactic category as these other types of nominal expressions. As a result, Type B languages do not differentiate between the category N^n and the syntactic category N^{n+1} posited in Type A languages in order to accommodate expressions containing nouns in construction with articles; hence, these languages can be said to lack the category N^{n+1}. The first typological correlate thus reflects the degree of NP-internal configurationality of Type A and Type B languages—the function of the definite and indefinite articles in Type A languages being to "raise" an expression from category N^n to category N^{n+1} and thereby increase the amount of NP-internal bar syntactic structure.

The second typological correlate involves the morphosyntactic expression of nominal plurality.

(2) a. Sam read the book(s)
    b. Susumu-ga   hon-o   yonda   (= (1b))
       Susumu-Nom book-Acc read-Perf

In Type A languages a large class of nouns, generally those characterized as count nouns, is obligatorily marked for number: if such a noun is marked as singular, it is interpreted as singular, and similarly for plural. In Type B languages, however, nouns not marked for number may be interpreted as either singular or plural, as *hon* is in (2b). Some Type B languages, such as Japanese, have no nominal plural marking whatsoever, whereas in other Type B languages plural marking may be optional (as in Tagalog), restricted to certain contexts (as in Turkish, where it occurs only when no overtly plural quantifier is present), or interpreted in special ways (as in Indonesian, where it refers to a plurality of kinds; compare English *wines*).

The second typological correlate is an immediate corollary of the count-mass parameter. Since the distinction between singular and plural presupposes countability, only Type A languages (that is, those possessing count nouns) may have obligatory nominal plurality marking. Type B languages, which treat all nouns as mass nouns, accordingly make much less use of nominal plurality markings; their status in such languages, if they are present at all, is generally peripheral.

The third typological correlate pertains to the existence and use of numeral classifier systems.

(3) a. Sam read three books
    b. Susumu-ga   sansatu no   hon-o   yonda
       Susumu-Nom three-Cl Cop book-Acc read-Perf

In Type A languages the use of a numeral classifier—for example, *volumes of*—in construction with count nouns is optional and generally avoided. (In fact, it may be questioned whether phrasal expressions such as *volumes of* should even be analyzed as numeral classifiers. If not, then English and other Type A languages would have no numeral classifiers for count nouns whatsoever.) Conversely, in Japanese and other Type B languages the use of numeral classifiers is obligatory for all nouns: numerals simply cannot occur without such a classifier.

This correlate, too, is a direct consequence of the count-mass parameter. Since count nouns come with a "natural" unit for enumeration, Type A languages, possessing count nouns, do not require a numeral classifier specifying such a unit. Mass nouns, however, have no such natural units; hence, Type B languages, possessing only mass nouns, must make use of a numeral classifier in order to establish appropriate units for enumeration. And, in fact, just as English offers a choice of classifying expressions for its mass nouns—for instance, *three drops/cups/gallons of water*—so Japanese offers a choice of classifiers for all its nouns—for instance, *sansatu no hon* 'three volumes of book' (three books), *sanmai no hon* 'three pages of book' (one or more three-paged books), *sansyoku no hon* 'three colors of book' (one or more three-colored books).

The fourth typological correlate involves a somewhat less well known construction type: adnominal distributive numerals. (For a detailed investigation into the syntax and semantics of distributive numerals, see Gil 1982.)

(4) a. Sam and Cyril carried $\left\{\begin{array}{l}\text{three books each}\\ \text{the books three at a time}\\ \text{the books in threes}\end{array}\right\}$

   b. Susumu to   Siro-ga   sansatuzutu no   hon-o   hakonda
      Susumu and Siro-Nom three-Cl-Dist Cop book-Acc carry-Perf

The form *sansatuzutu* in (4b) is a distributive numeral, obtained from the ordinary numeral-plus-classifier *sansatu* by suffixation of the distributive marker *-zutu;* it is an adnominal distributive numeral since it occurs in construction with a nominal head, *hon.* Sentence (4b) may be interpreted—subject to a certain amount of idiolectal variation—as synonymous with any or all of the three variants of English (4a). Only Type B languages possess adnominal distributive numerals: Type A languages require paraphrases such as those indicated in (4a). (However, Type A languages may possess adverbial distributive numerals, such as English *in threes* in (4a).)

The restriction of adnominal distributive numerals to Type B languages is a consequence of the configurationality parameter. In order to see why, it is first necessary to contrast the syntactic behavior of numerals in Type A and Type B languages. In Type A languages numerals are determiners, combining with expressions of category N^n to yield expressions of category N^{n+1}. (One piece of evidence in support of this claim is provided in the discussion of the sixth typological correlate—namely, that numerals do not stack.) However, in Type B languages NPs are nonconfigurational; hence, there is no distinction between the syntactic categories N^n and N^{n+1} and there can exist no syntactic category of determiner. Accordingly, in Type B languages numerals are either adjectival or nominal modifiers. (For more extensive discussion of the syntax of numerals in typologically diverse languages, see Gil 1982.)

Let us now take a somewhat closer look at the semantics of adnominal distributive numerals. As noted, sentence (4b) may potentially be interpreted according to any of the English paraphrases in (4a). In the first paraphrase, with *three . . . each,* the direct object NP distributes over the subject NP. In the second paraphrase, with *three at a time,* the direct object NP distributes over a set of events, arguably associated with the verb. However, the third paraphrase, with *in threes,* can be interpreted in two ways: either as synonymous with the second paraphrase (with *three at a time*) or as stipulating that Sam and Cyril (either separately or together) carried (in one or more events) an unspecified number of books arranged in sets of threes. For example, both men might have—jointly, in a single event—carried a large sack containing several packages, each of which, in turn, contained three books. It is this second interpretation of the third variant of (4a) that is important here. To begin with, it is—subject to a degree of idiolectal and cross-linguistic variation—the most common way of interpreting constructions such as (4b) containing adnominal distributive numerals (see Gil 1982:341, Universal 16). Moreover, it is the existence of this interpretation that entails that Type A languages cannot possess adnominal distributive numerals. The reason is as follows. In this interpretation the distributive numeral distributes, NP-internally, over its own nominal head. That is, in (4b) *sansatuzutu* distributes over *hon:* the books number three volumes per set, package, and so on. However, this interpretation entails that the distributive numeral cannot be a determiner. For, as proven by Keenan and Stavi (1986), determiners cannot distribute over their heads; this is a consequence of the fact that they are interpreted as functions from a Boolean algebra into its power set. Hence, Type A languages, in which numerals are determiners, cannot possess adnominal distributive numerals. Type B languages may, however, since here numerals are adjectival or nominal modifiers, and such modifiers are interpreted as functions from a Boolean algebra into itself: functions that may satisfy distributivity. (For a more general formulation of this argument, see Gil 1982:344–348.)

The fifth correlate of the NP typology pertains to constituent order. Consider the following constructions in which a nominal head is modified by a possessor phrase, a numeral, an adjective, and a relative clause.

(5) a. Sam's three blue books that Cyril read
    b. Susumu-no   sansatu no   aoi Siro-ga   yonda   hon
       Susumu-Gen three-Cl Cop blue Siro-Nom read-Perf book

Whereas in English the linear order of the four modifiers is rigid, as in (5a), in Japanese the order is free: in fact, all 4! = 24 permutations of the four prenominal modifiers in (5b) yield grammatical NPs. In general, NP-internal constituent order tends to be rigid in languages of Type A but free in languages of Type B.

This correlate is a straightforward corollary of the configurationality parameter. The phenomenon of free constituent order is an important factor in what triggered the development of syntactic theories of configurationality, such as those of Hale (1978) and Chomsky (1981).

The sixth typological correlate also involves a construction type not frequently alluded to in the linguistic literature: stacked numerals. Consider the phrases in (6).

(6) a. *three two books
 b. sansatu no   nisyoku no   hon
    three-Cl Cop two-Cl   Cop book

Whereas in Type A languages it is totally impossible for two adnominal numerals to quantify the same noun, in Japanese and other Type B languages stacked numeral constructions may occur freely. For example, the NP in (6b) has a range of interpretations similar to that of the English *three two-colored books* — in which one of the numerals quantifies not the noun but the adjective. (For further examples and analysis of stacked numeral constructions in other languages, see Gil 1982:229–241, 287–294.)

This correlate is also an immediate corollary of the configurationality parameter. As stated earlier, Type A languages possess NP-internal bar structure and determiners (expressions combining with N^n expressions to yield N^{n+1} expressions); that is, the presence of a determiner will obligatorily induce additional hierarchical structure. Numerals have properties of determiners in English. The most natural assumption is that they are in fact determiners and are interpreted as such. It follows then that numerals do not stack. I am assuming with Keenan (see chapter 12) and Keenan and Stavi (1986) that determiners are interpreted as functions from properties to sets of properties. As a consequence, in (6a) *two books* denotes such a set. Hence, it is not in the domain of the function interpreting *three,* and *three two books* is not assigned an interpretation. The fact that NPs such as *the two books* are possible is not incompatible with this approach, given Keenan's analysis of expressions such as *the n* as basic determiners (see chapter 12). On the other hand, since Type B languages lack a syntactic NP-internal bar structure, they also lack determiners in the sense used here: accordingly, numerals are adjectival or nominal modifiers and are interpreted as such. Hence, in Type B languages numerals — like adjectives and nouns — may be stacked.

The seventh and final correlate of the NP typology pertains to the interpretation of stacked adjective constructions, such as those in (7).

(7) a. small powerful engine   /   powerful small engine
 b. tiisai tayoi   enzin   /   tayoi   tiisai enzin
    small powerful engine   powerful small engine

Each of these four constructions—two English and two Japanese—
may be interpreted as referring to an engine that is both small and powerful relative to engines in general—that is, as synonymous with the
English expression *small and powerful* (or *powerful and small*) *engine*.
In fact, in Japanese this is the only possible interpretation: the two
phrases in (7b) are thus synonymous. However, in English an additional class of interpretations is also available. *Small powerful engine*
may also refer to an engine that is powerful relative to engines in general but small relative to powerful engines—not engines in general; this
phrase may thus denote an engine that is medium-sized or even large
with respect to engines in general. Conversely, *powerful small engine*
may also refer to an engine that is small relative to engines in general
but powerful relative to small engines—not engines in general; this
phrase may accordingly denote an engine that is actually rather weak
with respect to engines in general. In contrast to their Japanese counterparts, the two English phrases in (7a) are thus nonsynonymous. In
general, hierarchic interpretations—such as those of (7a) but not
(7b)—are available for stacked adjective constructions in Type A but
not Type B languages.

This typological correlate is also a consequence of the configurationality parameter. As argued in Gil 1983b, the configurationality parameter governs not only the existence of X′-structure but in fact the existence of hierarchic syntactic structure of any kind. Hence, if an NP is
configurational, A – A – N sequences may possess hierarchic structure
and be parsed A [A N]. However, if an NP is nonconfigurational,
A – A – N sequences will possess no internal constituent structure. Of
course, it is the existence of internal structuring that enables a stacked
adjective construction to be interpreted hierarchically—in such a way
that the outermost adjective A modifies the entire [A N] constituent.
Hence, Type A languages, with configurational NPs, possess hierarchic
interpretations of stacked adjective constructions, whereas Type B
languages, with nonconfigurational NPs, do not.

In illustrating the seven correlates of the NP typology, I have shown
English and Japanese to be typical exemplars of Type A and Type B
languages, respectively. However, like most linguistic typologies, the
NP typology is not exceptionless: alongside many "pure" languages
conforming entirely to the typology, there exist many languages of
"mixed" character, possessing some Type A and some Type B features. Table 10.2 presents a characterization of five languages in terms

Table 10.2
Pure and mixed languages

Language	Correlate						
	1	2	3	4	5	6	7
English	A	A	A	A	A	A	A
Hebrew	A	A	A	A	m	A	B
Russian	B	m	A	B	m	A	B
Georgian	B	m	A	B	m	B	B
Japanese	B	B	B	B	B	B	B

of the seven correlates of the NP typology. In this table A, B, and m indicate that the language behaves like a Type A language, like a Type B language, or in a mixed or unclear manner with respect to the typological correlate in question. Thus, for example, Hebrew patterns in mixed fashion with respect to the fifth correlate, free NP-internal constituent order, since, of the 4! = 24 permutations of the four modifiers in a construction corresponding to (5), more than one but fewer than twenty-four are grammatical. It patterns with Type A languages with respect to the sixth correlate, since it has no stacked adnominal numeral constructions, but it patterns with Type B languages with respect to the seventh correlate, since it has no hierarchic interpretations of stacked adjective constructions. As indicated in table 10.2, Hebrew, Russian, and Georgian are mixed languages with respect to the NP typology.

In order for the NP typology to retain its empirical force, it is necessary to investigate the constraints on the ways in which mixed languages may deviate from the pure typology. A fruitful way of constraining the existence of typologically mixed languages is by means of implicational universals. The following are three implicational universals governing the cooccurrence of obligatory marking of (in)definiteness and some of the other typological features.

(8) *Universal 1*
If a language has obligatory marking of (in)definiteness, then it has obligatory marking of nominal plurality (but not vice versa).

(9) *Universal 2*
If a language has obligatory marking of (in)definiteness, then it has no obligatory marking of numeral classification (but not vice versa).

(10) *Universal 3*
    If a language has obligatory marking of (in)definiteness, then it
    has no stacked adnominal numeral constructions (but not vice
    versa).

Universals 1–3 permit a language to pattern as Type B with respect to
the first correlate, obligatory marking of (in)definiteness, but as mixed
or Type A with respect to the second, third, and sixth correlates. As
indicated in table 10.2, these three options are exploited by a typologically mixed language, Russian, as illustrated by the following
constructions.

(11) Saša pročital   knigu
     Sasha Perf-read-Past-Sg:M book-Acc:Sg:F
     'Sasha read a/the book'
     (compare (1b))

(12) Saša pročital   knigi
     Sasha Perf-read-Past-Sg:M book-Acc:Pl
     'Sasha read (the) books'
     (compare (2a))

(13) Saša pročital   tri   knigi
     Sasha Perf-read-Past-Sg:M three-Acc book-Gen:Sg:F
     'Sasha read (the) three books'
     (compare (3a))

(14) *tri   dve   knigi
     three-Nom two-Nom:F book-Gen:Sg:F
     'three two books'
     (compare (6a))

As (11), (12), and (13) show, Russian patterns as Type B with respect to
the first correlate: like *hon* in (1b), *knigu* and *knigi* may—in the absence of an article—be interpreted as either definite or indefinite.
However, in accordance with Universal 1, Russian patterns as mixed
with respect to the second correlate: whereas in some contexts, as with
the bare nouns in (11) and (12), marking of nominal plurality is obligatory, in other contexts, as with a direct case in construction with the
numeral 2, 3, or 4, illustrated in (13), a (genitive) singular form of the
noun is interpreted as plural. Next, in accordance with Universal 2,
Russian patterns as Type A with respect to the third correlate: as (13)
shows, use of numeral classifiers is, as in English, optional and disfa-

vored. Finally, in accordance with Universal 3, Russian patterns as Type A with respect to the sixth correlate: it has no stacked adnominal numeral constructions.

While permitting the existence of typologically mixed languages such as Russian, Universals 1–3 rule out languages patterning as Type A with respect to the first correlate but as mixed or Type B with respect to the second, third, or sixth. That is, they rule out languages with obligatory marking of (in)definiteness and one or more of the following: no obligatory marking of nominal plurality, obligatory marking of numeral classification, and stacked adnominal numeral constructions. It should be noted, however, that these universals are based on a limited sample of languages: further investigation may produce either support or counterexamples—and, perhaps, reveal additional implicational universals.

10.2 Some Consequences of the Noun Phrase Typology

The NP typology has a number of important consequences for the substance and methodology of linguistic theory. First, it provides support for recent proposals that the configurationality parameter is an attribute not of grammars as a whole but rather of various subsystems of categories within the grammars of particular languages (Chomsky 1981; Szabolcsi 1983; Gil and Ritter 1984). Consider, for example, Japanese. Hoji (1982) has argued—against claims by Farmer (1980), Hale (1980), and Chomsky (1981)—that Japanese is in fact configurational at the clausal level. Coupled with Hoji's arguments, the results of this chapter would support the view that Japanese varies with respect to configurationality at clausal and phrasal levels—being configurational at the former level but nonconfigurational at the latter.

A second important effect of the NP typology is to underscore the inadequacy of linguistic theories based solely on the study of English. Much recent work in syntax and semantics relies crucially upon certain properties that are limited to Type A languages—specifically, some of the more familiar western European ones. Thus, for example, generalized quantification theory (Barwise and Cooper 1981; Keenan and Stavi 1986; Keenan and Moss 1985; Keenan, chapter 12 of this volume) is concerned with the formulation of a semantic characterization of determiners; however, the occurrence of determiners is restricted to Type A languages—Type B languages have none. The results of generalized quantification theory may thus be construed as representing the consequences of assigning certain particular values to the configurationality and count-mass parameters. However, in order to achieve universal validity—specifically, in order to come to grips with the existence of Type B languages—it is incumbent upon generalized quantification theory to offer analyses not just of determiners but also of quantifiers belonging to other syntactic categories, such as adjectives and nouns. In addition, generalized quantification theory must provide a suitable framework for a unified analysis of quantification over both count and mass domains.

A third, perhaps deeper issue raised by the NP typology pertains to the problem of delimiting the scope of grammatical theory. Let us consider in more detail the nature of the count-mass parameter—specifically, raising the question whether or not it is a proper part of grammatical theory. Following Chomsky (1976), I will assume that semantics is partly grammatical and partly extragrammatical (pertaining to other mental faculties such as common sense); the question is, then, to which of these two domains of semantics the count-mass parameter should be assigned. A reasonable method for adjudicating questions such as these is proposed by Lightfoot (1980): a linguistic phenomenon is to be characterized as grammatical if and only if it possesses no extralinguistic reflexes or parallels. Hence, in order to determine whether the count-mass parameter is grammatical, we must search for possible reflexes within various domains of nonverbal mental activity. If such reflexes are found, the parameter will be characterized as extragrammatical; if none are found, it will be said to fall within the scope of grammatical theory.

Applying this criterion to the count-mass parameter yields mixed results, suggesting that the parameter is partly grammatical, partly extragrammatical. The notion of countability itself would appear to be extragrammatical. Humans can compare the cardinalities of sets nonverbally, by setting up a one-to-one correspondence between them; this feat may also be accomplished by speakers of languages with impoverished numeral vocabularies, of the "one, two, three, many" variety. (This is not to deny the possibility, occasionally raised, that there may exist significant evolutionary and/or synchronic links between the arithmetical and verbal aptitudes of human beings; see Gil 1983a for discussion.)

The classification of particular nouns as either count or mass also depends on a variety of extragrammatical factors. Our conception of the world is such that some entities, such as books and concepts, are associated with a natural unit of enumeration, whereas other entities, such as water and sincerity, are not. As a result, some nouns, such as English *book, concept,* Hebrew *sefer, musag,* are treated by many languages as count, whereas other nouns, such as English *water, sincerity,* Hebrew *mayim, kenut,* are treated by all languages as basically mass. Moreover, the existence of a natural unit of enumeration quite obviously depends on a number of contextual factors. For example, a chemist may consider water to form natural units of one mole, or approximately 6.02×10^{23} molecules. A geographer may be more concerned with various natural configurations of water: rivers, lakes, seas, and so forth. And a connoisseur of mineral water may count different kinds of water—or, more simply, *waters.* In Type A languages, then, an appropriate context can be constructed to convert almost any mass noun into a count noun.

The classification of nouns into count or mass may also be governed by grammatical factors. Consider, for example, the fact that English *advice* is a mass noun, whereas its Hebrew counterpart ʕeyca is treated as count. No nonverbal conceptual difference would appear to be associated with this fact; it is, accordingly, a fact about grammar—specifically, about the lexicons of English and Hebrew. Indeed, Hebrew consistently allows more count nouns than English; for example, the Hebrew count nouns *leḥem, gir, rahit,* correspond to the English mass nouns *bread, chalk, furniture.* (I am aware of no opposite cases of Hebrew mass nouns corresponding to English count nouns.) The different classifications of count and mass nouns in English and Hebrew must accordingly be represented in the grammars of the two languages.

In general, though, the grammatical aspects of the count-mass parameter would seem to be of a more restricted nature than its extragrammatical aspects. I therefore conclude—albeit tentatively, and for want of more extensive investigation—that the count-mass parameter is largely extragrammatical, though possessing, in addition, some grammatical reflexes.

As we have seen, the count-mass parameter covaries with the configurationality parameter—a language distinguishes between count and mass nouns if and only if it possesses configurational NPs. Unlike the count-mass parameter, however, the configurationality parameter is quite clearly grammatical—in fact, syntactic. The NP typology accordingly reflects a state of affairs in which a grammatical parameter covaries with a parameter that is largely extragrammatical. Let us now examine the significance of this state of affairs.

Considerations of redundancy dictate that if two parameters covary, a more felicitous account of the facts should be sought: an account in which one parameter is characterized as primitive and the other is expressed in terms of it, or perhaps in which both parameters are reduced to a third, more fundamental parameter. Specifically, we may entertain three possible scenarios governing the relationship between the configurationality and count-mass parameters. According to *Scenario I*, the configurationality parameter is primitive, entailing the count-mass parameter. To the extent that the count-mass parameter is extragrammatical, this scenario supports a version of linguistic relativity whereby grammar determines world view (Humboldt 1903–1918; Whorf 1956). According to *Scenario II*, the count-mass parameter is more basic, entailing the configurationality parameter. This scenario is in the spirit of various pragmatically oriented theories that attempt to explain syntactic structures in terms of communicative function (for example, Givón 1979; Hopper and Thompson 1980). Finally, *Scenario III* asserts the existence of a third, deeper parameter underlying both the configurationality and the count-mass parameters—though what the nature of such a parameter may be remains an open question.

An adequate analysis of these scenarios lies beyond the scope of this chapter. Nevertheless, some preliminary comments may point to the tentative conclusion that Scenario I is closer to the truth. First, of the two parameters, the notion of configurationality is more general than the count-mass distinction. Thus, whereas the notion of configurationality is relevant to clauses, phrases, words, syllables—in fact, to just about any grammatical unit whatsoever—the count-mass distinction pertains primarily—though perhaps not exclusively—to nouns or NPs. However, according to Scenarios II and III, configurationality at the NP level—and the NP level alone—is a consequence of some other parameter: the count-mass distinction in the former case, a third, unspecified parameter in the latter. Hence, in Scenarios II and III configurationality at the NP level is accounted for in a unique fashion, totally different from whatever explanation it receives at other levels. As a result, Scenarios II and III obscure the underlying phenomenological unity of configurationality across various grammatical domains. The only scenario consistent with such unity is Scenario I, whereby configurationality at one particular level (that of the NP) determines the value of the count-mass parameter. Thus, if these tentative observations are correct, the NP typology would provide support for one version of Whorf's hypothesis of linguistic relativity.

Whichever scenario is in fact closer to the truth, the preceding observations have important consequences for linguistic methodology. The NP typology points to the need for linguistic theory to concern itself with patterns of cross-linguistic variation. Specifically, in order to provide a grammatical analysis of the morphosyntactic marking of (in)definiteness in English, it is necessary to investigate not only English but also Japanese and other languages, thereby constructing a Universal Grammar within which the marking of (in)definiteness in English will emerge as one of several consequences of a particular assignment of values to a certain parameter. However, in order to construct such a Universal Grammar, it is necessary, among other things, to adjudicate among the three scenarios just formulated, so as to determine which parameter it is that governs the morphosyntactic marking of (in)definiteness across languages. Moreover, since one of the parameters—the count-mass distinction—is largely extragrammatical, adjudication among the three scenarios must involve an investigation not only of grammar but also of other mental faculties—specifically, those pertaining to the notion of countability. Consequently, any explanatorily adequate account of the morphosyntactic marking of (in)definiteness in English must in turn be grounded not just in a theory of Universal Grammar but indeed in a theory of mind concerned—at the very least—with the structure of the various mental faculties underlying language.

This, then, is the major methodological moral to be derived from our study of (in)definiteness and the NP typology. That this moral has far-reaching consequences with regard to the daily practice of linguistics does not detract from its validity.

Note

I am indebted to Betsy Ritter for a number of lengthy discussions that assisted me in formulating some of the ideas presented in this chapter, and to several participants of the Fifth Groningen Round Table for various useful suggestions. I am also grateful to Edith Moravcsik, an anonymous MIT Press reviewer, and the editors of this volume, Eric Reuland and Alice ter Meulen, for a number of helpful comments on earlier drafts. The data cited herein were kindly provided by Manana Bat-Hana and Tamara Japaridze (Georgian), Baruch Podolsky and Ilan Roziner (Russian), and Kahoru Yoshikawa (Japanese). This chapter was written during July 1984 at Mylah's Nipa Hut in Puerto Galera; special thanks are due to all the people there—and in particular Robinson Arbilo and Joelito Arca—for providing an atmosphere stimulating and conducive to work.

Chapter 11

The Compositional Nature of (In)definiteness

Franciska de Jong

Traditionally most discussions on the distinction between definiteness and indefiniteness have in some sense a narrow scope: either the set of expressions under consideration is limited, or the set of contexts regarded as sensitive to the distinction. The rather extensive literature on (in)definiteness appears to lack a clear-cut definition of the categories involved. In part, this can be ascribed to the often rather coarse selection of data. A comparison of the distributional restrictions in two contexts that are assumed to be sensitive to (in)definiteness can clarify this diagnosis. The contexts are (a) sentences with initial *there* and (b) partitive NP-constructions. The following restrictions, presented here as filters, have been proposed.

(1) a. *there be [+def] N XP   (see Milsark 1977)
    b. *Det of [−def] N   (see Selkirk 1977)

With respect to *a*, *the*, and *some*, the reference to the feature [±def] in both (1a) and (1b) seems to reflect a correct generalization. The indefinite articles *a* and *some* can occur within the grammatical subject of (1a), whereas they cannot occupy the embedded determiner position in partitives. The definite article *the* shows the reverse possibilities: it cannot occur in the crucial position of (1a), whereas it can occupy the relevant position in (1b). However, if in the analysis of these two contexts one wishes to deal with the distributional peculiarities of other determiners as well, there appears to be a classificatory problem. This is illustrated by the observations in (2) and (3), which incorporate the distribution of *most, all, the,* and numerals like *three* and *twenty*. Like *the* and unlike numerals, *most* and *all* are blocked in *there*-sentences. But like numerals and unlike *the* and *all, most* is blocked in the crucial position of partitives as well.[1]

(2) There are $\begin{Bmatrix} \text{*the} \\ \text{*all} \\ \text{*most} \\ \text{three} \end{Bmatrix}$ boys in the garden

(3) a. Some of $\begin{Bmatrix} \text{the} \\ \text{*most} \\ \text{*twenty} \end{Bmatrix}$ boys are red-haired

b. Half of $\begin{Bmatrix} \text{the} \\ \text{all} \\ \text{*most} \\ \text{*twenty} \end{Bmatrix}$ boys are red-haired

This problem can be solved in several ways. First, since there is no independently motivated criterion for (in)definiteness, there is no need to think of the distinction between definites and indefinites as a dichotomy. If definiteness and indefiniteness are taken to be the two extreme values on a sliding scale, a third category of determiners, neither definite nor indefinite, is conceivable. If *most* is classified as a member of this third category, the problem that is posed by (2) and (3) in view of (1a) and (1b) need not arise.

This solution seems to be descriptively adequate, but its drawback is obvious. Not only does it explain very little, it also replaces an analysis that enables one to regard the subcategories among determiners as natural classes with an analysis that does not. Obviously, some improvement might be gained by adopting more than just one dichotomy. A solution along these lines—though not presented as such—can be found in Barwise and Cooper 1981.

Barwise and Cooper distinguish between a weak-strong contrast among determiners and a definite-indefinite contrast among NPs. The first contrast is said to be reflected in *there*-sentences, whereas the latter is regarded as relevant in relation to the partitive construction. Note that Milsark introduces *weak* and *strong* as neutral terms discriminating between those determiners that can occur in (1a) and those that cannot, whereas Barwise and Cooper introduce two criteria pertaining to two different syntactic categories, both of which are relevant to a specific context.[2] Consequently, the observations in (2) and (3) cannot be accounted for in a uniform way. Superficially, both (2) and (3) illustrate the same phenomenon, namely, that in certain contexts only a restricted set of determiners can be inserted. Hence, an account that does not a priori exclude a generalization over contexts and categories is to be preferred. Such an alternative will be proposed here. The classification of determiners to be proposed will be based on a system incorporating two features, provisionally referred to as $[\pm F_1]$ and $[\pm F_2]$. Each feature covers a true dichotomy. The four values involved contribute to the characterization of various natural classes among the set of determiners, by combining F_1-values with F_2-values. Empirical evidence for this proposal will be derived from the analysis of several other restrictive contexts. Because space is limited, the discussion will be restricted to simple determiners, but there are indications that the proposal to be developed can deal with the distribution of complex determiners as well. The features will be given model-theoretic definitions that contribute to a more explanatory account of the restrictions showing up in (2) and (3).

11.1 Extension of the Data

The data reviewed so far can be summarized as follows. The class of determiners blocked in *there*-sentences, *all, the,* and *most,* does not correspond to the class permitted in partitives. Just like numerals, *most* is not contained in the latter class. Within this restricted set of data one might question the importance of the contradictory distribution of *most* in view of the generally adopted filters in (1). However, even if we restrict attention to simple determiners, the need for at least a third class is strengthened by the distribution of *neither* and a comparison of the data for English in (2) and (3) with Dutch data.

The determiner *neither* shares its distributional properties with *most:* it is blocked in both (1a) and (1b). Dutch has no determiners that can be regarded as the counterparts of *most* and *neither.* (The meaning of *most* is expressed by the complex *de meeste.*) But it does have a determiner with identical distributional properties: *sommige* 'some of the' is also blocked in both contexts.

Just like the data for *most,* the distribution of *neither* and *sommige* motivates a revision of the traditional interpretation of $[\pm def]$ as corresponding to a division among determiners in two subclasses. My proposal will be based on two features instead of one, and, as noted, both contexts in (1) will be taken as sensitive to just one of them. Though the features still have no exact definitions, a summary of the data under consideration is given in matrix (4), where $[\pm F_1]$ corresponds to the distributional alternatives "±blocked in *there/er*-sentences" and [±F₂] to "±permitted in partitives."

(4)	F_1	F_2
the/de	+	+
all/alle	+	+
(the two)/beide	+	+
(some of the)/sommige	+	−
most/(de meeste)	+	−
neither	+	−
one, two, three . . .	−	−
some/enkele	−	−
many/vele	−	−
few/weinige	−	−
no/geen	−	−

Note that *every* and *both* are not subsumed under (4), in spite of their clear distribution: not permitted in either context. An analysis of the distribution of *both* and *every* would require the introduction of a third distinction, based on an idea of Ladusaw, that would bring about a subdivision in the set [±F₂]-determiners. As pointed out by Ladusaw (1982), determiners permitted in the embedded position of partitives should allow a group reading. Since my concern is to analyze the notion of (in)definiteness, I will not discuss this third distinction. Unlike *both*, Dutch *beide* is not exclusively distributive; hence, it can occur in partitives.³ Note also that no [−F₁, +F₂]-determiner shows up. For an explanation of this, see section 11.2.

Before turning to the interpretation of these features, I will present extra evidence for a classificatory system allowing the classes defined by the various feature combinations in (4) to be distinguished. This evidence is derived from the fact that the elements of the subclasses appear to behave homogeneously within other contexts as well.

The prenominal structure of NPs is a most convincing context. I assume that the syntactic structure preceding the head noun of an NP consists of a Det position, optionally followed by one or more adjectival positions. There is no need for a separate QP position, since the Det position is accessible to all determiners mentioned thus far, including numerals like *three* and *twenty*. See De Jong 1983 for arguments supporting these claims.

Given that attention is restricted to simple determiners, the following distributional alternatives can be observed.

(5) i. a. Not accepted in adjectival position $[+F_1]$
       b. Accepted in adjectival position $[-F_1]$
    ii. a. Possibly followed by a numeral $[+F_2]$
        b. Never followed by a numeral[4] $[-F_2]$

As illustrated in (6), the alternatives in (i) correspond to the feature $[\pm F_1]$, whereas the alternatives in (ii) correspond to $[\pm F_2]$. Property (ia) or its equivalent, "no preceding determiner allowed," holds for *all, the,* and *most,* which are all $[+F_1]$, whereas *three, twenty,* and *many,* all $[-F_1]$, permit a preceding determiner. On the other hand, the alternatives in (ii) correspond to $[\pm F_2]$, since (iia) holds for the $[+F_2]$-determiners, whereas (iib) holds for those that are $[-F_2]$, as shown in (7).

(6) a. *three all candidates
    b. *the most candidates
    c. all twenty candidates
    d. the many candidates

(7) a. all twenty participants
    b. the two participants
    c. *most three participants
    d. *twenty many participants

As (6) and (7) illustrate, the distributional restrictions in prenominal structure reflect the systematic role of the determiner classification implicit in (4). Once again the behavior of *most* conforms to pattern (4); also, the specifier structure of Dutch NPs reflects the correspondence of (5) to (4), evidenced in *sommige,* which like *most* is $[+F_1, -F_2]$. Compare *de drie/*sommige drie boeken* (*books*) and *de drie/*de sommige boeken.*

The other restrictive contexts involve only one feature at a time. As they need very little explanation, I will present them as filters. The filters (8a–f) and (8h) have Dutch equivalents; (8g) has no equivalent in English.

(8) a. *$[+F_1]$ years ago; *$[+F_1]$ meetings later; *$[+F_1]$ summers ago; *$[+F_1]$ streets ahead
    b. *The path is $[+F_1]$ meters long; *This box weighs $[+F_1]$ ton
    c. *It took $[+F_1]$ seconds (years, summers, meetings, etc.)
    d. *I have $[+F_1]$ brothers; *He has $[+F_1]$ warts
    e. *a house with $[+F_1]$ windows;[5] *a girl with $[+F_1]$ brothers/warts

f. *$[+F_1]$ questions came into his mind; *She draws $[+F_1]$ conclusions

g. *Ik zie er $[+F_1]$ (lit: I see there Det)

h. *$[-F_2]$ following books are sold out: . . .

Anticipating a general account of the data in (6), (7), and (8), we can draw some conclusions already. Whatever has been called (in)definiteness in connection with the contexts in (1) seems to be related to a more general phenomenon: the existence of various contexts restrictive to various subclasses of determiners. If one wishes to deal with (in)definiteness as part of this more general phenomenon, it should be reanalyzed as a notion covering more than one opposition. Definiteness should not be regarded as a monolithic concept. It can be decomposed into at least two factors.

Some of the $[+F_1]$-blocking noun phrases in (8) obviously have a syntactic status different from that of the noun phrases in (1a). Hence, any account of (1a) that crucially depends on the syntactic analysis usually assigned to *there*-sentences (that is, with VP dominating the noun phrase) will not be able to account for the observations in (8a–g) and must be regarded as inadequate from the explanatory point of view.

Apart from this, the preceding discussion shows that the distribution of *most, neither,* and *sommige* sheds an interesting light on the nature of the feature system for natural language determiners. Any theory of determiners that ignores these cases must therefore be regarded as biased.

Finally, note that contrary to what has often been claimed for other contexts, the determiner *all* (and where singular expressions are allowed, also *every* and *each*) appears to behave virtually identically to *the* in the contexts under discussion.

11.2 A Model-Theoretic Definition

In the preceding sections I argued for the necessity of distinguishing more than just two subclasses of determiners on a mere descriptive level. The following sections will be concerned with the possibility of providing a uniform explanation for the entire set of observations. It appears that a partial explanation might be obtained from the model-theoretical definitions that are assigned to determiners within the framework of generalized quantifiers. Following Barwise and Cooper

(1981) and Zwarts (1983), a sentence [[Det N] VP] is interpreted as $D_E AB$, where the determiner denotation D_E is a relation in E between two sets: the noun denotation A and the VP denotation B.

The first distinction to deal with—the one corresponding to $[\pm F_1]$—corresponds only indirectly to one of the oppositions in Barwise and Cooper 1981. The class of NPs that have a $[+F_1]$-determiner corresponds (one to one) to the class of strong NPs. However, strength is not a property that is defined in a uniform way. It appears in two forms, called *positive strength* and *negative strength*. As most examples of $[+F_1]$-determiners yield monotone increasing quantifiers, a case might be made to take $[\pm F_1]$ as "$\pm$positive strong." However, I wish to deal with the distinct behavior of the negative strong *neither* and the weak *no* as well. Consequently, a different opposition not unrelated to the weak-strong distinction will be taken to define $[\pm F_1]$ model-theoretically. My claim is that $[+F_1]$ characterizes the class of determiners that have a partial interpretation. These determiners have a denotation only in a model in which the noun-interpretation is not the empty set. For example, as $\|beide\|\ AB$ is defined only when the cardinality of A equals 2, *beide* belongs to the class of determiners that invoke a partial interpretation of the quantifier. With this criterion, we are able to generalize over both positive and negative strong NPs. The counterparts of the partially interpreted NPs, those that have a denotation in every model, all have a $[-F_1]$-determiner.

My proposal differs from that of Barwise and Cooper (1981) in its interpretation for *most, all,* and *every,* which is only defined when the presupposition $A \neq \emptyset$ is met. Several arguments favor a partial interpretation of these determiners (De Jong and Verkuyl 1985), arguments of both a theoretical and an empirical nature. A total interpretation for *all* and *every* seems to be based upon the marked usage of these determiners in sentences expressing a generic statement, for example, *All ravens are black* used as equivalent to *Ravens are black*. Assignment of a partial interpretation captures the presuppositional aspect of *all* occurring in nongeneric extensional statements. The *all N VP*–type sentences can always be interpreted as extensional statements, but a generic interpretation does not always make sense. For example, in *All seats are taken* or *All flowers are yellow* the determiner *all* cannot be deleted salva veritate. Hence, the extensional interpretation of *all N VP*–sentences should be regarded as unmarked, and it is therefore preferred as a basis for the interpretation of *all,* at least within a classificatory framework. Consequently, $\|all\|$ should be defined partially. For a more elaborate discussion of the arguments favoring a partial definition of $\|all\|$ $AB,$ see De Jong and Verkuyl 1985.[6]

If this point of view is correct, then $[\pm F_1]$ can be defined as follows.

Definition 1

A determiner D is $\left\{\begin{array}{l} [+F_1] \text{ iff the definition of } D_E AB \text{ presupposes} \\ \quad A \text{ to be a nonempty set} \\ [-F_1] \text{ otherwise} \end{array}\right\}$.

The second feature is easier to capture model-theoretically. All the $[+F_2]$-determiners, each regarded as a two-place function with A and B as its arguments, establish a relation that is antisymmetric (in the sense used in Zwarts 1983), whereas none of the $[-F_2]$-determiners does. To see the implications of this claim, expressed in Definition 2, consider Definition 3 and the definitions in (9). OU stands for *otherwise undefined;* E is the domain of discourse.

Definition 2

A determiner D is $\left\{\begin{array}{l} [+F_2] \text{ iff } D \text{ is antisymmetric} \\ [-F_2] \text{ otherwise} \end{array}\right\}$.

Definition 3

A determiner D is antisymmetric iff for every model in which $D_E AB$ & $D_E BA$ is true, $A = B$ is true as well.

(9) a. $the_E AB$ iff $A \subseteq B;$ $|A| \neq 0$, OU
   b. $all_E AB$ iff $A \subseteq B;$ $|A| \neq 0$, OU
   c. $beide_E AB$ iff $A \subseteq B;$ $|A| = 2$, OU
   d. $most_E AB$ iff $|A \cap B| > 1/2 |A|;$ $|A| \neq 0$, OU
   e. $sommige_E AB$ iff $|A \cap B| \geq 2;$ $|A| \geq 2$, OU
   f. $three_E AB$ iff $|A \cap B| \geq 3$
   g. $neither_E AB$ iff $|A \cap B| = 0;$ $|A| = 2$, OU
   h. $no_E AB$ iff $|A \cap B| = 0$

The three that are marked as $[+F_2]$ in (4) involve a requirement on the inclusion relation between A and B. As the inclusion relation is symmetric for identical arguments only, *the, all,* and *beide* are antisymmetric. An explanation for this correspondence between antisymmetry and the inclusion relation can be found in Zwarts 1983, where it is shown that antisymmetric determiners D are characterized by the fact that $D_E AB$ implies $A \subseteq B$. Alternatively, we might therefore call the antisymmetric determiners *inclusion determiners*. For the $[-F_1]$-determiners *most, sommige, neither, no,* and numerals the definition of the quantifier necessarily contains a condition on the cardinality of $A \cap B$.[7]

The definition of $[+F_2]$ also offers some insight into the reason for the fact that no $[-F_1,+F_2]$-determiners show up. All $[+F_2]$-determiners impose the same truth-conditions on $D_E AB$ as are imposed by *all* and, as already argued, *all* should be treated as presuppositional. Hence, its behavior as a $[+F_1]$-determiner is explained. Now, since for inclusion determiners the cardinality of $A \cap B$ is of no importance, only the assumption that they each impose a specific presupposition on the size of A can account for the intuition that, for example, *the* and *beide* are clearly distinct in meaning. So the uniformity of the truth-conditional part of the interpretation of antisymmetric determiners enforces their presuppositional nature and consequently their being $[+F_1]$.

As Definition 2 appears to bring about a distinction between inclusion determiners and what I will call *cardinality determiners* and as the notion of cardinality is quite often said to be relevant for the characterization of (in)definiteness, I will also make reference to the following definitions.

Definition 4

A determiner is $\begin{Bmatrix} [-F_2] \text{ iff it is a cardinality expression} \\ [+F_2] \text{ otherwise} \end{Bmatrix}$.

Definition 5

A determiner D is a cardinality expression iff $D_E AB$ can be true in a model, while $A \subseteq B$ is false.

This notion of cardinality, defined ex negativo, is here favored over other model-theoretic notions that are proposed in the literature to account for the restriction on partitives.[8] One reason for preferring this notion is that it should contribute to the explanation of the restriction on partitives as well as to the explanation of the restrictions on nonpartitive NPs mentioned below (5ii) (see section 11.3).

Until now I have restricted attention to simple determiners. But the distribution of complex determiners such as *almost all* and *all but one* appears to confirm the presumed correspondence of distributional and denotational properties. Obviously, the presuppositional nature of *all* is inherited by the complex determiners that contain *all*. According to Definition 1, they are to be considered as $[+F_1]$. On the other hand, *almost all* and *all but one* certainly do not denote the inclusion relation: according to Definitions 3 and 5, they classify as $[-F_2]$-determiners.

Semantically, then, these determiners belong to the class of *most* and *sommige*. Hence, the present proposal would predict that they can occur neither in (1a) nor in (1b). The following examples show that this prediction is borne out.

(10) a. *There are almost all boys in the garden
     b. *There is all but one boy in the garden

(11) a. *Half of almost all boys are red-haired
     b. *Half of all but one boy is red-haired

Since cardinality is a notion often related to (in)definiteness, it is worthwhile to reconsider the most well-known elaboration of this idea, that of Milsark (1977) in the light of Definitions 4 and 5. Milsark distinguishes between determiners expressing universal quantification (blocked in (1a)) and expressions of cardinality (permitted in (1a)). Since *most* (and also *sommige*) is not universally quantifying, it should be classified as a cardinality expression, in spite of its distribution. In order to prevent this, Milsark rejects the distinction between universal and nonuniversal quantification and he takes the quantificational nature of *most* to be a sufficient explanation of its being strong. For *sommige*, his proposal would incorrectly predict ambiguity. Just like *some*, it would receive a strong interpretation in addition to a primary cardinality interpretation. But the distribution of *sommige*, unlike that of *some*, parallels the distribution of the strong determiners in all relevant aspects. If Milsark's notion of cardinality is somehow to be related to antisymmetry or cardinality as defined here, distinguishing between $[+F_2]$-determiners and $[-F_2]$-determiners, then the observations on partitives would confirm the status of Milsark's distinction as a true opposition. However, since it is shown here that $[\pm F_2]$ is not the opposition that is relevant to (1a), $[\pm F_2]$ cannot be identified with the weak-strong distinction. Hence, Milsark seems correct in assigning a realistic status to the distinction between quantifying words and cardinality expressions, but he is not correct in regarding it as responsible for the restrictions in *there*-sentences.

11.3 The Explanatory Force of Model-Theory

The compositional nature of what is traditionally called (in)definiteness appears to be rather easy to define model-theoretically. Here I will relate the definitions given in the previous section to a more explanatory account of the restrictions to which the various subclasses are subject. I will begin by considering the contexts in (8) in more detail.

All the examples in (8a–c) contain some kind of measure phrase. As is clear from the examples with *summers, streets,* and so forth, it is not the noun itself that triggers the restrictive nature of (8a–c) but instead the occurrence of these nouns as the complement of certain verbs or adverbs. When a noun is modified by, for example, an adjective or a PP with predicational content, it loses the ability to function as a measuring unit: **many years of her life ago, *three narrow streets ahead.* Apparently the use of these nouns is parameterized. The context of use imposes restrictions on which parameters can be selected. Now regardless of how the rules of grammar interfere with this selection, it seems evident that the contexts in (8a–c) do not trigger the interpretation of nouns as sets of individual entities. In (8a–c) the nouns can only be interpreted as measure units. (I will ignore the question of whether and how measure units can be related to the set of individuals *E.*)

The claim that certain uses of a noun affect the nature of its interpretation and hence the possibility of its being preceded by certain determiners is relevant for the account of (8d–e) as well. To see this, note that the objects denoted by the nouns in (8d–e) have a rather complicated ontology. Things such as holes, warts, windows, and noses are inherently related to other objects. Their existence depends on the existence of the objects of which they are, metaphorically speaking, a part. In a way, then, the set denotation commonly assigned to count nouns is anomalous here, since it ignores this dependency. It presumes that, for instance, *hole* and *wart* are expressions denoting a function, whereas a relational interpretation would do more justice to the ontological complications. However, within certain contexts a functional interpretation is most natural. Consider, for example, *I can see (the) three holes in the roof* and *This picture shows the ten warts that I want to have removed.* These sentences involve quantification over sets of holes and warts, respectively.

A similar example of context-dependent typeshifting can be observed for the interpretation of nouns like *brother* and *colleague.* An individual referred to by these nouns is concurrently related to the individual that he or she is a brother or a colleague of. Only in case this relation is already established in the context is it possible to quantify over sets of brothers or colleagues. In (8d–e) the occurrence of *have* and *with* triggers the relational parameter.

This idea of parameterized noun interpretation suggests an account of the restriction on [+F₁]-determiners in (8): since none of the examples discussed thus far involves a set interpretation, the nonempty-set requirement associated with [+F₁]-determiners turns out to be trivial here. But although this generalization seems promising, it is bound to fail with respect to (8f–g): the contexts in (8f) do not resist a set interpretation of *questions* and *conclusions,* and the anaphoric nature of *er* in (8g) seems to be incompatible with the idea that blocking of [+F₁]-determiners is due to the failure of the nonempty-set requirement. To preserve the possibility of an overall account of the restriction on [+F₁]-determiners, I will reanalyze the data from a slightly different perspective, a perspective that bears on the distinction between predicational and presentational sentences already hinted at in Milsark 1977 and elaborated more formally in Heim 1982.

This distinction presumes a dynamic view of the process of semantic interpretation, since the domain of interpretation is not taken as static. Presentational sentences are distinguished from predicational sentences because of their function. They are supposed to accomplish a change or an extension of the domain, rather than to describe it, by asserting or denying the presence or coming into presence of (sets of) individual entities. From this perspective the analysis of (8f) would run as follows.

Unlike *[. . .] questions are written down carefully,* (8f) is not a predicational sentence but a sentence expressing that the subject denotation came into existence by the process referred to by the VP. Therefore, the occurrence of a presuppositional determiner forces the sentence to assert what is presupposed. This tautological result explains the intuition that inserting a [+F₁]-determiner in (8f) is blocked. In context (8f) *questions* does not refer to a set of objects that is present independently of what is predicated. Things change when a phrase like *just before he fell asleep* is added to the context. In that case a predicational interpretation and insertion of [+F₁]-determiners are no longer blocked.

There-sentences are presentational as well. They introduce or deny the presence of a certain set in the domain of discourse or, in case XP in (1a) is a locative adverbial phrase, in a context-relevant subdomain. Again, insertion of a presuppositional determiner would make the sentence assert or deny what is presupposed and hence yield a tautology or a contradiction (the latter in case *neither* is inserted). Barwise and Cooper (1981) also ascribe the ill-formedness of *there*-sentences with strong determiners to their tautological or contradictory nature. However, they presume in a rather ad hoc way that $||be\ NP||$ is identical to $||NP||$ and that E is the denotation of *there*.

The dynamic approach also gives some insight into (8g). Regardless of *er*, there is no noun in (8g) to which the determiner is attached; hence, there is nothing within the sentence to fulfill the nonempty-set requirement that would be introduced by $[+F_1]$-determiners. But whatever is accomplished by this conclusion, it does not solve the problem of what *er* does denote. Obviously, *er* is anaphoric in nature: the interpretation of *er* is determined by the context. In addition, I claim that *er* never refers to a specific subset of E, but rather to what Carlson (1977a) has called a *kind*. Actually, I claim that to know what *er* is referring to is to know the kind of objects that a certain piece of discourse is concerned with. The effect of using a sentence like (8g) is that a set corresponding to the kind that *er* is referring to becomes present in the (sub)domain of discourse. (In case *geen* 'no' is inserted in the context this set will be empty, whereas the kind might still be part of the context.) As a consequence of these assumptions, insertion of a $[+F_1]$-determiner is predicted to yield a tautologous or contradictory, and hence ill-formed, result.

Thus far the dynamic approach enables us to generalize over the restrictions in three different kinds of presentational sentences. Now I will indicate how it also applies to the account of (8a–e). The previous discussion of (8d–e) was based upon the observation that in these specific contexts *brother*, *wart*, and so forth, do not denote a set. But these statements can as well be taken as introducing the set corresponding to (for example) $||brother\ of\ NP||$ or $||wart\ of\ NP||$, where NP is meant as a variable that ranges over the subjects of *have*, for instance. This position is favored by the observation that the utterance of a sentence like *She has three brothers* can be followed by a sentence that presumes the presence of a set of brothers—for example, *One of the brothers is red-haired*, which involves quantification. Presuming that the derived set interpretation of nouns can be generated compositionally, this analysis allows us to regard (8d–e) as presentational and to treat them on a par with (8f–g) and (1a). That is, the restriction on $[+F_1]$-determiners can be taken as a consequence of the fact that they make the sentence assert or deny what is presupposed.

Something similar can be said with respect to (8a–c). The fact that these phrases do not admit a $[+F_1]$-determiner indicates that somehow a set interpretation is impossible. But the use of a measure phrase causes a change in the domain to the effect that a set of, for instance, weeks or streets becomes available. The following two sequences illustrate this: *You will find John's house five streets ahead; be careful and don't overlook the narrow streets, Within three weeks this manuscript must be finished and there is no time to work on it at present, so it will all depend on the third week.* Thus, sentences containing the measure phrases occurring in (8a–c) appear to be presentational as well. Hence, the account proposed for (8d,g) and (1a) applies to (8a–c) as well,[9] and it can be concluded that the dynamic approach appears to offer a general explanation for all the restrictions on $[+F_1]$-determiners.

This leaves us with the contexts sensitive to $[F_2]$: those involving an NP-internal aspect (namely, prenominal structure and partitive NPs) and one sensitive to $[F_2]$ only in relation to the context of the NP as a whole. Let us begin with the NP-internal restrictions. Unlike Barwise and Cooper (1981), I do not analyze numerals as part of the determiner. Stated in formal syntactic terms, numerals are $[+Det]$ as well as $[+A]$, whereas the other $[+Det]$-elements are $[-A]$. The correspondence of (5) to (4) supports this point of view. Now suppose the phrase structure rules specify the string $[Det_1$ of Det_2 N'$]$ for partitives and the string $[Det$ A ... N$]$ for nonpartitives, where N' is a projection of N that possibly dominates $[A$ N$]$, for example, *red-haired boys* or *twenty boys*. Furthermore, both contexts turn out to be ill formed if in more than one of the available positions preceding N a $[-F_2]$-element is inserted. As multiple numerical information is either redundant or contradictory, the interpretation assigned to $[F_2]$ contributes to an account of the NP-internal $[F_2]$-restrictions that generalizes over both NP types involved. Since in (8h) only one position is involved and since apart from the NP-internal cases it is until now the only context that I have found that is sensitive to the $[\pm F_2]$ distinction, any account would be ad hoc. Therefore, I will not try to explain this case here.

11.4 Concluding Remarks

I have argued here for the incorporation of the features $[\pm F_1]$ and $[\pm F_2]$ in the lexical specification of determiners. Though both features have been given a model-theoretic definition based upon the definitions in (9), my claim is not that the interpretations defined in (9) are relevant to every occurrence of a certain determiner. What I actually claim is that (a) the different interpretations of determiners in *Det N VP*-sentences reflect the existence of several determiner subclasses and (b) this subclassification plays a systematic role within the distribution of determiners. In view of this lexicalist approach to the model-theoretic notions involved, the one-to-one correspondence between the distributional and the semantic properties of determiners sheds some intriguing light on the role of the lexicon in relation to the learnability issue.

Notes

I would like to thank Anke Le Loux, Barbara Partee, Henk Verkuyl, and especially Dick de Jongh for their comments on an earlier draft of this chapter. The research for this chapter was partially supported by the Foundation for Linguistic Research, which is funded by the Netherlands Organization for the Advancement of Pure Research, ZWO.

1. There seem to be some subtle differences among partitive contexts with respect to the possibility of inserting *all*. Most speakers of English regard the occurrence of *all* in *some of all boys* or in *three of all boys* as ill formed. However, a comparison of these examples with those in (i) shows that it would be too strong a conclusion if *all* were to be regarded as excluded from the embedded position in partitives.

(i) a. At least ten of all children got lost
    b. Half of all participants failed to pass the exams
    c. Only three of all students succeeded
    d. Not more than four of all teachers were present

In these examples *all* fits perfectly well, whereas the insertion of *most* and numerals would lead to ill-formed results in all of the cases. Therefore, I propose to count *all* in the class of determiners that can occur in the embedded position of partitives.

2. In itself, definiteness is defined as property of a certain subset of the set of determiners. However, the restriction to partitive NPs is stated under reference to (a subset of) the set of definite NPs. See Barwise and Cooper 1981:184.

3. As a consequence of this restriction, the property associated with $[\pm F_2]$ in section 11.2 should be taken as a necessary rather than a sufficient condition for occurrence in partitives.

4. The exceptional distribution of *no* in this respect must be ascribed to the fact that *no* functions as a sentence operator.

5. This example is due to Irene Heim. See chapter 2, example (9).

6. Note that a partial definition of *all* and/or *every* makes it necessary to adopt the alternative formulation of truth-conditions proposed by Strawson (1952) in order to preserve the possibility of accounting for the property of antipersistence that intuitively is valid for $\|all\|$.

7. It might be argued that because $|A \cap B| = 0 \leftrightarrow A \cap B = \emptyset$, *neither* and *no* do not necessarily involve a condition on $A \cap B$. However, as $A \cap B = \emptyset$ cannot be stated by means of $A \subseteq B$ or its denial, I take the distinction between cardinality determiners and inclusion determiners to be a true opposition.

8. That nonantisymmetric determiners by necessity depend on the cardinality of $A \cap B$ will be argued more extensively elsewhere.

9. Not all the peculiarities of the nouns in (8a–c) are to be taken as a result of the assumed presentational status of the sentences they occur in. For example, the fact that they do not allow modification is independent of this status.

Chapter 12

A Semantic Definition of "Indefinite NP"

Edward L. Keenan

It is a long-standing observation that "indefinite" NPs naturally occur in *existential there* (ET) contexts.

(1) a. There is *at least one student* in the next room
   b. There are *fewer male than female students* who object to that
   c. There weren't *more men than women* enrolled in the course

But if NPs such as *John, every student,* or *the ten students* replace the italicized expressions in (1), the resulting expressions either are ungrammatical or receive an interpretation other than the "existential" (= existence assertion) reading.

The primary purpose of this chapter is to define the class of English NPs that naturally occur in ET contexts with the existential reading, a class of NPs that I will call *existential*. I propose my definition in section 12.2, basing it on the syntactic and semantic analysis of determiners given in section 12.1. In section 12.3 I address the question, Why should just those NPs defined to be existential occur in ET contexts? In section 12.4 I compare my approach with others, most extensively that of Barwise and Cooper (1981).

12.1 English Determiners

Based primarily on the more detailed studies in Keenan and Stavi 1986 and Keenan and Moss 1985, I treat determiners syntactically as expressions (often complex) that combine with an appropriate number of *common noun phrases* (CNPs) to form a full noun phrase (NP). Expressions such as *doctor, bald doctor,* and *bald doctor who Mary loves* are treated as CNPs, and ones such as *John, every doctor, all but two bald doctors,* and *more doctors than lawyers* are full NPs.

I treat expressions such as *some, more than two, all but six,* and *John's* as one-place determiners (Det₁'s), since they combine with one CNP to form an NP. I treat expressions such as *more . . . than . . . , at least as many . . . as . . . ,* and *more of John's . . . than of Mary's . . .* as two-place determiners (Det₂'s), since they combine with two CNPs to form an NP (*more students than teachers, more of John's cats than of Mary's dogs*). I even treat expressions such as *more . . . than . . . or . . .* as in *more students than teachers or deans* as Det₃'s, and in general for all k it is possible to give examples of k-place determiners (Det$_k$'s). An extensive list is given in the Appendix.

Semantically, I treat CNPs as denoting (= being interpreted as) *extensional properties*. Full NPs denote sets of properties, and a sentence such as *John is a doctor* is true in a state of affairs just in case the property denoted by *doctor* is a member of the set denoted by *John*. In such a case we will say that John *has* the doctor property. Similarly, *Every woman is a doctor* is true iff the set denoted by *every woman* has the doctor property as an element.

The property sets denotable by proper nouns (such as *John*) are called (here) *individuals*. Individuals are very special property sets. For example, if an individual John has the doctor property p and he also has the lawyer property $q,$ then he must also have the property of being both a doctor and a lawyer, noted by $(p \wedge q)$. Most property sets denotable by English NPs do not meet this condition. For example, it is quite possible that some teacher has the doctor property and that some teacher has the lawyer property but that some teacher fails to have the property of being both a doctor and a lawyer. This just says that the sentence *Some teacher is a doctor and some teacher is a lawyer* does not entail *Some teacher is both a doctor and a lawyer.* The entailment does obtain, however, if we replace each occurrence of *some teacher* by *John.*

In general, if p and q are properties—denoted, say, by *doctor* and *lawyer*—then $(p \wedge q)$ is a property denoted by expressions such as *doctor who is a lawyer* and *individual who is both a doctor and a lawyer.*

Extensional properties p,q are distinct just in case there is an individual with one of them but not the other. Typically, the properties denoted by *doctor, lawyer,* and *doctor who is a lawyer* are distinct since the individuals who are doctors, those who are lawyers, and those who are both may be three different sets of individuals. Extensional properties then correspond one by one to sets of individuals, and we may define such a property by stating just which individuals have it.

A certain trivial property will play an importanat role in what follows: namely, the property that all individuals have, noted simply as *property 1*. In what follows I will define *existential* NP in terms of the property 1. The definition is (formally) semantic, and for purposes of paraphrasing the intuition behind it in something like English it will be convenient (but not necessary) to use expressions of English that we may think of as denoting this property. For this purpose I will use the CNP *individual* and the VP *exist(s)*. That is, I will use the CNP *individual* to denote the property common to all the individuals in a state of affairs, and I will use *exist(s)* to denote the one-place predicate that is true of all the individuals. Note that I am establishing here a technical usage of these terms and not intending to make any significant claims concerning their uses in ordinary English. For example, individuals in this technical sense need not be human.

In this technical usage sentences such as *John exists* and *John is an individual* are trivially true. Each just says that the individual John has that property common to all individuals. Similarly, sentences of the form *Every CNP exists/is an individual* are trivially true. For such sentences to be false, there would have to be an individual with the CNP property that failed to be an individual.

I can now say somewhat more precisely what I mean by an *existential* (existence assertion) reading of ET sentences. To say that the (a)-sentences in (2) and (3) are understood on an existential reading is to say that they are true in the same conditions as the (b)-sentences, using the technical sense of *exist/individual*.

(2) a. There are more than two boys in the yard
     b. More than two boys in the yard exist/are individuals

(3) a. There is every student in the yard
     b. Every student in the yard exists/is an individual

(2a) is in fact understood on an existential reading, whereas it seems to me that, to the extent that speakers of English naturally assign a reading to (3a), it is not the existential reading. Rather, (3a) means *Every student is in the yard,* if it means anything at all.

Turning now to determiners, we will semantically interpret them as functions from properties to sets of properties (that is, as *generalized quantifiers*). For example, *exactly two* denotes the function that associates with each property q the set of those properties p such that the number of individual q's with p is exactly two. In general, where t is a property, we write $|t|$ for the number of individuals who have t. For example, $|q \wedge p|$ is the number of individuals with $(q \wedge p)$, that is, the number of q's with p (equivalently, the number of p's with q). Thus, we may say that *exactly two* denotes the function mapping each property q to $\{p: |q \wedge p| = 2\}$.

Similarly, consider a two-place determiner such as *more . . . than.* . . . It maps each pair (p,q) of properties to the set of those properties t such that the number of p's with t is greater than the number of q's with t. That is, $\{t: |p \wedge t| > |q \wedge t|\}$. Thus, *More doctors than lawyers are vegetarians* is true iff the number of doctors who are vegetarians is greater than the number of lawyers who are vegetarians.

In general, a k-place determiner semantically maps k-tuples of properties to sets of properties. In what follows I will give definitions and theorems just for one-place determiners and, where necessary, provide the straightforward generalization to k-place determiners in the Appendix.

12.2 Defining Existential NPs

In this section I define a class of NPs called *existential* and argue for the following Thesis.

Thesis
The existential NPs defined here are just those that occur in ET contexts with an existential reading.

I will define the existential NPs in terms of the notion *existential determiner*. As the determiners to be considered are quite complex and varied in structure, it will be convenient, in fact enlightening, to first define the notion *existential determiner* for a class of fairly simple, or *basic,* determiners and then extend that definition to the full class of determiners by showing how the property of being existential is preserved under the various ways of forming complex (nonbasic) determiners from simpler ones. I distinguish five ways of forming complex determiners from simpler ones:

(i) *Boolean combinations.* These are determiners of the form (Det_1 *and* Det_2), (Det_1 *or* Det_2), (*not* Det_1), (*neither* Det_1 *nor* Det_2), and variants thereof with (for example) *but, or else.*

(4) a. *Not more than two* students left early

    b. *At least two and/but not more than six* students left early

    c. *Neither every student's nor every teacher's* car was stolen

In (4a) *not more than two* is formed by negation from the determiner *more than two*.

(ii) *Composition with adjective phrases.* These are determiners of the form (*Det* + *AP*).

(5) a. *Most liberal and all conservative* delegates voted for Smith

    b. *More male* dogs *than female* cats were inoculated

In (5a) the entire determiner is a conjunction of two determiners, each of which consists of a determiner composed with an adjective. In (5b) I treat the determiner as the composition of the two-place determiner *more . . . than . . .* with the pair of APs (*male,female*) (see Keenan and Moss 1985).

I stress here that my purpose in including a large class of determiners is to have a large class of NPs about which to make predictions concerning their acceptability in ET contexts. Those who wish to analyze the internal structure of these NPs differently are free to do so and to modify their definition of existential NP accordingly.

(iii) *Exception determiners.* These are determiners of the form (*Det but X*) or (*Det . . . but X*).

(6) a. *All but (at most) two* cars were stolen

    b. *No* student *but John* left early

    c. *Every* student *but John* left early

(iv) *Partitive determiners.* These are determiners of the form (*Det*$_1$ *of Det*$_2$).

(7) a. *Exactly two of the ten* students left early

    b. *At least two of John's* students left early

(Most linguists would not assign the italicized expressions in (7) any category.)

(v) *Comparative determiners.* These are determiners of the form (*comp of Det*$_1$ *than/as of Det*$_2$).

(8) a. *More of John's than of Mary's* articles were accepted

    b. *At least as many of the male as of the female* students objected

Note that *John's (Mary's)* in (8a) is a determiner, as is *the male (the female)* in (8b).

I define a determiner to be *basic* just in case it is not built up from other determiners in any of the ways indicated in (i)–(v). Determiners that are basic on this definition are the one-word determiners and certain syntactically complex ones such as *at least two, John's,* and *more . . . than.* . . . I do not claim any independent syntactic status for the basic determiners but make the basic-complex distinction solely as a way of characterizing the full class of determiners.

The crucial definitions on which the ultimate definition of *existential NP* will depend may now be given as follows.

Definition 1
a. A basic determiner is called *existential* iff it is always interpreted by an existential function, where
b. A function f from properties to sets of properties is *existential* iff for all properties p,q
$$p \in f(q) \text{ iff } 1 \in f(q \wedge p)$$

Thus, to say that f is existential is to say that $f(q)$'s are p's iff $f(q$'s who are p's) exist (are individuals).[1]

To see that *some* is existential, for example, we must verify that (9a–b) are true in the same conditions.

(9) a. Some student is a vegetarian
    b. Some student who is a vegetarian exists

To see that *at least n* is existential for each cardinal number n, we must verify that (10a–b) are true in the same conditions.

(10) a. At least n students are vegetarians
     b. At least n students who are vegetarians exist

On the other hand, to see that *every* is not existential, we must verify that (11a–b) may differ in truth-value.

(11) a. Every student is a vegetarian
     b. Every student who is a vegetarian exists

By an earlier remark, (11b) is always true; but (11a) can be false.

And to see that *the ten* is not existential, observe that (12b) can be true in situations in which (12a) is not true. For example, imagine a situation in which there are twelve students, exactly ten of whom are vegetarians.

(12) a. The ten students are vegetarians
     b. The ten students who are vegetarians exist

Using these informal tests or the formal denotations given by Keenan and Stavi (1986), we may verify (13).

(13) *Some basic determiners that are existential*
    a. *Det₁'s:* some, a, no, almost no, several, a few, infinitely many, just finitely many, countably many, an infinite number of, an even number of, some number of, more male than female, at least as many male as female, at least *n*, exactly *n*, only *n*, more than *n*, at most *n*, fewer than *n*, *n* or more, approximately *n*, nearly *n*, between *n* and *m*
    b. *Detₖ's for k > 1:* more . . . than . . . , fewer . . . than . . . , at least as many . . . as . . . , exactly twice as many . . . as . . . , the same number of . . . as . . . , some . . . and . . . , no . . . or . . . , exactly two . . . and three . . . , more . . . than . . . or . . .

So far these results are quite pleasing, since obviously the existential NPs will include those formed from basic existential determiners and the appropriate number of CNPs. The Thesis claims, then, that NPs formed from the determiners in (13) will occur in ET contexts on an existential reading, and they do, as (14) partially illustrates.

(14) a. There are *infinitely many* unicorns in the garden
     b. There were *between five and ten* students accepted
     c. There are *exactly two* dogs *and three* cats in the pen
     d. There were *no* students *or* teachers who objected

The definitions also yield the following categorization.

(15) *Some basic determiners that are not existential*
    a. *Det₁'s:* every, each, all, both, neither, most, the, John's, the *n*, John's *n*, the *n* or more, John's *n* or more, almost all
    b. *Detₖ's for k > 1:* every . . . and . . . , the twenty . . . and . . . , John's . . . and . . .

These results are also pleasing, since the definition of existential NP will guarantee that NPs formed from basic determiners that are not existential are themselves not existential, and the determiners in (15) are among (in fact, they properly exhaust) those commonly cited as not occurring naturally in ET contexts.

Given these results, it is tempting to think that we can simply define the existential NPs as those formed from basic existential determiners with the appropriate number of CNPs. But this would not yield the desired result. For example, the NPs italicized in (16) occur naturally in ET contexts, but they do not consist merely of basic existential determiners and the requisite number of CNPs.

(16) a. There are *at least two dogs and more than ten cats* in the yard
   b. There are *at least two but not more than ten cats* in the yard
   c. There are *just two male but more than three female cats* in the yard
   d. There was *no student but John* in the building

The following definitions are adequate to cover these cases.

Definition 2
A determiner is called *existential* (simpliciter) iff either it is a basic existential determiner or it is built up from basic existential determiners by Boolean combinations, composition with adjective phrases, or the exception determiner operator (. . . *but John*).

Definition 3
a. A *basic existential* NP is one formed from an existential determiner and the appropriate number of CNPs.
b. The *existential* NPs are the basic existential ones together with those formed from them by Boolean combinations.

These definitions can be illustrated by showing that the NPs in (16) are existential. *At least two* is a basic existential determiner and hence an existential determiner by Definition 2, whence *at least two dogs* is a basic existential NP by Definition 3a and hence an existential NP by Definition 3b. Similarly, *more than ten cats* is an existential NP, so that by Definition 3b the conjunction of *at least two dogs* and *more than ten cats* is existential; therefore, the Thesis predicts (correctly) that (16a) is natural on an existence assertion reading.

Similarly, since *more than ten* is a basic existential determiner, it is existential by Definition 2; thus, *not more than ten* is existential (by Definition 2), and thus the NP in (16b) is a basic existential NP and (by Definition 3b) an existential NP.

In (16c) *just two* (= *only two*) is a basic existential determiner and thus existential by Definition 2, so its composition with the AP *male* is existential by Definition 2. By the same reasoning, *more than three fe-*

male is existential, so by Definition 2 again the conjunction of *just two male* and *more than three female* in (16c) is existential. As a result, by Definition 3a the NP in (16a) is a basic existential NP and therefore by Definition 3b an existential NP.

In (16d) *no* is a basic existential determiner, hence by Definition 2 an existential determiner. As a result, by Definition 2 *no . . . but John* is an existential determiner; hence, by Definition 3a *no student but John* is a basic existential NP and therefore by Definition 3b an existential NP.

12.2.1 Remarks on the Definitions

(i) The essential step in the definition of *basic existential determiner* is semantic: A basic determiner is existential if its semantic interpretation satisfies a certain condition, that of being an existential function as defined in Definition 1b. By contrast, Definitions 2 and 3 are purely syntactic. They are, however, semantically motivated as follows: Definition 2 says that the existential determiners are closed under the operations of Boolean combinations, composition with APs, and the exception determiner operator. This closure is motivated since it can be proved that if the determiners then apply to denote existential functions, then so do the ones they derive (see the Appendix). More explicitly:

Theorem 1

a. If d_1 and d_2 are determiners that always denote existential functions, then so do (d_1 *and* d_2), (d_1 *or* d_2), (*not* d_1) and (*neither* d_1 *nor* d_2).
b. If d is a determiner that always denotes an existential function, then so does ($d + a$) for any (absolute, extensional) adjective phrase a.
c. If d always denotes an existential function, then so does (d . . . *but John*).

(ii) By contrast, the semantic operations represented by partitive and comparative determiner formation (see Keenan and Stavi 1986) may lead from existential functions to nonexistential functions. Consequently, the set of existential determiners has not been formally closed under these syntactic operations. In fact, typically a partitive determiner formed from a basic existential one seems to be semantically anomalous, as in *more than two of at least ten* (students). This contrasts with the naturalness of partitives (and comparatives) formed from certain nonexistential determiners, such as *more than two of the ten* (students).

(iii) It might reasonably be asked why a determiner (however complex) is not simply defined to be existential just in case it always denotes an existential function. Why go through the trouble of distinguishing basic from nonbasic determiners? The reason is that certain "degenerate" complex determiners formed from basic nonexistential ones will in fact denote existential functions. Such determiners would then (wrongly) be predicted to form NPs that occur naturally in ET contexts. For example, according to the definitions proposed here, *either all or else not all* is classed as nonexistential. But the function it denotes sends each property q to the set P of all properties, since, no matter what property s we choose, either all q's have it or else not all q's have it. Now this function is easily seen to be existential. Thus, the apparently simpler definition would wrongly predict that NPs formed from *either all or else not all* would occur on existence assertion readings in ET contexts. (In section 12.4 we will see that we cannot use the "triviality" of *either all or else not all* as a basis for excluding it from being existential.)

12.2.2 Descriptive Adequacy of the Definitions

The proposed definitions have correctly, as per the Thesis, characterized a great many NPs as existential. They include many of those commonly cited as occurring naturally in ET contexts as well as many more not usually considered. In addition to those already cited, the following NPs are provably existential according to these definitions: *between five and ten dogs and more than twice that many cats, more than twice as many male as female cats, at least twenty students, teachers, and deans.*

Further, this approach correctly characterizes many NPs as not being existential. In addition to those formed from the basic nonexistential determiners in (15), the determiners in (17) are provably nonexistential.

(17) a. all but *n,* all but at most *n,* every . . . but John, every . . . but John's
b. some but not all, most but not all, either fewer than ten or else almost all
c. two out of three, every second, five percent of the, two-thirds of the
d. at least five of the ten, more of John's than of Mary's

In general, pretheoretical judgments accord reasonably well with the predictions made by the Thesis in these cases. So overall this solution may be counted as ranking fairly high on the scale of descriptive adequacy. Nonetheless, it has some insufficiencies.

12.2.3 Descriptive Inadequacies

First, to some extent the proposed analysis of partitives and possessives remains open. It forces partitives such as (18a) to be analyzed in such a way that (18b) occurs as a determiner.

(18) a. at least two of the ten students
     b. at least two of the ten

Along with most linguists who have considered these structures (Jackendoff 1977; Selkirk 1970; Ladusaw 1982), Barwise and Cooper (1981) would disagree with this analysis, treating *the ten students* in (18a) as a constituent of category NP. If we syntactically pursue the semantic analysis given by Barwise and Cooper for *of* in (18), we would treat the phrase *of the ten students* as a CNP. On such an analysis, (18a) would have the form [Det_1 + CNP], and on our definition of existential such NPs would be existential iff the Det_1 was existential. This analysis then would predict that sentences such as *There are at least two of the ten students in the garden* would be natural. My best judgment here, admittedly somewhat shaky, is that such sentences are not natural, and for that reason I prefer the analysis I have given. However, if further and more systematic judgments are elicited and accord such sentences a natural status, I would abandon this analysis in favor of the one suggested by Barwise and Cooper.

A second somewhat open case concerns possessive determiners of the form *some student's, every student's*. Since these determiners are basic on the proposed definition, whether they are existential or not depends crucially on how they are interpreted. But just how determiners of the form [Det_1 + CNP]*'s* are interpreted seems to vary in complicated ways as a function of the Det_1 and the number marking on the CNP as well as the number marking on the CNP the entire determiner combines with. Lacking the space to discuss this variation in detail, I offer only the following brief analysis: determiners such as *John's, John's two*, and *John's two or more* are clearly nonexistential, for the same reason that *the, the two*, and *the two or more* are nonexistential (for example, **John's two bikes = (the two)(bikes which John has))**.

For more complex cases, suppose we give the following definition.

(19) [(Det₁ student)'s] bike =$_{df}$ Det₁[student's bike]
where *student's bike* denotes a property an individual has iff it
has the bike property and is associated with "students" in some
appropriate way.

Then the determiner in (19) will be existential just in case Det₁ is. This
analysis is not unreasonable and predicts the naturalness of (20a) and
the unnaturalness of (20b), judgments that accord reasonably well with
our pretheoretical ones (see also Lyons 1982 and Woisetschlaeger
1983).

(20) a. There is some student's bike in the hallway
      b. There is every student's bike in the hallway

A second, more serious problem with the analysis is that there are
several determiners (and thus NPs) that it simply does not take into
account. So far I have considered only determiners that are *extensional*
(or, as I will call them, *transparent*). To say that a determiner *d* is
transparent is to say, for example, that whenever the doctors and the
lawyers happen to be the same individuals, then *d doctor(s)* and
d lawyer(s) denote the same property sets. To see that *every* is transparent, for example, it is sufficient to verify that (21a–b) have the same
truth-value whenever the doctors and the lawyers are the same.

(21) a. Every doctor attended the meeting
      b. Every lawyer attended the meeting

However, many determiners, in particular ones incorporating a value
judgment, fail to be transparent.

(22) *Some nontransparent determiners*
      a surprisingly high number of, a large number of, too many, too
      few, not enough, many, few

It is not difficult to imagine situations in which the doctors and the
lawyers are the same (perhaps quite unbeknownst to everyone) but in
which *A surprisingly high number of lawyers attended the meeting* is
true and *A surprisingly high number of doctors attended the meeting* is
false. (Suppose it is the annual meeting of a medical association.) (See
Keenan and Stavi 1986 for further discussion.)

Note that the determiners in (22) occur naturally in ET contexts. But
the analysis so far does not provide denotations for these (and cannot in
a purely extensional semantics); hence, it cannot predict them to be

existential. But it does give some basis for expecting the existential behavior of these determiners. Such determiners present two sorts of information: a cardinality claim and a value judgment claim. Thus, *A large number of doctors attended* means something like (1) Some number of doctors attended and (2) That number was large (by some criterion). Let us then think of the determiners in (22) as consisting of a cardinality determiner together with some sort of value judgment operator. Now value judgment operators are in general nontransparent. For example, compare APs like *skillful* (+value judgment) with ones like *female* (−value judgment). If the doctors and the lawyers are the same, then clearly the female doctors and the female lawyers are the same, so *female* is transparent; but the skillful doctors and the skillful lawyers need not be the same under those conditions, so *skillful* is not transparent. Cardinality determiners (such as *at least two, between five and ten, approximately thirty*) are transparent, as the reader may easily check by example. Thus, we may think of the determiners in (22) as consisting of a transparent part (the cardinality determiner) and a nontransparent part (the value judgment claim). And on an extension of the semantics we have assumed, we might define a basic determiner to be existential iff its transparent part is existential. This will guarantee that the determiners in (22) are existential since, as we will see, cardinality determiners are in general a proper subset of the existential ones.

To say that a determiner is a *cardinal* determiner is to say that it always denotes a *cardinal* function from properties to sets of properties. And informally, to say that a function f is cardinal is to say that whether $f(q)$'s are p's is determined by the number of individual q's who are p's. For example, *at least two* is cardinal since if we know how many q's are p's, then we know whether at least two q's are p's or not. This may be stated formally as follows.

Definition 4

A (one-place) function f from properties to sets of properties is *cardinal* iff for all properties p_1, p_2, q_1, q_2 if $|p_1 \wedge q_1| = |p_2 \wedge q_2|$ then $p_1 \in f(q_1)$ iff $p_2 \in f(q_2)$.

Theorem 2

a. Every cardinal function is existential, but the converse in general fails.

b. In a world of n individuals there are 2^{2^n} existential functions, only $2^{(n+1)}$ of which are cardinal.

We will return to cardinal determiners in section 12.4.

Finally, I have not explicitly treated indefinite plurals such as *fleas,* as in *There are fleas in this bed.* Such NPs occur with an existential reading in ET contexts and appear to have a cardinality interpretation there, meaning something like *some* or *at least two.* Treating the plural *s* as a determiner with that interpretation will of course classify such NPs as existential. But more would have to be said concerning their more "universal" interpretation in generic contexts, as in *John hates fleas.*

12.3 Explanatory Adequacy of the Analysis
12.3.1 Existential NPs in ET Sentences

So far I have merely defined a class of English NPs and claimed that that class correlates well with those NPs pretheoretically judged to occur in ET sentences on an existence assertion reading. I have made no commitments concerning the internal syntactic structure of ET sentences, nor have I provided any semantic interpretation for such sentences. One may then ask, without circularity, why just the NPs defined as existential should occur in ET sentences with the existence assertion reading. In what follows I claim to provide an explanation for that fact in terms of (1) the proposed definition of existential NP, (2) the motivated syntactic analysis of ET sentences, and (3) the principle of Compositionality—which I take here to mean that the semantic interpretation of an expression is given as a function of the interpretation of its immediate constituents.

I am not claiming (much less explaining) that ET sentences with nonexistential NPs are ungrammatical. I claim only that such expressions, if grammatical, are not understood on an existence assertion reading.

In presenting my explanation, I (herewith) assume that the use of *there* in ET sentences is the semantically empty use. That is, the truth-value of sentences like (23a) cannot vary according to whether *there* refers to different objects.

(23) a. There are several students who object to that
     b. Over there are several students who object to that

Arguably, for example, the truth of (23b) does vary with the location deictically indicated by *over there,* and there are doubtless grounds for considering that (23a) is ambiguous according to whether *there* is a locative deictic or is semantically empty. Here I do not treat sentences such as (23b) or the reading of (23a) on which it is understood like (23b) if it has such a reading.

My basic explanation proceeds in two steps, which I summarize and then justify.

Step 1: ET sentences have essentially the form given in (24).

(24)

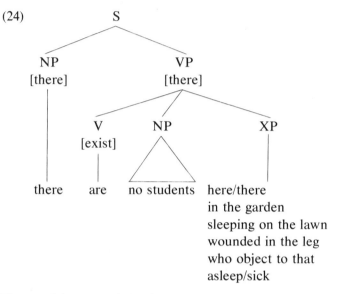

there   are   no students   here/there
                                in the garden
                                sleeping on the lawn
                                wounded in the leg
                                who object to that
                                asleep/sick

The crucial aspect of (24) for present purposes is that the *predicate* NP *no students* does not form a constituent with the XP. (My analysis contrasts in this respect with that of Barwise and Cooper, who assign (24) the gross structure [$_S$ there [$_{VP}$ be [$_{NP}$ no students in the garden]]]. Thus, on their analysis, the XP does form a constituent with the predicate NP.) Note that XP in (24) may be any of several categories: PP (*in the garden*), AP (*asleep, sick*), and so forth. What is important here is that the various sorts of expressions that can fill the XP slot semantically determine properties of individuals. For example, *in the garden* determines the property an individual has iff that individual is in the garden; *asleep* determines the property an individual has iff that individual is asleep. I will in general refer to this property by p_{XP}. Similarly, I will refer to the set of properties denoted by the predicate NP as Q_{NP}.

Step 2: From Compositionality, the only way to interpret sentences of the form [there [be NP XP]] in (24) is to say that Q_{NP}, the denotation of the predicate NP, has the property p_{XP} expressed by the XP.

I have not assumed in (24) that the predicate NP is existential. Therefore, Step 2 says that the (a)-sentences in (25) and (26) receive the same interpretations as the corresponding (b)-sentences.

(25) a. There are exactly two dogs and three cats in the yard
     b. Exactly two dogs and three cats are in the yard

(26) a. There is every student in the yard
     b. Every student is in the yard

Steps 1 and 2 yield the desired result as a theorem.

Theorem 3
ET sentences of the form in (27a) are logically equivalent to the existence assertion reading (27b) if and only if the determiner expression Det is always interpreted by an existential function.

(27) a. there [be [$_{\text{NP}}$ Det student] [$_{\text{XP}}$ in the garden]]
     b. [$_{\text{NP}}$ Det [$_{\text{CNP}}$ student in the garden]] exist
     c. 1 $\in$ (Det(**student** $\wedge$ **in the garden**))

((27c) states (27b) semantically, using boldface e for the semantic interpretation of *e*.) It remains then to establish Steps 1 and 2.

Step 1: I will provide four reasons to support the claim that the XP and the predicate NP in ET sentences form independent constituents. The first is taken from Barwise and Cooper (who note several other reasons). Namely, often the post-*be* phrases in ET sentences do not occur naturally in canonical NP positions, such as the subject position in (28b), and therefore should not be considered to be NPs.

(28) a. There are two students who object to that enrolled in the course
     b. ?*Two students who object to that enrolled in the course just came in

Equally (not noted by Barwise and Cooper) the post-*be* phrase in *There was no student but John in the building* occurs in virtually no unequivocal NP position.

Second, when the predicate NP is multiply headed, as with conjoined NPs (29c) or NPs formed from two-place determiners (29a–b), it is neither syntactically motivated nor semantically adequate (see Keenan and Moss 1985) to consider that the XP forms a constituent with each CNP head.

(29) a. There were fewer dogs than cats in every kennel
   b. There are exactly two tables and three chairs in some class-
      rooms
   c. There are between five and ten students and at most three
      teachers in some departments

Note that a compositional semantics yields incorrect interpretations for
the sentences in (29) if the XPs are construed as forming constituents
with the multiple CNP heads. For example, (29b) does not mean the
same as *There are exactly two tables in some classroom and three chairs
in some classroom.*

Third, in Det + CNP + XP collocations where it is known for independent reasons that the XP does not form a constituent with the CNP
(as in (30a)), the Det + CNP position relativizes, stranding the XP (as in
(30b)), and the entire Det + CNP + XP does not extract (as in (30c)).

(30) a. John put the books on the shelf
   b. the books which John put on the shelf
   c. *the books on the shelf which John put

Just the opposite pattern obtains in Det + CNP + XP collocations
where the XP does form a constituent with the CNP (as in (31a)). Here
the Det + CNP will not extract, stranding the XP (as in (31b)), and the
entire Det + CNP + XP position does extract (as in (31c)).

(31) a. John painted the shelves in my living room purple
   b. *the shelves that John painted in my living room purple
   c. the shelves in my living room that John painted purple

In these respects ET sentences behave like the cases in (30) where the
XP does not form a constituent with the CNP. The (a)-sentences in
(32)–(34) show that the predicate NP position can be relativized,
stranding the XP, and the (b)-sentences show that the entire Det +
CNP + XP sequence cannot be extracted.

(32) a. Not even *one* of the students$_i$ that there were i at the lecture
         could remember seeing John there
   b. *Not even *one* of [the students at the lecture]$_i$ that there were i
         could remember seeing John there

(33) a. Don't worry, John will help himself to whatever$_i$ there is i in
         the fridge
   b. *Don't worry, John will help himself to [whatever in the
         fridge]$_i$ there is i

(34) a.   Of [the thousands of lawyers]$_i$ that there are i in Washington, only one can tie his shoes without help, and he works as a doorman

   b.   ?*Of [the thousands of lawyers in Washington]$_i$ that there are i, only one can tie his shoes without help, and he works as a doorman

Fourth, it appears that the NP position in ET structures can be bound by a variable-binding operator, which implies that that position refers independently of the PP (but see Heim's remarks on this point in chapter 2). In fact, (32)–(34) illustrate this with relative clause binding. (35) and (36) illustrate other types of binding.

(35)   The campus authorities knew exactly which students$_i$ there were i at the party

(36)   A: Ten thousand students will attend the lecture tomorrow
       B: Don't be daft! That's more students$_i$ than there are i in the entire school

For these reasons, then, in addition to those given by Barwise and Cooper, I consider that the predicate NP and the XP in ET structures are syntactically independent as depicted in (24).

Step 2: A minimal compositional semantics for ET sentences must discriminate their truth and falsehood conditions as a function of the denotations of their immediate constituents. As the denotation of *there* is irrelevant, the distinction must be made on the basis of the interpretation of the VP[there], and that interpretation, again by Compositionality, must be given in terms of the denotations of *be*, the predicate NP, and the XP. But *be* has at most one interpretation, so the truth of an ET sentence cannot vary with its denotation. Thus, the truth and falsehood conditions must be determined on the basis of the denotations of the predicate NP and the XP, Q_{NP} and p_{XP}, respectively. But the only way we have to make a truth or falsehood distinction on the basis of an NP denotation and a property is to say that the NP denotation has (or fails to have) the property. And this is just what Step 2 says.

More formally, (37) provides a compositional semantics for VP[there]'s.

(37)   A VP[there] of the form [be, NP, XP] is true of an arbitrary NP denotation iff $p_{XP} \in Q_{XP}$.

(If we accept the degenerate case of VP[there]'s without XPs, then we interpret them as in (37), choosing p_{XP} = 1.) The semantics in (37) guarantees the equivalences in (25) and (26) and yields Theorem 3 (see the Appendix). This completes the formal analysis of the definiteness effect.

12.3.2 Additional Advantages of the Analysis

The proposed analysis has three additional advantages. First, it provides a basis for limiting the types of phrases that may occur in the XP slot: they must be ones that determine properties of individuals (though not all properties are equally accessible; see Stowell 1978 for some discussion). Note in particular that not all expressions of acceptable XP categories (such as the PPs in (38)) do determine properties of individuals.

(38) John spoke *about the problem*/ran *to the finish line*/won *by subterfuge*

It does not make much sense to say that John is about the problem, to the finish line, or by subterfuge. As a result, these PPs plausibly do not determine properties of individuals and hence on the proposed analysis cannot be interpreted in ET contexts (according to (37)). And this agrees with pretheoretical judgments: expressions such as *There are two students about the problem* make no more sense than *John is about the problem*.

Second, the proposed analysis provides an interpretation for ET sentences in which the predicate NP is not existential, and in several cases noted as problematic in the literature these predictions seem correct. As a simple case, the analysis predicts that (39a) should be interpreted as in (39b), rather than on the existence assertion reading in (39c).

(39) a. There were most of the students at the party
     b. Most of the students were at the party
     c. Most of the students at the party exist(ed)

The meaning predictions seem clearly correct in this case. A more interesting class of cases, noted variously by Hawkins (1978), Fauconnier (1979), and Holmback (1984), is that of superlatives, especially with an exclamatory intonation.

(40) a. There's the biggest dog in the garden!
   b. The biggest dog is in the garden!
   c. The biggest dog in the garden exists!

And indeed, as the analysis predicts, the natural interpretation of (40a) is (40b) and not the existence assertion claim in (40c). Note that (40a) is clearly grammatical and thus, in possible distinction to (39a), we do care to represent its meaning correctly. Moreover, on the natural way of interpreting *the biggest dog* (namely, as the unique dog bigger than all the other dogs if there is one, and the empty set of properties otherwise) that NP will not be existential. This constitutes support for not limiting predicate NPs to existential ones in the syntax.

Third, the proposed analysis also explains the distribution of determiners in another class of existential structures. To define that class, consider what Keenan and Faltz (1978) call *transitive* CNPs, such as *friend (of), brother (of), colleague (of)*. Syntactically, transitive CNPs combine with full NPs (such as *the president*) to form ordinary (complex) CNPs (*friend of the president*), which of course combine with ordinary determiners to form full NPs (*every friend of the president, no friend of the president,* and so forth). Semantically, transitive CNPs map NP denotations to properties.

Observe now that transitive CNPs may occur without an overtly expressed argument NP, in which case the entire sentence they occur in is usually construed so as to find an argument. For example, an assertion of *Two friends just came in* might be used to mean 'Two individuals who are friends of *us* just came in' (in which case the argument is found deictically), or it might be used to mean 'Two individuals who are friends of *each other* just came in'.

Semantically, then, we are motivated to treat expressions of the form [Det friends] as still requiring an argument. Let us call such expressions *transitive* NPs. Syntactically, they combine with full NPs to form full NPs, and semantically, they are maps from property sets to property sets, as defined informally in (41).

(41) [Det friend](John) $=_{df}$ Det [friend of (John)]

That is, (*[two friends](of) John*) denotes the same as *[two(friends (of) John)]*.

An interesting exception to this syntax and semantics is given by possessive determiners. *John's friends* is not a transitive NP and does

not require an argument. It is an ordinary NP and means roughly
the[friends which John has].

Now consider the sentences in (42), which contain transitive NPs
whose argument is provided by the subject of the sentence, *John*.

(42) a. John has several friends who work in the mines
 b. John has more male than female cousins in New York
 c. John has at least two sons and three daughters attending
    college

These sentences are understood on an existence assertion reading. For
example, (42a) is true in the same conditions as *Several friends of John
who work in the mines exist*. Let us refer to such constructions on this
reading as *existential have* (EH) sentences.

EH structures are similar in very many ways to ET structures. The
determiners that naturally occur in the EH NP slot seem to be just
those that we have called existential (other than possessives). If we
replace the determiners in (42) with ones like *every, the ten,* and *all but
three*, ungrammaticality or semantic anomaly results. Similarly, many
(though perhaps not all) of the XP expansions in ET structures apply in
EH structures, and many of the reasons for regarding the NP and the
XP as independent constituents carry over here as well. So let us adopt
(modulo details) the constituent structure analysis in (43) for EH
structures.

(43)

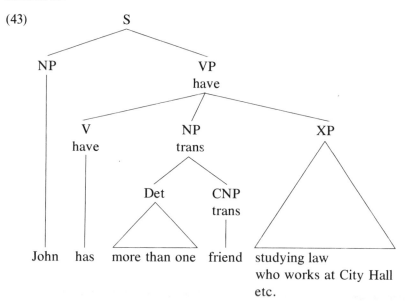

Now (43) is dissimilar to the corresponding structure for ET sentences in that it has a semantically referential subject. But the compositionality problem is essentially the same, since that subject "gets used up" as the argument of the transitive NP, leaving us, as before, in the position of having to define a sentence type denotation on the basis of an ordinary NP denotation and a property. So again, by Compositionality, essentially all we can say is that either the NP denotation has the property or it doesn't. This we may do as follows, using p_{XP} as before and F_{NP} for the function denoted by the transitive NP.

(44) Interpret a VP[have] of the form [have, NP, XP] as that
function mapping each individual J to *true* iff $P_{XP} \in F_{NP}(J)$.

Now the analogue of Theorem 3 follows.

Theorem 4
Sentences of the forms (45a) and (45b) are logically equivalent iff the determiner is always interpreted as an existential function.

(45) a. John has [$_{NP}$ Det friend][$_{XP}$ in Chicago]
       trans
    b. [$_{NP}$ Det [$_{CNP}$ friend of John in Chicago]] exist

12.4 Comparison with Other Treatments

Milsark (1974) proposes that the determiners natural in ET contexts are just cardinal ones (though his informal treatment of cardinality is not sufficient to represent decreasing cardinal determiners such as *fewer than six*). On the analysis proposed here, Theorem 2 shows that Milsark's intuition is correct as far as it goes (all cardinal determiners are existential) but that it does not go far enough (there are existential determiners that are not cardinal, such as *more male than female*).

But just how far does Milsark's intuition go? Theorem 2 tells us that in a world with more than two individuals the existential functions that are not cardinal vastly outnumber those that are. But this fact is misleading in an interesting way. Cardinal determiners are *logically constant*, which implies among other things that in a given universe of individuals a given cardinal determiner can be interpreted by only one function. But determiners such as *more male than female* are not logically constant. In a given universe there will typically be many functions that such a determiner can denote, depending on what functions *male* and *female* denote. Thus, if we took the set of functions needed to interpret just the cardinal determiners and then added in those needed to provide denotations for the single additional determiner *more male than female,* we would find that the resulting set of functions had increased by much more than one. It is this fact that accounts for the impression, scanning the existential determiners mentioned so far, that "most" existential determiners are in fact cardinal ones. And more can be said. The existential determiners that are not cardinal in the lists given earlier all appear to be not logically constant. I propose this as a semantic universal.

(46) *Universal*
    The logically constant existential determiners in a language are just the cardinal determiners.

(46) is empirically significant in that it does not (quite) follow from any other constraints on determiner interpretations. But we do have Theorem 5.

Theorem 5
In a finite universe the denotations of logically constant existential determiners are all cardinal functions.

The restriction of Theorem 5 to finite universes is, however, essential. For infinite universes there are existential functions that lie in the set in which the logical constants denote but that are not cardinal.

The universal then claims that natural languages do not present determiners always interpreted by such functions. The difficulty in expressing such functions does not lie in the fact that they make crucial reference to (in)finite properties. Such ordinary determiners as *infinitely many* and *all but finitely many* do that. The problem is rather that in deciding whether to put a property p in the set they associate with q, such determiners may make crucial reference not only to the number of individuals with $(q \wedge p)$, as do cardinal determiners, but also to the number of individuals that lack $(q \wedge p)$. In a finite universe the latter number is uniquely determined by the former, but this is not the case in an infinite universe.

I conclude this section with a comparison between my account and that given by Barwise and Cooper. Like my account, theirs treats (one-place) determiners as functions from properties to sets of properties, but unlike mine, theirs admits partial functions. For example, on their account, the function that interprets *the two* only assigns property sets to properties that exactly two individuals have. Thus, on their account, *the two students* has no denotation defined if there are not exactly two students, whereas on my account, it is the empty set $\emptyset$ of properties. My decision to limit determiner denotations to total functions is based largely on grounds of methodological simplicity rather than on ones of substance. Specifically, my account simply avoids the problem of having to decide in a principled way how to distinguish the case where a determiner denotation f fails to have a property q in its domain from the case where it has q in its domain but assigns it some trivial value, say, the empty set. Barwise and Cooper do not in fact provide a principled basis for making this decision, and this makes it difficult to extend their analysis to determiners they do not explicitly consider. Moreover, for the class of determiners they do consider, it turns out that my total function approach yields the same classification. So the additional complications attendant upon using the larger class of functions is not in fact necessary.

Now, the "Thesis" of Barwise and Cooper is that the NPs grammatical in ET sentences are just those formed from *weak* determiners, where Det is weak iff there are properties p,q in its domain such that *Det p's are p's* is true and *Det q's are q's* is false. Nonweak determiners are *strong: positive strong* if *Det p's are p's* is true for all p in the domain of Det, *negative strong* if *Det p's are p's* is false for all such p.

Barwise and Cooper's analysis and mine are close in several respects. For example, as noted earlier, the two analyses yield the same classification for the limited class of determiners they consider. But some divergences appear as this class is extended. Thus, consider the two classes of maximally trivial determiners in (47).

(47) a. at least zero, either zero or else more than zero, some
         number of, either at least *n* or else fewer than *n*, either
         infinitely many or else just finitely many
     b. fewer than zero, no number of, between seven and five,
         neither infinitely many nor finitely many, more male than
         male

The determiners in (47a) are existential and positive strong; all in fact are interpreted by the trivial function 1_{Det} that sends each q to P, the set of all properties. The determiners in (47b) are existential and negative strong, all being interpreted by the function 0_{Det} that sends each q to $\emptyset$. Thus, my analysis predicts that the determiners in (47) should occur naturally in ET contexts, and Barwise and Cooper's analysis makes the opposite prediction. (48a–b) shows that my analysis is preferable.

(48) a. Look, there were either zero or else more than zero students
there at the time. Now which is it?

b. Your argument is ingenious, Mr. Jones. It proves among
other things that there are fewer than zero perfect numbers

Like other obviously trivial expressions (contradictions, tautologies),
these determiners have natural uses that are emphatic, ironic, or
humorous.

Comparison of the two analyses with respect to more complex determiners is made difficult by the difficulty of applying the definition of
weak to new cases. One difficulty, for example, concerns its extension
to $k > 1$–place determiners. It would seem natural to say that a two-
place function f is positive strong iff $f(p,p)$'s are p's, for all appropriate
p. But then two-place existential determiners such as *at least as
many . . . as . . .* would wrongly be classed as positive strong and not
weak. For obviously the student property, indeed any property, is a
property that at least as many students as students have. Similarly,
determiners such as *more . . . than . . .* and *fewer . . . than . . .* would
be classed (wrongly by the ET test) as negative strong and thus not
weak. My analysis appears superior here since the definition of *existential* (on which, see the Appendix) applies uniformly to Det_k's for
all k.

Further difficulties in extending the application of *weak* derive from
the fact that to class a determiner as weak we must make crucial decisions concerning which properties are in the domain of the functions
that it may denote. Barwise and Cooper offer no criterion for making
this decision, and consequently there is no explicit way to extend this
approach to novel cases. For example, it might seem reasonable to
decide that the domain of any function that could interpret *John's* (singular, as in *John's hat*) would be the set of properties p such that John
"has" exactly one p. Then *John's hat is a hat* would be true whenever
John's hat was defined, so *John's* would (correctly) be classed as positive strong. But by the same intuition *someone's* (singular) should have
as domain the set of properties p such that someone has exactly one
p—whence *someone's* is also positive strong and thus wrongly predicted not to occur in ET sentences (*There's someone's hat on the table*
seems all right). We might solve this dilemma by setting the domain of
someone's to be the set of all properties, P. But clearly, to avoid the
charge of concocting the domains so as to make the ET test come out
right, we need a principled basis for deciding when an arbitrary prop-

erty is in the domain of an arbitrary determiner. As yet no clear criterion is available; hence, Barwise and Cooper's analysis is not satisfactory in this regard.

Moreover, the domain decisions that must be made to class a simple determiner as weak frequently involve crucial judgments about whether the 0 property (the nonexistence property, that property which no individual has) is in the domain of some determiner. For example, if 0 were not in the domains of *no, some, a, at least one,* these determiners would all be classed as strong. *No students are students* is clearly false whenever there are any students. The only way to class it as weak, then, is to say that it is true in the case where there are no individuals who are students, that is, where *student* denotes 0. Therefore, 0 must be in the domain of *no.* Similarly, *some* is positive strong if 0 is not in its domain, since the only case where *Some student is a student* can be false is where there are no students.

So our judgments here crucially involve assessing the meaning of NPs of the form [Det CNP], where the CNP denotes 0. But we would not normally assert a sentence of the form *Det students are ill* if we knew that there were no students. For who, in some sense, would we be talking about? Thus, the crucial decision in classifying determiners like *no* and *some* as weak requires judgments on the denotation of NPs precisely under conditions in which we would not normally use the NP, and thus under conditions where we may remain rather indifferent about what we consider it to denote. This seems a slim basis for establishing the weakness of *no* and *some,* yet these determiners are among the paradigm examples of determiners that occur naturally in ET contexts.

By contrast, no such messy judgments are involved in establishing *no* and *some* as existential. We must merely judge that (for example) *No students are vegetarians* is true in the same conditions as *No students who are vegetarians exist.*

Finally, the proposed analysis is preferable to Barwise and Cooper's on the grounds that the explanation of the definiteness effect induced by the former is more satisfactory than the explanation induced by the latter. Barwise and Cooper treat ET sentences as having the form [there[be NP]], interpreted as true iff *NP exist(s)* (that is, iff $1 \in Q_{NP}$ in the notation used here). They make the interesting observation that if *NP* has the form [Det CNP], where Det is strong, then *NP exist* is trivially true or trivially false (whenever **NP** is defined). Thus, if NPs with strong determiners occurred in ET sentences, the sentences would be logically trivial. These observations seem correct. But, as Barwise and Cooper acknowledge, they do not justify the inference that the ET sentences should be ungrammatical in such cases.

We have in fact already noted ET sentences that are logically trivial but clearly grammatical (see (48)). And grammatical but logically trivial sentences abound. Indeed, the very sentences we use to show that *NP exist* is trivial when the determiner is strong are a case in point. Thus, *Every student exists, Every student is a student* are logically trivial in just the way the corresponding ET sentence is with *every student* as the predicate NP. Barwise and Cooper's analysis then leaves unexplained why *Every student exists* should be grammatical but the corresponding ET sentence ungrammatical.

Appendix
Determiners Considered in This Study (Adapted from Keenan and Stavi 1986)
One-Place Determiners
1. *Simplex*
   a, some, six, no, several, a few, a score of, a dozen
   each, every, all, both, neither, most, the
   $this_i$, $that_j$, $these_p$, $those_q$, we_p, you_q, $them_p$, this $here_q$
2. *Possessives*
   John's, no student's, my_i, $your_p$, some student's and every dean's
3. *Adverb (etc.) + many*
   finitely many, infinitely many, uncountably many, aleph zero many
4. *a + AP + number of*
   an even number of, a prime number of, an infinite number of
5. *Approximative determiners*
   a hundred plus or minus ten, approximately thirty, about thirty, nearly thirty, practically no, almost no, hardly any, twenty-odd almost all, nearly all, most every
6. *Bounding determiners*
   between five and ten, exactly ten, only ten
   only SOME, exactly ten percent of the, just half the
   $THIS_i$, only $THIS_i$, $this_i$ and no other, only John's two, only John's biggest, only the LIBERAL, only the most liberal and the most conservative

7. *Modifier + numerical expression*
   at least ten, more than two, fewer than ten, exactly three, only
   six, five or more, a hundred or more, at most seven, over a
   hundred, at least finitely many
   the ten, the ten or more, the more than two hundred, all five, all
   the five, all the, the ten to twenty
   John's five, every student's two or more, these$_q$ five, all these$_q$
   five, these$_q$ five or more

8. *Exception determiners*
   all but five, all but finitely many, all but at most five
   every . . . but John, every . . . but John's, no . . . but John,
   all . . . but the two tallest

9. *Anaphoric determiners*
   (even) more, fewer, at least as many, not as many, twice as
   many, almost twice that many, not that many, half again as
   many

10. *Comparatives with APs*
    more male than female, fewer male than female, more than twice
    as many male as female, exactly as many male as female

11. *Det + AP*
    all liberal, most conservative, the five liberal, John's liberal
    exactly two male and three female, someone's two male and
    three female
    John's two biggest, the two biggest, neither the tallest nor the
    strongest
    whatever . . . are in the cupboard, any . . . that you write

12. *Comparatives with determiners*
    more of John's than of Mary's, fewer of the male than of the
    female, proportionately more of the student's than of the
    teacher's

13. *Proportional determiners*
    every other, every third, two out of three, more than two out of
    three, half the, more than half the, most, most of the, five
    percent of the, between five and ten percent of the, more than
    two-thirds of the, less than half the liberal

14. *Partitives*
    less than five of the ten, at most five of the ten, all of the ten
    less than five of John's, most of the liberal, the three tallest of
    the twenty or more, at least four of some student's, five percent
    of John's

15. *Boolean combinations*
not even one, not a, not more than five, not more than half of
John's, not every, not all the, no more than ten, no fewer than
ten, no more of the male than of the female, not more than two
out of three, not every student's, not only John's, not all of the,
not one of the ten, neither John's nor Mary's, neither the male
nor the female, neither exactly two nor exactly six
at least two and at most ten, at least two but no more than ten,
either exactly two or exactly ten, most but not all, some but not
all, John's but not Mary's, no more than twenty and no fewer
than ten, either fewer than ten or else more than a hundred

$k \geqslant 2$-*Place Determiners* (see Keenan and Moss 1985 for a more
detailed presentation)
more . . . than . . . , exactly twice as many . . . as . . . , more . . .
than . . . or . . . , no . . . or . . . , the ninety-odd . . . and . . . ,
some student's two . . . and three . . . , exactly half the . . .
and an even greater proportion of . . . , exactly two . . . and
three . . . , John's most aggressive . . . and . . .

Extensions to $k > 1$-Place Determiners
1. *Notation.* In what follows we generalize certain of the definitions
and theorems in the text to k-place functions. We write P for the set of
all properties (of a model) and P^* for the set of all sets of properties.
For each $k \geqslant 1$, p^k is the set of k-tuples of properties. A k-tuple
$(q_1, q_2, \ldots, q_k)$ of properties will usually be written $\bar{q}$. We write $(p \wedge \bar{q})$ for
the k-tuple $(q_1 \wedge p, q_2 \wedge p, \ldots, q_k \wedge p)$.

2. *Existential determiners.* A function f from P^k into P^* is *existential* iff
for all $p \in P$ and all $\bar{q} \in P^k$, $p \in f(\bar{q})$ iff $1 \in f(p \wedge \bar{q})$.

As an exercise using the definition we show that *more . . . than . . .*
as defined in the text is a two-place existential determiner. Note that for
any property t, $(t \wedge 1) = t$, since the individuals who are both t's and
individuals are just the individuals who are t's. Then we have that

$p \in$ *more q_1 than q_2* iff $|q_1 \wedge p| > |q_2 \wedge p|$ def *more . . . than . . .*
        iff $|q_1 \wedge p) \wedge 1| > |(q_2 \wedge p) \wedge 1|$
        iff $1 \in$ *more $(q_1 \wedge p)$ than $(q_2 \wedge p)$*
                       def *more . . . than . . .*

The first and last lines show that *more . . . than . . .* is existential.

3. *Theorem 1.* (a) If d_1 and d_2 are k-place determiners interpreted by f and g, respectively, then (d_1 *and* d_2), (d_1 *or* d_2), and (*not* d_1) are, respectively, interpreted by the functions ($f \wedge g$), ($f \vee g$), and f', defined by ($f \wedge g)(\bar{q}) = f(\bar{q}) \cap g(\bar{q})$, ($f \vee g)(\bar{q}) = f(\bar{q}) \cup g(\bar{q})$, and $f'(\bar{q}) = (f(\bar{q}))'$ (that is, $P - f(\bar{q})$). It is straightforward to show that these functions are existential whenever both f and g are.

(b) An absolute AP function h maps k-tuples of properties to k-tuples of properties by $h(\bar{q}) = h(1) \wedge \bar{q}$. For example, the male doctors are the male individuals who are doctors. Virtually all extensional APs in English are interpreted by absolute functions as above. Now, where f interprets a k-place existential determiner, the composition (fh) is seen to be existential as follows.

$p \in (fh)(\bar{q})$ iff $p \in f(h(\bar{q}))$

   iff $1 \in f[h(\bar{q}) \wedge p]$ f is existential

   iff $1 \in f[h(1) \wedge \bar{q} \wedge p]$ h is absolute

   iff $1 \in f[h(1) \wedge (p \wedge \bar{q})]$

   iff $1 \in f(h(p \wedge \bar{q}))$ h is absolute

   iff $1 \in (fh)(p \wedge \bar{q})$

(c) The exception determiner operator . . . *but John* applies to only two determiners, both one-place: *every* and *no*. Of these, only *no* is existential. (*no* . . . *but J*), for *J* any individual, is defined by $p \in$ (*no* . . . *but J*)(q) iff $(p \wedge q) = j$, where j is that property which *J* has to the exclusion of all other individuals. (That is, *No student but John left* is true iff John is the only student who left.) (*no* . . . *but J*) as defined is easily seen to be existential.

4. *Theorem 2.* Here $k = 1$ and n is assumed finite. There are 2^n properties and 2^{2^n} sets of properties. For each set of properties K, the function f_K defined by $p \in f_K(q)$ iff $(p \wedge q) \in K$ is easily seen to be existential, and every existential function f is an f_K for some K (choose $K = f(1)$). As different Ks give rise to different f_K's, we have that there are 2^{2^n} existential functions. Note in fact that the set of existential functions (one-place) is isomorphic to P^*, the set of full NP denotations.

The cardinal functions correspond one for one (see Keenan and Moss 1985 for details) to the sets of numbers drawn from $\{0,1,...,n\}$, so that there are only 2^{n+1} such functions. An *atomic* cardinal function f is f_K where K is the set of all properties of some fixed cardinality (between 0 and n, inclusively). Each cardinal function is a join of some atomic cardinal functions $f_{K_1},...,f_{K_j}$ and thus equals f_K for $K = K_1 \cup ... \cup K_j$.

5. *Theorem 3.* Assume first that **Det** is existential. Then

there be [Det student][in the garden] is true
iff (**in the garden**) $\in$ (**Det student**)	from def (37)
iff $1 \in$ **Det**(**student** $\wedge$ **in the garden**)	Det is existential
iff [Det(student in the garden)] exist	def. int. *exist*

Conversely, if **Det** is not existential, find properties p,q such that $p \in$ **Det**$(q) \leftrightarrow 1 \in$ Det$(q \wedge p)$ fails. Interpret *student* and *in the garden* as p and q, respectively, and show that the first and last lines of this proof have different truth-values.

6. *Theorem 5.* We show the case for $k = 1$. The logically constant determiners take their denotations in the *automorphism invariant* functions from P into P^*, where f is automorphism invariant (AI) iff $f(i(q)) = i[f(q)]$, all automorphisms i of P (that is, all permutations of the individuals). For a finite universe, any two properties s,t of the same cardinality are such that $i(s) = t$ for some automorphism i.

Now assume that f is AI and existential. We show f is cardinal. Let $|p_1 \wedge q_1| = |p_2 \wedge q_2|$. We must show $p_1 \in f(q_1)$ iff $p_2 \in f(q_2)$. Let $i(p_1 \wedge q_1) = p_2 \wedge q_2$. Then

$p_1 \in f(q_1)$ iff $1 \in f(q_1 \wedge p_1)$	f is existential
iff $i1 \in i[f(q_1 \wedge p_1)]$	
iff $1 \in f(i(q_1 \wedge p_1))$	$i1 = 1$ and f is AI
iff $1 \in f(q_2 \wedge p_2)$	
iff $p_2 \in f(q_2)$	f is existential

The generalization to k-place determiners is straightforward. See Keenan and Moss 1985 for the relevant definitions.

To see that the theorem fails for an infinite universe (and thus P infinite), let K be the set of infinite properties with finite complements and define the function f_K by $p \in f_K(q)$ iff $(p \wedge q) \in K$. Then f_K is easily shown to be AI and existential but not cardinal.

7. K-*place cardinal determiners.* A function f from P^k into P^* is *cardinal* iff for all $q,s \in P$ and all $\bar{q},\bar{s} \in P^K$, if $|q \wedge q_i| = |s \wedge s_i|$, all i between 1 and k, then $q \in f(\bar{q})$ iff $s \in f(\bar{s})$.

Notes

I am indebted to Steve Anderson and Susan Mordechay for critical discussions of the research reported here, and to the Max-Planck-Institut für Psycholinguistik for supporting the work on which this chapter is based.

1. Assuming that f is *conservative* $(p \in f(q) \leftrightarrow (p \wedge q) \in f(q))$, we have that f is existential iff f is *symmetric* $(p \in f(q) \leftrightarrow q \in f(p))$ iff f is *intersective* $(p \in f(q) \leftrightarrow p \in f(q \wedge p))$. From Keenan and Stavi we have that the denotations of all the determiners in the Appendix are conservative (in fact, they show that conservativity characterizes the possible determiner denotations). Thus, I could (for one-place functions) have taken the defining conditions for *existential* as those of *symmetry* or *intersective*. I did not, for two reasons: (1) *existential* is more basic in the sense that "f is existential" implies that f is conservative, symmetric, and intersective. But all the converses fail. (2) The notions *conservative, existential,* and *intersective* extend naturally to $k > 1$–place functions, preserving the equivalences noted above, but this does not hold for *symmetry*.

Bibliography

Andrews, A. (1975). "Studies in the Syntax of Comparative and Relative Clauses." Doctoral dissertation, MIT, Cambridge, Mass.

Aoun, J., N. Hornstein, and D. Sportiche (1981). "Aspects of Wide Scope Quantification." *Journal of Linguistic Research* 1, 67–95.

Aoun, J., and D. Lightfoot (1984). "Government and Contraction." *Linguistic Inquiry* 15, 465–473.

Aoun, J., and D. Sportiche (1982). "On the Formal Theory of Government." *The Linguistic Review* 2, 211–236.

Baker, C. L. (1970). "Notes on the Description of English Questions: The Role of an Abstract Question Morpheme." *Foundations of Language* 6, 197–219.

Baker, C. L. (1979). "Syntactic Theory and the Projection Problem." *Linguistic Inquiry* 10, 533–581.

Bartsch, R. (1973). "The Semantics and Syntax of Number and Numbers." In J. P. Kimball, ed., *Syntax and Semantics* 2. New York and London: Seminar Press.

Barwise, J., and R. Cooper (1981). "Generalized Quantifiers and Natural Language." *Linguistics and Philosophy* 4, 159–219.

Barwise, J., and J. Perry (1983). *Situations and Attitudes*. Cambridge, Mass.: MIT Press.

Belletti, A. (1985). "Unaccusatives as Case Assigners." Ms., MIT, Cambridge, Mass./Scuola Normale Superiore, Pisa.

Bergvall, V. (1984). "WH-Questions and Island Constraints in Kikuyu: A Reanalysis." In J. Kaye, H. Koopman, and D. Sportiche, eds., *Current Approaches to African Linguistics* II. Dordrecht: Foris.

Besten, H. den (1985). "The Ergative Hypothesis and Free Word Order in Dutch and German." In J. Toman, ed., *Studies in German Grammar*. Dordrecht: Foris.

Bolinger, D. (1972). *Degree Words*. The Hague: Mouton.

Bolinger, D. (1977). *Meaning and Form*. London and New York: Longmans.

Bolinger, D. (1978). "Asking More Than One Thing at a Time." In H. Hiż, ed., *Questions*. Dordrecht: Reidel.

Boolos, G. (1983). "To Be Is to Be a Value of a Variable (or to Be Some Values of Some Variables)." *The Journal of Philosophy* 81.8, 430–449.

Bordelois, I. (1974). "The Grammar of Spanish Causative Complements." Doctoral dissertation, MIT, Cambridge, Mass.

Bouchard, D. (1982). "On the Content of Empty Categories." Doctoral dissertation, MIT, Cambridge, Mass.

Bresnan, J. (1973). "Syntax of the Comparative Clause Construction in English." *Linguistic Inquiry* 4, 275–344.

Brody, M. (1984). "On Contextual Definitions and the Role of Chains." *Linguistic Inquiry* 15, 355–380.

Burzio, L. (1981). "Intransitive Verbs and Italian Auxiliaries." Doctoral dissertation, MIT, Cambridge, Mass.

Carden, G. (1978). "Backwards Anaphora in Discourse Context." Ms., Yale University, New Haven, Conn.

Carlson, G. (1977a). "Reference to Kinds in English." Doctoral dissertation, University of Massachusetts, Amherst. [New York: Garland (1980).]

Carlson, G. (1977b). "Amount Relatives." *Language* 53, 520–542.

Carlson, L. (1980). *Plural Quantification*. Ms., MIT, Cambridge, Mass. [To appear in *ACTA Philosophica Fennica* (1986).]

Chafe, W. L. (1976). "Givenness, Contrastiveness, Definiteness, Subjects, Topics and Point of View." In C. Li, ed., *Subject and Topic*. New York: Academic Press.

Chao, Y.-R. (1968). *A Grammar of Spoken Chinese*. Berkeley and Los Angeles: University of California Press.

Choe, J. W. (1984). "LF WH-Movement: A Case of Pied Piping?" Ms., University of Massachusetts, Amherst.

Chomsky, N. (1973). "Conditions on Transformations." In S. R. Anderson and P. Kiparsky, eds., *A Festschrift for Morris Halle*. New York: Holt, Rinehart and Winston. [Reprinted in N. Chomsky (1977). *Essays on Form and Interpretation*. New York: Elsevier North-Holland.]

Chomsky, N. (1975). *Reflections on Language*. New York: Pantheon Books.

Chomsky, N. (1976). "Conditions on Rules of Grammar." *Linguistic Analysis* 2, 303–351. [Reprinted in N. Chomsky (1977). *Essays on Form and Interpretation*. New York: Elsevier North-Holland.]

Chomsky, N. (1977). "On Wh-Movement." In P. W. Culicover, T. Wasow, and A. Akmajian, eds., *Formal Syntax*. New York: Academic Press.

Chomsky, N. (1980a). "On Binding." *Linguistic Inquiry* 11, 1–46.

Chomsky, N. (1980b). *Rules and Representations*. New York: Columbia University Press.

Chomsky, N. (1981). *Lectures on Government and Binding*. Dordrecht: Foris.

Chomsky, N. (1982a). *Some Concepts and Consequences of the Theory of Government and Binding*. Cambridge, Mass.: MIT Press.

Chomsky, N. (1982b). *The Generative Enterprise: A Discussion with Riny Huybregts and Henk van Riemsdijk*. Dordrecht: Foris.

Chomsky, N. (1985). *Barriers*. Cambridge, Mass.: MIT Press.

Chomsky, N. (1986). *Knowledge of Language: Its Nature, Origin, and Use*. New York: Praeger.

Chomsky, N., and H. Lasnik (1977). "Filters and Control." *Linguistic Inquiry* 8, 425–504.

Chung, S. (1981). "Transitivity and Surface Filters in Chamorro." In J. Hollyman and A. Pawley, eds., *Studies in Pacific Languages and Cultures in Honour of Bruce Biggs*. Auckland: Linguistic Society of New Zealand.

Chung, S. (1982a). "Unbounded Dependencies in Chamorro Grammar." *Linguistic Inquiry* 13, 39–77.

Chung, S. (1982b). "On Extending the Null Subject Parameter to NP's." In D. Flickinger, M. Macken, and N. Wiegand, eds., *Proceedings of the West Coast Conference on Formal Linguistics* 1. Stanford Linguistics Association, Department of Linguistics, Stanford University, Stanford, Calif.

Chung, S. (1983a). "Binding and Coexisting S-Structures in Chamorro." In M. Barlow, D. Flickinger, and M. Wescoat, eds., *Proceedings of the West Coast Conference on Formal Linguistics* 2. Stanford Linguistics Association, Department of Linguistics, Stanford University, Stanford, Calif.

Chung, S. (1983b). "The ECP and Government in Chamorro." *Natural Language and Linguistic Theory* 1, 207–244.

Chung, S. (1984). "Identifiability and Null Objects in Chamorro." In C. Brugman and M. Macaulay, eds., *Proceedings of the Tenth Annual Meeting of the Berkeley Linguistics Society*. Berkeley, Calif.

Chung, S., and J. McCloskey (1983). "On the Interpretation of Certain Island Facts in GPSG." *Linguistic Inquiry* 14, 704–713.

Cinque, G. (1985). "Bare Quantifiers, Quantified NPs, and the Notion of Operator at S-Structure." Ms., Università di Venezia. [To appear in the proceedings of the Workshop on Romance Syntax, Tromsö, Norway.]

Clark, E. (1978). "Locationals: Existential, Locative, and Possessive Constructions." In J. Greenberg, ed., *Universals of Human Language IV. Syntax*. Stanford, Calif.: Stanford University Press.

Cole, P. (1983). "Null Pronominals and the Structure of Headless Relative Clauses." Ms., University of Illinois, Urbana-Champaign.

Cooper, R. (1975). "Montague's Semantic Theory and Transformational Syntax." Doctoral dissertation, University of Massachusetts, Amherst.

Cooper, R. (1983a). "The Semantics of Existential Sentences." Ms., University of Texas, Austin.

Cooper, R. (1983b). *Quantification and Syntactic Theory*. Dordrecht: Reidel.

Cooreman, A. (1982). "Chamorro Texts." Ms., University of Oregon, Eugene.

Cooreman, A. (1983). "Chamorro Texts." Ms., Saipan, Commonwealth of the Northern Marianas.

Cormack, A. (1985). "Plural Indefinites as Variables." Ms., University of Reading, U.K.

Cormack, A., and R. M. Kempson (1984). "Are Indefinite NPs Names, Variables, or Neither?" Paper presented at the Fifth Groningen Round Table, Groningen, June 1984.

Costenoble, H. (1940). *Die Chamoro Sprache*. The Hague: M. Nijhoff.

Crain, C. (1979). "Advancements and Ascensions to Direct Object in Chamorro." In *Linguistic Notes from La Jolla* 7. Department of Linguistics, UCSD, La Jolla, Calif.

Cresswell, M. (1976). "The Semantics of Degree." In B. Partee, ed., *Montague Grammar*. New York: Academic Press.

Davidson, D. (1967). "The Logical Form of Action Sentences." In N. Rescher, ed., *The Logic of Decision and Action*. Pittsburgh, Pa.: University of Pittsburgh Press. [Reprinted in D. Davidson (1980). *Essays on Actions and Events*. Oxford: Oxford University Press.]

Davidson, D. (1982). "Communication and Convention." In *Inquiries into Truth and Interpretation*. Oxford: Oxford University Press.

Doron, E. (1983). "The Semantics of Existential Sentences." Ms., University of Texas, Austin.

Emonds, J. (1976). *A Transformational Approach to English Syntax*. New York: Academic Press.

Engdahl, E. (1980). "The Syntax and Semantics of Constituent Questions in Swedish." Doctoral dissertation, University of Massachusetts, Amherst.

Engdahl, E. (1982). "Constituent Questions, Topicalization, and Surface Structure Interpretation." In D. Flickinger, M. Macken, and N. Wiegand, eds., *Proceedings of the West Coast Conference on Formal Linguistics* 1. Stanford Linguistics Association, Department of Linguistics, Stanford University, Stanford, Calif.

Engdahl, E. (1983). "Parasitic Gaps, Subject Extractions and the ECP." *Working Papers in Scandinavian Syntax* 6. University of Trondheim, Norway.

Evans, G. (1980). "Pronouns." *Linguistic Inquiry* 11, 337–362.

Fan, F.-L. (1963). "Cun Zai Ju (On Existential Sentences in Chinese)." *Zhongguo Yuwen,* 386–395.

Farmer, A. (1980). "On the Interaction of Morphology and Syntax." Doctoral dissertation, MIT, Cambridge, Mass.

Fauconnier, G. (1979). "Implication Reversal in Natural Language." In F. Guenther and S. Schmidt, eds., *Formal Semantics for Natural Language.* Dordrecht: Reidel.

Fiengo, R. (1980). *Surface Structure: The Interface of Autonomous Components.* Cambridge, Mass.: Harvard University Press.

Fillmore, C. J. (1968). "The Case for Case." In E. Bach and R. Harms, eds., *Universals in Linguistic Theory.* New York: Holt, Rinehart and Winston.

Fodor, J. D. (1978). "Parsing Strategies and Constraints on Transformations." *Linguistic Inquiry* 9, 427–473.

Fodor, J. D., and I. Sag (1982). "Referential and Quantificational Indefinites." *Linguistics and Philosophy* 5, 355–398.

Frege, G. (1891). "Function and Concept." In P. Geach and M. Black, eds., *Translations from the Philosophical Writings of Gottlob Frege.* 3d ed. London: Basil Blackwell.

Gil, D. (1982). "Distributive Numerals." Doctoral dissertation, UCLA, Los Angeles, Calif.

Gil, D. (1983a). "Intuitionism, Transformational Generative Grammar, and Mental Acts." *Studies in History and Philosophy of Science* 14, 231–254.

Gil, D. (1983b). "Stacked Adjectives and Configurationality." *Linguistic Analysis* 12, 141–158.

Gil, D. (to appear). "On the Scope of Grammatical Theory." In S. Modgil and C. Modgil, eds., *Noam Chomsky, Nothing Wrong with Being Wrong, Consensus and Controversy.* Barcombe: The Falmer Press.

Gil, D., and E. Ritter (1984). "Evidence for Nonconfigurationality in Japanese Noun-Phrases." Ms., Tel Aviv University, Israel.

Givón, T. (1979). *On Understanding Grammar.* New York: Academic Press.

Grice, H. P. (1975). "Logic and Conversation." In D. Davidson and G. Harman, eds., *The Logic of Grammar.* Encino, Calif.: Dickenson.

Guéron, J. (1984). "Locative Small Clauses and the Definiteness Effect." Paper presented at the Fifth Groningen Round Table, Groningen, June 1984. [Ms., Université de Paris VIII, France.]

Guéron, J., and R. May (1984). "Extraposition and Logical Form." *Linguistic Inquiry* 15, 1–32.

Haïk, I. (1984). "Indirect Binding." *Linguistic Inquiry* 15, 185–224.

Hale, K. (1980). "Remarks on Japanese Phrase Structure: Comments on the Papers on Japanese Syntax." In Y. Otsu and A. Farmer, eds., *MIT Working Papers in Linguistics* 2. MIT, Cambridge, Mass.

Hale, K. (1981). *On the Position of Walbiri in a Typology of the Base.* Bloomington, Ind.: Indiana University Linguistics Club.

Hankamer, H. (1974). "On Wh Indexing." In E. Kaisse and J. Hankamer, eds., *Papers from the Fifth Annual Meeting, North Eastern Linguistic Society.* Harvard University, Cambridge, Mass. [Available from GLSA, University of Massachusetts, Amherst.]

Hasegawa, Y. (in press). "More Arguments for the Pied-Piping Analysis of *Wh*-Questions in Japanese." To appear in Kitagawa and Hasegawa, eds. (in press).

Hawkins, J. (1978). *Definiteness and Indefiniteness.* London: Croom Helm.

Heim, I. (1982). "The Semantics of Definite and Indefinite Noun Phrases." Doctoral dissertation, University of Massachusetts, Amherst.

Hendrick, R., and M. Rochemont (1982). "Complementation, Multiple WH and Echo Questions." Ms., University of California, Irvine, and University of North Carolina, Chapel Hill.

Higginbotham, J. (1981). "Reciprocal Interpretation." *Journal of Linguistic Research* 1, 97–117.

Higginbotham, J. (1982). "Comments on Hintikka's Paper." *Notre Dame Journal of Formal Logic* 23, 263–271.

Higginbotham, J. (1983a). "Logical Form, Binding, and Nominals." *Linguistic Inquiry* 14, 395–420.

Higginbotham, J. (1983b). "The Logic of Perceptual Reports: An Extensional Alternative to Situation Semantics." *The Journal of Philosophy* 80.2, 100–127.

Higginbotham, J. (1985). "On Semantics." *Linguistic Inquiry* 16, 547–594.

Hoji, H. (1982). "The $\bar{X}$-schema in Japanese and the * Parameter." Ms., University of Washington, Seattle, and MIT, Cambridge, Mass.

Hoji, H. (1984). "Discourse-Linked Quantifiers and Weak Crossover in Japanese." Ms., University of Massachusetts, Amherst.

Hoji, H. (1985). "Logical Form Constraints and Configurational Structures in Japanese." Doctoral dissertation, University of Washington.

Hoji, H., and M. Saito (1983). "Weak Crossover and Move α in Japanese." *Natural Language and Linguistic Theory* 1, 245–260.

Holmback, H. (1984). "An Interpretive Solution to the Definiteness Effect Problem." *Linguistic Analysis* 13, 195–216.

Hopper, P. J., and S. A. Thompson (1980). "Transitivity in Grammar and Discourse." *Language* 56, 251–299.

Hornstein, N. (1984). *Logic as Grammar*. Cambridge, Mass.: MIT Press.

Huang, C.-T. J. (1981). "Move WH in a Language without WH Movement." *The Linguistic Review* 1, 369–416.

Huang, C.-T. J. (1982). "Logical Relations in Chinese and the Theory of Grammar." Doctoral dissertation, MIT, Cambridge, Mass.

Huang, S.-F. (1967). "Subject and Object in Mandarin." *Project on Linguistic Analysis* 13. [Reprinted in S.-F. Huang (1983). *Papers in Chinese Syntax*. Taipei: Literary Crane Press.]

Humboldt, W. von (1903–1918). *Gesammelte Schriften*. A. Leitzmann, ed., Berlin: B. Behrs Verlag.

Jackendoff, R. (1972). *Semantic Interpretation in Generative Grammar*. Cambridge, Mass.: MIT Press.

Jackendoff, R. (1977). $\bar{X}$ *Syntax: A Study of Phrase Structure*. Cambridge, Mass.: MIT Press.

Jaeggli, O. (1980a). "On Some Phonologically Null Elements in Syntax." Doctoral dissertation, MIT, Cambridge, Mass.

Jaeggli, O. (1980b). "Remarks on *To* Contraction." *Linguistic Inquiry* 11, 239–245.

Jaeggli, O. (1982). *Topics in Romance Syntax*. Dordrecht: Foris.

Jenkins, L. (1972). "Modality in English Syntax." Doctoral dissertation, MIT, Cambridge, Mass.

Jenkins, L. (1975). *The English Existential*. Tübingen: Max Niemeyer Verlag.

Jong, F. M. G. de (1983). "Numerals as Determiners." In H. Bennis and W. U. S. van Lessen Kloeke, eds., *Linguistics in the Netherlands*. Dordrecht: Foris.

Jong, F. M. G. de, and H. J. Verkuyl (1985). "Generalized Quantifiers: The Properness of Their Strength." In J. van Benthem and A. ter Meulen, eds., *Generalized Quantifiers in Natural Language*. Dordrecht: Foris.

Kamp, H. (1981). "A Theory of Truth and Semantic Representation." In J. Groenendijk et al., eds., *Formal Methods in the Study of Language*. Amsterdam: Mathematical Center. [Reprinted in J. Groenendijk et al., eds. (1984). *Truth, Interpretation and Information*. Dordrecht: Foris.]

Karttunen, L. (1977). "Syntax and Semantics of Questions." *Linguistics and Philosophy* 1, 3–44.

Katz, J., and P. Postal (1964). *An Integrated Theory of Linguistic Description*. Cambridge, Mass.: MIT Press.

Kayne, R. (1972). "Subject Inversion in French Interrogatives." In J. Casagrande and B. Saciuk, eds., *Generative Studies in Romance Languages*. Rowley, Mass.: Newbury House.

Kayne, R. (1979). "Two Notes on the NIC." In A. Belletti, L. Brandi, and L. Rizzi, eds., *Theory of Markedness in Generative Grammar*, Scuola Normale Superiore di Pisa. [Reprinted in Kayne (1984).]

Kayne, R. (1981). "ECP Extensions." *Linguistic Inquiry* 12, 93–133.

Kayne, R. (1983). "Connectedness." *Linguistic Inquiry* 14, 223–249.

Kayne, R. (1984). *Connectedness and Binary Branching*. Dordrecht: Foris.

Keenan, E. (1978a). "Language Variation and the Logical Structure of Universal Grammar." In H. Seiler, ed., *Language Universals*. Tübingen: Günter Narr Verlag.

Keenan, E. (1978b). "Logical Semantics and Universal Grammar." *Theoretical Linguistics* 5, 83–107.

Keenan, E. (1982). "Parametric Variation in Universal Grammar." In R. Dirven and G. Radden, eds., *Issues in the Theory of Universal Grammar*. Tübingen: Günter Narr Verlag.

Keenan, E. (1983). "Parametric Variation in Universal Grammar." In S. Mordechay, ed., *UCLA Working Papers in Semantics*. UCLA, Los Angeles, Calif.

Keenan, E., and L. Faltz (1978). *Logical Types for Natural Language*. UCLA Occasional Papers in Syntax 3. UCLA, Los Angeles, Calif.

Keenan, E., and L. Moss (1985). "Generalized Quantifiers and the Expressive Power of Natural Languages." In J. van Benthem and A. ter Meulen, eds., *Generalized Quantifiers in Natural Language*. Dordrecht: Foris.

Keenan, E., and Y. Stavi (1986). "A Semantic Characterization of Natural Language Determiners." *Linguistics and Philosophy* 9, 253–326. [First published in S. Mordechay, ed. (1983). *UCLA Working Papers in Semantics*. UCLA, Los Angeles, Calif.]

Kempson, R. (1984). "Weak Crossover, Logical Form and Pragmatics." Paper presented at the GLOW colloquium, Copenhagen, April 1984.

Kirsner, R. (1979). *The Problem of Presentative Sentences in Modern Dutch*. New York: North-Holland.

Kitagawa, Y. (1984). "Superiority Effects in Japanese: An Argument for LF." Ms., University of Massachusetts, Amherst.

Kitagawa, Y., and N. Hasegawa, eds. (in press). *Papers in Oriental Linguistics: Proceedings from the 1985 WOOL Conference*. GLSA, University of Massachusetts, Amherst.

Klima, E. S. (1964). "Negation in English." In J. A. Fodor and J. J. Katz, eds., *The Structure of Language*. Englewood Cliffs, N.J.: Prentice-Hall.

Koopman, H., and D. Sportiche (1981). "Variables and the Bijection Principle." *The Linguistic Review* 2, 139–160.

Koster, J. (1975). "Dutch as an SOV Language." *Linguistic Analysis* 1, 111–136.

Koster, J. (1978). *Locality Principles in Syntax*. Dordrecht: Foris.

Koster, J. (1984). "Global Harmony." Ms., Tilburg University, The Netherlands.

Kuno, S. (1971). "The Position of Locatives in Existential Sentences." *Linguistic Inquiry* 2, 333–378.

Kuno, S. (1973). *The Structure of the Japanese Language*. Cambridge, Mass.: MIT Press.

Kuno, S. (1976). "Subject, Theme, and the Speaker's Empathy." In C. Li, ed., *Subject and Topic*. New York: Academic Press.

Kuno, S. (1982). "The Focus of the Question and the Focus of the Answer." In *Papers from the Parasession on Nondeclaratives, Chicago Linguistic Society*. Department of Linguistics, University of Chicago, Chicago, Ill.

Kuno, S., and K. Masunaga (1985). "Questions with WH Phrases in Islands." Ms., Harvard University. [To appear in Kitagawa and Hasegawa, eds. (in press).]

Kuno, S., and J. J. Robinson (1972). "Multiple WH-Questions." *Linguistic Inquiry* 3, 463–487.

Kurata, K. (1986). "Asymmetries in Japanese." Generals paper, University of Massachusetts, Amherst.

Kuroda, S.-Y. (1969). "English Relativization and Certain Related Problems." In D. Reibel and S. Schane, eds., *Modern Studies in English*. Englewood Cliffs, N.J.: Prentice-Hall.

Ladusaw, W. A. (1982). "Semantic Constraints on the English Partitive Construction." In D. Flickinger, M. Macken, and N. Wiegand, eds., *Proceedings of the West Coast Conference on Formal Linguistics* 1. Stanford Linguistics Association, Department of Linguistics, Stanford University, Stanford, Calif.

Ladusaw, W. A. (1983). "Logical Form and Conditions on Grammaticality." *Linguistics and Philosophy* 6, 373–392.

Lakoff, G. (1970). "Repartee, or A Reply to 'Negation, Conjunction, and Quantifiers'." *Foundations of Language* 6, 389–422.

Larson, R. (1983). "Restrictive Modification: Relative Clauses and Adverbs." Doctoral dissertation, University of Wisconsin, Madison.

Larson, R. (1985). "On the Syntax of Disjunction Scope." *Natural Language and Linguistic Theory* 3, 217–264.

Lasnik, H. (1981). "Restricting the Theory of Transformations." In N. Hornstein and D. Lightfoot, eds., *Explanation in Linguistics: The Logical Problem of Language Acquisition*. London: Longman.

Lasnik, H., and M. Saito (1984). "On the Nature of Proper Government." *Linguistic Inquiry* 15, 235–290.

Lee, H. S. (1982). "Asymmetry in Island Constraints in Korean." Ms., UCLA, Los Angeles, Calif.

Lehn, K. van (1978). "Determining the Scope of English Quantifiers." Master's thesis, MIT, Cambridge, Mass.

Lewis, D. (1975). "Adverbs of Quantification." In E. Keenan, ed., *Formal Semantics of Natural Language*. Cambridge: Cambridge University Press.

Li, C., and S. Thompson (1981). *Mandarin Chinese: A Functional Reference Grammar*. Berkeley and Los Angeles: University of California Press.

Lightfoot, D. (1980). "Trace Theory and Explanation." In E. A. Moravcsik and J. R. Wirth, eds., *Current Approaches to Syntax*. New York: Academic Press.

Löbner, S. (1984). "Indefinites, Counting, and the Background/Foreground Distinction." Paper presented at the Fifth Groningen Round Table, Groningen, June 1984. [Ms., University of Stuttgart, West Germany.]

Lyons, C. (1984). "Phrase Structure, Possessives and Definiteness." Paper presented at the Fifth Groningen Round Table, Groningen, June 1984. [Ms., University of Salford, U.K.]

McCloskey, J. (1979). *Transformational Syntax and Model Theoretic Semantics*. Dordrecht: D. Reidel.

May, R. (1977). "The Grammar of Quantification." Doctoral dissertation, MIT, Cambridge, Mass. [Distributed by the Indiana University Linguistics Club, Bloomington.]

May, R. (1985). *Logical Form: Its Structure and Derivation*. Cambridge, Mass.: MIT Press.

Mei, K. (1972). "Transformational Studies on Modern Standard Chinese." Doctoral dissertation, Harvard University, Cambridge, Mass.

Milsark, G. (1974). "Existential Sentences in English." Doctoral dissertation, MIT, Cambridge, Mass.

Milsark, G. (1977). "Toward an Explanation of Certain Peculiarities in the Existential Construction in English." *Linguistic Analysis* 3, 1–30.

Milsark, G., and K. Safir (1983). "On Adjacency in Phonological Form." Ms., Temple University, Philadelphia, and University of Pennsylvania, Philadelphia.

Montague, R. (1974). "The Proper Treatment of Quantification in Ordinary English." In R. Thomason, ed., *Formal Philosophy*. New Haven, Conn.: Yale University Press.

do Nascimento, M. (1984). *Sur la postposition du sujet dans le portugais de Brésil*. Doctorat de troisième cycle, Université de Paris VIII, France.

Nishigauchi, T. (1984). "Japanese LF: Subjacency vs. ECP." Ms., Shoin College, Kobe. [To appear in *Seoul Papers on Formal Grammar Theory*, Linguistic Society of Korea.]

Nishigauchi, T. (1985). "Addendum to Japanese LF." Ms., University of Massachusetts, Amherst.

Nishigauchi, T. (1986). "Quantification in Syntax." Doctoral dissertation, University of Massachusetts, Amherst.

Partee, B. H. (1973). "The Syntax and Semantics of Quotation." In S. R. Anderson and P. Kiparsky, eds., *A Festschrift for Morris Halle*. New York: Holt, Rinehart and Winston.

Partee, B. H., and M. Rooth (1982). "Conjunction, Type Ambiguity, and Wide Scope Or." *Proceedings of the West Coast Conference on Formal Linguistics* 1. Stanford Linguistic Association, Department of Linguistics, Stanford University, Stanford, Calif.

Perlmutter, D. (1978). "Impersonal Passives and the Unaccusative Hypothesis." In *Proceedings of the Fourth Annual Meeting of the Berkeley Linguistics Society*. Berkeley, Calif.

Perlmutter, D., and A. Zaenen (1984). "The Indefinite Extraposition Construction in Dutch and German." In D. Perlmutter, ed., *Relational Grammar II*. Chicago: University of Chicago Press.

Pesetsky, D. (1982). "Paths and Categories." Doctoral dissertation, MIT, Cambridge, Mass.

Pesetsky, D. (1985). "Reply to Kuno and Masunaga." Ms., University of Massachusetts, Amherst. [To appear in Kitagawa and Hasegawa, eds. (in press).]

Pesetsky, D. (forthcoming). *A Syntactic Theory of Paths*. Cambridge, Mass.: MIT Press.

Pollock, J.-Y. (1984). "Accord, chaines impersonnelles et variables." *Linguisticae Investigationes* 7, 131–181.

Postal, P. M., and G. K. Pullum (1982). "The Contraction Debate." *Linguistic Inquiry* 13, 122–150.

Pullum, G. K., and P. M. Postal (1979). "An Inadequate Defense of Trace Theory." *Linguistic Inquiry* 10, 689–706.

Rando, E., and D. J. Napoli (1978). "Definites in THERE-sentences." *Language* 54, 300–313.

Reinhart, T. (1983). *Anaphora and Semantic Interpretation*. London: Croom Helm. [Also published by University of Chicago Press, Chicago (1985).]

Reinhart, T. (1985). "Center and Periphery in the Grammar of Anaphora." In B. Lust, ed., *Studies in the Acquisition of Anaphora*. Dordrecht: D. Reidel.

Reinhart, T. (1986). "On the Interpretation of Donkey-Sentences." In E. Traugott et al., eds., *On Conditionals*. Cambridge: Cambridge University Press.

Renault, R. (1984). "Théorie de roles thématiques et cas morphologique de l'objet en finnois." *Recherches Linguistiques* 12, 125–172.

Reuland, E. J. (1983). "The Extended Projection Principle and the Definiteness Effect." In M. Barlow, D. Flickinger, and M. Wescoat, eds., *Proceedings of the West Coast Conference on Formal Linguistics* 2. Stanford Linguistics Association, Department of Linguistics, Stanford University, Stanford, Calif.

Reuland, E. J. (1985). "Representation at the Level of Logical Form and the Definiteness Effect." In J. Guéron, H.-G. Obenauer, and J.-Y. Pollock, eds., *Grammatical Representation*. Dordrecht: Foris.

Riemsdijk, H. van, and E. Williams (1981). "NP-Structure." *The Linguistic Review* 1, 171–217.

Rizzi, L. (1982). *Issues in Italian Syntax*. Dordrecht: Foris.

Ross, J. R. (1967). "Constraints on Variables in Syntax." Doctoral dissertation, MIT, Cambridge, Mass.

Rothstein, S. (1983). "The Syntactic Forms of Predication." Doctoral dissertation, MIT, Cambridge, Mass.

Rouveret, A., and J.-R. Vergnaud (1980). "Specifying Reference to the Subject." *Linguistic Inquiry* 11, 97–202.

Safir, K. (1982). "Syntactic Chains and the Definiteness Effect." Doctoral dissertation, MIT, Cambridge, Mass.

Safir, K. (1983a). "On Small Clauses as Constituents." *Linguistic Inquiry* 14, 730–735.

Safir, K. (1983b). "Postverbal Subjects and the Definiteness Effect." In P. Sells and C. Jones, eds., *Proceedings of the Thirteenth Annual Meeting of NELS*. GLSA, University of Massachusetts, Amherst.

Safir, K. (1984a). "Multiple Variable Binding." *Linguistic Inquiry* 15, 603–638.

Safir, K. (1984b). "So There! A Reply to Williams' Analysis of *There* Sentences." Ms., Rutgers University, New Brunswick, N.J.

Safir, K. (1985). *Syntactic Chains*. Cambridge: Cambridge University Press.

Safir, K. (1985). "Missing Subjects in German." In J. Toman, ed., *Studies in German Grammar*. Dordrecht: Foris.

Sag, I. A., G. Gazdar, T. Wasow, and S. Weisler (1984). "Coordination and How to Distinguish Categories." Ms., Center for the Study of Language and Information, Stanford University, Stanford, Calif.

Scha, R. (1981). "Distributive, Collective and Cumulative Quantification." In J. Groenendijk et al., eds., *Formal Methods in the Study of Language*. Amsterdam: Mathematical Center. [Reprinted in J. Groenendijk et al., eds. (1984). *Truth, Interpretation and Information*. Dordrecht: Foris.]

Schein, B. (1982). "Small Clauses and Predication." Ms., MIT, Cambridge, Mass.

Schein, B. (1984). "Reference to Events and Quantification." Paper presented at the Fifth Groningen Round Table, Groningen, June 1984. [Ms., MIT, Cambridge, Mass.]

Selkirk, E. (1970). "On the Determiner System of Noun Phrase and Adjective Phrase." Ms., MIT, Cambridge, Mass.

Selkirk, E. (1977). "Some Remarks on Noun Phrase Structure." In P. W. Culicover, T. Wasow, and A. Akmajian, eds., *Formal Syntax*. New York: Academic Press.

Sproat, R. (1985). "On Deriving the Lexicon." Doctoral dissertation, MIT, Cambridge, Mass.

Stechow, A. von (1980). "Modification of Noun Phrases: A Challenge for Compositional Semantics." *Theoretical Linguistics* 7, 57–109.

Stein, M. J. (1981). "Quantification in Thai." Doctoral dissertation, University of Massachusetts, Amherst.

Stockwell, R., P. Schachter, and B. Partee (1973). *The Major Syntactic Structures of English*. New York: Holt, Rinehart and Winston.

Stowell, T. (1978). "What Was There Before There Was There." In D. Farkas, W. Jacobson, and K. Todrys, eds., *Papers from the Fourteenth Regional Meeting of the Chicago Linguistic Society*. University of Chicago, Chicago, Ill.

Stowell, T. (1981). "Origins of Phrase Structure." Doctoral dissertation, MIT, Cambridge, Mass.

Stowell, T. (1984). "Subjects across Categories." *The Linguistic Review* 2, 285–312.

Strawson, P. F. (1952). *Introduction to Logical Theory*. New York: Wiley.

Strawson, P. F. (1964). "Identifying Reference and Truth Values." *Theoria* 30.

Suñer, M. (1983). *The Syntax and Semantics of Spanish Presentational Sentence-Types*. Washington, D.C.: Georgetown University Press.

Szabolcsi, A. (1983). "The Possessor that Ran Away from Home." Ms., The Hungarian Academy of Sciences, Budapest, Hungary, and the Max-Planck-Institut für Psycholinguistik, Nijmegen, The Netherlands.

Szabolcsi, A. (1984). "(In)definiteness Effects in Hungarian." Paper presented at the Fifth Groningen Round Table, Groningen, June 1984.

Szabolcsi, A. (1984). "From the Definiteness Effect to Lexical Integrity." In W. Abraham and J. de Mey, eds., *Topic, Focus and Configurationality*. Amsterdam: J. Benjamins.

Teng, S.-H. (1977). "Modification and the Structure of Existential Sentences." In T. C. Tang et al., eds., *Symposium on Chinese Linguistics*. Taipei: Student Book Co.

Thomason, R. (1985). "Some Issues Concerning the Interpretation of Derived and Gerundive Nominals." *Linguistics and Philosophy* 8, 73–80.

Toman, J. (1981). "Aspects of Multiple WH Movement in Polish and Czech." In J. Koster and R. May, eds., *Levels of Syntactic Representation*. Dordrecht: Foris.

Torrego, E. (1983). "A Look to Existential *there be* Sentences in English." Ms., University of Massachusetts, Boston.

Vergnaud, J.-R. (1974). "French Relative Clauses." Doctoral dissertation, MIT, Cambridge, Mass.

Wachowicz, K. (1974). "Against the Universality of a Single WH-Question Movement." *Foundations of Language* 11, 155–166.

Wang, P. W. (1981). "Existential Sentences in Chinese." Master's thesis, National Taiwan Normal University, Taiwan.

Wang, W. S.-Y. (1965). "Two Aspect Markers in Mandarin." *Language* 41, 457–471.

Whorf, B. L. (1956). *Language, Thought, and Reality*. J. B. Carroll, ed. Cambridge, Mass.: MIT Press.

Williams, E. (1975). "Small Clauses in English." In J. Kimball, ed., *Syntax and Semantics* 4. New York: Academic Press.

Williams, E. (1980). "Predication." *Linguistic Inquiry* 11, 203–238.

Williams, E. (1981). "Argument Structure and Morphology." *The Linguistic Review* 1, 81–114.

Williams, E. (1983). "Against Small Clauses." *Linguistic Inquiry* 14, 287–308.

Williams, E. (1984). "*There*-Insertion." *Linguistic Inquiry* 15, 131–153.

Williamson, J. (1984). "Studies in Lakhota Grammar." Doctoral dissertation, University of California at San Diego, La Jolla.

Woisetschlaeger, E. (1983). "On the Question of Definiteness in 'An Old Man's Book'," *Linguistic Inquiry* 14, 137–154.

Woolford, E. (1986). "The Distribution of Empty Nodes in Navajo: A Mapping Approach." *Linguistic Inquiry* 17, 301–330.

Zwarts, F. (1983). "Determiners: A Relational Perspective." In A. G. B. ter Meulen, ed., *Studies in Modeltheoretic Semantics*. Dordrecht: Foris.

Index